Syntax Analysis
and
Software Tools

INTERNATIONAL COMPUTER SCIENCE SERIES

Consulting editors **A D McGettrick** University of Strathclyde
J van Leeuwen University of Utrecht

OTHER TITLES IN THE SERIES

Syntax Analysis
and
Software Tools

K. John Gough

Queensland Institute of Technology,
Australia

ADDISON-WESLEY
PUBLISHING
COMPANY

Sydney · Wokingham, England · Reading, Massachusetts
Menlo Park, California · New York · Don Mills, Ontario
Amsterdam · Bonn · Singapore · Tokyo · Madrid
Bogota · Santiago · San Juan

The programs presented in this book have been included for their instructional value. They have been tested with care but are not guaranteed for any particular purpose. The publisher does not offer any warranties or representations, nor does it accept any liabilities with respect to the programs.

Cover graphic by Laurence M. Gartel
Typeset by Columns of Caversham, Reading, Berks.
Printed in Great Britain by TJ Press (Padstow) Ltd, Cornwall.

First Printed in 1988.

British Library Cataloguing in Publication Data

Gough, K. John
   Syntax analysis and software tools.–
   (International computer science series)
   1. Linguistics – Data processing
   I. Title II. Series
   418   P98

   ISBN 0–201–18048–0

Library of Congress Cataloging in Publication Data

Gough, K. John (Kevin John), 1942–
   Syntax analysis and software tools.

   (International computer science series)
   Bibliography: p.
   Includes index.
   1. Grammar, Comparative and general – Syntax – Data
processing. 2. Linguistics – Data processing. I. Title.
   II. Series.
P291.G67 1988   415′.028′5   87-17343
ISBN 0–201–18048–0

Preface

The ability to create syntax-directed software tools is a basic skill of the computer professional. However, the practical study of formal languages and their recognizers has invariably been associated with just one such tool. Programming language compilers are an important but extremely specialized example of software programs which involve the processing of formal languages. It is the central thesis of this book that the techniques of language processing should be taught earlier in the computer science curriculum, and quite separately from the specialized consideration of compilers.

This book is intended to be used for a one-semester course in language processing, but is sufficiently self-contained to be used for self-study as well. It is designed to be used in the junior year of the college computer science curriculum. However, it would be possible to place such a course even earlier in the programme in those colleges where the prerequisite material is covered in the first year.

Preliminary drafts of the material of this book have been used for such a course for some years in the Department of Computing Science at the Queensland Institute of Technology. The philosophy involved in introducing the subject matter separately from the compiler construction course was first expressed by the author in 1981 (Gough, 1981).

How to use this book

The material in this book is divided into thirteen chapters. The ordering of the material into chapters forms a sequence of topics which is a logical one, and one which is recommended where time permits. For a one-semester course, however, it is recommended that the optional sections, which are marked with a star in the table of contents, be omitted.

Chapters are divided into sections and subsections, and each section is followed by a brief review. This review summarizes the important notions in the section and repeats definitions in an accessible position. This particular style has been chosen as a convenience for the reader, and so that the body of each section is not broken up by frequent labels and subheadings.

Finally, each chapter is followed by a small number of exercises, which test knowledge of the material in the preceding chapter, and sometimes fill in details of results which were deliberately omitted from the text. It is recommended that at least some of these exercises be attempted at the conclusion of each chapter. In some cases, the exercises involve the writing of programs which may involve a fair amount of code. Certainly some of these should be attempted.

At the back of the book, there are model answers to all the exercises,

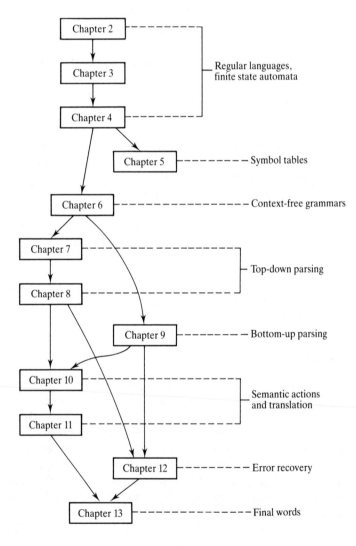

Figure 0.1 Prerequisite structure of chapters.

except for some which merely ask for verification of some result used in the text. Many of the model answers involve further discussion of the particular problem, and logically form part of the development in the main body of the text. In such cases the discussion has been deferred to the answer chapter so that the attempt to solve the problem motivates understanding of the discussion. The model answers thus merit a careful reading even for those exercises for which a solution has been easily obtained. In any case, the answers should be consulted for those exercises which have either not been attempted, or with which difficulties were encountered.

The relationship between the various chapters of the text is shown in Figure 0.1. An edge of the directed graph from Chapter i to Chapter j implies that the material in Chapter j depends on that in Chapter i.

There are three fairly substantial case studies distributed through the text, and a large number of fragments of other software tools. The number of possible applications of these techniques in the construction of software tools is so large that the book can do no more than attempt to point in the general direction of the applications, and deal with a few simple cases in some detail. In particular, many of the examples deal with applications in such areas as the recognition and processing of various kinds of expression languages, and tools which process Pascal program texts. This rather narrow range of applications is not intended to imply that these are the important areas of applications of these techniques. Rather these examples have been chosen simply because every reader of the book is assumed to possess some familiarity with arithmetic expressions and to be familiar with the Pascal language.

Concluding each chapter is a short section which details further reading on the particular topics treated in the chapter. In some cases these references are of historical interest, while in others they give a more advanced treatment which extends the coverage given in the book. There has, however, been no attempt to be encyclopaedic in the references to original work.

Acknowledgements

The idea of separating the study of syntax analysis from its traditional place in the compiler construction course first arose in discussions with John Staples in the late 1970s. Since that time many computer science educators have listened patiently to my exposition of the concept, and in turn have pointed out the necessity of having a suitable textbook to support any such course. Richard Austing was one of the first to do so.

A number of colleagues have commented on early drafts of the material in the book, and have contributed to the development of the courses which it supports. Steve Sugden and Melanie Dugdale both made valuable contributions in this way, as did many of the several hundred senior students who elected to take the course. Geoff Horne and Doug Merrett each helped by ironing out errors.

Several reviewers helped by pointing out errors and inconsistencies in the various versions of the draft, and Arthur Sale contributed valuable discussions of Pascal style, particularly the unique problems which arise when converting Modula-2 programs *back* to Pascal. Since I often ignored the good advice I received, I accept full responsibility for any remaining errors, idiosyncrasies and awkwardness.

Finally, much of the writing was done during weekends when I might otherwise have been walking in tropical rainforest, paddling on rivers or just being sociable. My sacrifice was uncomplainingly shared by Noeleen Atwell, whose support is gratefully acknowledged.

K John Gough
Brisbane, June 1987

Contents

Chapter 1 **Introduction**

1.1 Syntax-directed programming

Computer programs in which the analysis of the sequence of input symbols plays a central role in determining the program actions are **syntax-directed programs**. Editors, text formatters, command interpreters, and all manner of program text-manipulation tools fall within this classification. Programming language compilers are, of course, familiar examples of such programs, but are sufficiently specialized to warrant separate study.

In order to create syntax-directed software tools, it is necessary to understand something of the theory and practice of that part of the computer science generally called language processing.

Although we usually reserve the term 'syntax-directed' for programs in which the analysis of the input data format is the most obvious function of the program, there is a sense in which the techniques of syntax-directed programming are involved in a majority of programs. Any program which accepts free-form input, or involves the user in some kind of interactive dialogue, is syntax-directed in the widest sense.

A program which performs as simple a task as the reading of a sequence of free-form numbers is syntax-directed, since it must infer from the character stream where one number ends and another begins, which characters are exponents and which fraction parts, and so on. This is not to say that the techniques of language processing are necessary for the creation of such a simple program. What may be asserted, however, is that an understanding of syntax-directed programming gives a fresh perspective to the writing of all manner of programs, from the most simple to the most complex.

1.1.1 The importance of language processing

The material covered in this book has a special importance for at least three reasons.

Firstly, and most obviously, the study of this material allows the construction of all manner of useful software tools. The design of several

1

tools is discussed in the text, and fragments of many others are mentioned in passing.

Secondly, the ideas of language processing can, and should, be applied to the design of almost every program. In principle, any program, whether interactive or otherwise, defines an input language which it will accept and will process correctly. In many cases this language is almost trivially simple, consisting of perhaps just two possible strings ('Y' or 'N' perhaps, to choose a deprecated example). However, it is this book's contention that in all situations the input language of a program should be formally defined, and then implemented by systematic techniques. It is only by adopting such a formal approach that we may be relatively certain that the language that has been specified is the same as the actual language that is accepted by the program. Conversely, viewed from the perspective of producing accurate documentation, the formal approach is the only way in which we may be confident that the documented language is the same as the one which the program actually accepts.

Finally, the study of language processing is a foundation on which several of the more advanced, theoretical subjects in the computer science curriculum depend. In particular, the formal study of programming language syntax, complexity theory, automata theory, and, of course, compiler construction, all depend to some extent on the material introduced in the chapters of this book.

Despite the importance of the topic in this more general context, it has become traditional to isolate the teaching of language processing in courses in 'compiler construction'. This is a great pity, since the subject could easily be placed much earlier in the curriculum. Most aspects of the subject are well within the grasp of students who have had both an introduction to programming based on an algorithmic language, such as Pascal, an introduction to the theory of data structures, and who are slightly familiar with some of the notions of finite mathematics.

Having stressed the importance of the subject for its contribution to the understanding of theory, we should hasten to add that this is a practical rather than theoretical book. Certainly there is much theory, but it is introduced in as practical a way as possible. It is argued that the understanding of theory is an important goal, and one which for most students is best approached by first seeing a practical example which may then motivate the study of theory, and also forms a framework to which the formalism may be related.

There are a number of very deep theoretical results mentioned in the text, and in most cases some attempt has been made to make these results plausible. Those readers who already understand these results will look in vain for formal proofs. This is not because formal proofs are unnecessary. On the contrary, they are the only reliable basis on which new knowledge may be established. However, the intention is *not* to establish new knowledge but to spread the understanding of established theory and practice. The goal is to lead the reader to see why these results must be so, without becoming involved in either the fine detail or the notational complexities of completely rigorous proofs.

Nevertheless, there are certain sections of the book which are somewhat more difficult than others, and these are marked with an asterisk in the list of contents. These sections may be skipped on a first reading, since their content is not essential to what follows.

Apart from all else, writing syntax-directed programs is fun, and an infallible antidote for those who suffer from the pernicious notion that computing has somehow to do with numbers. In language processing, the concept of software as the symbol-manipulation system is central. Our syntax-directed software tools do not calculate, instead they extract 'meaning' from sequences of symbols, and then act on the basis of that meaning.

1.1.2 Choice of programming language

The algorithms and program fragments which appear in this book are all written in Pascal, although some mention is made of the changes which may need to be made in the implementation of the various algorithms when other languages are used. There can be no doubt, however, that the goal of introducing language processing early in the curriculum has been made possible, to a large extent, by the widespread adoption of Pascal as a teaching language for beginning computer science majors. The facilities which Pascal provides, for expressing both algorithms and data structures in a clear and elegant way, allows the student to concentrate on the essence of the material rather than on the syntactic oddities of the implementation.

The dialect of Pascal used for the examples is, with very few exceptions ISO Pascal as defined by ISO 7185. An attempt has been made to avoid those features of the standard, such as conformant arrays, which are not widely implemented.

One notational convention, which has been adopted throughout, is that comments within programs are enclosed in the '(*', '*)' form of comment delimiters. The alternative delimiters, '{', '}' are reserved exclusively for use in programs which are not fully elaborated, to describe the purpose of the code which is omitted. A typical program fragment might begin

```
begin
     {initialize tables};
```

to indicate that the omitted code performs an appropriate initialization.

There are also some departures from strict ISO Pascal standards where it is necessary to, say, define a character constant with a value corresponding to a non-printing character of the underlying character set. Different compilers for machines with differing character sets will have different methods of doing this. For example, the VAX/VMS Pascal compiler allows a declaration in the form

const *CR* = *CHR*(13);

while in Turbo Pascal the same effect may be obtained by

const *CR* = *^M*;

Neither is a standard notation.

In the final analysis, the choice of programming language is more important to the exposition of ideas than for the writing of programs. Once an algorithm is properly understood it may actually be coded in almost any language, albeit with a greater or lesser amount of effort. The ideal language for exposition in a book of this kind would be one which contains constructs which directly embody the abstractions with which the algorithms deal. It is our judgement that, of the widely known languages, Pascal most closely fits this requirement at present.

In spite of this support of Pascal, and its use throughout the text, there are languages which are more suitable for the purpose. As a general observation, an algorithmic language which provides facilities for the creation of abstract data types might be superior to Pascal, both for purposes of explanation and for implementation of the algorithms in this book. The various elements in language-processing programs may almost invariably be best understood as abstract data types which interact in quite well-defined ways. Indeed, the implementation of programs as multiple layers in a hierarchical structure is one of the themes which runs throughout language processing, and to which data abstraction is ideally suited.

Either Modula-2 or Ada would have been an excellent choice, but unfortunately neither of these is yet sufficiently well known nor widely available to be considered for the purpose. In the future, however, we may look forward to languages of this later generation being as widely used as Pascal is now. The adoption of these languages will surely bring about as profound an effect in the way that people think about programming tasks as Pascal did for programmers in the 1970s.

1.2 Language processing and compiler construction

The relationship between the material in this book and those books intended to support traditional courses in the theory of language compilers is an important one. Certainly, compilers are among the best known and most widely used syntax-directed software tools. Consequently, the material in this book is basic to the understanding of any language compiler. However, it does form only a part of the material in a course in compiler construction. Many would argue that the material here forms the bulk of many of the traditional courses in compilers. This is simply because the theory of formal languages and parsers occurs in such courses as a time-consuming preliminary which must be covered before the fascinating and challenging questions of compiler construction may be properly addressed.

This book, and the courses which it supports, are thus intended to allow the course in compiler construction to assume its rightful place in the advanced undergraduate and beginning post-graduate curriculum. Since the elementary notions of languages and their recognizers have been thoroughly covered (and probably applied in the interim) the compiler course is left free to deal with what are the real issues of compiler design and implementation.

The topics which are not treated here, but which form an important part of even the most cursory study of compiler construction, are: advanced aspects of symbol-table organization, code generation, run-time organization, and so-called optimization. Furthermore, any serious course dealing with the construction of compilers must address the question of formal definitions for the semantics of programming languages, and should probably only occur after some grounding has been obtained in the techniques of design and production of large software systems, i.e. a study of software engineering. All of these topics are conceptually separate to the subject matter of this book, and so are best treated separately and subsequently.

Indeed, this book places a rather different emphasis on several other topics, and treats some topics which are not covered in the traditional textbooks. The main reason for this is that the area of application for most of the techniques which are treated here is what might be called 'little languages', that is, those which are defined by a relatively small number of rules. There are any number of interesting and useful software tools which may be understood without becoming involved in the more advanced ideas of language compilation.

Many of the applications of small languages require only a very simple form of language which we shall call **regular languages**, and which are treated in the first part of the book. The kind of recognizers which are required for languages of this kind are called **finite state automata**. Even within the study of regular languages, some unusual topics are considered in some detail. For example, consideration is given to the direct implementation of what we shall call non-deterministic recognizers. This topic is of great importance in applications where 'throwaway' recognizers are required, but would be somewhat out of place in a compiler text.

Equally, when the more powerful language definition mechanisms are described, the book emphasizes recognition methods which are readily (and correctly) implemented by hand-written programs. Because of this, the emphasis in the latter part of the book is on the recursive descent method, which is well suited to hand coding. The 'bottom-up' methods, which are properly emphasized as the method of choice in contemporary compiler texts, are treated here in somewhat lesser detail.

In summary then, this book can be used as preparation for the study of compiler construction, but beyond that purpose is intended for use by all students of computing science, including those who choose not to make a special study of compilers.

Chapter 2 **Finite State Automata**

2.1 Strings, symbols, alphabets, and languages

In language processing we deal with strings, which are finite length, ordered sequences of symbols. The concepts of symbol and sequence are fundamental, and we do not attempt to define them formally here.

In any particular context the set of symbols which we consider form a collection which we call the **alphabet**. In some cases the alphabet will quite literally be the alphabet $a,b,c \ldots z$; in other circumstances the alphabet might be all ASCII characters, or all Pascal keywords, or the set $\{`0'..`9', `.', `E', `+', `-'\}$ and so on.

The important concept is that at any particular level of analysis the symbol is the atomic, indivisible unit from which the string is constructed. It does not matter that seen at a different level the symbols of the Pascal keyword-alphabet may be represented as being composed of alphabetic characters, or that the ASCII character set may be represented as a sequence of bits. If the alphabet is the printed character set used in this book we may treat the characters as indivisible units. However, the designer of an optical character recognizer might well consider a lower level in which characters are composed of straight and curved line segments.

We represent the alphabet Σ (the upper case Greek letter sigma), and all the strings formed by arbitrary finite sequences of symbols from Σ as Σ^+. Note that even though the cardinality of the set Σ is finite, the cardinality of the set of strings Σ^+ is infinite.

In order to deal consistently with strings of all finite lengths including zero we use a special symbol ε (Greek letter epsilon) to denote a string of zero length. This empty string ε is not an element of Σ nor of Σ^+, but we may define a new set of strings which does include ε. Σ^* is defined as the union of Σ^+ and the set containing just the empty string ε.

This new set of strings is called the closure of Σ. In symbols

$$\Sigma^* = \Sigma^+ \cup \{\varepsilon\}$$

It follows from the definition that Σ^* is the set of all finite strings of symbols from Σ of length zero or more.

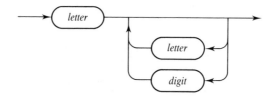

Figure 2.1   The syntax rule for the Pascal language.

In general, however, we are not interested in all strings in Σ^*, but only in some subsets which 'make sense' in some particular context. We are led, therefore, to define rules which determine which of the strings have meaning. These rules define a language, which is therefore a particular subset of Σ^*. The rules which define the language may be simple, like an enumeration of the acceptable strings, or require special constructs such as the Backus Naur Form (BNF) for their concise definition. If there are only a finite number of strings in the language then we say that the language is finite; all other languages are said to be infinite.

Consider the alphabet $A = \{I,V,X\}$. For this alphabet the closure of A is the infinite set

$$A^* = \{\varepsilon,I,V,X,II,IV,IX,VI,VV,VX,XI,XV,XX,III, \ldots\}$$

while the language $R(1..9)$ may be defined to be a finite subset of this, namely

$$R = \{I,II,III,IV,V,VI,VII,VIII,IX\}$$

R is the language of strings which form the legal Roman numbers corresponding to the natural numbers from one to nine. R is thus a finite language.

On the other hand, if the alphabet A is the alphanumeric character set, then we may define a subset of A^*, the Pascal identifier language, by the syntax diagram Figure 2.1. Note that in this example the language is infinite since we have placed no limitation on the string length.

Having defined languages in this way, a key problem to address is the algorithmic means for determining whether or not a particular string belongs to the language in question. In principle there is no difficulty for finite languages, since if the finite language is defined by an enumeration of acceptable strings then any candidate string may be compared with each of the valid strings in turn. However, such a string comparison method turns out to be rather inefficient in practice, and is in any case impossible in the case of infinite languages.

It is plausible to accept that the testing algorithm will be related in some fashion to the way in which the language defining rule is structured.

Certain mechanisms of language definition lead to simple recognition algorithms, while other mechanisms lead to more complex algorithms. One purpose of this book is to clarify this connection, so that sensible choices may be made when defining languages, and sufficiently powerful algorithms chosen when processing them by syntax-directed tools.

2.1.1 Section checklist and summary definitions

1. Assumed notions.
   - Symbol, and sequence.
2. Alphabet definitions.
   - An alphabet Σ is a finite set of symbols.
   - The cardinality of alphabet Σ is denoted $|\Sigma|$.
3. String definitions.
   - A string over alphabet Σ, is any finite sequence of symbols from alphabet Σ.
   - The length of a string α, denoted $|\alpha|$, is the number of symbols in the string.
   - The empty string, denoted ε, has length zero, i.e. $|\varepsilon| = 0$.
4. Definitions of closures.
   - The closure of some alphabet Σ is denoted Σ^*, and comprises all finite strings over alphabet Σ of length zero or more.
   - The positive closure of some alphabet Σ, denoted Σ^+, comprises all finite strings over alphabet Σ of length one or more.
5. Language definitions.
   - A language is a subset of Σ^*.
   - A language L is said to be infinite if the set L contains an infinite number of strings, otherwise it is said to be finite.
   - Finite languages may be defined by an enumeration of the strings which belong to the language.

2.2 The concept of state

The language recognition programs which we shall write may be thought of as examples of a particular kind of automatic mechanism. As an abstract model, we may think of a language recognizer as any device which accepts input symbols, one by one, and then finally answers *accept* or *reject*. Such a mechanism is called a **string-recognizing automaton**.

Our automata operate by examining each symbol of the input string in turn, from the start of the string to the end. For reasons which have more to do with history than with logic this is invariably referred to as **left to right scanning**.

At any intermediate instant during the recognition of a string the automaton must 'remember' certain information regarding that part of the string scanned so far. It is usually not necessary to store sufficient information to reconstruct the prefix string, but some lesser amount. An example may clarify this point.

Consider the two-member alphabet $B = \{T, F\}$, and a language E comprising all those finite strings from B^* which contain an *even* number of T symbols. We might call this the **even parity language**. Clearly E is an infinite language, and furthermore the acceptance or otherwise of any string depends on every single symbol in the string. However, it is not necessary for an automaton recognizing E to remember the identity of every symbol which it has encountered. It is sufficient for the automaton simply to remember whether it has seen an odd or even number of T symbols so far. In this case then, we conclude that the 'memory' of the automaton for past events comprises no more than a single Boolean-valued state variable which we might call **even so far**.

The information stored within the recognizing automaton corresponds to what we shall call the **state**. It is exactly the information which would need to be saved and restored if the task of recognition were to be interrupted and then resumed without error. The state thus represents and embodies all of the essential information about the part of the string seen so far at any intermediate point of the recognition process.

The concept of state occurs in a number of different contexts, with somewhat analogous meaning. To choose a physical example, in any dynamical system which changes its configuration with time, the state of the system is that part of the past history of the system which influences the future. For a single particle, this state consists of six coordinates, three of position, and three of velocity. Knowledge of these six components, and the future forces which will act on the particle, allows calculation of the future trajectory of that particle.

For our string recognizers we define the configuration of the automaton as the pair (*present state, remaining input string*). The present state encodes and encapsulates all necessary knowledge of the past input symbols, while the remainder of the input string contains all of the symbols still to be encountered.

There is always a distinguished state which we call the *start* state, so that the initial configuration, when an attempt to recognize a string α is about to begin, is (*start*, α). If the final state of the automaton after scanning string α is denoted *end*, then the final configuration is (*end*, ε). Of all possible final states arising from the scanning of strings from the alphabet, one or more belong to a set *accept*, corresponding to the configurations arising from strings which belong to the language. All final configurations containing states not belonging to *accept* correspond to strings which are not in the language, i.e. invalid strings. In the example given above of the even parity language, the accept set is just the single state *even so far*, which in this particular case is also the start state.

The nature of the state which an automaton must implement in order to recognize strings in a particular language depends on the way in which the rules of the language are structured. We shall be particularly interested in languages in which the state of the recognizing automaton is an element of a finite set. Such languages are called **regular languages**, and the automata which recognize them are called **finite state automata** (FSA). The chief attraction of this class of languages is the simplicity of their recognizers. Furthermore, as we shall see, there exist particularly evocative graphical representations for the behaviour of such systems, which makes their behaviour particularly easy to understand.

For programmed realizations of such FSA, the state, being a member of a finite set, may be represented by a single variable belonging to a scalar type in Pascal-like languages, or mapped onto a subrange of ordinal numbers in more primitive languages. The variable in such a programmed realization is called the **state variable**, and each state is a discrete value of that state variable.

2.2.1   Section checklist and summary definitions

1. Informal definition of state.
   - For a string-recognizing automaton, the state is a representation of the information derived from that part of the input string seen so far.
   - A finite state automaton has only a finite number of possible states.

2. Start state.
   - The start state of an automaton is the state of the automaton before reading the first symbol of any string.

3. Recognizer configuration.
   - The configuration of a recognizer at some point during a recognition attempt, is the pair (*present state, string remainder*).
   - The final configuration of an automaton after reading all of a string is (*end*, ε), where *end* is some state of the machine.

4. Accept states.
   - A subset of all states of an FSA is designated as an accept state.

- The complement of the accept set is the reject set.
- A string is accepted by an FSA if the final state belongs to the accept set, otherwise it is rejected.

2.3 State diagrams and the transition table

The distinguishing feature of finite state automata is that any implementation of such a machine has some kind of internal state variable to indicate the state of the machine. This state variable has only a finite number of permitted values, and there exists some function Φ (*state, symbol*), called the transition function, which defines a unique new state for each (*present state, alphabet symbol*) pair. This next state, called the successor state, replaces the present state. This behaviour can be represented and helpfully visualized, at least for FSA with few states, by a graphical device called a state diagram.

A state diagram is a directed graph composed of nodes, one node for each state, with directed edges leading from node to node. A label on each edge lists the symbol or symbols which cause the machine to make a transition from one node to another. Along any path in the graph, the string formed by concatenating edge symbols in the order in which they are traversed corresponds to the string of symbols in the language which causes that particular state sequence to arise. We say that the path **spells out** the string. The language defined by a state diagram is thus the set of all strings which spell out paths leading from the start state to any member of the accept state set.

A path in a graph which leads from some node back to the same node is called a **cycle**. It follows that any state diagram which has no cycles defines a finite language, since there is only a finite number of paths through any such graph. Conversely, any graph which has a cycle which is reachable from the start state, defines an infinite set of strings, since the closed path, once reached, may be traversed an arbitrary number of times.

As a first example of a state diagram, the FSA recognizing the even parity language of the last section corresponds to the diagram shown in Figure 2.2. The behaviour of the FSA may be understood directly from

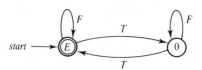

Figure 2.2   FSA recognizing the even parity language.

| Present | Symbol | |
state	T	F
even	odd	even
odd	even	odd

NextState

Figure 2.3   The transition table for language E.

the figure. The machine is initially in the state labelled E (for *even so far*), and any T symbol causes the machine to switch states to the state corresponding to *odd so far*. Any F symbol, however, causes the state of the automaton to remain unchanged, and hence does not cause a transition to a new state. Such null transitions which do not change the state are represented by self-loops in the state diagram which lead out of a state and back to the same state. By convention we represent all states belonging to the accept set by drawing them on the state diagram with a double circle. In Figure 2.2, as noted earlier, the start state is also the accept state.

The same information as is contained in the state diagram may also be represented in a transition table, which contains a next state entry for each (*state*, *symbol*) pair. The transition table is thus logically a two-dimensional table.

The transition table for the language E is shown in Figure 2.3. The row and column labels are the present state and the input symbol respectively, and the table entries are the successor states.

The state diagram for the Pascal identifier language defined by the syntax diagram, Figure 2.1, is shown in Figure 2.4.

If Figures 2.1 and 2.4 are compared, an interesting property of topological duality may be noted. Lines on Figure 2.1 correspond to the

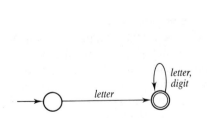

Figure 2.4   FSA recognizing the Pascal identifier language.

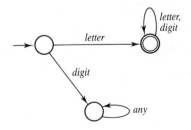

Figure 2.5   Complete FSA, including the error state.

| Present | Character type | |
state	alpha	numeric
start	accept	–
accept	accept	accept

NextState

Figure 2.6 Transition table for Pascal identifier language.

nodes of Figure 2.4, while the labelled shapes of Figure 2.1 correspond to the labelled edges of Figure 2.4. This is an example of a general form of duality which exists between syntax diagrams and state diagrams, which holds provided the syntax diagram is labelled only with symbols from the alphabet.

This last example raises an important question: what happens with an illegal string? In this state diagram there is no transition out of the start state labelled *digit*. The convention is that for all state diagrams which are incompletely specified there is an additional (usually undrawn) state called the error state. Any (*state, symbol*) pair which does not have a transition explicitly shown on the diagram corresponds to a transition to the error state. The error state is a *trap* state, since once the error state is entered, no exit to any non-error state is possible. Figure 2.5 is the complete state diagram corresponding to Figure 2.4, with the error state explicitly shown.

By convention, the state transition table corresponding to an incompletely specified state diagram usually does not show the error state. It is taken to be understood in such tables that if a valid transition is not explicitly given then the correct transition is to the implicit error state. Thus the transition for the Pascal identifer language is as shown in Figure 2.6.

2.3.1 The Roman numeral recognizer

Finally in this section we present a more complex example. The Roman numeral language $R(1..9)$ is recognized by the state diagram shown in Figure 2.7. Note that in this example the inclusion of the alternative, dubious form 'IIII' for the numeral *four* is easily admitted by including the additional transition shown by the dashed line. It is also apparent that the FSA not only recognizes the strings in the language, but also calculates the value of the string, since it is just the ordinal value of the final accept state.

The corresponding state transition table is shown in Figure 2.8. If the

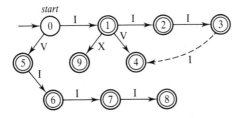

Figure 2.7   The Roman numeral language $R(1..9)$.

string 'IIII' is to be accepted, then the starred entry in Figure 2.8 should be changed to read 4.

In this example the very large proportion of blank entries corresponding to transitions to the error state should be noted. If a full table were to be given it would have an entry *error* in the place of each blank. This sparseness of the transition table is typical of the FSA which arise in practical applications. We may make good use of this characteristic in one form of programmed implementation of FSA, by using a compacted form of the table which only stores the non-error entries.

2.3.2 Section checklist and summary definitions

1. The transition function.
   - The transition function for an FSA defines the unique next state arising from every (*present state, input symbol*) pair.
   - The transition table is a tabular representation of the transition

Present state	Input symbol 'I'	'V'	'X'
0	1	5	–
1	2	4	9
2	3	–	–
3	–*	–	–
4	–	–	–
5	6	–	–
6	7	–	–
7	8	–	–
8	–	–	–
9	–	–	–

NextState

Figure 2.8   Transition table for the language $R(1..9)$.

function. The state diagram of an FSA is a graphical representation of the transition function.

2. State diagram conventions used in this book.

- A state diagram is a directed graph. Each node corresponds to a state, each directed edge to a transition.

- States are represented by solid circles, transitions by directed line segments connecting two nodes. Accept states are distinguished by being drawn with a double circle.

- Transitions are labelled by the symbol(s) which cause that transition to take place.

- If any particular state does not have an out-transition for some alphabet symbol, then there is an implicit transition on the omitted symbol, leading from that state to the error state. The error state itself may also be omitted from the diagram.

2.4 Languages defined by FSA

In Chapters 4 and 6 we shall deal with two different methods of specifying languages which may be recognized by finite state automata. In this section we explore some of the properties of such languages, which we shall presume for the moment are defined by state diagrams.

The members of the class of languages which may be recognized by finite state automata are called the **regular languages**. We first note that all finite languages are regular. An informal proof of this follows from noting the following constructive procedure, which actually demonstrates how to derive the state diagram to recognize a finite language. Let us first assume that the strings of the language are given some arbitrary ordinal numbering. Starting from an FSA consisting of just the start state we add the states required to recognize each string in turn until all the strings are recognized.

The state adding procedure is as follows. An attempt is made to recognize the new string with the partially constructed FSA. This attempt will terminate in one of two ways. In one case the string will end with the FSA in an already existing state, and that state is then marked as

Figure 2.9   Partially constructed FSA.

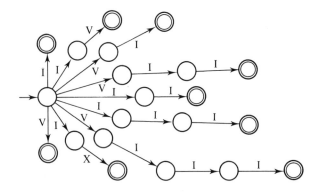

Figure 2.10   Non-deterministic FSA.

belonging to the accept set. The other possibility is that at some stage during the attempt to recognize a new string the partially constructed FSA will indicate an error transition. In this latter case a new chain of states is added, which starts from the current state, and which spells out the remainder of the current string. The final state of this newly added chain is marked as an accept state.

If this process is carried out for the language $R(1..9)$, then after the strings 'II', 'III' and 'V' have been inserted the partially constructed FSA is as shown in Figure 2.9.

It should be noted that the construction method which has been outlined requires the strings to be entered one at a time. An attempt simply to provide for all strings at once leads to a valid state diagram which is, however, **non-deterministic**. The result of such a method is shown in Figure 2.10.

The state diagram in Figure 2.10, and the FSA which it represents, are said to be non-deterministic because the rule relating the next state to the current (*state*, *symbol*) pair is multiple valued. In this example the possible successor states of the start state on the symbol 'I' are five in number. Later we shall study the systematic methods of removing such ambiguity from state diagrams, but at least for finite languages we can avoid the appearance of non-determinism at the outset.

The method given above for constructing an FSA to recognize a finite language does not necessarily lead to the 'simplest' FSA recognizing that particular language. For example, the FSA of Figure 2.7 was produced by the constructive method outlined above, but is not the simplest FSA which accepts the same language. Figure 2.11 is equivalent to the version of Figure 2.7 without the extra dashed transition. The reader is challenged to test the proposition that the FSA of Figure 2.11 accepts precisely the same language. A direct test that the same strings are accepted is quite feasible since there are only a finite number of strings

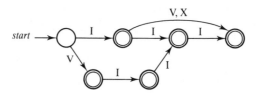

Figure 2.11   Minimal FSA for $R(1..9)$.

which are accepted. But how may one be sure that the same strings are rejected by each FSA?

We define two FSA as being **equivalent** if they accept precisely the same strings and reject the same strings. Equivalence in this particular sense implies that we cannot distinguish between the two automata on the basis of experiments with the acceptance of particular strings. For this reason, equivalent automata are also said to be **indistinguishable**. Given this definition, we are interested in finding from among all equivalent FSA one with the least number of states. It is an important result that just one, unique, minimal FSA does exist for any regular language. We may restate this result as the assertion that if two minimal FSA are equivalent then they are isomorphic[†] up to the naming of states. Although this result is not proved here, it has consequences for some of the later material.

In the event that two automata are not equivalent, there must be at least one string which one FSA accepts and the other rejects. Such a string is said to be a **distinguishing** string. One method of proof of the uniqueness property of minimal FSA has as a corollary the result that if two automata are not equivalent, and have n and m states respectively, then there is a distinguishing string of length at most $(n + m + 1)$.

Consideration of the finite languages has been useful, as it has provided an excuse for mentioning non-determinism, equivalence and minimization. However, almost all interesting languages are infinite. What may be deduced about the properties of languages which are infinite but may nevertheless be recognized by FSA?

2.4.1 The pumping lemma

It will be shown that all sufficiently long strings in a regular language have a simple repetitive property. Suppose that the FSA under consideration has a number of states n. Since our automaton is by assumption finite, it

---

[†] Two state diagrams are said to be isomorphic if every state in one corresponds to a unique state of the other.

is clear that such an n must certainly exist. Now, since by assumption the language which is accepted is infinite, there must exist strings in the language which are longer than n. Let us choose one such string, say β, where $\beta = c_1 c_2 c_3 \ldots c_m$, where the c_i are symbols from the alphabet Σ, and where m exceeds n.

If the state of the FSA after scanning i symbols is denoted S_i, then since there are more c_i than there are states, at least one state must have been visited more than once. Let us assume, to be definite that the state is the same after scanning c_i and c_j, where $j > i$. Thus the symbol sequence $c_{i+1}, \ldots c_j$ takes the FSA around a closed path in the state diagram which leads back to S_i. It follows that any string longer than n must include a loop-traversing substring. In fact a loop-traversing substring must be included somewhere in the string prior to the $(n + 1)$th symbol, for every sufficiently long string in the language. Clearly, this loop-traversing substring may be repeated any number of times without affecting the acceptability of the string.

The result obtained above is referred to as the **pumping lemma**, and may be obtained without recourse to a graphical argument. It is a powerful method for showing that certain language constructs are not regular, and hence require the use of recognizers which are not finite-state. The name pumping lemma is used because of the rather evocative concept involved in finding a loop-traversing substring, and using it to 'pump up' the string. The lemma assures us that for any sufficiently long string we can find such a substring, and by repeating it many times may pump the original string up to any length.

Clearly the above result cannot apply to finite languages, so we may conclude by way of corollary that in recognizing any finite language the number of states in the FSA must exceed the length of the longest string in the language. This result gives a crude lower limit to the number of states of an FSA, which is sometimes useful, but unfortunately says nothing at all about the minimal number of states required to recognize the more usual, infinite languages.

2.4.2   A non-regular language

We may use the pumping lemma to prove that any language which has nested parentheses cannot be regular, and hence cannot be recognized by an FSA. As a prototype of such languages, consider the infinite language given by

$$P = \{(x),((x)),(((x))), \ldots\}$$

We will show that this language cannot be recognized by an FSA with

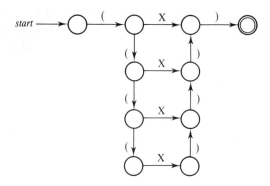

Figure 2.12   FSA for language with finite nesting levels.

only n states, no matter how large n is chosen to be. Consider the string

$$(((. . .(x))) . . .)$$

$(n + 1)$ parentheses

According to the pumping lemma, if the language is to be regular then somewhere in these first $(n + 1)$ symbols there is a substring which may be repeatedly traversed without affecting the legality of the string. Clearly, however, there is no substring in the first $(n + 1)$ symbols of the given string which may be repeated without upsetting the balance of the parentheses, and hence the acceptability of the string. We must regretfully conclude that this language is not recognized by any finite state automaton, and hence is not regular.

In general any language construct which involves the matching of brackets, or the balancing of equal numbers of **begins** and **ends**, or indeed any kind of recursively nested structure is not regular, and hence cannot be recognized by an FSA. Such constructs are not difficult to recognize, they simply require a different kind of automaton, and will be dealt with in detail later in the book. (See Chapters 6–9.)

It is an interesting observation, however, that if the nesting level is limited in the above example, then the language *is* finite and hence can be recognized by an FSA. The FSA which recognizes the language with a maximum nesting level of four is given in Figure 2.12.

It will be noted that the longest string recognized by the FSA of Figure 2.12 is '((((x))))', a string of length nine. Because of the corollary of the pumping lemma which was mentioned above, no finite language with a string of length nine may be recognized by an FSA with less than ten states. Since Figure 2.12 has exactly ten states, and in view of the uniqueness property mentioned above, we conclude that this is the minimal FSA recognizing the finite language. The reader may also easily see the mechanism which prevents the acceptance of the infinite version of this language by an FSA. As the permitted parenthesis nesting level is allowed to increase, a longer and longer 'ladder' of states grows downward in the diagram, so that when the nesting level becomes unbounded, then so does the number of states.

2.4.3 Section checklist and summary definitions.

1. Definition of a regular language.
   - A regular language is any language which may be recognized by a finite state automaton.

2. Finite and infinite languages.
   - Some infinite languages may be recognized by FSA and hence are regular. However, *every* finite language is regular.

3. The pumping lemma.
   - A pumpable substring is a substring of some valid string in a language, which may be repeated an arbitrary number of times without making the string invalid.
   - If a regular language is recognized by an FSA of n states, then every string in the language of length greater than n contains a pumpable substring.
   - Since there are many infinite languages in which there are no pumpable substrings, there are many languages which are not regular.

4. Equivalent automata.
   - Two automata are said to be equivalent if and only if they accept (and reject) precisely the same languages.
   - If two automata fail to be equivalent, then any string which one automaton accepts and the other rejects is called a distinguishing string.
   - Equivalent automata are said to be indistinguishable.
   - Among all equivalent FSA, there is a unique one with a minimal number of states.

2.5 Derived languages

Having defined a mechanism by which regular languages may be defined, we now take a brief look at the ways in which new languages may be derived from existing ones.

First, if we have a language L which is a subset of the closure of some alphabet Σ, then we define the complement of L as all the strings from Σ^* which do not belong to L. In symbols,

$$L' = \{\beta : \beta \in \Sigma^* \quad \text{and} \quad \beta \notin L\}$$

or in terms of the set difference operation

$$L' = \Sigma^* - L$$

It is an exercise for this chapter to prove that the complement of any regular language is also regular.

Note that if a language is finite, then its complement is necessarily infinite, but that if a language is infinite then its complement may be either finite or infinite. For example, the complement of the even parity language of Section 2.2 is infinite.

If we have two languages L_1 and L_2 defined over the same alphabet, then we may form new languages by performing set operations on the two. The union of the two languages is defined as the set of all those strings which belong to either one or other of the component languages, or to both.

$$L_1 \cup L_2 = \{\beta : \beta \in L_1 \quad \text{or} \quad \beta \in L_2\}$$

The intersection language is defined analogously as the set of all those strings which belong to both of the component languages.

$$L_1 \cap L_2 = \{\beta : \beta \in L_1 \quad \text{and} \quad \beta \in L_2\}$$

Note especially that the intersection of the two component languages may be empty. We designate such an empty language $\varnothing$, since its set of strings is the empty set. Such an empty language may be thought of as an extreme case of a finite language, being a language which contains exactly no strings at all.

We define the product of two languages $L_1 L_2$ as the set of strings in Σ^* which may be partitioned into two substrings the first of which belongs to L_1 and the second substring to L_2. $L_1 L_2$ is thus formed by concatenating strings from L_1 with those of L_2. In symbols

$$L_1 L_2 = \{\beta : \beta = \beta_1 \beta_2, \quad \text{where } \beta_1 \in L_1, \quad \text{and} \quad \beta_2 \in L_2\}$$

Clearly, in general $L_1 L_2 \neq L_2 L_1$ since the order in which the substrings are concatenated affects the strings of the language. Thus the product operation is not commutative. Of course if the two component languages are the same language, then the order of concatenation is immaterial. We may follow this particular path to define languages which are powers of a given language and which we denote, as one might expect, as L^2, L^3, and so on. Note that the product of two languages is infinite if either of the component languages is infinite, and is finite only if both of the component languages are finite.

By analogy with the definition of the product of two languages, we may define the quotient of two languages L_1/L_2 as the prefix strings left over when a suffix string belonging to L_2 is extracted from a string in L_1. Thus the quotient L_1/L_2 is the set of strings in Σ^* which can be concatenated with some string in L_2 to form a string in L_1. In symbols,

$$L_1/L_2 = \{\beta: \exists\ \beta_2 \in L_2 \quad \text{such that} \quad \beta\beta_2 \in L_1\}$$

The differences between the definitions of the language product and quotient should be noted. When a product is formed the derived language contains the strings formed by concatenating every string of the first language with every string from the second. On the other hand, a prefix string belongs to a quotient language if there is any single string in the 'divisor' language which may be removed from the right-hand end of a string in the other component language so as to leave the prefix. Product and quotient are thus not exactly inverse operations.

It is a fact that the union, intersection, product, and quotient of regular languages are also regular. Most of these results are proved in Section 4.3.4.

2.5.1   Section checklist and summary definitions

1. Operations on languages.
   - The complement of a language L is all the strings of Σ^* which are not in language L.
   - The union of two languages is the union of the two subsets of Σ^*.
   - The intersection of two languages is the intersection of the two subsets of Σ^*.
   - The product of two languages is the set of all strings formed by concatenating two strings, one from each language. The product is not commutative.

2. Derived regular languages.
   Suppose we have one or more languages, each of which, according to Section 2.1.1, is a subset of Σ^*, then we have the following results.
   - The complement of a regular language is a regular language.
   - The union of two regular languages is a regular language.
   - The intersection of two regular languages is a regular language.
   - The product of two regular languages is a regular language.

3. The empty language.
   - A special, limiting case of a finite language is the empty language $\varnothing$, which contains no strings at all.

Exercises

2.1 Verify that the FSA of Figures 2.7 and 2.11 accept exactly the same strings.

2.2 Carry out the constructive procedure of Section 2.4 for the Roman numeral language $R(1..9)$, verifying Figure 2.7.

2.3 Given an alphabet $\Sigma = \{a,b\}$ and a language L defined as all those strings in Σ^* which include three successive a symbols anywhere in their length, derive the state diagram of an FSA recognizing L.

2.4 Design a state diagram for an FSA which accepts identifiers which obey the following rules:
the first character must be alphabetic; following characters may be alphabetic, numeric or the underscore character; however, an underscore may not be the final character, and two underscores may not be adjacent.

2.5 A language is defined as the set of all numeric strings such that the natural number corresponding to the string is exactly divisible by seven. This language happens to be regular. Deduce how many states an automaton must have in order to recognize this language. [*Hint*: Do not try to form a state diagram, instead try to deduce the form and amount of information which the automaton must 'remember' between digits in a left to right scan.]

2.6 The complement of a language L, which we denote as L', is the set of all strings in Σ^* which are not in L. Derive a constructive procedure which starts with an FSA which recognizes L and modifies the FSA so that it finally recognizes L'. Hence show that the complement of any regular language is also regular.

2.7 Given the language $R(1..9)$ and a language $L = \{I,II,III\}$, calculate the quotient of R with respect to L, i.e. R/L.

2.8 Consider the two languages
$$X = \{x,xxx,xxxxx, \ldots\}$$
$$A = \{a,xa\}$$
Form the product language $P = XA$, and then the quotient language $Q = P/A$, to show that Q and X are not the same language and hence product and quotient are not inverse operations.

2.9 If two languages L_1 and L_2 are not disjoint, then their intersection contains at least one string. Show that the quotient of any two such languages includes the empty string, i.e. $\varepsilon \in L_1/L_2$.

Further reading

The theory of finite state automata is dealt with in a number of books. Hopcroft and Ullman (1979) is a modern introduction which deals with much of the theory in a much more rigorous fashion than does this book. Aho and Ullman (1972, 1973) is an older but still encyclopaedic treatment of the theory of this chapter and much else.

The hardware implementation of finite state or sequential machines has many parallels with the theory of FSA as it is applied to language recognition. McLuskey (1965) and Unger (1969) are relatively old switching theory texts which make interesting comparison with the material in this book. A more modern treatment of automata from a hardware point of view is found in Kohavi (1978).

Chapter 3 Implementing Finite State Automata

3.1 Table driven FSA

An FSA, as defined by a state diagram or any other mechanism, is an abstract automaton. An **implementation** of an FSA is a hardware device or software program which receives as its input a sequence of symbols from the alphabet Σ, and updates its internal state as specified by the transition function Φ. An implementation is thus a real object which behaves as specified by the FSA state diagram. For this reason we also refer to an implementation of an FSA as a **realization**.

We are chiefly interested in implementing FSA by software, but similar considerations apply in the case of implementation by programs stored in read-only memory, i.e. firmware. The techniques of direct realizations in hardware are allied, but lie beyond the scope of this book.

Conceptually the simplest method of implementing an FSA is to provide directly for a state variable to be updated by reference to a two-dimensional lookup table.

We assume that the representation of the transition function is a table indexed on the present state and current symbol, perhaps an array *NextState[state, symbol]*. The state is then updated by a cyclic process which we call the **interpretation cycle**. The interpretation cycle is shown in Figure 3.1.

A complete algorithm must also provide for initialization, including the setting of the machine to the start state, and for testing of whether or not the final state is in the accept set.

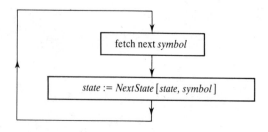

Figure 3.1 FSA interpretation cycle.

```
procedure FSAinterpret(var accept : BOOLEAN);
  {declarations}
begin
  {table initialization};
  state := Start;
  GetSymbol;
  while symbol in Alphabet do begin
    state := NextState[state,symbol];
    GetSymbol;
    end; (* string end has been found *)
  accept := state in AcceptStates;
end;
```

Figure 3.2   The FSA interpretation algorithm.

It is an important observation that the algorithm for interpreting the transition table of an FSA is the same for any FSA. To change from one FSA to another only requires the *NextState* table contents to be changed. This is of itself an important factor in favour of table-driven methods of language recognition, since it implies that modifications to the language may be made simply by changing table contents.

Written as a Pascal procedure, a complete table interpretation algorithm is given in Figure 3.2. Note the use of the Boolean expression in the last statement of the procedure to assign a value to the accept parameter. This is a programming idiom which occurs frequently in programs of this type.

It is assumed that the declarations include the state and symbol types, as well as the actual values of those variables, and the table structure. In this instance the algorithm assumes that the end of the string is marked by some non-alphabet symbol. The procedure *GetSymbol* fetches the next input symbol. In any particular application the *GetSymbol* procedure might be a simple *READ(ch)*, an assignment of a symbol from some buffer, or a procedure call to another FSA which recognizes the valid symbols in some lower-level alphabet.

3.1.1 The candybar vendor

Let us take as an example the control automaton for a candybar dispenser. The device has coin slots for nickels, dimes and quarters, and also two push-buttons marked 'reject' and 'vend'. The dispenser charges 30¢ for the bars, gives change and rejects all coins after the machine already has 30¢ or more deposited toward a transaction. The state

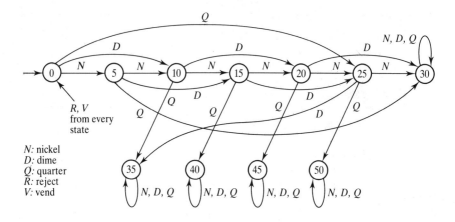

Figure 3.3   State diagram of the candybar vendor.

diagram of an FSA implementing the machine logic is shown in Figure 3.3. In this case the state of the machine needs to hold no information other than the amount of money presently credited towards the vending of a candybar. Thus in Figure 3.3 the states have been labelled so as to reflect the present credit amount in cents.

Of course, for such a machine it is not sufficient to accept a 'string' of money and push-button signals, we must arrange for appropriate output actions as well. We call such side-effects of the recognition process **semantic actions**, since they have to do with the meaning of the string rather than its grammatical structure or syntax.

Present state	nickel	dime	Input symbols quarter	reject	vend	
0	5/–	10/–	25/–	0/a	0/a	
5	10/–	15/–	30/–	0/a	0/a	
10	15/–	20/–	35/–	0/a	0/a	
15	20/–	25/–	40/–	0/a	0/a	
20	25/–	30/–	45/–	0/a	0/a	
25	30/–	35/–	50/–	0/a	0/a	*next state/action*
30	30/b	30/b	30/a	0/a	0/c	
35	35/b	35/b	35/b	0/a	0/d	
40	40/b	40/b	40/b	0/a	0/e	
45	45/b	45/b	45/b	0/a	0/f	
50	50/b	50/b	50/b	0/a	0/g	

Figure 3.4   The candybar vendor transition table.

a: return all coins
b: reject last coin
c: vend bar, no change
d: vend bar, a nickel change
e: vend bar, a dime change
f: vend bar, nickel and dime change
g: vend bar, two dimes change

Figure 3.5   Semantic actions for the candybar vendor.

The transition table for the candybar dispenser is given in Figure 3.4. It contains not only the next state, but also an index into a semantic action table. The table of semantic actions is shown in Figure 3.5, and indicates the action to be taken on each transaction.

Figure 3.6 is a Pascal program which emulates the candybar vendor machine. Most of the code in Figure 3.6 has to do with emulating the input process, the coin insertions and the button pushes from the keyboard of a terminal. The FSA interpreter requires only seven lines of Pascal code, if the action of printing explanations and prompts is not counted. The tables are presumed to be set up in a procedure body which is not shown. One array corresponds to the transition table Figure 3.4 while the other is an array of literal strings which indicate what the corresponding semantic action would be.

Figure 3.6 does not include the details of the table initializations, or the method by which the keyboard input is made to simulate the insertion of coins and pressing of buttons. In this simulation, the 'semantic action' is to print a message, rather than actually to dispense change and candy. This is completely fair of course, since the simulation does not insist on real money as input.

The candybar FSA example was chosen because it lends itself well to direct table interpretation, with the table stored as a complete two-dimensional array. In most cases of interest, however, the full tables are unnecessarily large, and it is preferable to compact the tables by omitting all the error transition entries by methods treated in Section 3.3.

3.1.2   Section checklist and summary definitions

1. Use of a state variable.
   - Since the state of an FSA is a member of a finite set, the states may be enumerated, and represented by a variable of ordinal type in the recognizing automaton.

```
    program CANDYBAR(INPUT,OUTPUT);
      type StateType = (S0,S5,S10,S15,S20,S25,S30,S35,S40,S45,S50);
           SymbolType = (Nickel,Dime,Quarter,Reject,Vend,Exit);
           MessageType = packed array[0..25] of CHAR;
      var deposited : StateType;
          input : SymbolType;
          TransitionTable :
             array [StateType,Nickel..Vend] of StateType;
          ActionTable :
             array [StateType,Nickel..Vend] of MessageType;

    procedure GetSymbol;
    begin { Simulate input from keyboard } end;

    procedure FormTables;
    begin { Set up tables } end;

    begin (* Main block *)
      FormTables;
      WriteLn;
      WriteLn('Emulation of candy-bar vendor.');
      WriteLn('N=Nickel,D=Dime,Q=Quarter,V=Vend,R=Reject,X to exit');
      deposited := S0;
      GetSymbol;
      while input <> Exit do begin
        WriteLn(ActionTable[Deposited,Input]); (* write message *)
        deposited := TransitionTable[deposited,input];
        GetSymbol;
      end; (* while *)
      WriteLn('Emulation ended.');
    end.
```

Figure 3.6   The candybar FSA emulator program.

2. The interpretation cycle.

- Recognition of a regular language is performed by loop which alternately fetches the next symbol, then updates the state variable as prescribed by the next state table.

3. The next state table.

- The next state table is a two-dimensional array indexed on the pair (*present state*, *input symbol*).

```
program FSAINT( . . . );
  { declarations . . . }
begin
  state := start;
  GetSymbol;
  while symbol in Alphabet do begin
    case state of
      start:  if token in LegalStart then
                case symbol of
                  t1: {update state and any semantic action};
                  t2: {update etc.}
                     .
                     .
                     .
                end (* case *)
              else state := error;
      one:  if symbol in LegalOne then
              case symbol of
                 .
                 .
                 .
              end (* case *)
            else state := error;
         .
         .
         .
      error: (* error is trap state so do nothing *);
      end (* outer case *)
    GetSymbol;
    end; (*while*)
  accept := state in AcceptStates;
end.
```

Figure 3.7   Skeleton of an FSA using nested **case** statements.

3.2 Programmed realizations of FSA

An alternative to the table-driven method of FSA implementation, as described in the last section, is directly to implement the machine as a high-level language program. One advantage of such an approach is that only the non-error entries in the transition table need to be programmed. In languages which have enumerated types a convenient mechanism is to use a variable such as the state variable, and to use a **case** statement to select the code relevant to the transitions out of each state. The most general structure of such a program consists of nested **case** statements.

Let us consider a general example of FSA which recognize strings from some alphabet, and where the strings are terminated by a non-alphabet symbol. We assume a scalar variable *state* has been declared, which takes the values *start, one, two, . . . n, error*. Further, we will assume that a number of sets of symbols have been declared, one for each value of the state type, corresponding to the symbols which give valid transitions out of that state.

The skeletal structure of the program to implement any such FSA is shown in Figure 3.7. Note that the inner **case** statements are protected by enclosing **if**s. This is as demanded by the syntax of standard Pascal. However, extended dialects which augment the case statement with **others, otherwise, else** or similar constructs considerably tidy up this detail. It should also be noted that if the number of cases is small then an **if** statement may be preferred to the **case** statement.

The figure also indicates the position in which semantic actions, if any, are conveniently placed. In Section 3.5 this point is addressed in more detail.

3.2.1 Recognizing Roman numerals

We now consider the recognition of Roman numerals. The state diagram for the recognition of the numerals 1..9 was shown in Figure 2.7. A straightforward application of the schema of Figure 3.7 leads to the procedure in Figure 3.8.

We may simplify the procedure in Figure 3.8 further, particularly by making use of the similarities in the **case** statement actions for states 2, 5, 6 and 7. However, instead we will consider the rather more interesting problem of dealing with Roman numbers of any size.

It turns out that the minimal state machine for recognizing Roman numerals of any size has only 16 non-error states, but a direct implementation of this FSA is not the most simple approach. Instead, we try to make use of the structure of the problem to suggest ways of decomposing the problem into parts. The key is to realize that the numbers 10,20, . . . 90 are structured exactly as for 1,2, . . . 9, except that the symbols 'X','L','C' replace 'I','V','X'. Similarly 100,200, . . . 900 have the same structure as 1,2, . . . 9 except that the corresponding symbols are 'C','D','M'. Finally, whole thousands are just indicated by repetitions of the symbol 'M'. For example the string MMMCMLXXIX is decomposed as shown here.

$$\underbrace{\text{MMM}}_{\text{thousands}} \quad \underbrace{\text{CM}}_{\text{hundreds}} \quad \underbrace{\text{LXX}}_{\text{tens}} \quad \underbrace{\text{IX}}_{\text{units}} \ = 3979$$

Notice that the thousands are terminated by the first non-'M' character, the hundreds by the first character not in the set {'C','D','M'}, and the

```
procedure RDIGIT(var Valid:BOOLEAN);
   const Error = 10; (* State 10 is error state *)
   var    state : 0..10;
          ch : CHAR;

begin
   Read(ch);
   state := 0;
   while ch in ['I','V','X'] do begin
     case state of
        0: case ch of
              'I': state := 1;
              'V': state := 5;
              'X': state := Error;
           end;
        1: case ch of
              'I': state := 2;
              'V': state := 4;
              'X': state := 9;
           end;
        2: if ch='I' then state := 3 else state := Error;
        5: if ch='I' then state := 6 else state := Error;
        6: if ch='I' then state := 7 else state := Error;
        7: if ch='I' then state := 8 else state := Error;
        3,4,8,9,10: state := Error;
     end; (* case *)
     Read(ch);
   end (* while *);
   Valid := state in [1..9];
end;
```

Figure 3.8   Recognizer for the language $R(1..9)$.

tens by the first character not in the set {'X','L','C'}. It is thus a relatively simple matter to detect the end of each digit-group, and to decompose the whole problem into the subproblems of recognizing the thousands, hundreds, tens, and units in turn.

The algorithm is:

```
begin
   while char = 'M' do {add the thousands};
   {find whole hundreds};
   {find whole tens};
   {find units}
end;
```

```
procedure ROMAN(var value:INTEGER; var valid:BOOLEAN);
  const Error = 10;
  var DVAL : INTEGER;
      OK : BOOLEAN;
      ch : CHAR;

  procedure RDIGIT(var digvalue:INTEGER; I,V,X:CHAR):
    var state : 0..10;
  begin
    state := 0;
    while ch in [I,V,X] do begin
      if ch = I then
        case state of
          0,1,2,5,6,7: state := state+1;
          3,4,8,9,10:  state := Error;
        end
      else if ch = V then
        case state of
          0: state := 5;
          1: state := 4;
          2,3,4,5,6,7,8,9,10: state := Error;
        end
      else (* ch=X *)
        if state = 1 then state := 9 else state := Error;
          if not EOLN then READ(ch);
    end (* while *);
    if state = Error
        then OK := FALSE
        else digvalue := state;
  end; (* RDIGIT *)
begin (* main block *)
  value := 0;
  OK := TRUE;
  if not EOLN then Read(ch);
  while ch = 'M' do begin
    value := value + 1000; Read(ch);
    end;
  RDIGIT(DVAL,'C','D','M'); (* fetch hundreds *)
  value := value + DVAL * 100;
  RDIGIT(DVAL,'X','L','C'); (* fetch tens *)
  value := value + DVAL * 10;
  RDIGIT(DVAL,'I','V','X'); (* fetch units *)
  value := value + DVAL;
  valid := OK and EOLN; (* check for terminator *)
  ReadLn;
end;
```

Figure 3.9   Complete Roman number recognizer.

Each of the *find* operations may be performed by a call to the same procedure, thus making use of the similarity of structure in the different digit groups. In order to achieve this generality the actual character sets which are used for each digit group are sent over as actual parameters to a digit-recognition procedure. In each case the digit-recognition procedure returns as soon as it encounters a character which does not belong to the 'subalphabet' for that particular digit group.

A complete procedure which recognizes Roman numbers of any size using this approach is shown in Figure 3.9. In this particular example, the choice has been made that an empty string denotes zero, so that in effect the language has been defined so that ε is a valid string.

There is a subtle trap involved in attempting to embed directly the single digit-recognizing procedure of Figure 3.8 in this larger problem. The inner **case** statements of Figure 3.8 work perfectly well with 'I','V' and 'X' as case labels, but the syntax of Pascal forbids the use of variables (and hence formal parameters) as case labels. The solution adopted in Figure 3.9 is to reverse the order of nesting so that the '**case** *ch* **of**' appears only once, as the outer branching construct, and then replace the **case** statement by a sequence of **if** statements.

Another nice point is that the Boolean *OK* is a '**sticky**' flag. A sticky flag is one which can be set to *false* by a number of different statements in a program, but is not set to *true* by any statement except during initialization. In this case *OK* may be set to *false* by any of the invocations of *RDIGIT*, but cannot be set back to true by any subsequent invocations, even if the substrings treated by the later calls happen to be error-free. Thus at the end of the recognition process the flag is *false* if any substring of the string was invalid. The sticky flag thus performs a kind of logical-**or** on the results of the substring analyses.

It should be noted that a good deal of compaction of the source code has been obtained by utilizing the fact that any valid 'I' character increments the ordinal number of the state by exactly one. It is always pleasing to find such special features in a particular problem which lead to simplification of the implementation. However, such features must be used with extreme caution, since the result may be to make the code obscure and consequently difficult to debug or modify.

3.2.2 A *real* number scanner

We treat one further example in this section, a useful FSA which we will consider in several variant forms.

One of the logical oddities of the Pascal environment is the rules which apply to the input of *real* numbers. In particular, a *real* number must contain a decimal point, with at least one digit on either side of it. There are very valid reasons why *real* numbers inside the program must adhere to rules such as this – the compiler would otherwise not be able to

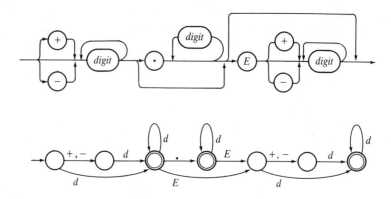

Figure 3.10   Syntax and state diagrams for *real* number FSA.

tell what type a numeric constant is supposed to be. However, there is very little reason to insist that this format also be used for program input. After all, the ultimate user of the program may not even know that the program is written in Pascal, let alone what format the *real* type is supposed to be.

The FSA which we will consider is a utility procedure which recognizes character strings which form *real* numbers in a fairly free format. We define the *real* number input language as consisting of:

An optional sign, followed by one or more decimal digits. These are followed by the optional fractional part which, if present, consists of a decimal point followed by zero or more digits. Finally an optional exponent part may appear. This exponent part consists of the letter 'E', followed by an optional sign character and one or more digits. The number is terminated by an end of line, and may be preceded by any number of blank characters.

In Chapter 4 we will look at a precise way of specifying regular languages using a formalism called regular expressions, and a method of systematically transforming these into state diagrams or transition tables. However, this particular example is sufficiently simple that it is possible, with a little effort, to verify that the syntax and state diagrams of Figure 3.10 correspond to the above word description.

Looking at the state diagram, it may be noted that a number of states share common successor states for a given input symbol group. For example, states 0,1,2 on symbol d, where symbol d is used to signify any digit character, '0'..'9'. Under these circumstances it seems that the code will be most compact if the transitions are sorted first by symbol group,

```
procedure ReadReal(var IsNum : BOOLEAN);
   const Error = 7;
   var    state : [0..7];
          ch : CHAR;

begin
   (* accept states are [2,3,6] *)
   state := 0; (* start state *)
   repeat
     Read(ch);
     if (state = 0) and (ch = ' ') then (*skip*)
     else if ch in ['0'..'9'] then
       case state of
          0,1 :   state := 2;
          4,5 :   state := 6;
          2,3,6,7 :   (* unchanged state *);
       end (*case*)
     else if ch in ['+','−'] then
       if state = 0 then state := 1
       else if state = 4 then state := 5
       else state := Error
     else if (ch = '.') and (state = 2) then
       state := 3
     else if (ch in ['E','e']) and (state in [2,3]) then
       state := 4
     else state := Error
     end; (*if*)
   until EOLN;
   IsNum := state in [2,3,6];
   ReadLn;
end;
```

Figure 3.11   The *real* input constant recognizer.

and then by present state. A procedure which recognizes strings in this *real* input language is given in Figure 3.11; it does not show any semantic actions but simply checks for validity of the strings. We consider the concurrent accumulation of the value of the number in a later section.

In this procedure, leading space characters are skipped only while the FSA is in state zero. The interpretation loop is terminated by the *EOLN* condition, and the Boolean flag *IsNum* set to indicate the validity or otherwise of the input string. This feature enables the calling program to test *IsNum* before making use of any returned value, and thereby prevent incorrect input from terminating the program.

3.2.4 Section checklist and summary definitions

Programmed implementations of FSA.

- Programmed realizations of FSA take advantage of the fact that many of the entries in the transition table are error transitions, by only requiring the non-error transitions to be coded.
- The most general program structure for a programmed implementation is a set of nested **case** statements, but very frequently some of these degenerate into **if** . . . **then** . . . constructions.

3.3 Sparse table techniques

The table-lookup method of implementing FSA has the virtue of simplicity and of easy modification. However the size of the arrays may become too large even in simple cases. For example, the *real* number recognizer treated in the last section, if implemented by a direct table lookup, would require a data structure

> *NextState*: **array**[0..7, *CHAR*] of *StateNum*;

If a full ASCII character set is implemented, this array is 1024 elements, of which all but 78 are error transitions. A possible alternative is to have a separate procedure, called by the FSA interpret procedure, which sorts the characters into groups which form the symbols for FSA interpret.

For the real number parser the symbol type might be declared as

> **type** *SymbolType* = (*digit,sign,blank,E,point,bad*);

and be fetched by a procedure such as the following procedure *GetSymbol*.

```
procedure GetSymbol(var symbol : SymbolType);
begin
  Read(ch);
  if (ch in ['0'..'9'] then symbol := digit
  else if (ch='+') or (ch='−') then symbol := sign
  else if (ch='E') or (ch ='e') then symbol := E
  else if ch='.' then symbol := point
  else symbol := bad
end;
```

This technique reduces the size of the array *NextState* to just 42 entries, a spectacular saving in space, but this must be offset against the program space used by the procedure which groups the characters. In any event, the transition table is still quite sparse, as may be seen from Figure 3.12.

In many circumstances the best solution is to store only the non-error

state	digit	sign	Symbol blank	E	point	bad
0	2	1	0	–	–	–
1	2	–	–	–	–	–
2	2	–	–	4	3	–
3	3	–	–	4	3	–
4	6	5	–	–	–	–
5	6	–	–	–	–	–
6	6	–	–	–	–	–
7	–	–	–	–	–	–

Figure 3.12   The *real* number FSA.

entries of the transition table in an indexed array. We will consider how to achieve this objective in the case of the table for the *real* number FSA.

The table may be represented by a one-dimensional array of non-error entries stored so that all transitions starting from the same state are adjacent. As shown in Figure 3.13, an index array indicates the starting position of each transition group in the array. In order to find the successor state from the table, with present state i and symbol t, the *NextState* table is indexed from *Start*[i] to one position short of *Start*[$i + 1$], and each symbol entry checked against t. If no match is found, then by default the next state must be the *error* state. The overall effect of this reorganization is to leave the FSA interpretation procedure unchanged except that the table lookup implied by the assignment

   state := *NextState*[*state*, *symbol*];

is replaced by a call to a *NextState* function which accesses the data structure and returns the successor value of the *state*. The function is invoked by the assignment

   state := *NextState*(*state*, *symbol*);

The similarities of the assignment statements in the two cases should be noted. So far as the FSA interpretation procedure is concerned the whole table system is an abstraction which has no other purpose than responding on demand with a successor state value. The actual mechanism used to implement this abstraction, whether direct table lookup or the searching of some compacted table, is irrelevant to the logic of the algorithm. In such cases, programming languages such as Ada and Modula-2, which support the construction of abstract data types, allow for the separation of abstraction from implementation in an elegant fashion.

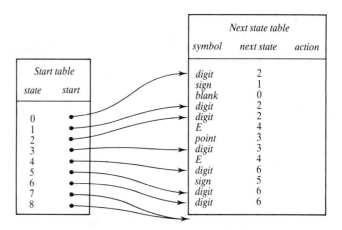

Figure 3.13 Compacted table for the *real* number FSA showing the index array *Start*, and the position of the semantic action entries.

The algorithm for a *NextState* function, suitable for accessing the data-structure in Figure 3.13, is given in Figure 3.14.

Several things should be noticed about the data structure in Figure 3.14 and the function which accesses it. Firstly, it is necessary to have an additional entry in the index table *start*, which points beyond the end of the valid token entries for the last state considered. Furthermore, for machines in which the appropriate semantic action depends on both the *state* and the *symbol*, a separate *action* field may be placed in the table records. Figure 3.13 indicates the position of such a field for those cases where it is required.

We may calculate the space savings due to the technique described by the last two figures under suitable assumptions regarding the size of the various data elements. Let us assume that the number of states, the number of symbols and the number of distinct semantic actions are all less than the cardinality of the type *CHAR* in the implementation used. The *symbol, next state*, and *action* entries may thus each be packed into a single byte. If N is the number of states, and M the number of symbols, then the full uncompacted table will have two bytes per entry, one each for the *Successor* and *Action* fields, and will occupy a total space equal to

$S(\text{uncompacted}) = 2NM$ bytes

Let us now suppose that the number of non-error entries is $L = \varrho NM$, where ϱ is defined as the density factor of the table, i.e. the fraction of the table entries which are not *error*. In this case the compacted table size will be $3L$ bytes, since there are L entries and each contains three single byte fields. The *Start* array is of length $(N + 1)$ and of width at most two

```
function NextState(state : StateType;
                      symbol : SymbolType) : StateType;
   var   index, endmark : 0..MaxIndex;
         found : BOOLEAN;
begin
   index := start[state];
   endmark := start[state + 1];
   found := FALSE;
   while not found and (index < endmark) do
      if table[index].sym = symbol then begin
         found := TRUE;
         NextState := table[index].next;
         end
      else
         index := index + 1;
   if not found then NextState := Error;
end;
```

Figure 3.14   The *NextState* function.

bytes. The total space required is thus

$S(\text{compacted}) = 3\varrho NM + 2(N + 1)$ bytes

In typical practical cases the density factor ϱ is of the order of 0.1, so that the formula shows that space savings of the order of 80% are attainable. Of course the size of the code for *NextState* must be accounted for, but this may be very small.

There are many alternative schemes which might be used to organize the compacted table. For example, each *start* table entry might contain a length field which specifies the number of entries in the *NextState* array which correspond to that *state*. If this is done then only a single access to *start* is required for each call of the *NextState* function, at the cost of an extra field in each *start* array record.

Another example of a modified form of data structure might place the entries in the table, for each state, in strict order of symbol collation sequence so that it is immediately apparent when the range of possible matches between the actual symbol and the token field entries has been exceeded. With this modification it is possible to go further, and to dispense with the *start* array altogether, by replacing each *successor* field entry with a starting index of the next *state* entry. These entries are in one-to-one correspondence with state ordinals, and thus serve perfectly well as distinguished values of the *state* variable. However, the table entries for distinct states must now be separated by dummy entries which contain a token field with a special *stop* symbol with an ordinal value greater than any alphabet symbol. For this particular form of compacted table there is no space saving compared to the scheme of Figure 3.13 since there will be ($\varrho NM + N$) entries which must each occupy 3 or even 4 bytes.

The possibility of greater width arises from the larger range of the starting index ordinal compared to the state ordinal which it replaces. However, this modified method may have advantages in terms of execution speed since it avoids an extra table access.

There are other, more specialized methods of organizing sparse tables, most of which trade off reduced space usage against slower execution. In many cases these methods require substantial human or machine labour to organize the tables, so we do not treat them here. However, there is a simple and generally applicable method of organization which minimizes the average execution time. Since the *NextState* function searches sequentially through the table looking for a symbol match, for each state the most probable symbols should be listed first.

3.3.1 Implicit state variable implementation of FSA

A question which naturally arises in connection with the implementation of FSA by means of sparse table lookup is whether it is actually necessary to have a state variable at all. For one of the variants of sparse table organization it was noted that merely keeping a pointer into the start point of the table for that particular state sufficed as a 'state variable'. A further extension of that idea involves the use of the **program counter** as state variable. Instead of the value of some state variable tracing out a path through the state diagram as recognition proceeds, the 'locus of control' threads through the code of the program. We may refer to such an implementation of an FSA as possessing an **implicit state variable**.

We may imagine the process of implementing an FSA using an implicit state variable as consisting of the following (where it is assumed that the programming environment permits the use of named labels). For every state in the state diagram we define a suitably named label. These labels may as well be *state1*, *state2* etc. At each labelled location we place code of the form

```
stateX: case smbl of
           a : goto stateY;
           b : goto stateZ;
               .
               .

           x,y, . . . : goto errorstate;
        end;
```

or some equivalent branching construct. In general each selected case would also perform some semantic action before taking the **goto**.

Such a program structure may make the purist blush, since it violates every tenet of good programming practice, but things may not actually be as bad as they appear. In the first place, such a structure implemented in assembly language will outperform any other type of FSA implementation on the same hardware and so must come into consideration for dedicated applications in which speed is the only criterion. Furthermore, when the state diagram is configured in certain special ways, the unstructured appearance of the prototype code entirely disappears and the FSA may be implemented without a single **goto**. The key observation is to note that a straight-line sequence of states may be implemented by a straight-line sequence of program statements, with control passing from statement to statement in normal sequence without any jumps. Side-loops through a sequence of states may be recognized by an appropriate structured loop, while alternate paths may be selected by following the selecting statement with straight-line code rather than a **goto** as was indicated above.

One of the less obvious corollaries of the material in Chapter 4 is that any regular language may be specified by using only the sequence, looping and selection constructs. Because of this result, it follows that any regular language may be implemented by an implicit state variable machine, without the use of **goto**s. In such cases we may perform the design without even generating a state diagram or transition table, for what we have finally ended up with is a non-recursive version of one of the types of language recognizer dealt with later in Section 8.2 (recursive descent). The concept of an implicit state variable thus provides an interesting and uniquely different way of looking at what is normally considered to be a completely separate recognition method.

3.3.2   Section checklist and summary definitions

1. Characteristics of compacted table implementations.

   - Compacted table implementations save table space by storing only the non-error transitions of the next state function.

   - Space savings may be large for very sparse tables, but the method requires the presence of some kind of subsidiary index array to point into the transition vector, and also requires that transition entries explicitly store the symbol on which they are predicated.

   - The usual two-dimensional table lookup for a table-driven implementation is replaced by a function call in the case of the sparse table method. The actual parameters which are sent to the function correspond to the indices used in the table lookup.

- In most cases, use of a sparse table implies a trade-off, in which speed of access is sacrificed in order to save table space.

2. Implicit state implementations.

- It is possible to implement FSA without having any explicit state variable. In such a case the locus of control of the program implicitly traces out the sequence of 'states'.

3.4   Multi-level FSA; lexical scanners

We have already met examples of recognizers which are multi-level automata, in which the lower-level FSA recognizes strings which then form the atomic symbols of the higher-level automaton. By analogy with the names which are used for components of compilers of programming languages we call the lowest level a **lexical scanner**. In programming languages the rules which specify the ways in which strings of characters make up the symbols of the language are almost always specified so as to lead to regular languages, and hence to recognition by FSA. On the other hand, the language rules which specify how those symbols may be used to build programs are usually not regular and hence cannot be recognized by FSA. These rules for the upper level are usually said to specify the **syntax** of the language.

The terms **lexical** and **syntactic** are borrowed from standard English usage, where lexical means 'having to do with the way in which words are formed', while syntactic means 'having to do with the way in which sentences are constructed from words'. The analogy is quite a close one. Sentences are indeed built up from words as their atomic units, while on a lower level the words are made up of the lower-level units, the alphabetic characters.

The examples which we have considered so far have used the lower-level recognizer to group characters into convenient lexical categories, and thereby reduce the complexity of a higher-level recognizer. However, in many cases the lower-level FSA needs to recognize substrings in the language. On detecting the end of any valid substring the lower level is required to report to the higher-level recognizer as to which symbol has been found, usually on the basis of the final state in which the FSA has been left. Thus different accept states in the FSA may correspond to the recognition of different symbols of the higher-level language, or **tokens** as we shall usually call them.

There is a subtle but significant difference between an FSA which recognizes complete strings in a language, and any lower-level FSA used to pick out the lexical entities from within a character string. The difference is that the lexical scanning FSA must be able to infer the end of a substring making up a token, even though the input character string has not ended.

The need to recognize embedded strings, and the added complexity which it causes, is related to the overall problem of detecting the end of strings for any FSA. So far, the FSA considered have had the benefit of language rules which make the detection of the end of the string simple. We have generally assumed that the string-end is marked by any non-alphabet symbol, so that the interpretation loop may be controlled by constructs such as

> **while** *smbl* **in** *alphabet* **do begin**
>
> .
>
> .
>
> .
>
>   *GetSymbol*;
> **end**; (* while *)

This particular construction may be used for lexical scanners provided that a set of symbols is reserved for no other purpose than to act as separators. For example, a scanner which accepts numbers separated by characters belonging to some explicit set of characters might be implemented by

> **procedure** *ReadNum*(**var** *value* : *NumType*;**var** *valid* : *BOOLEAN*);
>   **var** *ch* : CHAR; *state* : *StateType*;
> **begin**
>   *Read*(*ch*);
>   *state* := *start*;
>   **while not** *ch* **in** *SeparatorSet* **do begin**
>
> .
>
> .
>
> .
>
>   *Read*(*ch*);
>   **end**;
>   *valid* := *state* **in** *AcceptStates*;
> **end**;(* ReadNum *)

However, there are circumstances in which it is not possible to reserve a set of symbols for use as separators. In general, the fact that a particular symbol signifies the end of the substring making up a token must be inferred from the context in which the symbol occurs. In particular, the symbol which indicates the completion of one substring may be the first symbol of the next token to be recognized.

In Pascal, for example, the end of the token identifier is signalled by the occurrence of any character which is neither alphanumeric, nor the underscore character. The terminating character may be a separator such as space or a line-end marker, but may equally well be the first character

```
procedure GetToken;
  var ended : BOOLEAN;
begin (* a symbol has already been fetched *)
  ended := FALSE;
  repeat
    case state of

      .
      .
      n : case symbol of

            .
            .
            x, . . . : ended := TRUE;
          end; (* case symbol of *)

      .
      .
    end; (* case state of *)
    if not ended then GetNext Symbol;
  until ended;
  (* assert: current symbol does not belong to token *)

  .
  .
end; (* GetToken *)
```

Figure 3.15   Typical lexical scanner procedure with prefetched symbol.

of the following token, for instance a colon character, ':'. This possibility implies that a scanner may not know that the last token has finished until it has actually read the first symbol of the next token.

3.4.1   Lookahead techniques

There are two distinct conventions which a lexical scanner may adopt in dealing with its symbol input stream. These two conventions lead to rather different mechanisms for detecting the ends of tokens.

Firstly, it may be convenient to adopt the rule that the scanner always reads one symbol past the end of the token which it has just recognized. Each call to the scanner procedure will then assume that the first symbol has already been read, and will therefore not begin with a symbol fetch statement. Note that in this case the *symbol* variable cannot be a local variable of the scanning procedure, since its value must be preserved between the return of one invocation of the *GetToken* procedure and the next call of the procedure. This choice of convention leads to a procedure skeleton which has the general form shown in Figure 3.15.

```
procedure GetToken;
  var ended : BOOLEAN;
begin
  ended := FALSE;
  repeat
    GetNextSymbol;
    case state of

        .
        .
      n : if input^ in [x, . . . ] then
            ended := TRUE
          else . . . ;

        .
        .
    end; (* case state of *)
  until ended;
  (* assert: current symbol is last of token *)
    .
    .
end; (* GetToken *)
```

Figure 3.16   Lexical scanner procedure without prefetched symbol.

It must always be remembered that when using this method the very first symbol must be prefetched prior to the very first call of *GetToken*. It is usual to do this by means of some scanner initialization procedure.

Rules which apply at the call and return of a procedure such as *GetToken*, are called **preconditions** and **postconditions** respectively. In each case, since the procedure is to be called repeatedly, we must ensure that the precondition required by the next procedure call is guaranteed by the postcondition on the current procedure return. In this case we ensure that the precondition is met for the first call by an explicit initialization, and that thereafter the post- and preconditions match.

The beauty of the prefetch convention is that a single symbol lookahead is provided 'for free', since it is possible to view the next symbol without having any responsibility to actually process it.

The other possible input convention for a lexical scanner to adopt is for the *GetToken* procedure to always return with the final symbol of the recognized token in the *symbol* variable. In this case, the *GetToken* procedure will always begin with a call to the procedure which reads the next symbol. This second convention is sometimes useful, particularly when a large number of the tokens do not require a symbol lookahead to determine that they have ended. In those cases for which a lookahead is required, it must be obtained explicitly. In ISO Pascal it is always possible

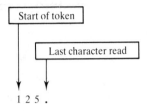

Figure 3.17   A situation requiring a further lookahead.

to view the next input record by explicitly accessing the file buffer *input^*.
A lexical scanner procedure using this method is outlined in Figure 3.16.

Some widely used Pascal programming environments do not implement the file buffer mechanism. In such cases it is necessary to explicitly
read a symbol, and then 'push' it back onto the input stream if it is found
that it does not belong to the current symbol.

Unfortunately, there may be cases where a single character may not
uniquely determine whether or not a token has ended. Examples of such
difficulties abound in the lexical conventions of programming languages.
These difficulties may even occur for the small languages which are the
particular interest of this book. An example from Pascal is the problem
which faces a lexical scanner which tries to detect *integer* and *real*
constants as separate tokens. Consider the situation illustrated in Figure
3.17.

It is not possible to tell whether the token is the *integer* literal '125',
and thus is already ended, or is instead the start of a *real* literal. The
ambiguity is resolved by another character of lookahead. If the next
character is another '.' then the first choice is correct, while if the next
character is a numeric digit, then the token is not yet complete but is the
start of a *real* literal.

It is possible to obtain a two symbol lookahead in a programmed
implementation of an FSA, by using a combination of both of the
techniques mentioned earlier. A typical skeleton is

case *State* **of**

  .

  .

  .

  n : **if** (*symbol* = *x*) **and** (*input^* = *y*) **then** *ended* := *TRUE*
    else . . .

  .

  .

end; (* case *)
if not *ended* **then** *GetNextSymbol*;
(* assert: at exit, *symbol* belongs to next token *)

For even more difficult cases, it may be necessary to embed more complex end-detection tests into the recognizer, in the same position as shown in the skeleton code.

To build such a lookahead action into a table-driven FSA is quite a different matter, however. In this case any lookahead tests should probably be supplied by means of procedure calls, which may be invoked as necessary. Since a table-driven automaton will usually have an *action* field in the table for semantic action selection, the lookahead action may be included inline with such code. Certainly the tables should not be indexed on the triple (*present state*, *present symbol*, *lookahead symbol*) just to provide a lookahead facility for what is probably a tiny fraction of machine configurations, since this would add enormously to the size of the tables.

It should be obvious that it is preferable, when designing languages, to adopt lexical conventions which avoid the necessity for difficult lookaheads. However, the need for lookahead sometimes arises because of the way in which the overall recognition task is split between the various levels of a multi-level recognizer.

What should be avoided, if at all possible, are the extremely long lookaheads which may become necessary to resolve lexical ambiguities in some programming languages. For example, in FORTRAN very long lookaheads may be required to determine whether a substring *FORMAT* is actually the familiar keyword or the result of a programmer quite legitimately (if rather unwisely) choosing to use *FORMAT* as an array identifier.

In most cases such ambiguities may be resolved by simply demanding that keywords be reserved. However, this may not always be possible. Consider the design of a command language for a file utility. It does not seem reasonable to attempt to separate the command verbs from the possible filenames by demanding that the command verbs are to be reserved, so the two possible meanings of a substring must be disentangled by other means. One method is to use additional contextual information in order to resolve the token to which a particular substring belongs, either by means of further lookahead, or possibly by querying the upper-level recognizer for some detail of its state.

This last method is sometimes necessary, but must be adopted with some caution, since it increases the complexity of interaction between the levels, considerably compromising the structural simplicity of the overall recognizer. Perhaps in such cases a more satisfactory method is to allow the lexical scanner to report all such occurrences as the single token *identifier*, and leave it to the upper level to deduce the function of the identifier from the greater contextual information which it normally possesses.

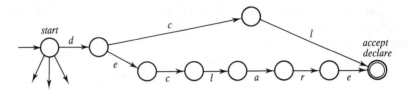

Figure 3.18   Synonym recognizer.

3.4.2 Synonymous token recognition

The lexical level of a multi-level recognizer is usually the correct place to build in the recognition of token synonyms. This is certainly the case whenever the lower level of the recognizer is able to ascertain the token to which every substring belongs. The advantage of this approach is that the upper levels need only deal with the abstract token values, without concern for the way in which the tokens are actually represented in the source string in any particular case. Even in small command languages it is often convenient to allow token synonyms so that, for instance, either abbreviated or full versions of command names may be used. The recognition of synonyms is easily built into an FSA by having alternative paths in the state diagram which lead to the recognition of the same token. For example, Figure 3.18 shows a fragment of the state diagram of a lexical scanner which treats *dcl* and *declare* as synonyms.

An often-used synonym mechanism in command languages is to accept truncated versions of keywords, provided they exceed a certain minimum length which is defined in each case, and to insist that the keyword be spelled correctly as far as it does appear. This policy is used in many operating system command languages.

As an example of this, in some command languages the strings *DIR*, *DIRE*, *DIREC*, . . . *DIRECTORY* are all synonyms. Recognition of these synonyms may be cast as a problem in string prefix matching, but recognition by an FSA is also quite straightforward. A partial state diagram is shown in Figure 3.19.

In this particular example the token *directory* is reported if a separator character {'/',*SP*,*CR*} is detected on lookahead when the FSA is in any of the accept states of Figure 3.19. Notice, however, that not just

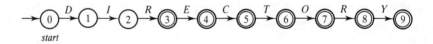

Figure 3.19   Synonym recognition.

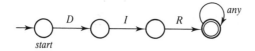

Figure 3.20 Deprecated form of prefix recognizer.

any prefix of *DIRECTORY* is acceptable. There must be some minimum length required to distinguish the string from all other commands which begin similarly.

The policy of demanding correct spelling of permissible prefixes is much safer than merely checking for a match on the minimal length prefix of a command verb, as would be implied by a state diagram such as Figure 3.20. The point is that the FSA of Figure 3.20 might erroneously recognize some totally random word which just happened to start off *DIR* . . . as the valid command token directory.

This seems an obvious point, and yet a special case of this dangerous construction is often seen in programs which accept string responses to queries and only then proceed to check whether the first character which was input was a *Y*, or any other character. A safe form of query recognizer is described in the following section.

3.4.3 The safe query-response recognizer

The machine illustrated in Figure 3.21 accepts *Y*, *y*, *YES*, *yeS*, etc. as an affirmative response, and corresponding strings for the negative. It will not accept any random response which just happens to start with a *Y*, and neither will it reject a sensible response just because it happens to begin with one or more spaces.

The price which has to be paid in code complexity for the added safety and friendlier user interface may be gauged from the procedure *GetResponse* in Figure 3.22.

This procedure typically compiles to less than 300 bytes of code for a

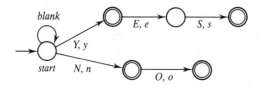

Figure 3.21 The safe query-response recognizer.

```
    var  RESPONSE:(YES,NO,INVALID);
           .
           .
           .

procedure GetResponse(var result : RESPONSE);
  const Error = 6;
  var   state:0..6;
        ch:CHAR;
begin (* assert: first character not yet read *)
  repeat Read(ch) until ch <> ' ';
  state := 0;
  repeat
    case state of
      0: if (ch='Y') or (ch='y') then state := 1
         else if (ch='N') or (ch='n') then state := 4
         else state := Error;
      1: if (ch='E') or (ch='e') then state := 2
         else state := Error;
      2: if (ch='S') or (ch='s') then state := 3
         else state := Error;
      4: if (ch='O') or (ch='o') then state := 5
         else state := Error;
      3,5,6: state := Error
    end (* case *);
    if not EOLN then Read(ch);
  until EOLN;
  ReadLn;
  if state in [1,3] then result := YES
  else if state in [4,5] then result := NO
  else result := INVALID ;
end (* GetResponse *);
```

Figure 3.22   Code for query-response recognizer.

16-bit computer. If declared at a global level, such a procedure might be used throughout a program, and hence add very little space on a per-call basis.

A typical user call might be

WRITE(' some prompt '); GetResponse(answer);
if *answer = YES* **then** . . .
else if *answer = NO* **then** . . .
else (* invalid *) . . . ;

It is left as an exercise for the reader to modify the FSA in Figures 3.21

and 3.22 so that they accept strings with trailing as well as leading spaces.

In general the whole idea of the inquisitorial style of interactive program, which demands yes/no answers, is a little suspect. However, when such style truly is appropriate, the use of a flexible query recognizer such as *GetResponse* is strongly advocated.

3.4.4 Section checklist and summary definitions

1. Lexical scanner definition.
   - A lexical scanner is a recognizer which takes an input string and recognizes embedded substrings which form the input tokens for a higher-level language recognizer.

2. Multi-level recognizers.
   - The lower level of a multi-level recognizer is the logical place to deal with symbol synonyms.
   - A lexical scanner must be able to recognize the logical end of a token substring, even though its own input string has not ended. In order to do this it frequently must read one symbol past the end of the recognized substring.
   - In the interests of simplicity and correctness, it is essential that a lexical scanner provide a uniform postcondition on its input stream after each token recognition. Two widely practised but mutually exclusive conventions are:
     a) the current symbol on exit is always the first symbol of the following token, or
     b) the current symbol on exit is the final symbol of the recognized token.

   The second of these may necessitate the occasional use of an input *unget* procedure in cases where a symbol lookahead is logically unavoidable.

3.5 Semantic actions

Some of the preceding examples have briefly indicated where semantic actions might be fitted into the recognition process. We now consider this aspect in more detail.

There are two distinct patterns along which FSA language recognizers might be designed. One pattern is exemplified by the recognizer for the Roman number-digit recognizer $R(1..9)$, in which the semantic result of the recognition process may be inferred from the final state of the recognizer. The other type of behaviour is demonstrated by a real-number recognizer which accumulates the value of the number as the character string is scanned.

With lexical scanners, the result of the recognition process is often implicit in the identity of the final accept state, but there is often a need for additional side-effects during the recognition of at least some of the tokens. An example of such a side-effect might be the accumulation of a character string in a buffer. Often, for a multi-level recognizer, the function of the lowest level is to sort input substrings into convenient lexical categories. For example, in a software tool which operates on computer program source files, the lowest level might contain a number recognizer, so that the upper level need only be aware that the current token belongs to the lexical category *number*, say. Clearly, from the point of view of the syntactic correctness of the program, any number may be equivalent.

However, when semantic actions are to be performed, it is often necessary to know more than just the lexical category of a token. In the example of the programming language tool, it might be necessary not only to know that a particular character string belongs to the category *number*, but also to know the value of the number which it represents. In such cases, we are led to a structured solution in which the information required for recognition and for semantic action are separated. The information required for recognition is the token identity, which in some cases might be a lexical category such as *number*, or *identifier*. The additional information which is required for semantic action is held in a separate variable, which we shall call a **lexical attribute**. In the case of a number the attribute would be the numerical value, while for an identifier token the lexical attribute might be the character string which represents it.

3.5.1 Moore and Mealy machines

For FSA which do include semantic actions during the recognition process there are at least two distinct models of behaviour. In one model, the Moore machine, the semantic actions are associated with each state, and therefore the number of distinct, different semantic actions may be no greater than the number of states in the machine. The alternative model, the Mealy machine, attaches semantic actions to each transition, and hence selects actions on the (*state*, *symbol*) pair. The terms refer to the names of two pioneering researchers in automata theory, who studied the theory of sequential state machines with output corresponding to the two models. In those theories the concept of machine output is an equivalent to our concept of semantic action.

It is an important result of automata theory that there is a Mealy machine which is functionally equivalent to any Moore machine, and conversely. In this context, two automata are said to be equivalent if they produce identical output actions when presented with the same input strings. There may be a delay of one state update step between the output for the two equivalent machines. Nevertheless, this result implies that any recognition task which may be performed by any one type of recognizer may equally be performed by either. However, it is usually more natural and therefore easier to associate semantic actions with transitions, as in the Mealy model. Furthermore, the Moore machine which is equivalent to a given Mealy machine almost invariably requires a significantly larger number of states. It must be concluded that, in almost all cases, actions should be associated with transitions.

To implement semantic actions in the manner of a Mealy machine, the various actions may be incorporated into a programmed implementation alongside the state updating assignments. If there is significant duplication of code, or if the actions are complex, then each semantic action should be implemented as a procedure call. Such a policy keeps the code nicely structured, and avoids cluttering the interpreter loop with distracting details. In the case of table-driven automata, a semantic action table paralleling the *next state* table is declared and is used as a jump table. In Pascal, an ordinal variable may be used as an index of the various semantic actions, and then used as a **case** statement selector.

A typical table-driven interpreter, with semantic actions implemented in Pascal, has the skeleton shown in Figure 3.23. The table entry selecting the semantic action is some scalar or subrange type, as is the state variable.

In this example, the table entries for the *next state* and *semantic action* selectors are held in an array of records. A single function call returns the index of the selected record, so that the appropriate fields may then be selected. There are, of course, a host of alternative data structures to the one given in this example.

It is difficult to give general advice about the incorporation of semantic actions. In any particular application the programmer's ingenuity must be used to ensure that the actions are both simply implemented and correct.

It is important to note that a semantic action is not necessarily completed all at once. Rather the semantic action attached to a particular transition may be to assign values to the elements of some data structure, with these values causing other specific actions to take place later in the recognition process. A typical example of this phenomenon occurs in the recognition of free-form numbers. The first character encountered may be an optional sign. Suppose that this sign happens to be a '−' character. An appropriate semantic action would be to set some Boolean flag *negative* to the value *true*. The real semantic action is, of course, to negate the value of the number which follows, but this cannot be performed until after the value has been accumulated. In this case, the semantic action which we

```
type StateAndAction = record
                            NextState : StateType;
                            NextAction: ActionType;
                    end;

var Table : array[TableIndex] of StateAndAction;

procedure FSAINT(var accept:BOOLEAN);
    .
    .
    function NEXT(PresentState: StateType;
                        CurrentSymbol:SymbolType) :TableIndex;
    begin { find index of next StateAndAction record } end;

    procedure Perform(semaction : ActionType);
    begin
      case semaction of
        1 : {first action};
        2 : {next action};
          .
          .
          .
      end (* case *)
    end; (* Action *)

begin (* fsaint *)
  state := start;
  GetSymbol;
  while symbol in Alphabet do begin
    with Table[NEXT(state,smbl)] do begin
      state := NextState;
      Perform(NextAction)
      end; (* with *)
    GetSymbol;
  end; (* while *)
  . . .
end; (* FSAINT *)
```

Figure 3.23   FSA interpreter for compacted table, showing semantic action
selection.

attach to the state transition is the setting of the flag, while the logical effect of the semantic action is not performed until the very last step in the recognition process.

3.5.2 The *real* number recognizer revisited

We are now in a position to complete the free-form *real* number recognizer in Figure 3.11, by including the semantic actions which accumulate the value of the number. The FSA exactly implements the state diagram of Figure 3.10, and is shown in Figure 3.24. In this case we have a single-level recognizer. Notice in particular that, as foreshadowed above, the second to last line of Figure 3.24 performs the real semantic action of negating the value of the number if the flag *neg* was set to *true* at the very start of the recognition process.

The method of incorporating the effect of non-zero exponents in Figure 3.24 is likely to make the numerical analyst flinch. There are many methods of performing this calculation which are more time efficient than the method chosen. Perhaps the simplest method to use, in the absence of an exponentiation operator, is to code a function *Power* which returns the real value of any positive integer power of 10. The final value may then be obtained by the statement

> **if** *expNeg*
> > **then** *val* := *val* / *Power(expValue)*
> > **else** *val* := *val* * *Power(expValue)*

The function *Power* may perform the computation in a number of steps which is proportional to the number of significant bits in *expValue*, a great improvement on the behaviour of the simple code in Figure 3.24.

An example of another recognizer for essentially this same real number language occurs in case study 2, at the end of Chapter 8. This later version differs in three significant ways from the example in Figure 3.24. It is a multi-level recognizer, it uses an efficient method of computing exponents, and it is implemented as an implicit state FSA. Figure 3.24 should therefore be reviewed at that time.

3.5.3 Section checklist and summary definitions

1. Semantic action definitions.
   - Semantic actions are deliberate side-effects of language recognition. Semantic actions for an FSA may be attached to states or to state transitions.
   - In the more usual case, where actions are attached to transitions, a two-dimensional action table may parallel the next state table, or a

```
procedure ReadReal(var value : REAL; var IsNum : BOOLEAN);
  const Error = 7;
  var    state : [0..7];
         ch : CHAR; neg, expNeg : BOOLEAN;
         digValue, expValue : INTEGER;
         factor : REAL;
begin (* accept states are [2,3,6] *)
  state := 0; factor := 1.0;
  neg := FALSE; expNeg := FALSE;
  repeat
    Read(ch);
    if (state = 0) and (ch = ' ') then (*skip*)
    else if ch in ['0'..'9'] then begin
      digValue := ORD(ch) − ORD('0')
      case state of
        0,1 : begin
                  state := 2;
                  value := digValue;
              end;
        4,5 : begin
                  state := 6;
                  expValue := digValue;
              end;
        2 :   value := value * 10.0 + digValue;
        3 :   begin
                  factor := factor / 0.1;
                  value := value + digValue * factor;
              end;
        6 :   expValue := expValue * 10 + digValue;
        7 :   (* unchanged state *);
        end (* case *)
      end
    else if ch in ['+','−'] then
      if state = 0 then begin
        state := 1;
        neg := (ch = '−');
      end
      else if state = 4 then begin
        state := 5;
        expNeg := (ch = '−');
      else state := Error
    else if (ch = '.') and (state = 2) then state := 3
    else if (ch in ['E','e']) and (state in [2,3]) then
      state := 4
    else state := Error
    end; (*if*)
  until EOLN;
```

```
      IsNum := state in [2,3,6];
      ReadLn;
      if state = 6 then begin
        if expNeg then factor := 0.1 else factor := 10.0;
        while expValue > 0 do begin
          val := val * factor;
          expValue := expValue - 1;
          end;
        end; (* if state=6 *)
      if neg then val := -val;
    end;
```

Figure 3.24   *ReadReal* with semantic actions included.

combined table may exist, with record fields holding next state and semantic action values.

2. Lexical attributes.
   - In cases of multi-level recognizers, the semantic actions may utilize information available from the lexical level, which is not logically necessary merely to test string validity. Any such item of additional information is called a lexical attribute.
   - Typical lexical attributes are the source representation of an identifier, the value of a number, etc.

3. Deferral of effect.
   - The logical effect of a semantic action may be deferred well beyond the point at which the action is inserted into the code of the recognizer. Typically, the manifest semantic action is to set up some data value which will cause a particular action to be performed later in the recognition, or even at its completion.

3.6   Introduction to error handling

One of the most important semantic actions, which must be incorporated into any syntax-directed software tool, involves the handling of errors. This is a difficult area of design which may be tackled at a number of different levels. We distinguish between several different strategies: at the simple end of the spectrum a recognizer may just detect that something about the input string was erroneous and report that simple fact. For certain applications such an error-detection policy may be adequate; for example some editors have a single diagnostic message, '?'. The circumstances in which such an approach is appropriate are when the input language is relatively simple, the input strings short, and the level of sophistication of the users high.

At an intermediate level of complexity, the recognizer may give a diagnostic message which specifies the reason for the rejection of the string, and the position in the string at which the error was first detected. For an FSA it is also simple (although not always helpful) to inform the user of the alphabet symbols which would have been acceptable at the error site. Systems which work at this intermediate level of complexity may be characterized as error-diagnosing.

Finally, the recognizer may attempt to recover from, or even repair the error by making suitable assumptions about the real intentions of the user. Some such error-recovery strategy must be used for the compilers of programming languages in order that the rest of the syntax checking may proceed. This is clearly necessary because of the significant possibility that more than one error may be present. In cases where semantic actions are associated with the recognition, it is common to stop performing such actions after a first error has been encountered, but to continue to attempt recognition of the remainder of the string. The reason is that it may be too dangerous to perform actions which are based on dubious assumptions regarding the actual intent of a defective input string. Nevertheless, in circumstances where multiple errors should be detected, some kind of error-recovery strategy is mandatory.

Note that both of the simpler approaches outlined above can only detect the first error in any input string, and thus can detect at most one error per recognition attempt. At this stage we shall be content with treating error detection and diagnosis, leaving the more difficult considerations until Chapter 12.

Error detection, and appropriate actions, are particularly easy to incorporate into an FSA. In essence the program prints a warning if the string terminates with the automaton in a non-accept state. If the FSA has actually entered the error state it is simple, and usually helpful, to indicate the position in the input string of the symbol which caused the error transition.

Some ingenuity may be called for in cases where it is advisable to check that a complete input string is valid before initiating any irrevocable semantic action. This is the case for certain text editors which accept command strings, and must check that the whole string is valid before performing any editing action. One option is to scan the string twice: the first time just to check for correctness, and a second time in order to perform the semantic actions. Another option is to use a single scan to recognize the string, and to perform semantic actions which translate the string into some internal command string format. If the whole input string is successfully translated and the recognizer signals

Figure 3.25   Conceptual state diagram.

acceptance, then the command string is executed. The concept involves including finalization code of the form

>**if** *state* **in** *AcceptStateSet* **then**
>   *EXECUTE*(. . . . .)
>**else** *WRITE*('error in input string');

The error diagnosis strategy is far less trivial to implement than is simple error detection, and warrants careful consideration. One immediate problem is that if a unique semantic action is to be attached to every error transition in the transition table, then the table sparseness is immediately lost.

It is thus necessary to select particular error diagnosing actions which are not held in a nice two-dimensional array along with the *next state* entries. The information which is readily available for diagnosis and reporting comprises the position in the input string at which the error transition was selected, and the identity of the last non-error state. This information is sufficient to allow formation of a list of symbols which would have been acceptable in the error position, and may be enough to decide on the true nature of the error. There is an outstanding problem which may occur and which is even more acute in the case of several of the other types of recognizers treated later in the book. This is the possibility that the 'real' error in the input string may in fact have occurred several symbols prior to the symbol which actually precipitated the error transition and was flagged with the diagnostic message.

One technique which is sometimes useful, in the context of table-driven FSA, involves the use of an index into a table of error actions, with the index being updated from time to time as recognition proceeds. This technique is a flexible one on which to build error diagnostics, since the diagnostic message may be varied according to the stage of completion which the recognition attempt reached prior to the error transition.

However, the main advantage of having such an index into an error action table is the possibility of using it to perform a crude type of error recovery. Consider, as an example, a command language which accepts strings in a regular language, with the overall form of the string being:

><command> <options> <file_specifications>

If an error is detected during the recognition of the command, then the

```
case errorIndex of
   0 : begin
         WriteLn('invalid command');
         state := 0;
         Write(InitialPrompt);
      end;
   1 : begin
         WriteLn('invalid options');
         state := 10;
         Write('options & fileSpec ->>');
      end;
   2 : begin
         WriteLn('invalid fileSpec.');
         state := 20;
         Write('fileSpec. ->> ');
      end;
end; (* case *)
```

Figure 3.26   Alternative error re-entry scheme.

FSA should restart at the *start* state after some diagnostic message and an appropriate prompt. On the other hand, an error during the file specification part should only prompt for new filespecs and restart the recognition at that point. We assume a state diagram with the overall form of Figure 3.25.

On initialization the error-index is set to 0, while on entry to state 10, the index is set to 1. Likewise on entry to state 20 the error-index is set to 2. The error actions are then coded somewhat after the fashion of Figure 3.26.

3.6.1 Section checklist and summary definitions

Definition of error-handling alternatives.

- A language recognizer which merely reports on the acceptance or otherwise of a submitted input string is said to perform error detection and reporting.

- A language recognizer which displays a variety of different messages depending on the nature of the (first) error is said to perform error diagnosis.

- A language recognizer which attempts to recover from errors so that the remainder of the input string may be scanned is said to perform error recovery.

3.7   Case study 1: A keyword bold-printer

3.7.1   Introduction and design considerations

This case study concerns the design and implementation of a simple, syntax-directed tool. The purpose of the tool is to produce a printed file of a computer program, in this case written in the Pascal language, in which the reserved words of the language are made 'bold' by multiple overstriking in the printing process. The techniques used in the implementation involve simple finite-state automata, but nevertheless illustrate a number of very important design principles.

There are a number of ways in which the effect of bold printing may be obtained. Some dot-matrix printers are able to automatically produce this effect in response to 'escape sequences' which are embedded in the character stream. Some character-by-character printers are able to increase character density by backspacing and overstriking.

However, in this particular case, the bold effect is obtained by finding all those lines which contain any keywords, and creating an auxiliary line which contains just the keywords. As well as printing the original line, the auxiliary line is overprinted, twice, to accentuate the keywords. This particular method may be used with any lineprinter capable of performing a carriage return without a line feed.

The overall plan involved in the tool is to read characters from the input file, copying them into a line buffer. Concurrently, the character stream is checked for the presence of keywords, copying any which are found into an otherwise blank overstrike-line buffer. Care must be taken to ensure that the keywords appear in the original and overstrike buffers in exactly the same character positions. Finally, if any keywords have been found, the line buffer is written to the output, together with two copies of the overstrike line, all printed on the same line. In the event that the line contains no keywords, the line buffer is written to the output in the normal way.

It is possible to construct a single FSA which accepts the finite language comprising all Pascal keyword tokens, using chains of transitions which spell out the Pascal keywords. This approach leads to the fastest possible program, but in the interests of simplicity we use a string-matching approach instead.

Keywords in Pascal are only distinguished from identifiers by the fact that they are pre-defined and reserved. In other words, if a string occurs which matches a keyword, we may be sure that it is the keyword, and not just an identifier with the same character sequence. We may therefore use a simple FSA which isolates substrings in the input stream which are either identifiers or keywords. We find out which category the string falls into by performing a lookup in a table which contains the keyword strings.

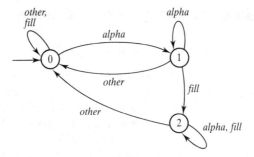

Figure 3.27   State diagram for identifier recognizer (simple version).

The character case-conventions are important, since Pascal is not case-sensitive, and keywords might be either entirely upper case, lower case, or even a mixture of cases. In order to simplify the table lookup, the keywords are stored in one single case. Before a string is compared with the reserved words in the table, it is converted to the standard case. It would still be possible to print out the keyword in the original case in which it appears in the source file, but it seems more sensible to print all keywords in a uniform case. In this example, upper case has been chosen, but lower case would be equally simple.

3.7.2 The simple solution

As a first attempt at finding identifier substrings in Pascal programs, we note that identifiers always start with an alphabetic character, and are terminated by any following character which is non-alphanumeric. Identifiers may be terminated either by a space or end of line, or by any special character such as the punctuation characters, the operators, or any of the bracket characters. In the interests of wasting as little time as possible in futile table lookups, we distinguish between identifier strings which are entirely alphabetic, and those which contain non-alphabetic, 'filler' characters, such as numeric digits or the underscore character. We only bother to search for a match in the purely alphabetic case.

Note that although the use of embedded underscores within identifiers is not in accordance with the Pascal standard, the extension is so widely implemented that it is almost mandatory to allow it.

We are led, therefore, to the state diagram shown in Figure 3.27, where it is assumed that a lower-level recognizer separates all input characters into three categories, *alpha*, *fill*, and *other*, for alphabetic, filler, and all other characters, and turns the *EOLN* and *EOF* conditions into pseudo-symbols *eol* and *stopper*.

```
RESET(inFile);
REWRITE(outFile);
state := 0;
ClearLineBuffers;
keywordsFound := FALSE;
repeat (* until EOF *)
   GetPutChar; (* fetch and copy first character *)
   case state of
      0 : if charType = alpha then begin
            ResetId; (* start keyword copy *)
            StoreChar; (* save first char *)
            state := 1;
            end;
          (* else no change *)
      1 : case charType of
            alpha : StoreChar;
            fill    : state := 2;
            other, eol, stopper : begin
                        if StringPresent then begin
                           CopyKeyword;
                           keywords Found := TRUE;
                           end;
                         state := 0;
                         end;
         end;
      2 : if charType >= other then state := 0;
   end; (* case, now is it end of line? *)
   if charType = eol then begin
      if keywordsFound then begin
         OverPrint(overstrike);
         OverPrint(overstrike);
         keywordsFound := FALSE;
         end;
      LineOut(original);
      ClearLineBuffers;
      state := 0;
      end;
until charType = stopper;
```

Figure 3.28   Simple FSA for keyword overstriking.

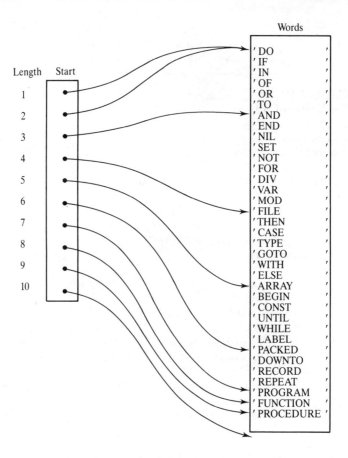

Figure 3.29   Data structure for reserved word lookup.

The semantic action which initiates the accumulation of an identifier string is attached to the initial transition, from state 0 to state 1 in the figure. The self-loop on state 1 causes the accumulation of a further character in the string to be tested, while the testing step itself is attached to the return transition from state 1 to state 0.

An outline of the kernel of the algorithm is given in Figure 3.28. In the figure, we have deliberately glossed over the way in which the overprinting is achieved. Unfortunately, there is no standard way of doing this in Pascal, and the means of effecting overprinting vary according to the conventions of the file system. In systems which have character-stream oriented file systems, sending a carriage return chararacter without a linefeed produces the required effect. In this particular case we declare the output file as a **file of** *CHAR*, so that we may insert our own line delimiters.

There are a number of different methods by which the table lookup might be arranged. In particular, a string array indexed on length is quite attractive since it is only necessary to check the search string against keywords of the same length. Since very few keywords have the same length, the number of comparisons may be kept quite short.

What is involved is a data structure which is very reminiscent of the sparse-table data structures of Section 3.3. A comparison between the keyword table in Figure 3.29 and the sparse FSA table in Figure 3.13 will make the analogy clear.

The code of the *StringPresent* function accesses the *start* table for the keywords which are equal in length to the test string, and comparisons are made until either the string is found, or the index reaches the start of the list for the next greater length. In the worst possible case, a string of length 3, the algorithm will check nine strings before declaring an identifier not to be a reserved word, but in most cases the comparison operation will fail after checking just one character. In Chapter 5 we will consider a much more efficient table lookup mechanism, but for the moment we will use the structure in Figure 3.29.

3.7.3   A correct solution

A much more important limitation of the simple solution concerns the fact that the simple FSA in Figure 3.27 erroneously recognizes keywords which appear inside comments, or inside literal strings. We must consider a more complex state diagram which ignores alphabetic strings which start inside literals or comments.

Figure 3.30 shows a state diagram which acts in the required fashion. In this complete version of the FSA we have an enumerated type for the variable *charType* which is defined as

type *CharClass* = (*alpha,fill,quote,comstart,comend,other,eol,stopper*);

The figure shows the states identified by their ordinal numbers. However, the code of the algorithm is much more readable if the states are named according to their functions. A suitable definition is as follows.

type *StateType* = (*waiting,inIdent,skipping,inString,inComment*);

The machine is in the *waiting* state (state 0 in the diagram) except when the last input character belongs to an identifier, a keyword, a literal string or a comment. The state *inIdent* (state 1) is used for the accumulation of identifier strings in the case that the string is purely alphabetic. If a numeric character or an underscore occurs, the machine state becomes *skipping*. The machine enters the *inString* state when the opening quote of a literal string is encountered. Notice that although it is possible that

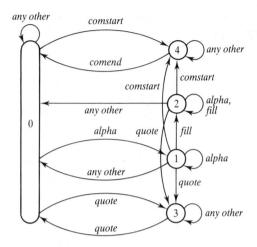

Figure 3.30   State diagram for identifier recognizer (complete version).

quote characters may occur within a literal string, when they do so they always occur in pairs, so that the *skipping* state is re-entered immediately. Finally, state 4, *inComment*, implements the recognition of comments. It should be noted that if it is desired that the particular form of the comment start and end characters should match, then it might be simplest to have two comment states, *inACurlyComment* and *inABracketStar-Comment*, for instance. Existing Pascal compilers differ in their treatment of these matters, so no more will be said of the various possibilities.

When the end of an identifier string is encountered, the current state, which must be either *inIdent* or *skipping*, is exited. As discussed for the simpler example earlier, an exit from the *inIdent* state has an attached semantic action which checks for the presence of the accumulated string in the keyword table. It should be carefully noted that an identifier may be terminated quite legitimately either by the start of a literal string or by the start of a comment. A deadly but plausible error would be always to return to *waiting* on identifier termination. Instead, the successor state should be *waiting*, *inString* or *inComment*, according to the type of the terminating character.

It is possible to devise a state diagram which deals directly with symbols from the ASCII set, but the recognition of comments is quite complex. Since we have planned to implement a lower-level recognizer to classify characters into the various classes, we may use the *GetChar* procedure to merge the synonyms '{' and '(*' and so on.

As usual, when a multi-level recognizer is designed, it is important to ensure that the symbols of each level are kept well separate. It would be a mistake to allow the FSA interpreter to deal directly with the reading and writing of characters, since these belong properly at the lower, lexical-scanner level.

In the final code it should be noted carefully that although the semantic actions of the FSA make use of the character values, all control flow actions of the FSA depend only on the variable *charType* which is of the enumerated type. In addition, we take advantage of the lexical scanner to turn the *EOLN* and *EOF* predicates into 'pseudo-symbols'. This choice makes the design of the upper level much simpler, and is a technique which is very widely practised for the grammar recognizers in the later chapters of this book.

The convention which has been adopted for the lexical scanner, since some of the tokens involve differing numbers of characters, is that at the return of *GetString* the current character is the last character of the recognized token. Of course, other conventions are possible, but the important point in the design process is to decide what the convention is to be, and to keep rigidly to it.

Figure 3.31 is a complete listing of the tool. It necessarily includes a small number of implementation-dependent statements which are involved in accessing the file system of the computer.

3.7.4 Possible extensions

The Pascal keyword bold-printer program may be extended and improved in a number of ways. Firstly, the keyword lookup procedure may be made very much more efficient by use of a hash table. This point is taken up again in Chapter 5.

Perhaps even more interesting, however, is the possibility of incorporating the highlighting of keywords as part of a software tool which performs a standard reformatting of the Pascal source program. This particular class of tools is discussed in a later case study.

Exercises

3.1   Modify the Roman number recognizer so as to accept 'IIII' for four, 'XXXX' for forty, etc.

3.2   Derive a state diagram for an FSA which accepts unsigned integers with optional formatting spaces. A number may be completely free of spaces, but if spaces are present they must be used consistently and must separate digits into groups of three, starting from the right-hand end of the number. The number is to be terminated by either an end of line, or two successive space characters.

Implement your FSA in Pascal, and test the program.

cont. on p. 75

```pascal
program BoldPrinter(input,output); (* kjg 1985 *)


(* This program prints out Pascal programs, with all standard keywords
   made bold by overstriking. It is a simple example of the use of a finite
   state automaton. *)

(* Some of the file-handling statements will be operating system
   dependent. The mechanism for determining filenames has been
   omitted. On some systems it would be preferred to pass filenames
   from the command level. Otherwise the program should prompt for
   filenames in the first line of the main block of the program. *)

const    LineMax = 80;

           (**** these constants for ASCII only ****)
           (**** change for other character sets ****)

           CR = CHR(13); (* carriage return *)
           LF = CHR(10); (* line feed char. *)
           HT = CHR (09); (* horizontal tab *)
           CaseOffset = 32;(* = ORD('a') − ORD ('A') *)

type     CharClass = (alpha, fill, quote, comstart,
                         comend, other, eol, stopper );
           StateType = (waiting, inIdent, skipping,
                         inString, inComment);

           Line = packed array [0..LineMax] of CHAR;
           String9 = packed array [1..9] of CHAR;

var       ch : CHAR;
           state      : StateType;
           charType : CharClass;
           keywords : BOOLEAN;

           original    : Line; (* original line *)
           overstrike : Line; (* overprint line *)

           ptr      : 0..LineMax; (* current line pos *)
           idStart : 0..LineMax; (* position in line of identifier start *)

           identifier : String9;
           length   : INTEGER;        (* length of id *)

           start    : array [1..10] of INTEGER; (* index *)
           word    : array [0..34] of String9; (* keys *)
```

```
    inFile   : TEXT;
    outFile : file of CHAR;

      (* These declarations are for the standard Pascal keywords.
         If extensions are added, then array parameters may need
         to be changed. *)

(* buffer management procedures for both lines, and the ident buffer *)

  procedure ClearLineBuffers;
    var I : INTEGER;
  begin
    for I := 0 to LineMax do begin
      original[I] := ' '; overstrike[I] := ' ';
      ptr := 0; (* char pointer is at start *)
    end;
    keywords := FALSE;
  end; (* ClearLineBuffers *)

  procedure ResetId; (* init. identifier buffer *)
    var I : INTEGER;
  begin
    for I := 1 to 9 do identifier[I] := ' ';
      idStart := ptr - 1; (* start position *)
      length := 0; (* init. id. length *)
  end; (* ResetId *)

  procedure StoreChar; (* store upper case id-character *)
  begin
    (* assert: ch is alphabetic *)
    length := length + 1;
    if length <= 9 then
      if ch in ['a'..'z'] then (* convert to upper case *)
        identifier[length] := CHR(ORD)(ch)-CaseOffset)
      else identifier[length] := ch;
  end; (* StoreChar *)

  procedure CopyKeyword; (* copy keyword into line-buffers *)
    var I, pos : INTEGER;
  begin
    pos := idStart - 1;
    for I := 1 to length do begin
      (* copy upper-case version *)
      original[pos+I] := identifier[I];
      overstrike[pos+I] := identifier[I];
      (* modify to leave case unchanged *)
    end;
  end; (* CopyKeyword *)
```

cont. overleaf

Figure 3.31   *cont.*

```
procedure WriteLine(ln : Line);
  var I : INTEGER;
begin (* assert: linelength = ptr *)
  for I := 0 to ptr − 1 do
    Write(outFile,ln[I]);
end;


    (* test identifiers against entries in the keyword table *)


    function StringFound : BOOLEAN;
      var   found : BOOLEAN;
            index, max : INTEGER;


    begin
      found := FALSE;
      if length <= 9 then begin
        index := start[length];
        max   := start[length+1];
        while not found and (index<max) do
          if identifier = word[index] then found := TRUE
          else index := index+1;
        end; (* outer if *)
      StringFound := found;
    end; (* StringFound *)


    procedure GetChar; (* lexical scanner for charType *)
    (* precondition: ch belongs to previous token *)
    (* postcondition: ch is last char of new token *)


      procedure GetPutChar(var ch : CHAR);
      begin
        Read(inFile,ch);
        original[ptr] := ch;
        if ch = HT then overstrike[ptr] := ch;
        ptr := ptr + 1;
      end;


    begin
      if EOF(inFile) then charType := stopper
      else if EOLN(inFile) then begin
        charType := eol; ReadLn(inFile);
        end
      else begin
        GetPutChar(ch);
        if ch in ['a'..'z','A'..'Z'] then charType := alpha
        else if ch in ['0'..'9','_'] then charType := fill
        else if ch in ['''','{','}','(','*'] then
```

```
            case ch of
                '''' : charType := quote;
                '{' :  charType := comstart;
                '}' :  charType := comend;
                '(' :  (* lookahead !! *)
                        if inFile^ = '*' then begin
                            GetPutChar(ch); charType := comstart
                            end
                        else charType = other;
                '*' :  (* lookahead again *)
                        if inFile^ = ')' then begin
                            GetPutChar(ch); charType := comend
                            end
                        else charType := other;
                end (* case *)
            else charType = other;
        end; (* outer if *)
    end; (* GetChar *)
```

(* initialize the keyword string-tables for standard keywords *)

```
procedure InitTables;
begin
                        (* index array *)
    start[1] := 0;      start[2] := 0;      start[3] := 6;
    start[4] := 15;     start[5] := 22;     start[6] := 28;
    start[7] := 32;     start[8] := 33;     start[9] := 34;
    start[10]:= 35;


                        (* string table *)

    word[00] := 'DO        ';   word[01] := 'IF        ';
    word[02] := 'IN        ';   word[03] := 'OF        ';
    word[04] := 'OR        ';   word[05] := 'TO        ';
    word[06] := 'AND       ';   word[07] := 'END       ';
    word[08] := 'NIL       ';   word[09] := 'SET       ';
    word[10] := 'NOT       ';   word[11] := 'FOR       ';
    word[12] := 'DIV       ';   word[13] := 'VAR       ';
    word[14] := 'MOD       ';   word[15] := 'FILE      ';
    word[16] := 'THEN      ';   word[17] := 'CASE      ';
    word[18] := 'TYPE      ';   word[19] := 'GOTO      ';
    word[20] := 'WITH      ';   word[21] := 'ELSE      ';
    word[22] := 'ARRAY     ';   word[23] := 'BEGIN     ';
    word[24] := 'CONST     ';   word[25] := 'UNTIL     ';
    word[26] := 'WHILE     ';   word[27] := 'LABEL     ';
    word[28] := 'PACKED    ';   word[29] := 'DOWNTO    ';
    word[30] := 'RECORD    ';   word[31] := 'REPEAT    ';
    word[32] := 'PROGRAM   ';   word[33] := 'FUNCTION  ';
    word[34] := 'PROCEDURE ';

end; (* InitTables *)
```

cont. overleaf

Figure 3.31   *cont.*

```
begin (* main line *)
  (* file opening procedures may be system dependent *)
  Open(inFile, . . . );
  Open(outFile, . . . );
  Reset(inFile);
  Rewrite(outFile);
  InitTables;

  (* fsa interpreter: Figure 3.29 *)
  state := waiting;
  ClearLineBuffers;
  repeat (* until charType = stopper *)
    GetChar; (* fetch first character *)
    case state of
      waiting :
        if charType = alpha then begin
          ResetId; (* start string copy *)
          StoreChar; (* store first char *)
          state := inIdent;
          end
        else if charType = quote then state := inString
        else if charType = comstart then state := inComment
        (* else no change of state *);
      inIdent :
        if charType = alpha then StoreChar
        else if charType = fill then state := skipping
        else begin (* an id. has been found *)
          if StringFound then begin
            CopyKeyword;
            keywords := TRUE;
            end; (* now, what is nextstate? *)
          if charType = comstart then state := inString
          else if charType = comstart then state := inComment
          else state := waiting;
          end;
      skipping :
        if charType <= fill then (* nothing *)
        else if charType = quote then state := inString
        else if charType = comstart then state := inComment
        else state := waiting;
      inString : if charType = quote then state := waiting;
      inComment : if charType = comend then state := waiting;
    end; (* case *)
    (* now check for end of line *)
    if charType = eol then begin
      if keywords then begin
        WriteLine(overstrike); Write(outFile,CR);
        WriteLine(overstrike); Write(outFile,CR);
        end;
```

```
        WriteLine(original); Write(outFile,CR,LF);
        ClearLineBuffers;
        end; (* if end-of-line *)
    until charType = stopper;
    (* end of fsa interpreter *)
    Close(inFile);
    Close(outFile);
  end.
```

Figure 3.31   The Pascal keyword bold-printer.

cont. from p. 69

3.3 Find out, if possible. how your local Pascal compiler implements the **case** statement, and then formulate criteria to choose between the use of a **case** statement or successive **if** statements in the programmed implementation of any FSA. The remark on page 31 of Jensen and Wirth's *Pascal User Manual and Report* may be helpful.

When the successive **if** form is chosen, and where some notion of the relative frequency of various transitions is known, how should the tests be ordered to minimize the mean execution time?

3.4 Rewrite the procedure *RDIGIT* used in Figure 3.9 so as to implement the minimal FSA for $R(1..9)$. The state diagram for the minimal machine was given in Figure 2.11.

Would you consider the decrease in the number of states to be an advantage in this case, bearing in mind the relative difficulty of incorporating semantic actions?

3.5 Modify the safe query-response recognizer so that it permits trailing whitespace. Try to do this without destroying the safe nature of the machine. Input strings should now be terminated by the *EOLN* condition becoming true.

Code your FSA, and test it.

3.6 A Mealy machine has semantic actions attached to each transition, while a Moore machine has actions which depend on the state. Devise an informal argument which shows that if given the transition and action table for a Mealy machine, an equivalent Moore machine may be constructed.

[*Hint*: Consider a machine with a state-labelling policy which identifies states by a label corresponding to a Mealy machine transition.]

Further reading

The standard texts on automata theory, mentioned at the conclusion of Chapter 2, treat 'FSA with output' in a manner closer to the original spirit of the pioneers Mealy and Moore than this chapter has done. The original references are Moore (1956) and Mealy (1955).

String recognizers which attempt to repair errors are treated in Backhouse (1979), which presents some new results in this rather difficult field.

Further methods of sparse-table reduction are treated in Aho and Ullman, (1978), Chapter 3.

Chapter 4 **Regular Expressions**

4.1 Definition of regular expressions

So far we have dealt with regular languages which were sufficiently simple that the translation from the word-statement definition of the language to the state diagram was either intuitively obvious, or at least easily verified. In this chapter we deal with a formal mechanism for defining regular expressions in a particularly convenient way. This mechanism is an algebra of regular expressions.

Regular expressions are strings of symbols taken from an alphabet which consists of the union of a target alphabet and a set of operator symbols and grouping constructs. Every well-formed regular expression defines a regular language from the closure of the target alphabet. For example, a regular expression which defines the identifier language which was the basis of Exercise 2.4 is

$$a(a|n|\_a|\_a|\_n)^*$$

where a stands for an alphabetic character, n for a numeric digit and the underscore stands for itself. All of the remaining characters, the parentheses, the bars and the asterisk, are operators or grouping symbols.

A **meta-language** is a language which is used to define languages. Although it is most useful, at this point, to think of regular expressions as belonging to an algebra, they do also belong to a language with well-defined syntactical rules. Since every regular expression defines a regular language, it follows that a regular expression may be considered to be a meta-language as well as an algebra.

In this chapter we give systematic methods for transforming regular expressions into finite state automata. Throughout the chapter we use upper-case Roman letters to indicate regular expressions, and lower-case Greek letters for strings from the alphabet Σ. Lower-case Roman letters are used for the symbols of the target alphabet. The alphabet Σ is referred to as the **target alphabet**, since defining strings from this alphabet is our objective. Individual symbols from the target alphabet are called **atoms**, since they are the indivisible units from which the strings are constructed.

We indicate that a string β belongs to the language defined by a regular expression E by the notation

$$\beta \in L(E)$$

The simplest regular expression is just a single atomic symbol from the alphabet Σ. It defines a regular language consisting of a single string of length one, the atomic symbol itself. Suppose, for example, that the target alphabet is the set $\Sigma = \{a,b,c, \ldots \}$ so that symbols from this target alphabet are the atoms of the regular expression language. The regular expression b then defines a language comprising the single string 'b'. In symbols

$$L(b) = \{b\}$$

and so on.

In ordinary algebra, complex expressions are formed by taking simpler expressions and compounding them together by arithmetic operators, such as multiplication, and raising to a power. In the algebra of regular expressions, more complex expressions are formed by connecting subexpressions together by the operations of **concatenation**, **alternation**, and **closure**. These operations correspond to the concatenation of strings, the choice between alternative forms, and the repetition of subexpressions zero or more times.

In the notation used in this book, closure is indicated by a superscript asterisk symbol. When applied to an atomic symbol it designates the repeating of the atomic symbol on which it operates zero or more times. For example, the language corresponding to the regular expression b^* is all strings consisting of zero or more repetitions of the symbol 'b'. No matter which alphabet symbol is chosen, a string consisting of exactly zero repetitions of that symbol must be the empty string ε, so that for any alphabet symbol b we have the result

$$L(b^*) = \{\varepsilon,b,bb,bbb, \ldots \}$$

Concatenation of subexpressions in a regular expression defines a language of strings formed by concatenating strings belonging to the languages defined by the subexpressions. In the case of concatenated single atoms, for example, the language defined by the regular expression ab has just one string, 'ab'. In symbols

$$L(ab) = \{ab\}.$$

Note that no explicit symbol is used in a regular expression to denote concatenation. The subexpressions are just placed in juxtaposition. This may be thought of as being analogous to the suppression of 'multiply' signs in certain arithmetic notations.

Alternation is the construct which allows alternative subexpressions to be chosen. It is indicated by listing the alternatives separated by the symbol '|', the solid vertical rule or **bar** symbol. The language defined by the alternation of atoms in a regular expression is just the strings consisting of all of the various alternatives. For example, the regular expression $(b|a)$ defines a language consisting of just the two strings 'b', and 'a'. In symbols

$$L(b|a) = \{a,b\}$$

Note the use of parentheses to group together the items over which the alternation is to range.

We must now explore the consequences of applying the basic operations to subexpressions which are more complicated than single atoms. First, however, since the language consisting of just the empty string is a particular case of a finite (and hence regular) language, we must have a regular expression to denote it. We define ε to be a regular expression, denoting the language consisting of exactly the empty string ε,

$$L(\varepsilon) = \{\varepsilon\}.$$

The closure of some expression E, written E^*, defines a language consisting of the concatenation of zero or more strings from $L(E)$. If E defines a language with only one string, $E = bc$, for example, then $L(E^*)$ consists of the strings

$$L((bc)^*) = \{\varepsilon,bc,bcbc,bcbcbc, \ldots \}$$

However, if $L(E)$ possesses more than one string, then the language of E^* does display a more complex repetitive pattern than that of the last example.

Suppose that $E=(a|b)$, then

$$L(E) = L(a|b) = \{a,b\}$$

and

$$L(E^*) = L((a|b)^*) = \{\varepsilon,a,b,aa,ab,ba,bb,aaa, \ldots \}$$

Obviously, an informal statement, such as that the closure consists of the concatenation of zero or more strings from the language, is less than satisfactory as a rigorous definition. To define the closure precisely, recursion must be resorted to, as in the following rules

If E is some regular expression, then

a) ε belongs to $L(E^*)$;
b) if α is some string that belongs to $L(E^*)$, and β is any string that belongs to $L(E)$, then the string $\alpha\beta$ belongs to $L(E^*)$

Concatenation of expressions defines a product language of all those strings formed by concatenating any string from the language of the first expression with any string taken from the language defined by the second. Thus if E_1 and E_2 are regular expressions, then E_1E_2 defines a language of strings $\alpha\beta$ where

$$\alpha \in L(E_1) \quad \text{and} \quad \beta \in L(E_2)$$

To take a definite example, the expression $E = (a|b)c^*$ defines a language which includes all the strings

$$\{a,b,ac,bc,acc,bcc,accc,bccc, \ldots\}$$

as may be verified by noting that

$$L(a|b) = \{a,b\}$$
$$L(c^*) = \{\varepsilon,c,cc,ccc, \ldots\}$$

and implicitly using the result that for any string α, $\varepsilon\alpha = \alpha\varepsilon = \alpha$.

Alternation of expressions defines a language which is the union of the languages of the constituent expressions. Thus

$$L(E_1|E_2) = L(E_1) \cup L(E_2)$$

For example, if $E_1 = ab^*$ and $E_2 = a^*b$, then

$$L(E_1) = \{a,ab,abb,abbb, \ldots\},$$

and

$$L(E_2) = \{b,ab,aab,aaab, \ldots\}$$

so that

$$L(E_1|E_2) = L(ab^*|a^*b) = \{a,b,ab,aab,abb, \ldots\}$$

A final, technical point relates to the possibility that a regular language may be empty, that is, have no strings at all. Since we wish to have our notation powerful enough to define any regular language, it is necessary to define a symbol for the regular expression which defines such a language. We therefore define the symbol $\emptyset$ to denote a regular expression, specifying the language consisting of no strings at all.

It is an important point to note that ε and $\emptyset$ define quite different languages. $L(\emptyset) = \{\}$, is the empty set, while $L(\varepsilon)$ defines a set of cardinality one, $\{\varepsilon\}$. It may seem paradoxical that the empty language is not the same as the language consisting of just the empty string. However, it is quite obvious when seen in terms of the state diagrams which define the two languages. Any state diagram which contains no accept state which is reachable from the start state accepts no strings at all, and hence implements the empty language $\emptyset$. On the other hand, any state diagram in which the start state is a member of the accept state set accepts the empty string, perhaps among other possibilities. This is illustrated in Figure 4.1.

$E=\emptyset$ $E=\varepsilon$

Figure 4.1   State diagram for FSA recognizing $\emptyset$ and ε.

4.1.1 The extended operators

The three basic operations of closure, concatenation, and alternation are sufficient to define any regular expression. However, it is convenient to introduce additional operators which allow a more compact representation for **positive closure** and for **optionality**.

Positive closure of an expression E, is denoted by E^+, and specifies a language consisting of strings formed by concatenating one or more strings from $L(E)$. This is to be contrasted with the rule for the (ordinary) closure which permits the empty string ε. It follows that

$$E^+ = EE^*$$

Corresponding to the more careful definition of the closure, we might define the positive closure as follows.

If E is some regular expression, then

a) every string from $L(E)$ belongs to $L(E^+)$;
b) if α is some string that belongs to $L(E^*)$, and β is any string that belongs to $L(E)$, then the string $\alpha\beta$ belongs to $L(E^+)$

Optionality of a subexpression within a regular expression merely specifies that the subexpression is in alternation with the empty expression. We denote this by placing the optional subexpression within square brackets. Thus

$$[E] = (\varepsilon|E)$$

so that

$$L([E]) = L(E) \cup \{\varepsilon\}$$

and

$$L([E^+]) = L(E^*)$$

As an example of the correspondence between the basic notation and the extended notation which includes the additional operators, consider the *real* number language defined in words in Section 3.2, and implemented by the FSA in Figure 3.10. The regular expression for this

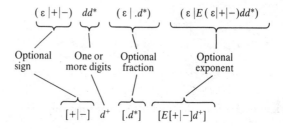

Figure 4.2   Regular expression for real numbers, basic form, and extended notation.

language is given in Figure 4.2, using the symbol '*d*' to signify any decimal digit.

4.1.2 Algebraic properties

Generally, we do not need to perform algebraic manipulation on regular expressions. Instead it is normal to write down regular expressions in whatever fashion is most obvious in terms of defining the language which is intended, and then directly to transform into a finite state automaton. There is nevertheless occasionally a need for such manipulation.

The algebraic laws which may sometimes assist in the manipulation of regular expressions are as follows, where A, B, C denote regular expressions, and it is assumed that in our notation that concatenation takes precedence over alternation.

1. Distributive law of concatenation over alternation.
   $A(B|C) = AB|AC$

2. Associative laws for concatenation and alternation.
   $A|(B|C) = (A|B)|C = A|B|C$
   $A(BC) = (AB)C = ABC$

3. Commutative law for alternation.
   $A|B = B|A$

Note carefully, however, that concatenation is not commutative, for the same reason that the product operation applied to languages is not.

There are a number of special results for closure

4. $(A^*)^* = A^*$

5. $(A^*B^*)^* = (A|B)^*$

Finally there are the following special properties of the null and empty expressions

6. $A|\varepsilon = A$, for any A

7. $A\emptyset = \emptyset A = \emptyset$, for any A

8. $A\varepsilon = \varepsilon A = A$, for any A

Two regular expressions are defined as being equivalent if they define the same regular language. However, because of the difficulty of manipulating regular expressions algebraically, the problem of deciding when two regular expressions are equivalent is difficult. In effect, the question of equivalence must be answered indirectly, by finding the FSA which correspond to the two regular expressions, and seeing if they lead to isomorphic minimal FSA. The property that every regular language possesses a unique FSA with a minimal number of states thus indirectly provides a sort of canonical form for regular expressions.

The results of the next two sections, in effect, provide a proof that every regular expression corresponds to a regular language. The proof proceeds by showing exactly how to derive the corresponding finite state automaton. The converse result is also true; every regular language defines a regular expression. However, the proof turns out to be surprisingly tortuous. Interested readers are referred to McNaughton and Yamada (1960).

4.1.3 Section checklist and summary definitions

1. Meta-language.

   - A meta-language is a language which is used to formally define languages.

2. Definition of regular expression.

   A regular expression over an alphabet Σ is recursively defined by the following rules.

   - Every symbol of the alphabet Σ is a regular expression, and defines the language $L(a) = \{a\}$.

   - The symbol designating the empty string, ε, is a regular expression, and defines the language $L(\varepsilon) = \{\varepsilon\}$.

   - The symbol designating the empty language, $\emptyset$, is a regular expression, and defines the language $L(\emptyset) = \{\}$, the empty set.

   - The concatenation of two regular expressions, A and B, is a regular expression and defines the language $L(AB) = \{\beta: \beta=\beta_1\beta_2$, where $\beta_1 \in L(A)$ and $\beta_2 \in L(B)$.

   - The alternation of two regular expressions, A and B, is a regular expression, and defines the language consisting of the union of the component languages, $L(A|B) = L(A) \cup L(B)$.

   - The closure of a regular expression, A, is a regular expression, and defines the language according to the following rules.

    a) $\varepsilon \in L(A^*)$
    b) if $\alpha \in L(A^*)$ and $\beta \in L(A)$, then $\alpha\beta \in L(A^*)$.

3. Meta-symbol notation conventions.

- Concatenation is implicit, being indicated by the immediate juxtaposition of symbols.

- Alternation is indicated by separating the alternatives by the solid vertical rule, '|', with the complete set of alternatives placed in parentheses if necessary.

- Closure is indicated by the superscript asterisk, '*'. Unless the closure is on a single atomic symbol, the subexpression is placed in parentheses.

- The positive closure of a regular expression, A, is indicated by a super-script plus symbol, and defines the language $L(A^+) = L(A^*) - \{\varepsilon\}$.

- Optionality is indicated by placing the optional subexpression in square brackets. By definition, $L([A]) = L(\varepsilon|A)$.

4.2 Transforming regular expressions into FSA

4.2.1 Non-deterministic FSA

Every regular expression defines an FSA and hence a regular language. However, the transformation between the expression and the FSA is performed in two distinct steps. The first step is to construct a state diagram equivalent to the regular expression. Usually, however, a state diagram so formed is non-deterministic, by which we mean that the next state function is not uniquely defined for all possible (*state, symbol*) pairs. We call such a non-deterministic finite-state automaton an 'NFSA'.

    The non-determinism in the state diagram arises in two different ways. Firstly, it may appear because of the presence of transitions labelled by the empty string. Alternatively, two or more transitions out of a particular state may be labelled with the same alphabet symbol. For example, a regular expression for optionally signed integers is $E = (\varepsilon|+|-)dd^*$, where d is any decimal digit '0'..'9'. The straight-

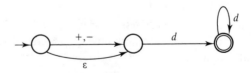

Figure 4.3 NFSA for $(\varepsilon|+|-)dd^*$.

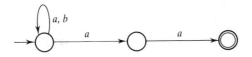

Figure 4.4   NFSA for $(a|b)^*aa$.

forward methods of this section form the non-deterministic state diagram shown in Figure 4.3 from this expression.

The method by which such a state diagram is derived is given shortly, but for the moment it should be noted that every possible path from the start state to the accept state in Figure 4.3 does spell out a valid string in the language, exactly as for the deterministic state diagrams of the previous chapters. The difference between Figure 4.3 and previous state diagrams is that no transition table may be formed from Figure 4.3, because one of the transitions is labelled with the empty string ε, which is not an alphabet symbol.

A simple example of the second type of non-determinism occurs with the expression $E = (a|b)^*aa$, which defines a language of strings from the alphabet $\{a,b\}$ which end in two successive 'a' symbols. The non-deterministic state diagram corresponding to this expression is shown in Figure 4.4.

Notice that there are two successor states for the (*state*, *symbol*) pair $(0,a)$, either state 1 or state 0 being possible successors. Nevertheless, every possible path from *start* to *accept* does spell out a valid string in the language.

The methods of Chapter 3 cannot be used to interpret state diagrams which have either of the non-deterministic features demonstrated. It is possible, however, to interpret such a state diagram by means of a backtracking automaton.

A backtracking automaton is an FSA which, when faced with a choice of several possible successor states, arbitrarily chooses one. If at some later state in the recognition attempt no valid transition can be found, there are two possible conclusions. Either the string being tested actually is invalid, or at some previous point of choice the wrong path was chosen. Before the string may be rejected as invalid, the second possibility must be exhausted.

The algorithm may be stated, rather informally, as follows:

So long as legal successor states exist choose one arbitrarily. If no legal successor remains, then back up both the state and the input string to the previous configuration at which a choice was made, and choose again. If all such choices have been exhausted, then backtrack to the previous point of choice.

The algorithm will terminate in one of two ways. The string may terminate with the automaton in an accept state, in which case the string is accepted. Alternatively, the automaton may run out of backtracking moves by backing up all the way to the start state, thus signifying rejection of the string.

Backtracking automata are particularly inefficient, and far better methods of directly implementing NFSA are dealt with in Section 4.4. Nevertheless backtracking algorithms are an interesting challenge to the programmer, so a simple exercise is included at the end of this chapter.

4.2.2 Converting a regular expression to an NFSA

We now consider the systematic transformation of regular expressions into NFSA.

The state diagram which accepts a single atom b is given by

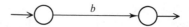

where the partial transitions indicate the (relative) start and accept states. More complex expressions are formed from the atoms by concatenation, closure, and alternation, so it is necessary only to show how these operations cause component subdiagrams to be interconnected. We use the following notation for the (partial) NFSA state diagram which accepts the strings in the language defined by some (sub)expression E.

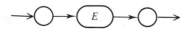

If we form an expression E_1E_2, then the NFSA accepting the strings in E_1E_2 is shown in Figure 4.5.

The correctness of Figure 4.5 may be verified by noting that only strings in E_1 permit passage from state 0 to state 1, while only strings in E_2 allow passage to state 2. Thus only strings in the product language E_1E_2 define valid paths from state 0 to state 2.

A simple example of the above rule occurs when each subexpression

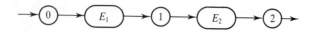

Figure 4.5   NFSA for E_1E_2.

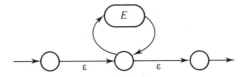

Figure 4.6   NFSA for E^*.

is just a single atom. Suppose $E = ab$. The state diagram is as expected:

The closure operation on a subexpression leads to a state diagram containing a loop. For any general expression E, the state diagram for E^* is shown in Figure 4.6.

Finally, the alternation operation results in the component diagrams being interconnected 'in parallel'. The state diagram for $(E_1|E_2)$ is shown in Figure 4.7.

4.2.3 Eliminating redundant ε-transitions

The standard construction for closure, as shown in Figure 4.6, results in the incorporation of a large number of ε-transitions into the NFSA. These empty transitions may often be removed by simply merging the states at either end of the ε-transition into a single state. It is usually possible to determine when such merging is permissible by inspection.

The key observation is that an ε-transition may be removed provided that the two end states do not both possess both *in*- and *out*-transitions exclusive of the ε-transition under consideration. Thus in Figure 4.8 the ε-transitions may be removed in cases (i) and (ii), but not in case (iii).

Various specific cases showing why this prohibition is necessary are given in Figure 4.9. In diagram (i), if the ε-transition is removed the

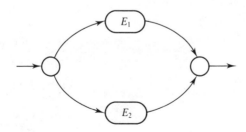

Figure 4.7   NFSA for $(E_1|E_2)$.

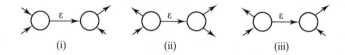

Figure 4.8   Various cases of ε-transitions.

accepted language becomes $L(a(a|b)*)$, which is clearly a different language to $L(aa*b*)$. A distinguishing string is *'aba'*, for example.

In diagram (ii) of Figure 4.9, the removal of the ε-transition by merging states 0 and 1 would change the regular expression from $(a|b*c)$ to $b*(a|c)$. These two expressions are distinguished by the string *ba*, for example. Note especially that in this case the prohibition on merging arises because the state 0 has an implicit in-transition since it is the start state, as well as the explicit out-edge labelled *a*. Diagrams (iii) and (iv), without the ε-transitions, would correspond to non-equivalent regular expressions, being distinguished by the string *bcab* in the case of (iii), and *a* in the case of (iv).

The reader should redraw each of the diagrams in Figure 4.9 with the empty transitions removed by state-merging operations. Tracing through the paths followed by the distinguishing strings should indicate the necessity of the retention of the empty transition as a sort of one-way 'valve'.

It should be noted that failure to detect and remove redundant ε-transitions is never fatal to the process of forming the FSA. The systematic methods of the next section remove non-determinism caused by any remaining empty transitions. The only point in removing the transitions, as indicated above, is to obtain a slightly simpler NFSA to start with. This may make the process a little quicker if the algorithm is

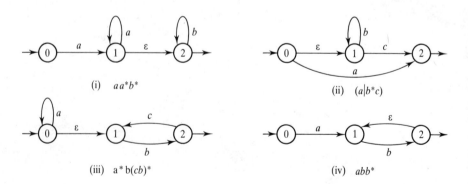

Figure 4.9   Various examples of non-redundant ε-transitions.

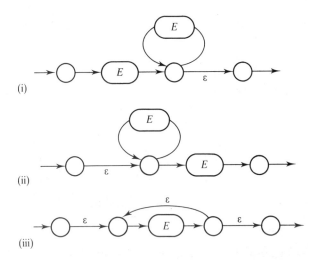

Figure 4.10   Various NFSA for a positive closure.

implemented by hand. However, if there is any doubt as to the validity of merging any two states, the safe approach is to leave the diagram exactly as implied by the regular expression.

4.2.4 Positive closure of a subexpression

Another useful building block to use in the transformation of regular expressions to NFSA is the form which arises from the positive closure of an expression. In our notation, $EE^* = E^*E = E^+$, and the state diagrams corresponding to these three equivalent forms are given in Figure 4.10.

The simplification involved in using the third form for the positive closure can often be significant if the subexpression E is more complex than a single atom. The considerations involved in deleting the possibly redundant ε-transitions are identical to those discussed for the ordinary closure.

Figure 4.11 shows the result of applying the methods of this section to the real number language given in the previous section. Diagram (i) is obtained directly from the regular expression, while diagram (ii) has all redundant ε-transitions removed.

Figure 4.12 gives the corresponding diagrams, but these arise from the use of the positive closure construct on the extended form of regular expression.

All of the examples of NFSA shown so far have in common that only a single accept state appears in each state diagram. This is a necessary result of the method used. However, the application of the methods of

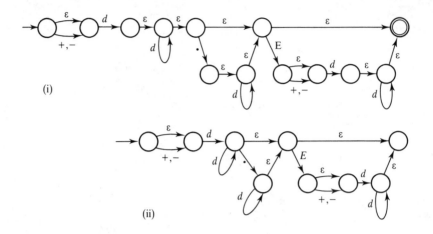

Figure 4.11   NFSA for the *real* number language.

the next section usually results in the appearance of multiple accept states in the deterministic versions of these same diagrams.

4.2.5   Section checklist and summary definitions

1. Non-deterministic FSA (NFSA) definitions.
   - An NFSA defines a 'transition function', but with the limitation that the next state is not uniquely defined for every (*present state, input symbol*) pair. Nevertheless, every path from the start state to an accept state of an NFSA spells out a string in the language.
   - An FSA may be non-deterministic for either of two reasons: some state transitions may not require the consumption of any input symbol (i.e. there may be 'ε-transitions'), or there may be multiple transitions out of some state which are predicated on the same input symbol.

2. Transforming to NFSA.
   - A single atom, *a*, in a regular expression is recognized by a transition from start to accept states predicated on symbol *a*.
   - An empty string, ε, is recognized by an ε-transition from start to accept states.
   - The concatenation of two regular expressions is recognized by an FSA which connects together the two component FSAs so that the accept state of the first is the start state of the second.
   - The alternation of two regular expressions is recognized by an FSA

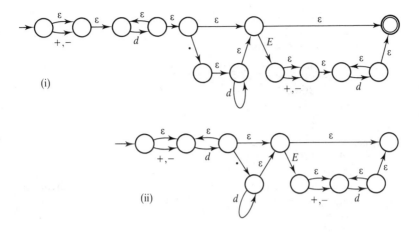

Figure 4.12 NFSA for the *real* number language using the positive closure construct.

which connects together the two component FSAs so that they share a common start state and a common accept state.

- If the start and accept states of an FSA are merged together, and ε-transitions connect a new start state to the merged state, and the merged state to a new accept state, then the new FSA recognizes the closure of the regular expression recognized by the original.

4.3   Elimination of non-determinism

The transformation from an NFSA to an equivalent deterministic-FSA can always be carried out successfully, and thus the methods of this section provide the final step in a constructive proof that every regular expression corresponds to an FSA (and hence by definition to a regular language). To avoid confusion between deterministic and non-deterministic automata, we will refer to ordinary, deterministic-FSA as 'DFSA'.

The basic idea behind the algorithm which removes the non-determinism is to generate a transition function which takes as argument the subset of all the possible NFSA states of the automaton. For each input symbol and possible set of present states the set of possible successor states is calculated. Each of these sets will, in general, be a subset of the complete set of NFSA states. By starting from the start state, and successively calculating possible successor state subsets, the transition table is gradually filled in. The number of possible subsets is bounded, since if the number of NFSA sets is N, the cardinality of the

```
type NfsaState = 0..K;
     DfsaState = set of NfsaState;

procedure EpsilonClosure(var S : DfsaState);
   var Ended : BOOLEAN;
       Element : NfsaState;
begin
  repeat
    Ended := TRUE;
    for {every Element in the set S} do
       {Consider all epsilon-transitions starting from state Element. If
        target state is not already in S then include it, and set Ended to
        FALSE.}
  until Ended; (*i.e. a complete sweep without an addition*)
end (* EpsilonClosure*);
```

Figure 4.13   ε-closure algorithm.

powerset is 2^N. Finally, we associate each reachable subset of NFSA states with a state of a DFSA.

4.3.1 The ε-closure

Since we wish to deal with NFSA which include ε-transitions, it is necessary to introduce the notion of the **ε-closure** of a set of states. If at any point in our procedure we calculate that a particular state, s_i say, is a possible state for the automaton to be in, then it follows that any state which is reachable from s_i by ε-transitions is also a possible state.

We define the ε-closure of a set of states S as

$$\varepsilon\text{-}closure(S) = \{s_i : s_i \in S \quad \text{or} \quad s_i \text{ is reachable from some} \\ s_j \in S \text{ by } \varepsilon\text{-transitions}\}$$

Note carefully the possibility that a particular s belonging to the closure may be reachable by multiple ε-transitions from a member of S. This fact complicates the algorithmic determination of the ε-closure.

We must repeatedly scan the states of S, adding new states reachable by ε-transitions as they are found. Only when a complete scan of S does not add any new states to the set does the algorithm terminate. Figure 4.13 gives a crude but straightforward algorithm, where the unelaborated details depend on the particular data structure used to represent the set. For a more elegant view of the possible algorithms, see the exercises at the end of this chapter.

4.3.2 The subset construction procedure

The generation of the DFSA transition table will now be described as it is implemented by hand. Implementation of the algorithm by machine is considered later.

The transition table is generated row by row, each row being labelled by a subset of NFSA states, and with the actual subsets generated explicitly during the process. The first row is labelled with the ε-closure of the start state of the NFSA. This subset will become the start state of the resulting DFSA.

For each row in turn, the successor state subset is generated for each input symbol in the alphabet. This successor state subset is calculated by first finding all the successor states of the present state subset which may be reached by means of a single transition labelled by the input symbol under consideration. The ε-closure of this subset is the required successor state subset, and is entered in the corresponding position in the table.

Whenever a successor state subset is formed, it must be checked against all of the row-labels generated so far. If the subset is new then it must be entered in the table as a new row-label, since by construction it is a reachable subset of the NFSA states. As remarked above, since the number of subsets of a finite set is bounded, the generation of new rows must ultimately terminate.

Finally, we associate a DFSA state with each row of the subset table, by renaming the subsets with DFSA state identifiers. Each DFSA state which includes any accept state of the original NFSA is labelled as an accept state of the DFSA. Any empty state subset implies that there is no possible valid NFSA state corresponding to that configuration, and hence corresponds to the error state of the DFSA.

We now perform the process in detail for two examples. The first is the NFSA previously given in Figure 4.4, $(a|b)^*aa$. Since this example contains no ε-transitions, no ε-closures are required. This example, shown in Figure 4.14, should be fully understood before the next example is attempted. Note that since the state subset $\{0,1,2\}$ is the only reachable subset which includes the NFSA accept state 2, DFSA state C is the only accept state of the DFSA.

4.3.3 A more substantial example

The example in Figure 4.15 is much more substantial than the previous example. It shows the construction of a real number recognizer DFSA from the NFSA of Figure 4.12 (ii).

In this example the ε-closure of the start state is $\{0,1\}$, and this subset of NFSA states is thus the start state of the DFSA. Considering the possible transitions on symbol d, we see that NFSA state 2 is the only

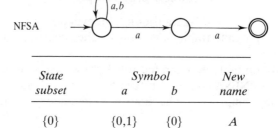

State subset	Symbol a	b	New name
{0}	{0,1}	{0}	A
{0,1}	{0,1,2}	{0}	B
{0,1,2}	{0,1,2}	{0}	C

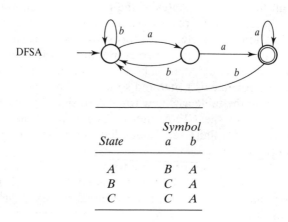

State	Symbol a	b
A	B	A
B	C	A
C	C	A

Figure 4.14   Subset construction for $(a|b)^*aa$.

direct successor. However, application of the ε-closure adds states 1, 4 and 8, so that the successor subset is {1,2,4,8}. The other table entries follow similarly. DFSA states 2,3 and 6 all correspond to subsets of the NFSA states which include NFSA state 8, so all of these are accept states of the DFSA, as shown in the table.

Both of the above examples produce DFSA of similar complexity to the original NFSA, at least as measured by the number of states. This is quite a common situation; however, there are simple examples where the complexity of the DFSA is very much greater than that of the corresponding NFSA.

4.3.4   Using FSA to form derived languages

We are now in a position to show that the union, product, and intersection of any two regular languages are also regular languages, as claimed in Section 2.5. The proof that the complement of any regular

NFSA

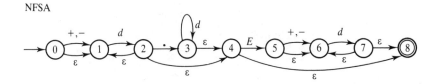

State subset	Symbol				New name	Accept state?
	d	$+,-$	$.$	E		
{0,1}	{1,2,4,8}	{1}	{}	{}	0	no
{1}	{1,2,4,8}	{}	{}	{}	1	no
{1,2,4,8}	{1,2,4,8}	{}	{3,4,8}	{5,6}	2	yes
{3,4,8}	{3,4,8}	{}	{}	{5,6}	3	yes
{5,6}	{6,7,8}	{6}	{}	{}	4	no
{6}	{6,7,8}	{}	{}	{}	5	no
{6,7,8}	{6,7,8}	{}	{}	{}	6	yes

DFSA

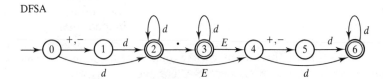

Figure 4.15   Subset construction for *real* number NFSA.

language is regular was required in Chapter 2, Exercise 2.6.

If two languages are each defined by regular expressions, A and B say, then the union language is defined by the regular expression $(A|B)$. Since any regular expression defines a regular language, we conclude that the union language must be regular.

Similarly, the concatenation of two regular expressions, AB say, defines the product language $L(A).L(B)$. Since AB is a well-formed regular expression, we conclude that the product language is regular.

In order to prove that the intersection of two regular languages is regular we must resort to a stratagem. From the DFSA for the two languages, we construct a compound NFSA as indicated in Figure 4.16. A shared start state leads, via ε-transitions, to the start state of the component DFSA. Two 'accept' states, labelled S_A and S_B, are then constructed. All accept states in the DFSA for regular expression A are connected to state S_A via empty transitions, and all the accept states of the DFSA B are likewise connected to state S_B. It follows that a string is in the intersection language if and only if it spells out paths which take the NFSA from the common start state to *both* accept states.

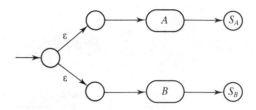

Figure 4.16   NFSA for an intersection language.

We now apply the subset construction procedure to the compound NFSA shown in Figure 4.16. If any of the resulting state subsets contain both of the accept states S_A and S_B, then the corresponding DFSA states are labelled 'accept'. All other states are labelled as non-accept states. If no accept state is constructed, then the DFSA accepts the regular language $\varnothing$. If there is one or more accept state in the DFSA, then the constructed automaton recognizes the intersection language. It is clear that since the subset construction always generates a bounded number of DFSA states, the resulting automaton does indeed define a regular language.

It may be seen that when two regular languages are combined by union or product the resulting FSA complexity, as measured by the number of states, is at worst equal to the sum of the individual complexities. However, in the case of the intersection language it is not difficult to see that the resulting automaton may have a number of states which might approach the product of the number of states of the component automata.

4.3.5   Section checklist and summary definitions

1. NFSA to DFSA conversion.
   - Every non-deterministic FSA may be converted into a deterministic-FSA (DFSA).

2. Epsilon-closure definition.
   - The ε-closure of a set of NFSA states is the set of all states which are reachable from the original set along ε-transition paths of length zero or more.
   - Since paths of length zero are specifically permitted, all of the states of a set are also in the epsilon-closure of that set.

3. The subset construction procedure.
   The subset construction procedure finds all reachable subsets of the

set of NFSA states. The procedure iteratively finds all subsets reachable from a known reachable subset, according to the following rules.

- The ε-closure of the state set which contains just the start state is a reachable subset.
- If S is a reachable subset, then the subset which is reached from S on symbol a, is the ε-closure of the set of states which are the direct successors of states in S, on symbol a.
- Every reachable subset corresponds to a unique state of a DFSA which accepts the same language as the original NFSA.
- DFSA states which correspond to subsets which include one or more accept states of the NFSA are accept states of the DFSA.

4.4   Direct realization of non-deterministic FSA

Normally when a regular language is defined, either by a regular expression or a regular grammar, it is converted into a deterministic state machine and implemented by one of the various methods treated in Chapter 3. For simple languages the elimination of non-determinism may be done by hand, while for larger languages the same algorithms may be implemented by machine.

There are certain classes of problems, however, where the language is defined by some kind of interactive process, and the resulting FSA is used only once. For example, some text-editors permit search strings which are defined by simple regular expressions or some equivalent construct. In such problems, the computation involved in generating the transition table for the DFSA may greatly exceed the computation involved in directly recognizing a single string with the original NFSA. For such 'throw-away' languages a direct realization of the non-deterministic FSA, although less efficient than an equivalent DFSA, may make more sense than the usual approach.

Realizations of NFSA using backtracking techniques are generally not practicable because the time taken to recognize a string may increase as a power of string length. However, there are alternative approaches which lead to automata for which the time taken is proportional to string length, and are only small factors slower than the equivalent DFSA. These algorithms are closely related to those which are used for converting from NFSA to DFSA, and are easily programmed in languages either with set constructors, such as Pascal, or Boolean arrays, such as Ada. A general explanation of the technique is given first, and then a particular, simple example is treated in some detail.

A direct implementation of an NFSA is a deterministic machine defined over an input alphabet Σ, with a state variable declared to be of

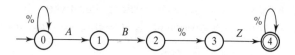

Figure 4.17   State diagram for '$*AB\%Z$'.

type **set of** *NfsaState*. Unlike the DFSA obtained by applying the algorithms of this chapter to the NFSA, we do not attempt to calculate the transition function for every possible (*present state, input symbol*) pair. Instead we evaluate the transition function as required for those pairs which actually occur during the operation of the machine. We may think of the machine as 'interpreting' the NFSA, rather than 'executing' the DFSA formed by 'compiling' the NFSA into the deterministic form.

By setting up a machine with a state variable of set type, we introduce a state space of high cardinality. In fact, if there are n states in the NFSA, there are 2^n states in the direct implementation. Of course only a tiny fraction of these states is accessible from the start state, and possibly even fewer will actually be constructed during the interpretation.

The algorithm for calculating the value of the transition function Φ for any actually occurring pair of arguments (S,a) is identical to that used in the subset construction procedure used for finding the equivalent DFSA. Suppose we denote the present state set by S, and we wish to find the successor state S' on a given input symbol a. The new set is constructed by considering all possible transitions on symbol a out of each of the elements of S in turn. This direct successor set is then augmented by taking the ε-closure, so as to include states which may be reached along paths which involve one or more empty transitions. The state of the automaton is then updated by replacing the present state set by the new state set just calculated.

It should be noted that so long as the successor state set is not the empty set the machine is in a non-error configuration. If S' becomes empty, however, then the situation corresponds to that which arises when an equivalent DFSA enters the error state, or when a backtracking automaton runs out of alternative states to back up to.

In the applications where direct interpretation of an NFSA is warranted, the most difficult area for the implementor is the design of the input meta-language which will specify the language to be recognized. There are also important questions of internal representation of the NFSA in a suitable data-structure. Fortunately, in many practical cases there are restrictions on the input language which lead to restrictions on the topology of the NFSA. In such cases the special structure of the NFSA may lead to efficient updating algorithms and simple data-structures.

Possible states	Current symbol	Unused input	Successor state set
{0}	A	AKABZZ	{0,1}
{0,1}	A	KABZZ	{0,1}
{0,1}	K	ABZZ	{0}
{0}	A	BZZ	{0,1}
{0,1}	B	ZZ	{0,2}
{0,2}	Z	Z	{0,3}
{0,3}	Z	ε	{0,4}

Figure 4.18   Simulation of direct implementation.

4.4.1   The wildcard language *W*

Consider a meta-language used in an operating system to specify filenames containing wildcards. The language consists of strings from a character set $T = \{`A'..`Z',`0'..`9'\}$ together with the meta-symbols '*' and '%'. The purpose of the wildcard symbol '*' is to signify any sequence of zero or more characters from the alphabet T, while '%' stands for any single character from T. Strings in the meta-language are equivalent to simple regular expressions. For example, the wildcard string '*AB%Z*' is equivalent to the regular expression

$$(A|B|C| \ldots)^*AB(A|B|C| \ldots)Z(A|B|C| \ldots)^*$$

which is recognized by the NFSA in Figure 4.17. In this diagram the transitions labelled '%' are taken on the occurrence of any symbol from T.

The structure of this state diagram is particularly simple, and the fact that it is non-deterministic may be verified by noting that there are two transitions out of state 0 on the input symbol A, since A is included in the 'any-character' symbol %.

Let us now simulate the direct interpretation of this NFSA, using the string '*AAKABZZ*' as a test string. Later we will return to derive the algorithms which map any string in the wildcard language onto a suitable data-structure, and interpret the NFSA using the stored values. The table in Figure 4.18 sets out the configuration of the process after each step, including the 'set of possible NFSA states'. It may be noted that, since the final state set in the table includes the NFSA state 4, the implementation accepts the test string.

One of the exercises of this chapter is to show that Figure 4.19 is the DFSA corresponding to the NFSA in Figure 4.17.

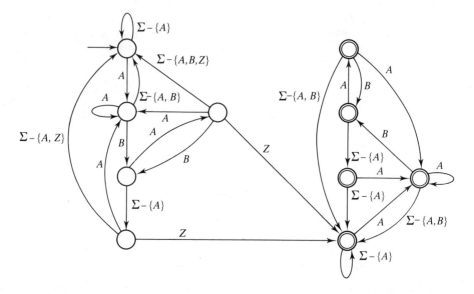

Figure 4.19   State diagram of DFSA recognizing the wildcard string *AB%Z*.

All the strings in the wildcard meta-language W have NFSA state diagrams with very similar topologies. In particular all of the state diagrams turn out to comprise a single chain of states with the forward transitions labelled by the non-'*' characters of the wildcard string in order. There is only one accept state, and every non-accept state has either a single 'advance' transition only, which goes to the next sequential state, or an advance transition and a self-loop. In the event that a state does have a self-loop, it may only be labelled with the 'any-character' symbol %.

Two additional examples of wildcard strings and their corresponding state diagrams are shown in Figure 4.20. This figure also suggests a tabular form for representing the information necessary to interpret the NFSA directly.

Because of the very restricted topology of the state diagram, the representation of the NFSA may be very simple. Each state has an *advance* symbol associated with it, and a Boolean which indicates the presence or otherwise of a self-loop on any-character.

Having devised a suitable data-structure to represent the NFSA, we now need two algorithms: one to interpret the table in a direct realization, and another to parse the wildcard string and build the table for the interpreter to use. The interpretation of the table is particularly simple, and the algorithm is shown in Figure 4.21. We assume some convenient maximum number of states $(K + 1)$, which also corresponds to the maximum number of non-'*' symbols in the permitted W-strings.

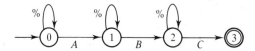

NFSA for wildcard string '*A*B*C'

NFSA state	Advance character	Self loop
0	A	true
1	B	true
2	C	true
3	–	false

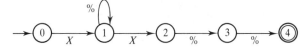

NFSA for wildcard string 'X*X%%'

NFSA state	Advance character	Self loop
0	X	false
1	X	true
2	%	false
3	%	false
4	–	false

Figure 4.20   *W*-strings, NFSA state diagrams, and corresponding tables.

The cardinality of the base type of the state set must be no smaller than this number if a Pascal **set** type is to be used to represent the state variable. Finally we define a variable *ENDNUM*, which is the ordinal of the accept state of the NFSA.

4.4.2 Creating the tables for the *W*-strings

The procedure which recognizes the strings in the wildcard meta-language *W* and builds the table representation of the NFSA is straightforward. The code is shown in Figure 4.22. We define two symbol alphabets: *INPUTSET*, which is the acceptable characters in a *W*-string, including

```
function WILDSCAN : BOOLEAN;
  (* The enclosing block declares NfsaState = 0..K,
     the arrays AdvanceChar and SelfLoop,
     the set ALPHABET, and the procedure GetChar. *)

  type DfsaState = set of NfsaState;
  varstate     : DfsaState;
     ENDNUM : NfsaState;
     ch        : CHAR;

  procedure UpdateState(var present : DfsaState; ch : CHAR);
  (* Forms the successor state of present *)
     var element : NfsaState;
        next    : DfsaState;
  begin
    next := []; (* initially empty *)
    for element := 0 to ENDNUM do begin
      if element in present then begin
        if SelfLoop[element] then next := next + [element];
        if (AdvanceChar[element] = ch) or
           (AdvanceChar[element] = '%')
          then next := next + [element + 1];
        end; (* outer if *)
      end; (* for *)
    present := next;
  end; (* UpdateState *)

begin (* Wildscan *)
  state := [0]; (* start state set *)
  GetChar(ch);
  while ch in ALPHABET do begin
    UpdateState(state,ch);
    GetChar(ch)
  end; (* while *)
  WILDSCAN := (ENDNUM in state);
end (* Wildscan *);
```

Figure 4.21   Function to directly interpret wildcard NFSA.

the wildcard meta-characters, and *ALPHABET*, which is the symbol set for the strings to be tested.

The meta-language *W* is a particularly simple choice and corresponds to a very restricted class of regular expressions. More general classes of meta-language require more general data structures to represent the NFSA, and require more complex recognizers to build their tables.

```
type NfsaState = O..K;
var  INPUTSET, ALPHABET : set of CHAR;
     AdvanceChar : array[NfsaState] of CHAR;
     SelfLoop     : array[NfsaState] of BOOLEAN;
     ENDNUM     : NfsaState;

procedure BUILDTABLE;
  var inpt : CHAR;
      CurrentState : NfsaState;
begin
  CurrentState := 0;
  SelfLoop[CurrentState] := FALSE;
  Read(inpt);
  while inpt in INPUTSET do begin
    if inpt = '*' then SelfLoop[CurrentState] := TRUE
      else begin
        AdvanceChar[CurrentState] := inpt;
        CurrentState := CurrentState + 1;
        SelfLoop[CurrentState] := FALSE;
        end; (* else *)
    Read(inpt);
    end; (* while *)
  (* W-string has finished, mark endstate with NUL *)
  ENDNUM := CurrentState;
  AdvanceChar[CurrentState] := CHR(0);
end (* Buildtable *);
```

Figure 4.22   Procedure to build NFSA table for direct interpretation.

The principles involved in direct interpretation of the more complex forms of NFSA table are similar to those which were used in the ordinary wildcard language example. However, almost any more general form of regular expression used to specify a language of acceptable strings will involve the use of parentheses to group symbols. Since these parentheses, in general, will be able to be nested, it follows that any such meta-language will not itself be regular. This is a direct consequence of the pumping lemma for regular languages, as discussed in Chapter 2.

We are, therefore, faced with a rather paradoxical situation. We have a meta-language which is not regular, but every string in the meta-language defines a language which *is* regular. Thus although the algorithm which interprets the NFSA table implements a finite state machine, the procedure which recognizes the specification string and inserts the data in the table must implement a more powerful class of recognizer.

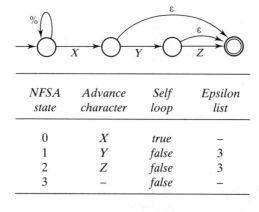

NFSA state	Advance character	Self loop	Epsilon list
0	X	true	–
1	Y	false	3
2	Z	false	3
3	–	false	–

Figure 4.23 NFSA recognizing the language of *WildOption* string '*X[Y[Z]]*'.

The wildcard language W in the previous example is quite atypical, in that the wildcard language is itself regular, being defined by the regular expression

$$('*'|'\%'|'A'|'B'| \ldots |'0'|'1'| \ldots |'9')*$$

possibly with an implementation-defined restriction on maximum string length.

4.4.3   The wildcard language with optional substrings, *WildOption*

We now consider an extension of the wildcard language which illustrates some of the above points. The extension to be considered allows for the specification of optional substrings. Optionality is indicated in the meta-language by the use of square brackets, '[' and ']', exactly as for the extended forms of general regular expressions. We call this extended version of the W meta-language *WildOption*.

It should be noted that although the *WildOption* language illustrates the considerations involved in handling nested parentheses, it still falls far short of being able to specify an arbitrary regular language since there is no provision for alternation.

WildOption permits specification strings such as '*X[Y[Z]]*', which specifies a language which would contain all of the strings belonging to the (previous) W-string languages '*X*', '*XY*', and '*XYZ*'. The NFSA state diagram for this language is shown in Figure 4.23.

Every state diagram arising from a string in *WildOption* has a straight chain of states, just as in the simpler case. However, in this case each state, as well as having an *advance-character* and an optional *self-loop*,

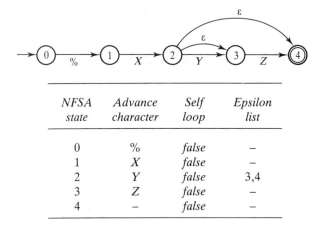

NFSA state	Advance character	Self loop	Epsilon list
0	%	false	–
1	X	false	–
2	Y	false	3,4
3	Z	false	–
4	–	false	–

Figure 4.24   NFSA recognizing the language of *WildOption* string '%*X*[[*Y*]*Z*]'.

also has a set of ε-transitions. Each element of this set, which may be empty, specifies an empty transition leading to a higher numbered state and implements the bypassing of one of the substrings which has been specified as optional.

A suitable data-structure provides a record for each state, with fields for the advance character, a Boolean to indicate the presence or otherwise of a self-loop on '%', and a list of the target states for ε-transitions, if any.

Figure 4.24 gives another example of a *WildOption* string, and its corresponding NFSA and interpreter table. In this second example, because two open parentheses occur together there are two empty transitions which leave from the same state.

The algorithm for interpreting the tables built for strings in the *WildOption* language is very little changed from the one given in Figure 4.21 for the *W*-language. The function corresponding to Figure 4.21 is given in Figure 4.25. The main body of the function is identical to the previous version except for two calls to a procedure *EpsilonClosure*.

EpsilonClosure is called, initially, to form the closure of the start state, and then is called after each return of *UpdateState* within the main interpretation loop. The procedure *UpdateState* is completely unchanged from the previous version, since the same fields are present in the data structure in each case.

The procedure *EpsilonClosure* is particularly simple in the case of the *WildOption* language because the ε-transitions can only lead to higher numbered states. This fortuitous circumstance allows the closure to be formed in a single sweep through the states of the set. The algorithm given in Figure 4.26 should be compared with the generally applicable

```
    function WOptionScan : BOOLEAN;
      (* The enclosing block declares NfsaState = 0..K,
          the arrays AdvanceChar and SelfLoop, the set ALPHABET,
          and the procedure GetChar.*)

    type DfsaState = set of NfsaState;
    var  state       : DfsaState;
         ENDNUM : NfsaState;
         ch          : CHAR;

      procedure UpdateState (var present : DfsaState; ch : CHAR);
        {code not shown here};
      procedure EpsilonClosure(var present : DfsaState);
        {code not shown here});

    begin (* WOptionScan *)
      state := [0];
      EpsilonClosure(state); (* start state set *)
      GetChar(ch);
      while ch in ALPHABET do begin
        UpdateState(state,ch);
        EpsilonClosure(state);
        GetChar(ch)
      end; (* while *)
      WOptionScan := (ENDNUM in state);
    end (* WOptionScan *);
```

Figure 4.25   Modified version of WILDSCAN which permits optional substrings.

ε-closure algorithm given in Figure 4.13, and also with the more efficient methods treated in the exercises.

The unelaborated details of the algorithm of Figure 4.26 depend on the way in which the ε-lists are actually represented. However, since the *WildOption* meta-language is not regular we defer any treatment of the algorithm which builds the tables until Chapter 8.

It is important to note that the kinds of regular expression which we have treated in the examples of this section have an extremely restricted topology. The classes of regular expressions which lead to 'straight line' NFSA are quite important, and do allow efficient interpretation to consider only these simplified cases. In the case of a more general NFSA with a graph-like structure, the data structures required are more complex and the algorithms which access them appropriately changed. Exercise 4.8 asks for a data structure to be designed for a completely general NFSA, and it is an interesting exercise to try to adapt the algorithm of Figure 4.21 to work with such a structure.

```
procedure EpsilonClosure(var present : DfsaState);
  var element : NfsaState;
begin
  for element := 0 to K do
    if element in present then
      {add epsilon-list elements to present state set}
end (* epsilon-closure *);
```

Figure 4.26   Special version of ε-closure algorithm.

4.4.4   Section checklist and summary definitions

Direct NFSA interpretation.

- An NFSA may be directly interpreted by implementing a state variable which corresponds to the set of possible NFSA states. This set is updated in a manner analogous to each step in the subset construction procedure.

- In a direct interpretation, the state is updated by finding that subset of the NFSA states which is reachable from the current possible-state set by transitions on the current input symbol. This reachable subset replaces the current possible-state set.

- For NFSA of restricted topology, direct interpretation algorithms may show important gains in speed and simplicity over the general case.

Exercises

4.1   Find the DFSA equivalent to the NFSA of Figure 4.3.

4.2   Write a regular expression for numerical constants which conform to the following list of restrictions.

a) At least one digit precedes the decimal point.
b) The decimal point is optional, but if present is followed by at least one digit.
c) Except as demanded by rules (a) and (b), leading and trailing zero digits are not permitted.

[Your regular expression should permit such strings as '25', '27.3', '0', '0.0', '0.54', etc.]

4.3   Draw a 'railroad' syntax diagram for the language in question 4.2, and find the state diagrams of the corresponding NFSA and DFSA.

4.4   Numbers in Algol-60 are given by the regular expression

$[+|-](d^+[.d^+] |_{10} [+|-]d^+ | d^+[.d^+]_{10}[+|-]d^+)$

Derive a DFSA to recognize this language. Note that '$_{10}$' is a single character in the lexical alphabet of Algol-60.

4.5   Verify that Figure 4.19 is the state diagram of the DFSA corresponding to the NFSA in Figure 4.17.

4.6   Deduce a regular expression for the language of strings from the alphabet $\Sigma = \{a,b\}$, such that the fourth-to-last symbol in the permitted strings is an *a*. Form the NFSA and DFSA.

[This is an example of a language for which the complexity of the DFSA far exceeds that of the NFSA.]

4.7   Write a program which recognizes strings in a language defined by the *wildcard* meta-language of Section 4.4, using a backtracking algorithm.

4.8   Devise a suitable compacted data-structure to represent NFSA, which takes advantage of the typical sparsity of the transition table. Ensure that your structure does not depend on any particular ordering of the state ordinals and permits an arbitrary number of out-edges for each state.

4.9   The ε-closure algorithm given in Figure 4.13 is far too inefficient in the general case. A better algorithm works as follows. Two 'sets' of states are maintained, one the set of states being accumulated as the ε-closure, the other a 'fringe' set of states which have been added to the closure, but have not yet had their out-transitions considered. A state may be added to the fringe only once, and only the states on the fringe have their transitions scanned. The search terminates when the fringe becomes empty.

Work out the details of an algorithm which works in this way, and code your algorithm for the particular data structure given in your answer to question 4.8.

4.10 Write a program equivalent to Figures 4.21 and 4.22, but which allows multiple wildcard strings to be searched for at once. The permissible input format should be

string ('|' string)*

where the strings are the conventional wildcard strings discussed in Section 4.4, including '%' and '*' characters.

As a possible extension, consider the implementation of an escape mechanism so that the *W*-strings may specify searching for patterns which include the meta-characters '*' and '%'.

4.11 The standard NFSA fragment which implements a closure was shown in Figure 4.6. However, none of the NFSA in Section 4.4 include the ε-transitions which separate the state with the loop from its neighbours. Why is this?

Does the same reasoning apply to NFSA which arise from the *WildOption* language of Section 4.4, and if not, under what circumstances must the ε-transitions be retained?

[*Hint*: Consider the operation of the NFSA which arises from the *WildOption* string 'a[*b*]c'.]

4.12 The major inefficiency in the wildscan interpreter of Figure 4.21 is in the procedure *UpdateState*. This procedure is called once for every character in the file to be scanned, and performs a loop of *ENDNUM* iterations for each call. One improvement which leads to an immediate speed-up is to use an alternative data structure to store the self-loop information so that all elements of *next* which arise from self-loops are found in a single (set) operation. Work out the detailed modifications for Figures 4.21 and 4.22 to implement this improvement.

4.13 An improvement is possible in the speed of the *UpdateState* procedure which far exceeds the effect of the changes proposed in the previous exercise. Seek this improvement.

[*Hint*: The solution involves a function on sets, *Shift*( ), which it is not possible to express in Pascal except as a loop. The operation may be defined by

function *Shift*(*S* : *DfsaState*) : *DfsaState*;

with a body which performs the set construction

$$Shift(S) = \{ j : (j - 1) \in S \} \qquad\qquad]$$

Further reading

Many texts deal with the theory of regular expressions, including Aho and Ullman (1972,1973) and Hopcroft and Ullman (1979). The algebra of regular expressions is dealt with in detail in Brzozski (1962, 1964).

The method of deriving a regular expression for a given FSA is due to McNaughton and Yamada (1960), a pioneering paper in this area, while efficient methods of computing the transitive closure of an expression such as the ε-closure are given by Warshall (1962).

Applications of finite automata methods to string-searching and bibliographic search are given by Knuth *et al.* (1977), while the direct implementation of NFSA for that purpose is treated in Thompson (1968).

Chapter 5 **Symbol Table Organization**

5.1   Simple symbol table organization

Many different syntax-directed software tools deal with languages in which the underlying alphabet has one or more symbols with an attribute type of very large or possibly even infinite cardinality. For example, in programming languages, the alphabet symbol *identifier* has a lexical attribute corresponding to the representation string of the identifier. Similarly, the 'value' attribute for a numeric symbol may have an extremely large cardinality in languages which have literal numeric symbols.

Note that in such cases, we do not pretend that the alphabet is very large. Instead, we use a single value of type *SymbolType* to represent any token of this lexical category, and use a separate attribute to distinguish between different instances of the syntactically equivalent symbols.

Although, from the point of view of the upper-level recognizer, any identifier symbol is syntactically equivalent, for semantic actions the attribute is usually required also. Typically, we must be able to retrieve the attribute so that we may perform tests to determine which other occurrences of the symbol *identifier* refer to the same object. In order to do this it is, at the very least, necessary to keep a record of the lexical attributes of identifiers which have already been encountered. The data structure which is used to answer such questions is called a **symbol table**.

For our purposes, a symbol table may be thought of as a mapping from string-valued lexical attributes to the semantic attributes of objects. In some particular instances the only information which it is necessary to know about an object is that it appears in the table. In other applications there may be many additional attributes which need to be stored. In any case, from the point of view of the stored lexical attribute, the symbol table may be thought of as an implementation of an unordered aggregate abstraction, with elements which are strings in most cases. An unordered aggregate is a primitive kind of 'set' abstraction which does not supply the full range of set operations. The only operations which the abstraction must supply are a membership test and an insertion operation. In most cases, we do not need a deletion operation. However, it is fair to comment that when the module which uses the symbol table is but one part of a larger program, we may wish to have a disposal operation which reclaims all of the symbol table space.

The topic of symbol table organization can be quite complex in the case of software tools which deal with languages with complex rules for the visibility of identifiers and the like. There is a voluminous literature dealing with these aspects as they arise in the context of programming language compilers. However, in this section we deal with the rather simpler symbol table organizations which are required to implement the software tools used as examples in the text. In the final section of this chapter we deal with just one more complicated case.

Although the following discussion is specifically aimed at symbol tables which deal with symbols with lexical attributes which are character strings, similar techniques are used for symbols which have numeric attributes.

We will assume, in the interests of generality, that we deal with a symbol *identifier*, which has a lexical attribute which is a string of characters, possibly of great length. The case of limited length may be treated as a special case. We will, however, assume that the attribute space is 'flat', which is to say that all identifiers are visible throughout the input sentence. In particular, only one object with a given lexical attribute may occur in the symbol table. We are, therefore, specifically excluding the complications which arise in the case of those languages which have nested scopes, and rules for resolving clashes of identifiers.

Note that although this restriction would appear to rule out syntax-directed tools such as pretty-printers for languages like Pascal, this is not the case. Clearly, in a Pascal program, although different occurrences of the same identifier name may not refer to the same object, the source representations are the same, and the objects may as well be the same, as far as the semantic action of producing output is concerned. However, in the case of tools such as cross-reference generators for Pascal, the block structure does matter, and a more complex organization than that which is described here might be preferable.

Symbol tables may also be used for resolving lexical issues such as whether or not a particular 'identifier-like' string is actually a keyword. In such cases the symbol table may permanently hold the keywords, and require a membership test but no insertion operation. Such a structure was used for the keyword recognizer which occurred in the case-study at the end of Chapter 3. We shall look at the design differences which arise in this specific case in Section 5.2.

There are two plausible data-structures which might be used for symbol tables of the type to be considered. One structure is based on hash-functions and the other is based on tree structures. For the simple applications considered here we will prefer the hash-function method.

We consider data structures which consist of some kind of identifier search structure, together with an unstructured string-table to store the

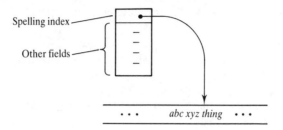

Figure 5.1   Identifier descriptor with spelling index.

actual character representations of the various identifiers. This table is simply an array of characters. The strings corresponding to various identifiers are entered into this table as they are found, and are separated by some distinguished character which cannot otherwise occur. Any character which does not occur within the strings is a suitable marker, but we will assume here that the ASCII character *NUL,CHR*(0), is used.

Identifier strings are retrieved by means of a so-called **spelling index**, which is an array index which points to the first character of the particular string in the string table. The string is terminated by the marker character. The strings thus take up only one more character position in the string-table than their length, and the length of individual strings is not limited. Furthermore, even in the case of languages which have bounded identifier length, space may be saved, since short identifiers do not use up unnecessary space.

Each identifier entered into the symbol table has a record associated with it. This record is the descriptor of the object to which the identifier refers, and contains whatever fields are required for that purpose. The record also contains a spelling index which allows retrieval of the string-valued lexical attribute. A diagramatic representation of a typical descriptor is shown in Figure 5.1. These descriptors may reside in an actual table, or may be distributed throughout a syntax tree in a manner which is described in Chapter 10.

For tables of even moderate size, the use of sequential search through a list of descriptors is too inefficient to be considered. We therefore resort to indices based on hash functions.

There are many different search techniques which are based on hash functions. We treat one particular variant, **open hashing**, which is suitable for this application. The standard data-structure texts deal with the topic in much greater generality.

A hash function is an arbitrary function which maps attribute values belonging to a base type of high cardinality into values belonging to some small subrange type. The purpose of the hash function is to partition the space of all possible attribute values into a relatively small number of

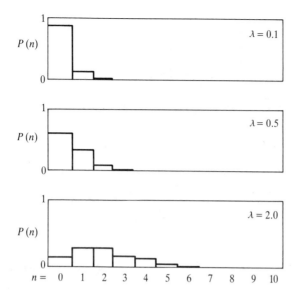

Figure 5.2 Hash bucket occupancy for various loading factors for an ideal hash function.

equivalence classes, which we call **hash buckets**. The function chosen should ensure that 'similar' attribute values map onto quite different ordinal values, so that identifiers are randomly distributed among the hash buckets to the greatest extent possible.

In order to find out if a descriptor with a particular attribute string is in the table, the hash function is applied to the search string, thereby producing some characteristic hash value. The search string need only be compared with those strings which belong to descriptors in the same hash-bucket as the search string. The point in performing this step is to ensure that if the number of hash-buckets is much larger than the number of identifier descriptors entered in the table, then most buckets will contain either no descriptors at all, or perhaps just one. In such a case the mean number of string comparisons which are necessary to find a given string in the table is close to one. Better still, in the case that the searched-for string is not in the table, the fact that the selected bucket is empty indicates that the lookup has failed without even a single comparison operation having to be performed.

In theory, an ideal hash function would distribute attribute values among the various hash buckets so that the probability of bucket occupancy obeys a Poisson distribution. The formula for the probability that a particular hash bucket will contain exactly n descriptors is given by

$$P(n) = \frac{\lambda^n e^{-\lambda}}{n!}$$

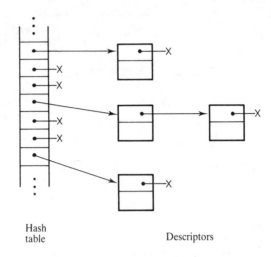

Hash
table   Descriptors

Figure 5.3   Hash table with collision overflow chains.

where λ, the loading factor, is equal to the number of descriptors inserted into the table divided by the number of buckets. Histograms for this function, for a few representative values of λ, are given in Figure 5.2.

Even for quite low loading factors, there is a possibility of more than one descriptor appearing in the same bucket. We must, therefore, have some method of dealing with the situation when two or more values 'collide in the hash table'.

The different methods of dealing with such collisions distinguish the various hash table algorithms. In this particular case, we take the approach that each hash bucket is implemented by a singly linked list. Initially, every hash bucket is empty, and has a list header which comprises a **nil**-valued pointer. Whenever an insertion operation maps an attribute value into a particular bucket, the descriptor with that attribute value is linked to the head of that bucket's list. This method of treating collisions is called **open hashing**. It has the advantage of being able, if necessary, to operate with loading factors greater than one. Figure 5.3 illustrates a fragment of an implementation of this data structure.

In the case that several descriptors appear in the same hash bucket, it is still necessary to perform a matching operation between the search string and each attribute in the bucket. The search terminates either when a match is found, or when the list is exhausted.

With the Poisson distribution, in the worse case, when the search is unsuccessful, the mean number of comparisons which need to be made when searching for the descriptor with some random attribute value, is exactly λ.

In the case that the descriptor is known to be present in the table, the

```
const  BucketMax = 499; (* bucket # should be prime *)
       StringMax = 2048; (* string table size in bytes *)

type   Buckets    = 0..BucketMax-1;
       Spellix    = 0..StringMax-1;
       DescPtr    = ^Descriptor;
       Descriptor = record
                         next : DescPtr; (* next in hash chain *)
                         spix : Spellix; (* string start index *)
                         . . . (* other attributes as required *)
                      end;
       StringType = packed array . . . of CHAR; (* as required *)

var    hashTable : array [Buckets] of DescPtr;
       stringTable: array [Spellix] of CHAR;
       top        : 0..StringMax; (* next free character position *)
       I          : INTEGER;

function HASH(s : StringType):Buckets;
  var total,I : INTEGER;
begin
  { . . .}
end;

function Lookup(string : StringType):DescPtr;
  (* returns DescPtr=nil if not found *)
  var ptr : DescPtr;
      bkt : Buckets;
      found : BOOLEAN;

          function Compare(lexAtt:Spellix) : BOOLEAN;
          begin
              {Compare lexAtt with string. Details depend on
               string format, case sensitivity etc.}
          end (* Compare *)

begin
  found := FALSE;
  bkt := HASH(string);
  ptr := hashTable[bkt];
  while not found and (ptr <> nil) do begin
     found := Compare(ptr^.spix);
     if not found then ptr := ptr^.next;
     end; (* if not found then exit is with ptr=nil *)
  Lookup := ptr;
end; (* Lookup *);
```

Figure 5.4   *cont. overleaf*

Figure 5.4 *cont.*

```
    procedure Insert(string: StringType);
    begin
        { . . .}
    end; (* Insert *)

begin (* initialization *)
    top := 0;
    for I := 0 to BucketMax do hashTable[I] := nil;
    { . . .}
end.
```

Figure 5.4   Outline of a hash table algorithm.

mean number of comparisons required to locate it, is given by $(1 + \lambda/2)$. This formula indicates that when loading factors are predominantly very small, a single comparison is all that is required. For the other extreme, when the loading factor is very large and every bucket has several descriptors in its chain, the average search is half the mean chain-length.

A typical implementation of the lookup procedure used in this technique is given in Figure 5.4. The details of the hash function have been omitted from the figure, as have the comparison and insertion procedure-bodies. Some actual hash functions are given later, while the details of the comparison procedure depend on the string conventions which are adopted. In the code, string parameters are assumed to belong to some fixed-length array type. In the case that the actual parameters do not use the whole length, the end of the actual parameter string is assumed to be marked in some fashion.

Many implementations of Pascal provide language extensions to make the handling of character strings a little less awkward, and program modules such as symbol tables can often make good use of such extensions, but at the cost of a loss of program portability.

It is quite possible to implement these procedures efficiently within the confines of standard Pascal, however. The most important point is to ensure that string-valued attributes which are packed into fixed-length arrays have an explicit end-marker character. In this way, the comparison procedure may be coded so that it only compares the relevant part of the strings, and that only the significant part of any new string gets copied into the string table. These conventions must be taken into account when the comparison procedure is written. It would also be a common (if somewhat suspect) practice to pass the string parameters by reference, by declaring them as **var** parameters, since this leads to much faster code for simple Pascal compilers.

```
procedure Insert(string: StringType);
   var  desc : DescPtr;
        bkt  : Buckets;

           procedure CopyString;
              var I : INTEGER;
           begin
             I := min;
             while {string not ended} do begin
               stringTable[top] := string[I];
               I := I+1;
               top := top+1;
               if top > StringMax then error('Table Overflow');
             end;
             stringTable[top] := MarkerChar;
             top := top+1;
             if top > StringMax then error('Table Overflow');
           end; (* CopyString *)

   begin (* assert: string is not already in table *)
     bkt := HASH(string);
     NEW(desc);
     with desc^ do begin (* link new descr. *)
       next := hashTable[bkt];
       spix := top;
       {assign other attributes}
     end; (* with *)
     hashTable[bkt] := desc;
     CopyString; (* and adjust top *)
   end (* Insert *);
```

Figure 5.5   Insertion procedure for a hash table.

The insert procedure is fairly straightforward, and is shown in Figure 5.5. In this particular example the procedure *Insert* does not check whether or not a descriptor with the same string already exists in the table. In cases where it is possible that multiple insertions of the same descriptor could be attempted, the assertion that no such descriptor exists must be tested, by a call to *Lookup*.

As a final topic for this section, we consider the possible ways in which the actual hash functions may be formed.

The only real requirement that a hash function must fulfil is to produce an apparently random result when sent some arbitrary string as argument. Most functions attempt to do this by 'jumbling' the bits of the

```
function HASH(string: StringType):Buckets;
   var total,I:INTEGER;
begin
  I := min;
  total := ORD(string[I]); I := I+1;
  while {string not ended} do begin
    (*$T- turn off overflow tests *)
    total := total*127 + ORD(string[I]);
    I := I+1
    (*$T= restore overflow tests *)
    end;
  HASH := (total mod BucketMax)
end;
```

Figure 5.6   A hash function in Pascal.

string, perhaps by treating it as some kind of arithmetic type. There is certainly no requirement that the function makes any kind of arithmetic sense.

Using assembly language, it is usually relatively simple to perform some arbitrary operation on a character string. For example, one might take several of the characters of the string at a time and treat them as unsigned numbers. After turning off arithmetic overflow detection, rotated versions of the numbers might be added together, and the result reduced modulo some prime number corresponding to the number of hash buckets.

If it is required that the hash function be written entirely in a high-level language, then the best policy is to turn off overflow detection by whatever compiler directive is required, and make lavish use of *ORD*() functions and **mod** operations. A typical such function is given in Figure 5.6. This function is well tested but perhaps rather slow.

In the case of attributes which are of some numerical type, it is usually sufficient to take the attribute value, or some part of its internal machine representation, and to apply a **mod** operation to it, to produce a bucket value. It is always good policy in such cases to choose a number of buckets which is a prime number.

In the case of real arithmetic types, it is normal to take some part of the real number which includes the most significant mantissa bits and treat it as though it were an integer. This may require the use of an undistinguished variant record type, to trick the compiler into allowing the 'nonsensical' type conversion.

For almost all of the hash function generation methods mentioned here, the code will be non-portable. Essentially all of the methods depend at least on the format of the data representations, and thus are machine dependent to a greater or lesser extent.

5.1.1   Section checklist and summary definitions

1. Hash functions and symbol tables.
   - If an attribute type has very large cardinality, but the number of objects with the attribute is small, we say that the attribute space is sparse.
   - A hash function provides a mechanism for indexing objects which sparsely populate some attribute space. All possible attribute values are mapped into a relatively small set of equivalence classes, called hash buckets.
   - The ratio of entries in the table to the number of buckets is called the loading factor. For fastest lookup, loading factors of less than one are desirable.
   - Whenever a lookup has to be performed, the attribute value being sought need only be compared with the value for objects which appear in the same hash bucket.

2. Handling hash table collisions.
   - When an object is being inserted into a hash table, and the generated hash bucket is not empty, a collision is said to have occurred.
   - Open hashing handles the possibility of hash table collisions by defining a list structure to hold all of the objects in the same hash bucket. In general insertions are performed at the head of the list, and the lookup procedure must scan the whole list looking for a match on the attribute value.

3. String-valued attributes and string tables.
   - An economical way of storing strings of varying size is to use a string table. This is a large array of characters.
   - Strings in the table may be accessed by means of a spelling index, which indicates the starting position of the associated string. Strings are usually separated by means of some marker or sentinel character.

4. Hash function choice.
   - An ideal hash function should distribute a set of random attribute values evenly among the hash buckets.
   - In the case of string values, typical hash functions perform

arithmetic operations on the character strings, finally reducing the generated integer modulo the number of buckets.

- For attributes of numerical type, in most cases a suitable hash function is obtained by treating the attribute as an integer, and reducing it modulo an appropriately large prime number.

5.2   Symbol tables for keyword lookup

The situation which arises when a symbol table is used to identify keywords is slightly different to the case considered in the previous section. A typical application of such a symbol table is in command interpreters which recognize a lexicon of command verbs and option names. In many such cases, there are no strings in the table except for the predeclared ones, so that no insertion operation needs to be implemented.

The Pascal reserved-word table lookup which occurs in case study 1, at the end of Chapter 3, is a classic example. We only wish to know whether or not a particular search string is in the table, and we wish to obtain this information with the least possible computational effort. A simple application of the methods of the last section may lead to a significant speedup over the sequential search technique actually used in the case study. However, we may do even better by taking account of the special circumstances which apply to predefined tables.

In this case, since the table contents are static, and known in advance, it is worthwhile spending some effort in finding a hash function with particularly good properties. In particular, a function which maps every attribute to a different bucket would be ideal, since then a single comparison would always suffice, and we might also dispense with the overhead of the linked lists. Such a hash function is said to be **perfect** (for a particular data set).

The method of finding a perfect hash function for a given set of attribute values may involve a great deal of trial and error, and a heavy computational effort. As an example, we seek a perfect hash function for the Pascal keywords used in the case study, using the ASCII character set. We would like to find a quickly computable function which maps the 35 keyword strings into a number of bucket ordinals which is of the order of one hundred or so. In this way, the low loading factor of the table would ensure that a majority of non-keyword strings map to empty buckets, so that no comparison is necessary.

As a first attempt, we might try the function

$$bucket = (ORD(ch[first]) + ORD(ch[last] + length) \textbf{ mod } n$$

where $ch[first]$ and $ch[last]$ are the uppercase characters corresponding to

m	n
32	164
64	147
128	161
256	–
512	158

Figure 5.7   Coefficient values for a hash function for the Pascal keywords.

the first and last characters of the string, and *n* is the number of buckets in the table.

Unfortunately, when using the ASCII character set, this function has collisions for the Pascal keywords for all values of *n*, so we next try a function with an additional parameter. As it turns out, the function

$$bucket = (ORD(ch[first])*m + ORD(ch[last]) + length) \textbf{ mod } n \qquad (1)$$

is a perfect hash function for the Pascal keywords, for some moderate values of *n*, for almost all values of *m* greater than about 20. For example, if the multiplying factor *m* is chosen as 38, then *n* = 97 is a suitable choice.

However, it is even more interesting that function (1) is a perfect hash function for several values of *m* which are powers of two. This implies that the 'multiplication' may be performed by a shift operation, which, on most machines, will be somewhat faster. Corresponding values of *m* and *n* which make formula (1) a perfect hash function for the Pascal keywords are given in Figure 5.7.

If the values *m* = 64 and *n* = 147 are chosen, then the loading factor of the table, with 35 keywords, is less than 0.25, leading to a very rapid decision.

We will assume that the data structure will be a string table, in this case holding 180 characters. The hash table will hold pointers into this table, with the value zero being reserved to indicate an empty bucket. An outline of the relevant pieces of code are given in Figure 5.8.

In this example, it is assumed that the scanner has loaded an upper case version of the search string into the array *id*, has set the *length* variable to the correct value, and has terminated the string with the *MarkerChar* character. The string comparison function compares characters until either a mismatch is found, or the strings terminate. As indicated above, in a majority of cases no comparison is required, since the selected hash bucket will be empty.

We have glossed over the question of how the string table and the hash table are to be loaded. Within the confines of standard Pascal, the

```
const   MarkerChar= CHR(0); (* implementation dependent ! *)

type    CharIndex = 1..180; (* characters in string table *)
        Buckets   = 0..146; (* exactly 147 hash buckets *)

var     stringTable : array [CharIndex] of CHAR;
        hashTable  : array [Buckets] of INTEGER;
                    (* zero entry => empty bucket *)

        id : array [1..MaxLength] of CHAR; (* string to test *)
        length : INTEGER; (* always, id[length+1] = NUL *)

function StringPresent : BOOLEAN;
var index : INTEGER;

    function HASH : Buckets;
    begin
      HASH :=((ORD(id[1])*64 + ORD(id[length] + length) mod 147);
    end;

    function CompareResult(ix : CharIndex) : BOOLEAN;
    var    I : INTEGER;
         same : BOOLEAN;
    begin
      I :=0;
      repeat I :=I+1;
        same :=(id[I] = StringTable[ix]);
        ix :=ix+1;
      until not same or (id[I] = MarkerChar);
      CompareResult :=same;
    end;
begin (* StringPresent *)
  index := hashTable[HASH];
  if index = 0 then StringPresent := FALSE
  else StringPresent := CompareResult(index);
end; (* StringPresent *)
```

Figure 5.8   Code for perfect hash table lookup, for the standard Pascal keyword set.

simplest solution is probably to implement an *insert* function, and to call an initialization procedure which inserts the keywords. This is a little annoying, since, other than for the initialization, we would not have to implement insertion. Therefore, extensions of Pascal which allow such data to be initialized at compile time might be used, if available, unless portability is a pressing concern.

The inclusion of this code into software tools such as the keyword bold-printer, Case study 1, will lead to substantial gains in efficiency. However, in general, some caution is advised. In particular, the amount of computation which is required to find a perfect hash function needs to be justified by the increase in runtime efficiency, and the lifetime of the program. If it is possible that the table contents are going to be changed at some time in the future, then it is not at all clear that the same hash function will work for the changed data.

Even in the case of the Pascal keyword table, the addition of a non-standard keyword such as **loop**, or **otherwise** might require a new hash function to be sought. In case of doubt, the best compromise might be to implement a standard hash function with overflow chains, and to live with the slightly slower execution.

5.2.1 Section checklist and summary definitions

- A perfect hash function, for a given set of attribute values, is one in which no more than one attribute value appears in any hash bucket.

- With a perfect hash function, no lookup requires more than a single attribute comparison.

5.3 Symbol tables for nested scopes

The implementation of symbol tables in languages which have restricted visibility of names is somewhat outside our main concerns. Nevertheless, software tools which operate on Pascal program texts are likely to be one of the areas of application of the techniques of this book. Therefore, we briefly consider the ways in which the symbol table techniques of this chapter may be adapted to support nested identifier scopes.

Firstly, however, a disclaimer. It should be noted that we are only concerned here with scope rules which implement simple nesting. The more complex and more flexible identifier visibility rules of languages, such as Ada and Modula-2, are not treated here at all. Furthermore, of the literally dozens of ways in which nested scopes may be implemented, just one is described. This method is reasonably efficient, and gives some feeling for the issues involved. Perhaps that is all that may be reasonably attempted.

By nested scopes we mean identifier visibility rules which follow the pattern first used in Algol-60, and subsequently used in Pascal and many other block-structured languages. In languages which support nested identifier scopes, an identifier is visible in a particular block if it is declared within that block, or if it is declared in a block which textually encloses that particular block. In the event that objects with the same identifier are declared at several different levels, a clash of identifiers is said to occur. In that case, a used occurrence of an identifier is held to refer to the object, with that identifier, with the most local declaration level. In effect, in order to find the object associated with a particular identifier string, the local symbol table is searched first, followed by that of the immediately enclosing scope, and so on, until either a match is found or the global level is reached.

We would like to modify the data structures of Section 5.1, so as to implement these visibility rules in some simple way. The use of hash functions with overflow chains can lead to a simple implementation of the rule which resolves clashes of identifiers. Clearly, objects with the same string-valued attribute will necessarily hash into the same bucket. Therefore, if we use each hash chain as a stack, with the latest identifiers added to the head of the list, then the first symbol match which is located will necessarily be the most local descriptor with that attribute. The search through the symbol tables of the enclosing scopes thus takes place within a single hash bucket, and the lookup function is unaltered from that given in Section 5.1.

The major question which remains unanswered is: how are the descriptors of local objects to be removed from the hash chains when the processing of a block is completed? Clearly, on block exit, it is necessary to remove the descriptors of all of the local objects from the access paths,

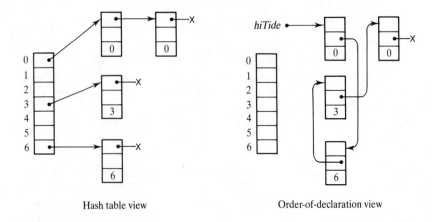

Hash table view   Order-of-declaration view

Figure 5.9   Hash table with independent lists.

```
type   DescPtr    : ^ Descriptor;
       Descriptor : record
                        hashNext : DescPtr; (* next in hash chain *)
                        listNext  : DescPtr; (* next in LIFO list *)
                        hashIndx : Buckets; (* hash table index *)
                        spix      : Spellix; (* string table entry *)
                        { other fields as required . . .}
                    end;
```

Figure 5.10   Descriptor declaration for nested scopes.

and to restore the hash table pointers to exactly the values which they held prior to entry into the block which is now being left.

We may note that, for some tools, it may be appropriate to dispose of the descriptors completely, and to reclaim the space which they occupy. More usual, however, is a situation in which the descriptor remains in use for some other purposes; it might, for example, be permanently linked into some kind of syntax tree. What is required is just that the descriptor be no longer visible to the lookup procedure. So the descriptor must at least be unlinked from the hash table chains which provide access to it.

It would be quite simple just to keep a copy of the previous hash table pointer array, but considerations of size immediately rule this out, except for tables with extremely high loading factors. Instead, we must devise some scheme which keeps track of just those buckets which have actually been altered.

The solution advocated here, is to set up a descriptor data structure in which every descriptor appears on two separate lists. One list is the hash overflow chain belonging to the bucket in which the identifier appears. The other is a list of all visible objects, kept in order of declaration. The second list allows us to remove descriptors from the list (and from their particular hash chain list) in exactly last-in-first-out (LIFO) order. Figure 5.9 shows a small hash table with a few descriptors, seen from the point of view of each of the two lists.

It may be noted, as an aside, that since the order-of-declaration list links descriptors in LIFO order, in cases where the descriptors are disposed of as well as being unlinked, a stack may be used, and pointers are not required. However, in the code given below we will adopt a conventional linked-list approach.

Each descriptor must hold a record field which indicates the hash table index to which it belongs, so that it may be unlinked correctly from its hash chain. The descriptor declarations are shown in Figure 5.10.

On entry into a block, a pointer must be saved which points to the current head of the order-of-declaration list; we will call it *old high tide*.

```
procedure Insert(string : StringType;
                 var d : DescPtr);

   var bkt : Buckets;
       old : DescPtr;

          procedure CopyString;
          begin
            { . . . }
          end; (* CopyString *)

   begin (* first check if this string exists already *)
     old := Lookup(string);
     NEW(d); (* but get a new descriptor anyway *)
     with d^ do begin
             (* link to LIFO list *)
       listNext := hiTide^;
       hiTide := d;
             (* link to hash list *)
       hashNext := hashTable[bkt];
       hashIndx := bkt;
       hashTable[bkt] := d;
             (* now enter string *)
       if old <> nil then (* use same string entry *)
         spix := old^.spix
       else begin (* make new entry *)
         spix := top;
         CopyString; (* and adjust top *)
         end (* if *)
       end; (* with *)
   end (* Insert *);
```

Figure 5.11   Insert procedure for nested scopes.

This pointer marks the point at which unlinking will be stopped, on exit from the block. These pointers must be stored in a way which takes into account the possibility of nested blocks.

When an insertion is made in the table, the code of Figure 5.11 will be executed to create and link the new descriptor. The procedure returns a descriptor pointer to the caller, so that the other fields of the descriptor may be assigned appropriate values.

Note that a simple economy has been implemented in Figure 5.11. Every identifier which is inserted has a new descriptor allocated, but if an identifier with the same string representation is already known, then both

```
procedure CutBack(oldHi : DescPtr);
begin
  while hiTide <> oldHi do begin
    with hiTide^ do begin
      (* unlink from hash chain *)
      hashTable[hashIndx] := hashNext;
      end; (* with *)
    (* unlink from LIFO list *)
    hiTide := hiTide^.listNext;
    end; (* while *)
end; (* CutBack *)
```

Figure 5.12   Descriptor unlinking procedure for symbol tables with nested scopes.

descriptors share the same spelling index value, pointing to the same string table entry.

Finally, on block exit, all of the descriptors between the current high tide marker and the old high tide mark on the LIFO list must be unlinked. Figure 5.12 shows typical code for this purpose.

The code for the procedure in Figure 5.12 is for the case where the descriptors are to remain in some data structure, in spite of being removed from access in the symbol table.

5.3.1 Section checklist and summary definitions

1. Nested scopes.

   - Languages such as Pascal, in which the identifiers declared in lexically enclosing blocks are visible in the enclosed block, are said to have nested scope rules.

   - The rule that, in case of a clash of identifers, the most local declaration takes precedence over more global objects with the same name, is automatically implemented by symbol table organizations which resolve hash table collisions by inserting entries at the head of the overflow chain.

2. Deleting local entries on block exit.

   - One way of deleting local entries on block exit is to hold all entries in two separate list structures. One holds the entries in order of declaration, so that they may be accessed in last-in-first-out order. The other is the normal overflow chain list organization.

- On exit from a block, the local declarations must be removed from the overflow chains, and all the hash bucket list-headers restored to the values held prior to the corresponding block entry.

Exercises

5.1 In a symbol table in which strings are looked up, and then inserted if not present, strings may be copied twice. First, the scanner will copy the characters into the string *id*, and then the string will be copied again into the string table.

Consider an organization in which the identifier string is copied directly into the top of the string table by the scanner, and the *top* value is adjusted to discard or retain the new value after the lookup has been performed. Modify the *Insert* and *Compare* procedures to reflect this change.

5.2 In performing the subset construction procedure for NFSA to DFSA conversion, each constructed set must be compared with all previous sets to see if the set is new, or is just a repetition of a previously constructed set. For many FSA, the number of DFSA states is comparable with the number of NFSA states, N say, but the number of possible subsets is 2^N. The DFSA states thus populate the space of possible subsets very sparsely.

Devise a way of using a hash table to look up the list of previously constructed sets, taking into account that in most implementations the size of the set representation will exceed that of the type *integer*.

5.3 In 1915, in a light-hearted exchange with a colleague, the mathematician Ramanujan was asked to defend his hypothesis that every number is 'special'. He was challenged to state what special property the apparently ordinary number 1729 might have, as an example. He replied immediately that 1729 is the smallest of those numbers which may be expressed as the sum of two cubes two different ways. This happens to be a fact.

Write a program which uses a hash table technique to efficiently find all of the other numbers, between 0 and *maxint* for your local Pascal implementation, which share this property.

5.4 The economy measure implemented in Figure 5.11 is an attempt to save on string table space by reusing the same strings for separate objects with the same identifier representation string. However, the code given fails to share space in the event that two local objects of non-overlapping scopes use the same representation string. Devise a method which does not have this drawback.

5.5 Write a program which finds a perfect hash function for the Pascal keyword set, including the non-standard keywords **loop**, **exit**, and **otherwise**. [Note that your program will have to use a simple trial and error search, and so may run for some time. Note also that the values given in the text apply to the ASCII character set and may need to be different for other collating sequences.]

5.6 Consider the detail of an alternative organization of symbol tables, based on tree data-structures. What are its likely advantages and disadvantages compared to the hash function method?

Further reading

Almost all introductory books on compiler construction include at least one chapter on symbol table organization (Aho *et al.*, 1986). The standard data-structure texts deal in the theory of hash functions in much more detail than is possible here (Aho *et al.*, 1983).

There is a number of papers on the generation of perfect hash functions. See Sagar (1985) for a recent paper with a comprehensive bibliography. Most of the work in this area, however, has been concerned with the construction of perfect hash functions which are minimal, in the sense that the number of hash buckets is equal to, or at most slightly greater than, the number of entries. In fact, unless space considerations predominate, a low loading factor will lead to faster lookups, since in most cases string comparisons are avoided entirely.

An excellent discussion of the table construction considerations involved in the design of the hash functions for spelling-checker programs is given in Bentley (1985).

Chapter 6   **Grammars**

6.1   Grammars, productions, and derivations

The languages considered so far in this book are insufficiently powerful to provide the facilities required for many command languages. The restricted form of strings in the regular languages, as demonstrated by the pumping lemma, excludes nesting of parentheses and many other useful constructs. In this chapter we introduce a new mechanism for defining languages which permits a greater generality. This mechanism defines phrase-structure grammars, which we immediately restrict to one special case, the **context-free grammars** (CFGs).

The CFGs are sufficiently powerful to describe most of the syntactic rules of command and programming languages, and correspond to a particular kind of recognizer, the **push-down automaton** (PDA). It turns out that the regular languages are a simple, special case of the languages described by CFGs, so an alternative method of specifying regular languages is obtained also.

A grammar is a set of rules which determines the form of sentences in a language. Of all possible ways of specifying the syntax of languages we are interested in those which are stated as replacement rules for objects which we call **syntactic categories**, or synonomously **non-terminals**.

6.1.1   Syntactic categories and replacement rules

The introduction of syntactic categories is an abstraction which permits discussion of the form of a sentence without regard to its detail. This use is familiar from the study of natural languages where 'noun' and 'verb' are syntactic categories. We may speak of the relationship between the noun and verb of a sentence in a way which is independent of whether the noun is a simple noun such as 'Jack' or a noun-phrase such as 'the rat that ate the malt that lay in the house that Jack built'. In the second case the noun has further substructure which involves the use of other grammatical rules. However, from the point of view of the sentences in which they appear, both quoted strings belong to the syntactic category noun.

Because of this analogy with usage in the discussion of natural languages, we often refer to the recognizers of phrase-structured languages as **parsers**. In effect, the recognizers attempt to validate the structure of each sentence by ascribing syntactic categories to the substrings which are the phrases of the sentence.

The replacement rules which form the basis of the phrase-structure grammars are stated in terms of the syntactic categories, and the symbols from some target alphabet Σ. We introduce a symbol which corresponds to each syntactic category, and call the set of such symbols the non-terminal alphabet, N. We refer to the union of N and Σ as the **vocabulary** of the grammar, V. The rules, which we call **productions**, are of the form

$$\alpha \to \beta$$

where α and β are strings from the vocabulary, with a further restriction that the left-hand-side string α must contain at least one symbol which represents a syntactic category.

The production rules define the way in which string (or substring) replacements may validly be carried out. If an embedded substring of some string matches the left-hand side of some production, then we may replace that substring by the right-hand side of the production. We say that the production rule has **derived** the final string from the original.

The set of productions define a language by showing how strings may be validly derived starting from a single, distinguished member of the non-terminal alphabet, N, which we call the **goal** symbol. If the goal symbol is denoted S, then any string which is derived from the goal symbol by the possibly repeated use of the productions of the grammar is called a **sentential form**. If the replacement rules finally lead to a string which contains only symbols from the target alphabet, Σ, then that string is said to be a **sentence** in the language.

We stress the synonymous use of the phrases 'non-terminal symbol' and 'syntactic category' for the members of the set N, and the phrases 'terminal symbol' and 'target alphabet symbol' for members of Σ.

A sentential form is a string from the vocabulary, V, which may be validly derived using the production rules, but in which the derivation process has not been carried through to its intended conclusion: the derivation of a string from the target alphabet alone. A sentential form may thus appear as an intermediate form during the process of sentence derivation.

6.1.2 Context-free grammars

The phrase-structure grammars are too general for our purposes, and we henceforth restrict consideration to the context-free grammars (CFGs). These grammars are phrase-structure grammars with the restriction that the left-hand side of any production rule may only be a single non-terminal symbol:

$$A \rightarrow \alpha$$

where $A \in N$, and $\alpha \in V^*$. We call such a production string 'context free' because if A occurs in any string, say $\beta A \gamma$, then we may use the above production to effect the derivation step

$$\beta A \gamma => \beta \alpha \gamma$$

without any regard for the context (prefix string β and suffix string γ) in which the A occurred.

We use the notation $\alpha =>^k \beta$ to show that string β is derived from α by use of the production numbered k. In cases where the actual production used is irrelevant, the production index may be omitted. In particular, if some string α_2 is derived by a chain of one or more derivation steps from α_1, we write

$$\alpha_1 =>^+ \alpha_2$$

while if α_2 is derived from α_1 in zero or more steps, we write

$$\alpha_1 =>^* \alpha_2$$

The special case of a derivation in zero steps corresponds to the situation where α_1 and α_2 are the same string.

We may thus succinctly describe the language defined by a set of production rules as all those strings in Σ^* derived from the goal symbol G in one or more derivation steps,

$$L(G) = \{w : w \in \Sigma^* \quad \text{and} \quad G =>^+ w\}$$

Let us now look at a simple example of a grammar which generates a language which we have already proved is not regular. In defining this grammer we adopt the convention that symbols not enclosed in quotes denote syntactic categories, while quoted strings are literals belonging to the terminal alphabet Σ.

The non-terminal set contains a single syntactic category only, which must therefore also be the goal symbol.

$$N = \{balancedString\}$$

The target alphabet has three symbols,

$$\Sigma = \{'x', '(', ')'\}$$

The productions are

balancedString → '(' 'x' ')'
balancedString → '(' balancedString ')'

The first production states that '(x)' is a sentence in the language, while the second rule states that any balanced string may be enclosed in parentheses to form another string which is also a sentence in the language. This definition of the balanced string language is recursive, and generates the language

$$\{'(x)', '((x))', '(((x)))', \ldots \}$$

6.1.3 Limitations on context-free languages

Before introducing any further examples of languages defined by context-free grammars it is necessary to stress certain points of terminology. A language is said to be context-free if a CFG may be used to define it (possibly among many alternative definitions). Therefore, if a non-context-free definition is given for a particular language, it does not necessarily imply that the language is not context-free, but may merely indicate that a context-free method for defining that particular language has yet to be found. In general, it is quite difficult to show that a given language feature is necessarily non-context-free, but there are a few examples which should be mentioned.

The language wvw, where the two 'w's are repetitions of the same string from Σ^*, is not context-free. This particular result indirectly implies that the programming language rule that formal and actual parameters must match in number and order cannot be described by a CFG. The same result also rules out the possibility of expressing the 'declaration before use' rule by means of a CFG.

Another simple case of a language which cannot be described by a CFG is $\{a^k b^k c^k\}$, where the notation a^k means k repetitions of 'a'. In Chapter 13 it is shown that this language is not context-free.

In many applications, these limitations on the expressive power of CFGs must be overcome by some means or another. In practical language recognizers, those parts of a language specification which cannot be described by means of a CFG must be checked by means of separate procedures.

There is a rather arbitrary distinction introduced between those parts of the language specification which may be tested by a context-free recognizing automaton, and consequently thought of as 'syntactic' rules, and those which are tested by semantic action procedures, and hence thought of as 'semantic'. Both sorts of rule may nevertheless be 'grammatical' rules in a wider sense.

As a first example of the process of transforming from a precise word definition of a language to a CFG consider the following definition of a palindrome language. (A palindrome, in informal terms, is a string which, like 'Ada' or 'madam', reads the same forwards or backwards.)

1. The empty string is a palindrome.
2. Any alphabet symbol is a palindrome.

3. If any alphabet symbol is added as both suffix and prefix to any palindrome, then the result is a palindrome.
4. Nothing else is a palindrome.

We may convert this word definition into a CFG for any given alphabet, Σ. For example, if $\Sigma = \{a,b\}$, and the empty string is denoted by ε as usual, then a suitable set of productions is

$$P \rightarrow \varepsilon \tag{1}$$
$$\rightarrow a \tag{2}$$
$$\rightarrow b \tag{3}$$
$$\rightarrow aPa \tag{4}$$
$$\rightarrow bPb. \tag{5}$$

In the above, we have adopted the convention that where a number of productions for the same non-terminal symbol follow each other, the left-hand side of the production is not repeated. Thus each of the above productions specify possible replacement strings for P. The production (1) follows directly from rule 1; productions (2 and 3) follow from rule 2; while (4) and (5) are due to rule 3. Rule 4 does not give rise to any explicit productions, but guarantees that the productions (1) to (5) derive all the strings in the language.

In order to show that the string 'abaaba' is a palindrome, we may explicitly show the derivation process.

$$P =>^4 aPa =>^5 abPba =>^4 abaPaba =>^1 abaaba.$$

In general, when a sentence is being derived in some context-free language, some of the intermediate sentential forms may contain several non-terminal symbols, that is, there may be several syntactic categories represented. We may adopt several different conventions as to a standard order in which the substitutions for those non-terminals is to take place. If we always replace the leftmost non-terminal first, then we obtain what we describe as a **leftmost derivation**. Conversely, if the rightmost non-terminal is always replaced first, then we obtain a **rightmost derivation**. In the example of the palindrome grammar there is only ever a single non-terminal in any sentential form, and so any derivation in this grammar is simultaneously leftmost and rightmost.

Let us now summarize the notation which we will use to represent CFGs. Each non-terminal symbol of a grammar has one or more productions. The first of these is written

$$L \rightarrow \alpha$$

where L is a member of the non-terminal alphabet N, and α is a string from the vocabulary, i.e. a string from V^*. Each subsequent production is written without repeating the left-hand-side symbol,

$$\rightarrow \beta$$

with the final production for any particular non-terminal being terminated by a fullstop '.'. In the event that a right-hand side is empty we use the notation

$$L \rightarrow \varepsilon$$

so that the symbol ε is a meta-symbol of the grammar indicating an empty right-hand side, and the erasure of the non-terminal symbol which it replaces. For this reason, such a production is sometimes called an **erasure**.

An alternative notation, which we very often use for convenience, is to list the alternative right-hand sides, for any given non-terminal symbol, separated by the solid vertical rule '|', just as is done for alternative subexpressions in a regular expression. In this case also, the final right-hand side is terminated by a fullstop.

In most of the 'model' grammars which we utilize in the next few chapters, when we wish to reason about the form of the productions, we invent single-character names for symbols in the vocabulary. We have a simple default naming strategy for these symbols.

- Upper-case letters early in the Roman alphabet, A, B, C, . . . denote non-terminal symbols, with G denoting the goal symbol.
- Lower-case letters early in the Roman alphabet, a, b, c, . . ., denote symbols from the alphabet Σ.
- Lower-case letters toward the end of the Roman alphabet, u, v, w, . . ., denote strings of terminal symbols.
- Lower-case Greek letters, α, β, γ . . ., denote strings from the vocabulary.
- When it is necessary to denote a single vocabulary symbol which might be either a terminal or non-terminal, we use upper-case letters towards the end of the Roman alphabet, X, Y, . . .

These conventions are adequate for model grammars, but other considerations apply when dealing with grammars in applications. Firstly, the terminal symbols are often arbitrary, predetermined character strings. Furthermore, in such cases it is also usually desirable to adopt meaningful, multi-character identifiers for the syntactic categories.

In cases where ambiguity arises, either because some meta-symbol of the grammar occurs also as a symbol in the target alphabet, or because both terminal and non-terminal symbols are represented by multi-character strings, we adopt the convention that character strings in quotes are terminal strings, representing themselves. In this convention, any unquoted strings have the usual meanings, and are names or meta-symbols as the case may be. This convention is necessary for the definition of meta-languages such as regular expressions, for example. In this case the epsilon symbol 'ε' may occur not only as a symbol in the target alphabet, indicating the regular expression 'empty', but also as a grammar meta-symbol signifying the possibility of erasure of some non-terminal symbol. Another simple example of the necessity of this convention occurs whenever a target language has a single fullstop '.' as an alphabet symbol. In this case we must distinguish between the use of the fullstop as the terminal symbol, and its use as the meta-symbol ending a sequence of production right-hand sides. According to the convention given above, a fullstop in quotes signifies the literal, symbol 'fullstop', while any occurrence of a stop on its own is the end-mark meta-symbol.

6.1.4 Section checklist and summary definitions

1. CFG definitions.
   - The terminal alphabet, denoted Σ, is the target alphabet of the grammar.
   - The non-terminal alphabet, denoted N, is the set of syntactic categories of the grammar.
   - One non-terminal symbol is distinguished, and is called the goal symbol of the grammar.
   - The union of the terminal and non-terminal alphabets is called the vocabulary, and is denoted V.
   - A production rule of a context-free grammar (CFG) specifies a string from V^*, which may validly replace a particular non-terminal symbol in any string in which the non-terminal appears.

2. Derivation definitions.
   - When a production rule is used to replace a non-terminal symbol in a string, we say that a derivation step has been performed.
   - If a particular string over V^* may be derived from the goal symbol in a finite number of steps, then we call that string a sentential form.
   - A special case of a sentential form in which all the symbols belong to the terminal alphabet Σ, is called a sentence.
   - The language defined by a CFG is the set of all sentences which may be derived from the goal symbol by use of the productions.

3. Leftmost and rightmost derivations.
   - A rightmost derivation is one in which a sentence is derived by systematically choosing the rightmost non-terminal symbol of the sentential form for replacement at each step.
   - A leftmost derivation is one in which a sentence is derived by systematically choosing the leftmost non-terminal symbol of the sentential form for replacement at each step.

4. Synonyms.
   - 'Sentence' and 'string in the language'.
   - 'Non-terminal symbol' and 'syntactic category'.
   - 'Terminal symbol' and 'target alphabet symbol'.

5. Notational conventions.
   - The first production rule for a non-terminal symbol A is written
     $A \rightarrow \varrho$
     where ϱ is a string from the vocabulary V.
   - Subsequent production rules for the same non-terminal symbol may immediately follow, omitting the left-hand-side symbol,
     $\rightarrow \alpha$.
   - Alternatively, right-hand-side strings may be separated by the alternation symbol,
     $A \rightarrow \alpha \mid \beta \mid \gamma$.
   - In all cases, the final production rule for a given non-terminal symbol is terminated by a fullstop meta-symbol.

6. Use of single-character names.

   For most of the examples in this book, the following notation is adopted for single-character names
   - Upper-case letters, A, B, . . ., denote members of N.
   - Lower-case letters, a, b, . . ., denote members of Σ.
   - Lower-case letters, u, v, . . ., denote strings from Σ.
   - Greek symbols, α, β, . . ., denote strings from the vocabulary V.
   - Upper-case letters, X, Y, . . ., denote members of either N or Σ, i.e. members of V.

7. Special cases.
   - An empty production $A \rightarrow \varepsilon$ is called an erasure.
   - A production such as $A \rightarrow B$, in which one non-terminal symbol replaces another is called a unit production.

6.2 Derivation trees

An alternative method of displaying the process of replacement by which a sentence is derived from the goal symbol is to use a **derivation tree**. In these trees, each node is labelled by a single symbol from the vocabulary.

To each production in a grammar, we associate a simple subtree. For example, for the palindrome grammar of the last section, the subtrees are as shown in Figure 6.1.

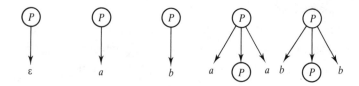

Figure 6.1   Subtrees for the palindrome grammar.

We use subtree attachment as an analogue of the replacement effected by any single step in the derivation of a sentence. The correspondence between the various trees in some derivation sequence and the various sentential forms in the string replacement sequence is given by the **frontier** of the tree. In any tree, the frontier of the tree is simply the string formed by the labels of the leaf nodes, taken left-to-right.

We wish for the frontier of any tree to correspond to a valid sentential form. We therefore begin our tree derivation process with a single root node labelled with the goal symbol. The frontier of this tree is the length one string *goal*, which is a perfectly valid sentential form. Having started with a valid sentential form, it is necessary to ensure that the permitted subtree grafting operations leave the frontier validity invariant.

Suppose we now take some leaf node of a tree, which is labelled by a non-terminal symbol, and attach to that node a subtree corresponding to one of the productions for that syntactic category. This attachment will have the effect of making that leaf node into an interior node, and replacing the non-terminal symbol in the previous frontier by the substring spelled out by the frontier of the attached subtree. Such subtree attachments thus correspond to valid string replacements, and leave the tree in a state corresponding to a sentential form.

When the subtree attachment operations result in a tree with all the leaf nodes labelled with terminal symbols (or possibly the empty-string symbol ε), no further attachments are possible, and the frontier of the tree is a sentence of the language. For example, the derivation of the string 'abaaba' in the palindrome language is represented by the tree shown in Figure 6.2.

The importance of the derivation tree as a method of representing a sentence of a context-free language is that the tree not only spells out the sentence on its frontier, but also, by its interior nodes, makes explicit every single derivation step which was used in deriving that sentence from the goal symbol. Note, however, that the tree only imposes a partial ordering on the derivation steps, and cannot distinguish between a leftmost or rightmost derivation for sentences for which these are different.

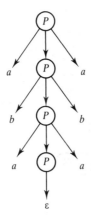

Figure 6.2   Derivation of '*abaaba*'.

6.2.1   Ambiguous and unambiguous grammars

The question of the uniqueness of the derivation tree for any sentence is an important one. If, for some grammar, every sentence in the language has only one possible derivation tree, then we call that grammar **unambiguous**. If there are two or more derivation trees for some string in the language, then we say that the grammar is **ambiguous**.

It might seem that if our objective is merely to check whether or not a given string is a sentence, then it does not matter if there are multiple derivations of that string. However, if semantic actions are to be attached to every derivation step, then the results might differ for distinct derivations. Furthermore, as we shall see later, the important recognizing automata need unambiguous grammars.

6.2.2   An ambiguous expression grammar

Consider a simple grammar for arithmetic expressions, given by

$$
\begin{aligned}
Expression &\rightarrow number & (1)\\
&\rightarrow \text{'(' } Expression \text{ ')'} & (2)\\
&\rightarrow Expression \text{ '+' } Expression & (3)\\
&\rightarrow Expression \text{ '*' } Expression \text{ .} & (4)
\end{aligned}
$$

Note that the substructure of the numbers has been hidden away in the lexical category *number*.

This grammar correctly generates the language of arithmetic expressions using addition, multiplication, and parentheses, and does not generate any strings which are not well formed. However, the grammar is

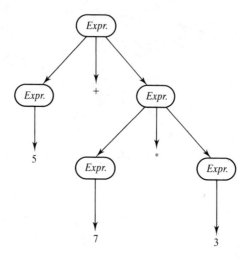

Figure 6.3   First derivation of '5 + 7 * 3'.

hopelessly ambiguous, as may be seen from the fact that two distinct leftmost derivations exist for a simple string such as '5 + 7 * 3'. The first derivation is:

Expression $=>^3$ *Expression + Expression* $=>^1$ *5 + Expression*
$=>^4$ *5 + Expression * Expression* $=>^1$ *5 + 7 * Expression*
$=>^1$ *5 + 7 * 3.*

The second derivation is:

Expression $=>^4$ *Expression * Expression*
$=>^3$ *Expression + Expression * Expression*
$=>^1$ *5 + Expression * Expression* $=>^1$ *5 + 7 * Expression*
$=>^1$ *5 + 7 * 3.*

The two derivation trees are shown in Figures 6.3 and 6.4 respectively. They each show that the string is a valid sentence in the language. However, suppose that the derivation trees are to be used to evaluate the expressions by starting at the numerical leaves and performing binary operations on pairs of values acording to the groupings shown in the trees. The value of the expression according to Figure 6.3 would be 26, while Figure 6.4 would imply a value of 36.

Both of the derivations given above are leftmost, and there are corresponding rightmost derivations.

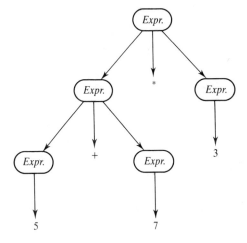

Figure 6.4   Second derivation of '5 + 7 * 3'.

6.2.3   An unambiguous expression grammar

What is required to make the grammar unambiguous is a method of forcing the addition rule to be used in any derivation before any production rule which introduces a multiplication. This may be achieved by the introduction of further syntactic categories *Term* and *Factor*.

A revised and unambiguous grammar for the same language is

Expression → *Term*	(1)
→ *Expression* '+' *Term*.	(2)
Term → *Factor*	(3)
→ *Term* '*' *Factor*.	(4)
Factor → *number*	(5)
→ '(' *Expression* ')'.	(6)

By forcing the additions to be derived first, the multiplications occur further down the tree, and thus correspond to the usual arithmetic conventions for operator precedence. Production (6), which causes a parenthesized expression to be treated as a *Factor*, causes evaluation inside parentheses to be performed first.

The unique leftmost derivation of the string '5 + 7 * 3' in this revised grammar is as follows:

$$\textit{Expression} =>^2 \textit{Expression} + \textit{Term} =>^1 \textit{Term} + \textit{Term}$$
$$=>^3 \textit{Factor} + \textit{Term} =>^5 5 + \textit{Term} =>^4 5 + \textit{Term} * \textit{Factor}$$
$$=>^3 5 + \textit{Factor} * \textit{Factor} =>^5 5 + 7 * \textit{Factor} =>^5 5 + 7 * 3.$$

The reader may verify that this derivation is indeed unique, and that it

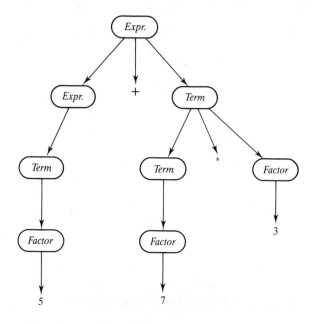

Figure 6.5   Unambiguous derivation of '5 + 7 * 3'.

corresponds to the derivation tree of Figure 6.5, where once again abbreviated forms of the non-terminal symbol names have been used.

This modified grammar leads to the usual rules of precedence for the two arithmetic operators. Also, it should be noted that this particular grammar enforces a left-to-right order of evaluation of sums and products, as is shown in Figure 6.6.

Figure 6.6 demonstrates that '3 * 3 * 5' is evaluated as (3 * 3) * 5. It is possible to modify the grammar so that the implied order of evaluation is right-to-left, if this is what is required. In the example grammar, since the operators are associative it does not make much difference, but if the language possessed non-associative operators such as subtraction or division then the grammar would need to be chosen with care.

6.2.4   Section checklist and summary definitions

Tree definitions
- The frontier of a derivation tree is the string from V^*, spelled out by the labels of the leaves of the tree, taken in left-to-right order.
- If it is possible to construct two different derivation trees for the same

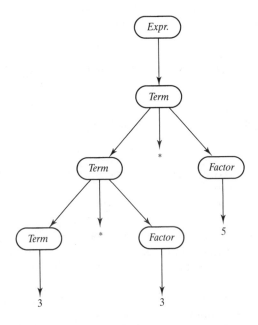

Figure 6.6 Derivation tree for '3 * 3 * 5', demonstrating that evaluation will be
(3 * 3) * 5.

sentence in a CFG, then we say that the grammar is ambiguous.
Conversely, if no such different derivation trees may exist for any
string in the language, then the grammar is said to be unambiguous.

6.3 Regular grammars

It turns out that regular languages are described by a simple, special case
of context-free grammars. A right-linear grammer is a CFG with a further
restriction on the permitted form of the productions. The only permitted
forms for the production are

$$A \rightarrow aB$$
$$A \rightarrow a$$

where in each case $A, B \in N$, and $a \in \Sigma$. Note that these rules
imply that no production right-hand-side may be empty, since ε is not a
member of either N or Σ.

Productions may replace a non-terminal symbol either by a single
terminal symbol, or by a single terminal followed by a non-terminal.
Using such a grammar, and starting from the goal symbol, it is impossible
to have more than one non-terminal symbol in any sentential form.

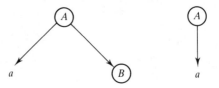

Figure 6.7   Subtrees for right-linear productions.

Therefore every derivation of a sentence in such a grammar is both leftmost and rightmost.

It follows that, whenever a derivation is performed using a regular grammar, each derivation step which uses a production of the form $A \rightarrow aB$, leaves the number of non-terminals unchanged at one. However, when a production of the form $A \rightarrow a$ is chosen, the last non-terminal is replaced, and the derivation process is complete.

For a regular grammar the productions correspond to derivation subtrees which have one of the two forms shown in Figure 6.7. The derivation trees of sentences in regular languages thus have a rather restricted topology. The shape is as shown in Figure 6.8.

In general, the specification of a regular language by means of a regular grammar is less natural, and hence less evocative, than the use of a regular expression for the same task. For example, a regular grammar for a language of signed integer numbers is given by

$$
\begin{aligned}
S &\rightarrow \text{'+'}\ U \\
  &\rightarrow \text{'--'}\ U \\
  &\rightarrow d\ U \\
  &\rightarrow d\ . \\
U &\rightarrow d\ U \\
  &\rightarrow d\ .
\end{aligned}
$$

where $d = \{\text{'0'}..\text{'9'}\}$, $\Sigma = \{+,-,0..9\}$, $N = \{S,U\}$, and S is the goal symbol. The regular expression for the same language is $[+|-]d^+$.

6.3.1   Converting regular grammars to NFSA

The conversion between a right-linear regular grammar and an NFSA is quite simple. A state is created for every non-terminal symbol with the state corresponding to the goal symbol being marked *start*. One additional state is created, marked *accept*, and is the only state in the accept state set.

Every production in the grammar provides a single transition in the NFSA. For example, the production $A \rightarrow aB$ provides a transition from the state corresponding to non-terminal A to the state corresponding to

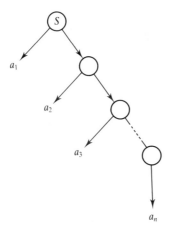

Figure 6.8   Derivation tree for a regular grammar.

non-terminal *B*. This transition is labelled with the terminal symbol *a*. Any production $A \rightarrow a$, provides a transition from state *A* to the accept state, labelled with the symbol *a*.

It follows from the above construction that it is possible to think of the syntactic categories of a right-linear grammar as being labels for the 'language construct yet to be recognized'. At each transition a single symbol is recognized and a new state corresponds to the syntactic category of the string suffix which remains to be recognized. The accept state does not correspond to any syntactic category, since at that point there is nothing left to be recognized. Similarly, the *start* state corresponds to the goal symbol because the whole of the string has yet to be recognized.

The grammar for the signed integer number language is translated by the given procedure into the state diagram shown in Figure 6.9.

It should be noted that the translation of a regular grammar into an NFSA will never produce a state diagram with any ε-transitions. The only reason that the state diagrams which result are non-deterministic is the possibility that two or more productions for the same non-terminal symbol might start with the same terminal symbol. This is exactly what has happened in our example, where both *S* and *U* have two productions starting with the symbol *d*, and hence each of the corresponding states has two separate out-transitions labelled *d*. This implies that the process of transforming the NFSA into a DFSA is simpler than is the general subset construction, since no ε-closures are ever needed.

Since every regular grammar may be transformed into an NFSA, and thence by the use of the subset construction procedure into a DFSA, it follows that every regular grammar defines a regular language. The

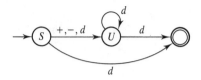

Figure 6.9   NFSA for signed integer language.

converse result is 'almost' true. Almost every regular language has a regular grammar which defines it. The exceptions are the empty language $L(\varnothing)$, and any language which includes the empty string ε. We may state the result as follows: the language defined by any DFSA which has a reachable accept state, and for which the start state does not belong to the accept-state set, may be defined by a regular grammar.

6.3.2   Converting DFSA to regular grammars

We may demonstrate the validity of this converse result by showing how an arbitrary DFSA may generate a regular grammar. Suppose we have a DFSA with states named A, B, C . . ., where A is the start state and, by assumption, is not a member of the accept-state set. We divide all accept states into two groups: the **dead-end states** with no out-transitions, and the **live-end states** which do have out-transitions. We first create a syntactic category symbol for every state which is not a dead-end accept state, that is, for every non-accept state, and for every live-end state. The syntactic category corresponding to the start state will be the goal symbol of the grammar.

For every transition which ends in a non-accept state, say from state A to state B on symbol a, we introduce a production $A \rightarrow aB$. For every transition which ends in a dead-end accept state, say from state C to state D on symbol b, we introduce a production $C \rightarrow b$. Finally, for every transition which ends in a live-end state we introduce two productions. Suppose the transition is from state E to state F on symbol c. The productions are $E \rightarrow cF$ and $E \rightarrow c$. The grammar which results from this procedure is clearly in the right-linear form.

In order to show that this grammar does derive the same strings as the original DFSA, we must show that the NFSA corresponding to this grammar is equivalent to the original DFSA. We briefly sketch the argument.

Applying our previous grammar-to-NFSA conversion procedure to any generated grammar clearly leads to an FSA which is identical to the original except for two features. All of the dead-end accept states will have been merged into the single accept state of the new NFSA, and

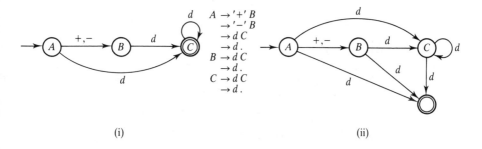

$$
\begin{aligned}
A &\to\ '+'\,B \\
  &\to\ '-'\,B \\
  &\to d\,C \\
  &\to d\ . \\
B &\to d\,C \\
  &\to d\ . \\
C &\to d\,C \\
  &\to d\ .
\end{aligned}
$$

(i)   (ii)

Figure 6.10   (i) Regular grammar obtained for a DFSA.
(ii) NFSA obtained from a regular grammar.

every transition to a live-end state in the original DFSA will reappear as two transitions in the NFSA, each out of the same state, and each on the same symbol. One of these transitions will go to *accept* while the other will go to the NFSA state corresponding to the original live-end state.

The merging of the dead-end states causes no difficulty, since all such states of the DFSA are indistinguishable, and neither does the reappearance of a single transition in the original DFSA as a pair of transitions in the NFSA. Since the two transitions in question lead out of the same state on the same symbol, it is clear that the application of the subset construction procedure to the NFSA will reform a subset of states equivalent to the original live-end state.

If a regular grammar is converted into an NFSA, thence to a DFSA, and the DFSA finally used to generate a regular grammar, then the regular grammar will be equivalent to the original, in that it generates the same language. However, the resulting grammar will not necessarily be identical to the original.

For example, the DFSA for the signed integer language is shown in Figure 6.10(i), together with the regular grammar which it generates. This grammar is clearly not the same as the original. If this regular grammar is once again converted to an NFSA, Figure 6.10(ii) results. Although this NFSA is different to that of Figure 6.9, application of the subset construction procedure regenerates the same DFSA, as was argued above.

We may summarize all of the above by stating that the classes of languages which may be defined by NFSA, DFSA, regular expressions, and regular grammars are identical, except for the small restriction which applies to the regular grammars. In most practical cases the use of a regular expression turns out to be more convenient than the use of a regular grammar to initially specify a regular language. Nevertheless, the equivalence of the two methods has important theoretical implications as we shall see.

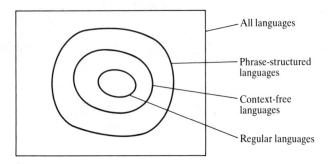

Figure 6.11   Venn diagram of language classes.

As an aside, we may note that the apparent restriction on the regular languages which may be defined by regular grammars is of little practical consequence. We may always imagine that we have modified our alphabet, so that all strings end with some explicit *stopper* symbol. The effect of this change is to ensure that the (previously) empty string is now of length-one in the augmented alphabet. Since we must be able to tell, by some means or another, when a string has finished, it is convenient, for purposes of analysis, to pretend that the termination condition is an explicit symbol. As we shall see, it is also quite common to assume the presence of an explicit string end-marker for other reasons.

6.3.3   Left-linear grammars

All of the above discussion of regular grammars has been stated in terms of the right-linear grammars, so called because of the similarity in form between the productions and right-linear algebraic equations. However, a completely dual development may be performed with left-linear productions of the form $A \rightarrow Ba$. In this case, each syntactic category corresponds to the part of the string already recognized, the accept state corresponds to the goal symbol, and it is the start state which is anonymous. We leave further exploration of this duality to the exercises.

The relationship between the various language classes which we have defined in this chapter is illustrated in Figure 6.11. The phrase-structured languages properly contain the context-free languages, while the regular languages are properly included in the context-free languages.

6.3.4 Section checklist and summary definitions

1. Right-linear production.
   - A right-linear production is a production of either of the forms $A \rightarrow aB$, or $A \rightarrow a$, where A and B are any symbols from N, and a is a terminal symbol.

2. Left-linear production.
   - A left-linear production is a production of either of the forms $A \rightarrow Ba$, or $A \rightarrow a$, where A and B are any symbols from N and a is a terminal symbol.

3. Regular grammar.
   - A grammar in which all productions are either left-linear or right-linear, is said to be a regular grammar.

4. Conversion from right-linear grammar to an NFSA.
   - One state is defined for each non-terminal symbol, with one additional state defined and labelled accept.
   - Every production in the grammar leads to exactly one transition in the state diagram. A production $A \rightarrow aB$ defines a transition from state A to state B labelled with symbol a. A production $A \rightarrow a$ defines a transition from state A to the accept state, labelled a.

5. Equivalent mechanisms for regular language definition.
   - Every non-empty regular language which does not include the empty string may be defined by either an NFSA, a DFSA, a regular expression, a right-linear regular grammar or a left-linear regular grammar.
   - Every non-empty regular language may be made to fulfil the requirements for definition by all the equivalent mechanisms, by augmenting the language so that every string is terminated by an explicit stopper symbol.

6.4 Push-down automata and context-free grammars

Just as regular grammars have a class of automaton which may recognize them, so the context-free languages have a corresponding class of automaton, the **push-down automaton** (PDA). Push-down automata, in some form or another, form the basis of all of CFG recognizers, or parsers as we shall call them.

A push-down automaton is an abstract automaton consisting of an input alphabet, a finite state controller, and a stack. The stack is of indefinite size and contains symbols from a stack alphabet. The permissible operations on the stack are: to push an element from the stack alphabet onto the stack, to examine the top of stack symbol, and to pop one or more elements from the top of the stack.

The operation of the automaton associates an action with each triple (*top of stack, controller state, input symbol*). The possible actions are the stacking or unstacking of one or more stack symbols, the reading of one more input symbol, and the transition of the finite state controller to a new state. If the action of the automaton is uniquely determined by the triple (*TOS, state, symbol*), then we call the automaton a **deterministic PDA**, and in case the action is not uniquely determined we refer to the PDA as **non-deterministic**.

It is a classic result of automata theory that every CFG has a corresponding PDA. We will not prove that result here, but will give an example of a PDA which recognizes a language which is known not to be regular.

6.4.1 A first PDA example

A partial state diagram and the action table for the finite state controller for a PDA which recognizes the balanced parenthesis language is shown in Figure 6.12. Omitted from the state diagram is the fact that the *next state* may depend on the top of stack as well as the input symbol. The grammar is given by

$$goal \qquad\qquad \rightarrow balancedString \vdash.$$
$$balancedString \rightarrow (\; x \;)$$
$$\qquad\qquad\quad \rightarrow (\; balancedString \;).$$

where the terminal alphabet Σ is $\{(,), x, \vdash\}$.

In this example two new concepts have been introduced. Firstly, the original grammar has been augmented by the addition of a production for a non-terminal **goal**. The purpose of this extra production is to introduce a new alphabet symbol, a **stopper** symbol which we denote $\vdash$, to mark the end of the input string. The other innovation is to create a stack alphabet which contains an explicit marker symbol which indicates that the stack is empty. We call this symbol **bottom**, and denote it $\perp$.

The whole point in introducing the symbols *stopper* and *bottom* into the input and stack alphabets, respectively, is to make all of the PDA activities depend uniformly on the (*TOS, state, symbol*) triple, and avoid the need for subsidiary conditions such as '**if** *string-has-ended*' and '**if** *stack-not-empty*'. In any implementation the actual conditions may be tested by a lower level and the pseudo-symbol returned to the PDA. Thus these additional symbols are abstractions which may actually be implemented in a variety of ways.

In the example, the starting configuration of the PDA has the

State	Stack top	Input symbol			
		(	x	)	⊢
0	⊥	0,push'('	error,–	error,–	error,–	
0	(	0,push'('	1,–	error,–	error,–	next state,
1	⊥	error,–	error,–	error,–	1,accept	action
1	(	error,–	error,–	1,pop1	error,–	

Figure 6.12 State diagram, and *nextState* and action table of PDA to recognize the balanced parenthesis language.

controller in state 0, and the top-of-stack marked by the bottom symbol ⊥. The automaton accepts the input string only if the final configuration has an empty stack (as shown by the top of stack being the bottom marker), the controller state is 1, and the string is ended (as shown by the input symbol being the stopper symbol).

In general terms, the recognizer works by pushing the left parentheses onto the stack as they are encountered in the input string. When the centre marker, *x*, is found the controller switches into an unstacking mode. In the unstacking mode, as right parentheses are found the matching left parentheses will be on the top of the stack and may be popped off as the matching process proceeds.

6.4.2 Recognizing palindromes

An example of apparently similar complexity is provided by an automaton to recognize the palindrome language of Section 6.2. The grammar might be

$S \rightarrow P\vdash.$
$P \rightarrow \varepsilon$
$\quad \rightarrow a$
$\quad \rightarrow b$
$\quad \rightarrow aPa$
$\quad \rightarrow bPb.$

Once again we might envisage a recognizer with two states. In the stacking state, the input symbols are pushed onto the stack as they are recognized. In the unstacking state, the input symbols are matched against the top of stack symbols. A failure to match indicates an error, while a successful match causes the stack to be popped, and a new input symbol read. Again, the string should be accepted if the string ends with the controller in the unstacking state and the stack empty.

Unfortunately, in this example there is no way that the PDA can tell that it has reached the middle of the string so as to switch from the stacking to the unstacking state. The algorithm envisaged works correctly, but is non-deterministic since the position of the middle of the string can only be guessed at. Consider the dilemma confronting the controller when the input symbol matches the top-of-stack while in the stacking state. The input symbol might belong to the second half of the string, in which case the stack should be popped. On the other hand, it might be just another first-half symbol which should be pushed onto the stack.

The palindrome grammar which we have devised cannot be recognized by *any* deterministic PDA, so the fault does not lie with the particular algorithm which we have considered. It is unfortunate that there is no systematic way of transforming a non-deterministic PDA into a deterministic one. This situation must be contrasted with the situation with regular language recognizers, where there is always a deterministic automaton.

6.4.3   Palindromes with centre marker

The palindrome language is a tantalizing example, since a very similar language which contains an explicit centre marker symbol may be recognized by a quite simple deterministic PDA. The grammar is

$$S \rightarrow P\vdash.$$
$$P \rightarrow c$$
$$\rightarrow aPa$$
$$\rightarrow bPb.$$

where c is the centre marking symbol.

Figure 6.13 is the action table for this automaton. State S is the stacking state, U the unstacking state. The special terminal symbol $\vdash$ is used as the explicit string end-marker *stopper*.

We must conclude that the context-free languages are too wide a class of language for use in practical recognizers. Firstly, there are context-free languages for which no unambiguous CFGs exist. Furthermore there are unambiguous grammars for which no deterministic PDAs may be constructed. Therefore, in the following chapters we concentrate on those particular CFGs which do permit simple and deterministic recognizers to be constructed. Much of what follows concerns the characterization of the additional properties which the grammar must possess in order that this goal is achieved.

State	Stack		Input symbol		
	top	a	b	c	⊢
S	⊥	S,push a	S,push b	U,–	error,–	
S	a	S,push a	S,push b	U,–	error,–	
S	b	S,push a	S,push b	U,–	error,–	next state,
U	⊥	error,–	error,–	error,–	U,accept	action
U	a	U,pop1	error,–	error,–	error,–	
U	b	error,–	U,pop1	error,–	error,–	

Figure 6.13   Deterministic PDA for palindrome language with centre marker.

6.4.4 Useful and useless productions

There is one property of CFGs which should be developed immediately, however, so that the notion may be used in later material. A production of a CFG is **useful** if it is used in the derivation of at least one sentence in the language. If a particular production is not used in the derivation of any sentence in the language it is **useless**, and the grammar to which it belongs is **dirty**.

In the following chapters we often need to assume that the grammars with which we work are clean, so it is necessary to devise methods for detecting the presence of useless productions, and cleaning up the grammar by deleting them.

The definition of usefulness given above is of limited use in checking the property, so we seek a different way of characterizing usefulness. A non-terminal symbol, A say, is said to be **reachable** if there is a derivation sequence which results in a sentential form containing A, i.e.

$$S =>^* \alpha A \beta$$

where α, $\beta \in V^*$. A string from the vocabulary, $\alpha \in V^*$ say, is said to be **terminating** if α derives at least one terminal string, i.e.

$$\alpha =>^* w$$

where $w \in \Sigma^*$. In order for a production to be useful, its left-hand-side symbol must be reachable, and its right-hand-side string must be terminating. Each of these properties may be readily tested, although neither algorithm is trivial.

6.4.5 Testing for the terminating property

We define a non-terminal *symbol* as being terminating if it possesses at least one production with a right-hand side which is terminating.

Consequently, a production right-hand-side is terminating if every non-terminal symbol in it is terminating. This rather circular definition leads to an algorithm which is closely related to the transitive closure algorithms discussed in the solution to Exercise 4.9.

An outline of the algorithm, minus the implementation details of the list data structures, is shown in Figure 6.14. The algorithm utilizes a data structure which maintains a record for each production. Each record contains an index field, *prodLHS*, indicating the non-terminal symbol to which the production belongs, and a numerical field, *suspectCount*, which indicates how many of the right-hand-side symbols are not yet known to be terminating. Initially the *suspectCount* value will be equal to the number of non-terminals in the production right-hand-side. As execution of the algorithm proceeds, some of these non-terminal symbols will be found to be terminating, and the counter value will be decremented accordingly.

The grammar must be scanned in order to initialize the *suspectCount* field for each production, and at the same time a list is constructed for

```
procedure TestTerminating;

type   NTIndex    = 0..k;
       ProdIndex  = 0..N;

       ProdInfo   = record
                       prodLHS : NTIndex;
                       suspectCount : INTEGER
                    end;

       NonTermInfo = record
                       terminating : BOOLEAN;
                       usedOccurrences : {List of ProdIndex}
                     end;

var    productions : array[ProdIndex] of ProdInfo;
       synCats     : array[NTIndex] of NonTermInfo;
       fringe      : {stack of NTIndex};
       deleteSmbl  : NTIndex;
       pIndex      : ProdIndex;

begin
   { read in the grammar, initializing the suspectCount field to indicate
     the number of RHS non-terminals. Also, create a list of used
     occurrences of each NT symbol, and set every terminating field
     false.};
```

```
(* initialize the fringe stack *)
{set fringe to the empty stack};
for pIndex := 0 to N do (* for every production *)
   with productions[pIndex] do
      if (suspectCount = 0) and
            not synCats[prodLHS].terminating
      then begin
         synCats[prodLHS].terminating := TRUE;
         {push prodLHS on fringe stack};
      end; (* if, with and for *)

(* pop a terminating NT and decrement counts on its list *)
while {fringe not empty} do begin
   delSymbol := {pop of fringe};
   for {every prodIndex pIndex on the list for delSymbol} do
      with productions[pIndex] do begin
         suspectCount := suspectCount − 1;
         if (suspectCount = 0) and
               not synCats[prodLHS].terminating
         then begin
            synCats[prodLHS].terminating := TRUE;
            {push prodLHS on fringe stack};
         end (* if *)
      end (* with and for *)
end; (* while *)
{output diagnostics for non-terminating productions}
end;
```

Figure 6.14   Body of the algorithm to detect non-terminating productions.

each non-terminal symbol. The list for each such symbol contains the indices of all those productions which possess a right-hand-side occurrence of that particular symbol. If a production contains multiple occurrences of a particular non-terminal, then that production appears on the corresponding list several times.

The idea of the algorithm is that whenever a non-terminal symbol is discovered to be terminating, all productions on the list for that symbol must have their associated count value decremented. If a count should reach zero as a result of such a step, and if the corresponding left-hand-side symbol was not previously known to be terminating, then the left-hand-side symbol must be marked as terminating, and placed on a *fringe* stack of symbols whose used-occurrence lists must subsequently be processed.

```
type  ProdInfo = record
                    prodLHS  : NTIndex;
                    RhsNTs   : {List of NTIndex};
                 end;

var   production : array [NTIndex] of ProdInfo;
      reached     : set of NTIndex;
      fringe      : {stack of NTIndex};
      current, NTsymbol : NTIndex;

begin

  { Read in productions and initialize data structure };

  (* initialize stack with goal symbol *)
  {push NTIndex of goal symbol on the fringe stack};
  reached := [goal]; (* initially, only the goal is reached *)

  (* main loop of algorithm *)
  while {fringe not empty} do begin
    current := {pop of fringe};
    for {every production-RHS of current} do
      for {every NTsymbol on RhsNTs list} do
        if not (NTsymbol in reached) then begin
          reached := reached + [NTsymbol];
          {push NTsymbol on fringe};
          end; (* if *)
    end; (* while *)

  {output diagnostic message for all non-reachable symbols}
end.
```

Figure 6.15   Algorithm to compute reachable symbols.

At termination of the algorithm, all productions with non-zero *suspectCounts* are known to be non-terminating and should be removed from the grammar.

6.4.6 Testing for the reachable property

We find the reachable non-terminal symbols by using the following reasoning. Any non-terminal symbol is reachable if it occurs in the right-hand-side string of a production of a non-terminal which is itself reachable. Initially, the goal symbol is known to be reachable.

We use a very straightforward version of a transitive closure algorithm to perform the task. (Figure 6.15 has most of the details.) The data structure required involves a record for each production. This record stores the left-hand-side symbol for the productions, and a list of non-terminal symbols which appear on the right-hand side of the production. The details of the implementation of the list are omitted, but several possibilities exist, particularly if the maximum length of the list is bounded by a small number. The algorithm works by setting up a *fringe* stack, of all the symbols which are known to be reachable, but whose right-hand-side strings have yet to become processed. The algorithm terminates when the fringe becomes empty.

Among the unelaborated details of this algorithm are the data structure details which enable the two '**for** {*every* . . .}' loops to be controlled. Either some ordering of the productions or some kind of index is required for the first loop, while for the second the details depend on the implementation of the list structures.

The overall task of cleaning up a grammar is thus performed in two steps. The productions with non-terminating right-hand-side strings are detected and removed from the grammar. The remaining productions are then input to the reachability algorithm. Any symbols which prove to be unreachable must then have all their productions removed.

6.4.7 Section checklist and summary definitions

1. Parsers and parsing.
   - A recognizer for a CFG is called a parser.

2. Push-down automata (PDA).
   - A push-down automaton consists of a stack, stack alphabet, input alphabet, and a finite-state controller.
   - A PDA move consists of examining the input symbols and the top of stack symbol, and performing one or more of the following actions: pushing one or more elements of the stack alphabet onto the stack, popping one or more elements off the stack, or consuming an input symbol.
   - If the action is uniquely determined for each (*top of stack*, *controller state*, *input symbol*[s]), triple, then the PDA is said to be deterministic.
   - Every language defined by a CFG may be recognized by a (possibly non-deterministic) PDA.
   - Not every non-deterministic PDA may be converted into a deterministic PDA.

3. Clean and dirty grammars.

- A useful production is one which may be used in the derivation of a sentence in the language defined by the CFG.

- In order to be useful, a production must be both terminating and reachable.

- A production is terminating if, starting from its right-hand side, it is possible to derive a string consisting entirely of terminal symbols.

- A production is reachable if it is possible to derive a sentential form which contains the left-hand-side symbol of the production.

- A CFG which contains useless productions is said to be dirty. Removal of all such productions leads to a grammar which is said to be clean.

Exercises

6.1 Find all rightmost derivations of '5 + 7 * 3', using the ambiguous grammar

$Expression$ → *number*
    → *'(' Expression ')'*
    → *Expression '+' Expression*
    → *Expression '*' Expression.*

6.2 The overall structure of the command language for an editor is described as follows.

1. A valid editor command consists of a command string followed by the terminator '$$'.
2. There are various atomic commands which we here will call **command terms**.
3. One or more command terms may be concatenated to form a valid **command string**.
4. Any command string may be enclosed in brackets, '<' and '>', and preceded by a repeat count. Such a bracketed construction is a valid command term.

Choose suitable terminal and non-terminal alphabets, and devise a CFG for the language.

Is this language regular?

6.3 Suppose you are given an NFSA which has a reachable accept state, and no accept state is in the ε-closure of the start state. Can you adapt the method of Section 6.3, which generates a regular grammar from a DFSA, so as to work directly with the NFSA?

Separately consider the cases where the NFSA does and does not contain empty transitions.

6.4 Devise a grammar for a language which models the normal conventions for the nesting of parentheses in text. Suppose that two kinds of brackets are used, round and square, which must match pairwise. The outermost brackets in any text must be round, any nesting of parentheses must thereafter alternate between square and round as the nesting level increases. As an example, using W to represent a word in the text, one of the valid strings in this language would be 'W(WW[W][W(WW)]W)WW'.

6.5 Devise an action table for a PDA which accepts the language described in question 6.4.

[*Hint*: Use a stack alphabet $\{(,[,\perp\}$, and note that if your grammar permits empty strings, the finite-state controller requires only a single state.]

6.6 The rules for generating a regular grammar from a DFSA make no mention of the reachability of any accept state. What is to stop this procedure from being applied to a DFSA which accepts the empty language?

6.7 Starting from the comment at the end of Section 6.3, provide the rules for converting between FSA and left-linear regular grammars.

6.8 One of the more irritating aspects of standard Pascal is that comments may not be nested. An attempt to 'comment out' a section of code, therefore, will fail with a syntax error if the commented-out section already includes a comment.

It would appear that the ability to recognize nested comments requires the full power of a CFG recognizer, since the language is certainly not regular. However, show that the introduction of a *nesting level variable* allows the end of nested comments to be recognized by a program similar to a regular language recognizer.

Further reading

The material in this chapter is covered in the standard texts on automata. Hopcroft and Ullman (1979), for example, deal with PDA and with the more general Turing Machine model which is required to recognize general phrase-structured grammars. However, the study of these more general types of automata finds more application in complexity theory than it does in practical language recognizers.

The classification of languages according to the grammars which may be used to define them is due to Chomsky (1959), who was primarily interested in models for the grammatical structure of natural languages.

Meta-languages which use the productions of CFGs to define programming languages were introduced in the Algol Report (Naur, 1960, 1963). The meta-syntax introduced for this purpose was called the Backus Naur Form (BNF). The modified form of BNF which we use here, and in an extended form in later chapters, is essentially that of Wirth (1977).

Chapter 7 **Top-down Parsing**

7.1 Predictive parsing

To demonstrate the validity of a string in a context-free grammar, it is sufficient to produce a derivation tree with the given string as frontier. We may attempt to produce this tree in a step-by-step fashion, either by working upward from the leaves of the tree towards the root, or by starting with the root and attempting to grow the tree downwards to meet the existing leaves. We would like to be able to construct such a tree in a single left-to-right scan over the input string, without having to backtrack. The ability to achieve this goal depends on detailed properties of the particular grammar.

There are thus two major parsing methods for CFGs. It transpires that the most powerful of the bottom-up parsing methods, the so-called LR(k) parsers, accept a wider class of languages than do the most powerful top-down parsers. However, the top-down parsers, which work down from the root toward the leaves of the derivation tree, are simpler to implement and easier to understand. The top-down methods are emphasized here, but the bottom-up methods are given a substantial introduction in Chapter 9.

The top-down methods work by predicting the production to be used in the replacement of any non-terminal in the interim sentential form. The prediction must finally be validated, by matching the tree leaves against the symbols of the input string. For this reason the top-down parsers are referred to as **predictive parsers**.

Predictive parsers generate leftmost derivation trees in the following manner. For the leftmost non-terminal in the sentential form, which is the first non-terminal on the frontier of the partially constructed tree, a production is predicted, and its subtree attached to the non-terminal node. This step is iterated until finally terminal symbols are produced. These terminal symbols are matched against the input string, from left to right, with more productions being predicted and the corresponding subtrees attached to the tree as required, to derive leaves to match the later symbols of the input string.

If, at any stage in the process, a terminal leaf symbol of the partially derived tree fails to match the next symbol of the input string, then two explanations might be advanced: either the input string is invalid, or maybe an incorrect prediction was made at some previous step in the procedure. If the prediction method is non-deterministic, the second explanation cannot be ruled out and a backtracking step is required.

Since backtracking algorithms are potentially very inefficient, we are interested in discovering those properties of a CFG which allow unique, deterministic predictions to be made. It turns out that the class of languages which are able to be parsed by deterministic, predictive parsers are sufficiently powerful for our purposes, and indeed are powerful enough to describe the syntax of programming languages such as Pascal.

We must first explore the relationship between predictive parsing and push-down automata. Consider a PDA which has a stack alphabet consisting of the entire vocabulary, V, together with a special bottom-of-stack marker, *bottom*. The control algorithm is reminiscent of the palindrome recognizer of Chapter 6. When a terminal symbol is on the top of the stack, and it matches the input symbol, the stack is popped and a new input symbol fetched.

However, when a non-terminal appears on the top of the stack, a replacing production is predicted and the right-hand side of that production is pushed on the stack as a substitute for the original non-terminal symbol. The symbols of the production are pushed in reverse order, so that the last-in-first-out discipline of the stack will return the symbols in the order in which they will be encountered in a left-to-right scan along the input string.

At any stage of the recognition process the stack holds the yet-to-be-recognized part of the tree frontier, including all of the non-terminal symbols. This part is called the **open part** of the parse. The remainder of the frontier, the **closed part** of the parse, is the part of the input string which has already been scanned and matched against non-terminals popped from the stack.

7.1.1 A Polish expression recognizer

We will work through a detailed example of a PDA recognizing strings in a 'Polish string language', defined by the following grammar.

$$S \rightarrow E \vdash. \tag{1}$$
$$E \rightarrow num \tag{2}$$
$$\rightarrow op\ E\ E. \tag{3}$$

where S is the goal symbol and E is an expression. Numbers and operators are designated *num* and *op*, respectively, and are terminal symbols of the grammar, as is the special endmarker $\vdash$.

Suppose that the symbol string to be recognized is '+ 5 * 6 3 $\vdash$', then the configuration of the PDA at various times is as shown in Figure 7.1. In this figure we have omitted the explicit bottom-of-stack marker, but have explicitly displayed the derivation tree which is implicitly being built up by the replacement operations.

In this example it is not difficult to see how the prediction is to be made. If the top-of-stack symbol is an E, and the next input symbol is a number, then $E \rightarrow num$ is predicted, while if the next input symbol is an operator, then $E \rightarrow op\ E\ E$ is chosen.

This method of predicting the production based on looking ahead at the input string symbols is the basis of the methods of both this chapter and the next. However, the need to perform this prediction umambiguously places quite severe restrictions on the form of the grammar. For instance, the grammar similar to the one in the example, but which generates the more familiar 'reverse Polish expressions', is

$$S \rightarrow E \vdash. \tag{1}$$
$$E \rightarrow num \tag{2}$$
$$ \rightarrow E\ E\ op. \tag{3}$$

This grammar cannot be recognized by a predictive parser working as suggested, no matter how long a finite lookahead is permitted. That is not to say that an infinite lookahead could not make a correct prediction, but just that for any permitted lookahead a string can always be chosen for which that lookahead is inadequate.

Worse still, a backtracking PDA algorithm which chooses between productions (2) and (3) in some arbitrary order will get caught in an endless loop, no matter which production it chooses first. The trap is obvious if the first choice is the production $E \rightarrow E\ E\ op$. The reader is invited to simulate the situation which arises if the first choice is always $E \rightarrow num$ by trying to recognize the string '2 3 * 4 *', which happens to be a valid sentence in the language.

The problem is that if the automaton backtracks to the point of last choice this will not necessarily be the site of the incorrect decision, but may nevertheless precipitate a search down an infinite decision tree. If the backtracking is done to the first point of choice then the strategy does work for this particular grammar, although it does not for a general CFG. In this particular case, the effect of backtracking to the point of earliest choice is to generate all of the strings in the infinite language, in order of increasing length, until finally a match is found.

The culprit in the case of the reverse Polish string grammar is production (3), $E \rightarrow E\ E\ op$. This production is said to be **left-recursive**, since the left-hand-side symbol appears as the first symbol of the right-hand side. In general, top-down methods do not permit left-recursive productions.

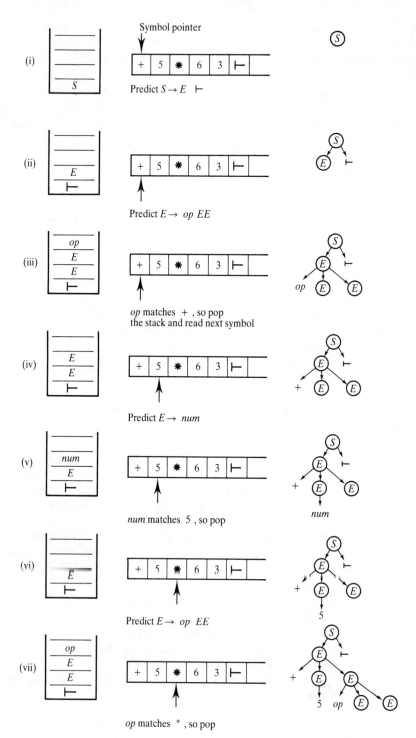

(i)

Symbol pointer

Predict $S \rightarrow E \vdash$

(ii)

Predict $E \rightarrow op\ EE$

(iii)

op matches + , so pop
the stack and read next symbol

(iv)

Predict $E \rightarrow num$

(v)

num matches 5 , so pop

(vi)

Predict $E \rightarrow op\ EE$

(vii)

op matches * , so pop

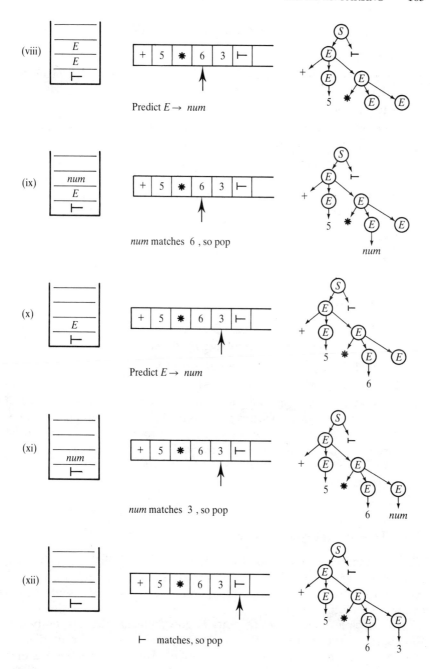

The stack is empty and the string ends, so the string is accepted

Figure 7.1   PDA recognizing a Polish expression.

7.1.2 Section checklist and summary definitions

1. Top-down and bottom-up parsing.

   - Two classes of methods may be used in an attempt to produce a derivation tree for a given string.

   - Top-down methods try to perform derivation steps starting from the goal symbol, growing a tree downwards so that the leaves of the frontier match the symbols of the given string.

   - Bottom-up methods try to find patterns of symbols in the string which may be identified as the leaves of a forest of trees, the roots of which may be attached to other subtrees, until finally a single root node exists which is labelled by the goal symbol.

2. Predictive parsing.

   - Top-down methods inherently necessitate prediction of the production to be used to expand the leftmost non-terminal symbol on the frontier of the interim derivation tree. Top-down parsers are, therefore, synonymously called predictive parsers.

3. Predictive parsing and PDA.

   A PDA may perform a predictive parse as follows.

   - Initially, the parser stack holds just the goal symbol.

   - At each step in the parse, terminal symbols which appear on the top of the stack are popped off and matched against a symbol of the input string. However, whenever a non-terminal symbol appears on the top of the stack, a production is predicted to replace that non-terminal. The symbol is then popped from the stack and replaced by the right-hand-side string of the predicted production.

7.2 The LL(k) grammars

The grammars which lead to deterministic, predictive push-down automata have the property that a unique choice of production may be based on the triple: stack-top symbol, controller state, and a finite length of input-string lookahead.

In principle, there is no difficulty in encompassing the possibility that the choice of production might require knowledge of a finite number of stack symbols, and not just the top symbol. However, knowledge of a finite number of stack symbols may just as easily be represented by the state of the controller, since the controller may update its state as it pushes the symbols onto the stack. When the choice of a correct production logically requires knowledge of the complete stack contents the method is insufficiently powerful, since by assumption the stack is unbounded but the controller has only a finite number of states.

We define the LL(k) grammars as comprising the class of grammars for which a correct, unique choice of production may be made in a top-down parser, on the basis of the stack-top symbol, the controller state, and no more than k symbols of input string lookahead.

7.2.1 Strong and weak LL grammars

If the grammar may be recognized by a deterministic automaton with only a single state in the PDA controller, then we say that the grammar is **strong LL(k)**. If the controller requires more than one state, possibly to represent additional information regarding the stack configuration below the top, then we say the grammar is **weak LL(k)**. We will chiefly be interested in the simplest case of all, the (strong) LL(1) grammars.

The name 'LL(.)' is an abbreviation for 'Left-to-right scan, Leftmost derivation'. We already noted in the previous section that a predictive parser inherently produces a derivation tree in leftmost order, starting from the goal symbol as root. The popular varieties of bottom-up parsers produce a rightmost derivation during their left-to-right scan of a string, and for that reason are referred to as LR(.) parsers.

We now consider the detailed properties of grammars which allow LL(k) parsing. We first make explicit the prohibition on left-recursion. A production which has the form

$$A \rightarrow A\alpha$$

where $A \in N$, and $\alpha \in V^*$, is said to be left-recursive, since when a non-terminal symbol is replaced in a derivation step, the same non-terminal symbol appears at the left-hand end of the substituted string. If a clean grammar has a left-recursive production, then it cannot be strong LL(k) for any finite k. The reason for this restriction may be understood by considering the situation confronting a deterministic PDA which attempts to use such a production. By assumption, the grammar is strong LL(k), so that the controller has only a single state. Suppose that the PDA is in a configuration where an A symbol is on the top of the stack, and the k-symbol lookahead in the input string predicts the production $A \rightarrow A\alpha$. The A symbol must be popped from the stack and replaced by the symbols of the production right-hand-side string, that is, the symbols of string α followed finally by the symbol A.

The final configuration of the PDA thus has the same stack-top symbol as before the replacement, and since no input symbols have been consumed, the k-symbol lookahead is also unchanged. The controller will therefore predict the same production once again, and then again and again!

This reasoning shows that any left-recursive production will trap a strong-LL(k) parser in an endless loop. The reasoning does not apply directly to weak-LL(k) algorithms since, in principle, the controller state might be changed after the first derivation step so as to prevent the same production being selected repeatedly.

The prohibition against left-recursive productions if the grammar is to be strong LL(k) applies equally well to situations where a group of productions is indirectly left-recursive. For example, if the grammar possesses two productions

$$A \rightarrow B\beta,$$
$$B \rightarrow A\alpha,$$

then the productions are indirectly left-recursive, and will trap the PDA just as surely as if A was directly left-recursive. In general, if there is some derivation sequence such that

$$A =>^+ A\alpha,$$

where $A \in N$ and $\alpha \in V^*$, then A is left-recursive, and the grammar is not strong LL(k).

The reason that the grammar was assumed to be clean in the above argument is simply that the presence of a useless left-recursive production cannot cause a problem, since that production cannot be used in the derivation of any sentence. A useless production may thus raise a false alarm regarding the acceptability of the grammar.

7.2.2 The LL(*k*) condition

In principle, in order to test whether or not a grammar is LL(k), it is necessary to consider the sets of terminal strings which may be derived starting from the right-hand side of each production. The procedure would be simple if each right-hand side derived strings which were always at least as long as k. In that case, the k-length prefixes of all derived strings could be compared to see if any two productions of the same non-terminal symbol derived strings which began identically. If no such identical prefixes occur, i.e. all sets of k-length prefixes of derived strings are pairwise disjoint for productions belonging to the same non-terminal symbol, then the prefixes would be an unerring indication of the correct production.

Unfortunately for the above analysis, some production right-hand-sides might derive strings of terminal symbols which are shorter than k. Indeed, for many grammars it is possible for some productions to derive the empty string ε, which has length zero. We must, therefore, not only take into account the strings which may derive from a particular production right-hand-side, but also consider the possibility of encountering terminal symbols in the lookahead which belong to vocabulary symbols further down the stack of the PDA.

In the case that a non-terminal symbol A derives a string of length m, where m is less than k, the k-lookaheads for the production of A will include strings in which only the first m symbols are derived from A. The remaining $(k - m)$ symbols of some lookaheads will be the length $(k - m)$ lookaheads of all those strings which may follow A in a sentential form.

Let us consider the reverse Polish grammar of Section 7.1, which as we have remarked is not strong LL(k) for any k. The productions are

$$S \rightarrow E \vdash \vdash. \tag{1}$$
$$E \rightarrow num \tag{2}$$
$$\rightarrow E\,E\,op. \tag{3}$$

where we have included a second *stopper* symbol on production (1) in order to ensure that every production has a 3-lookahead. We will calculate the 3-lookaheads for each production in this grammar.

The language derived from the right-hand side of production (2) is just the set {*num*}. Production (3), however, has strings beginning *num num op* . . ., and also *num num num* . . . . Since it is not possible to derive strings shorter than three symbols using this production, the 3-lookahead of production (3) is {*num num op, num num num*}.

The 3-lookahead of production (2), on the other hand, is composed of strings starting with *num*, but continuing with another two symbols belonging to any string which may validly follow an E in a sentential form. It may be seen that there are three separate possibilities:

1. the end symbols '$\vdash \vdash$' may follow an E;
2. another $E\,op$ may follow an E;
3. an *op* may follow an E, and in turn be followed by some other string which may validly follow an E.

Taking into account the recursion inherent in the last two possibilities, we finally arrive at the 3-lookahead set

{*num op* $\vdash$, *num* $\vdash \vdash$, *num num op*, *num num num*, *num op op*, *num op num*}.

The intersection of the 3-lookahead sets of productions (2) and (3) contains the common elements *num num num* and *num num op*, which shows that a 3-lookahead is insufficient information to allow a choice to be made between these two productions when the stack-top symbol is an E. Hence we conclude that the grammar cannot be strong LL(3).

In practice we are almost exclusively interested in the LL(1) grammars. The reason for this specialization is to keep the size of the PDA tables within reasonable bounds. For example, if a language is LL(k), and the size of the terminal and non-terminal alphabets is $|\Sigma|$ and

$|N|$, respectively, then the size of an uncompacted PDA table is

$$|N|.|\Sigma|^k$$

if the grammar is strong LL(k). However, if the grammar is weak LL(k), then the situation is even worse. If the PDA controller has n states, then the size of the uncompacted tables will be

$$n.|N|.|\Sigma|^k$$

Even taking into account the probable sparsity of these tables, the dependence of size on the index k will make any grammar with $k > 1$ most unattractive.

An added virtue of the LL(1) case follows from the result that any LL(1) grammar is necessarily strong LL(1). This result, which is not proved here, implies that a two-dimensional lookup table will suffice for any LL(1) grammar. This table will be indexed on the pair (*top of stack, input symbol*).

7.2.3 Section checklist and summary definitions

1. Open and closed parts of a parse.
   - Part-way through a predictive parse, a partially formed derivation tree has been implicitly produced, and the leftmost leaves of the frontier have been matched up with symbols on the left-hand end of the target string.
   - The part of the tree frontier which has been matched with symbols of the input string is called the closed part of the parse.
   - The part of the tree frontier which begins with the first non-terminal symbol, and has yet to be completely expanded, is called the open part of the parse.
   - At each point in a predictive parse, the stack of the PDA holds the symbols of the open part of the frontier of the implicit derivation tree.

2. LL(k) language definition.
   - An LL(k) language is one in which the strings are able to be predictively parsed by a PDA which looks ahead at no more than k symbols of the input string.
   - Equivalently, an LL(k) PDA is able to make a unique prediction of production, based on the triple:
     (*top of stack symbol, controller state, next k input symbols*).

3. Strong and weak LL(k) grammars.
   - If a grammar defines a language which may be deterministically parsed by an LL(k) PDA with a single controller state, then the grammar is said to be strong LL(k).

- If a grammar defines a language which may be deterministically parsed by an LL(k) PDA, but the PDA has more than one controller state, then the grammar is said to be weak LL(k).
- Strong LL(k) grammars are to be preferred, since the predicted production is a function of two discrete variables only, rather than three, as in the weak LL(k) case.
- Every LL(1) grammar is necessarily strong LL(1).

7.3 Checking the LL(1) condition

This section provides a basis for determining whether or not a particular grammar is LL(1), and discusses grammar transformations which may be used in cases where the grammar does not meet the LL(1) condition. The procedures given here are a somewhat modified special case of the methods used for checking the LL(k) condition in cases where $k > 1$.

7.3.1 Augmenting the grammar

The first step in checking a grammar for the LL(1) condition, is to check whether or not the grammar has an explicit end-of-string symbol. If it does not, then it may be necessary to augment the grammar with one additional production. If the goal symbol of the original grammar is S, then a new goal symbol G is introduced, with the single production

$G \rightarrow S\vdash$.

The augmentation of the grammar is simply an artifice to ensure that the various tests may always be performed. For example, if S happens (among other possibilities) to derive the empty string, then the 1-lookahead of G is well defined in the augmented grammar, where it includes the explicit stopper symbol $\vdash$.

For every production of the augmented grammar we derive a set of possible 1-lookahead symbols, which we call the **director set** for that production. If and only if the director sets for different productions of the same non-terminal are disjoint, i.e. have no common elements, is the grammar LL(1).

The grammar for the Polish string language of Section 7.1 is a particularly simple example. The director sets may be written down by inspection:

$$S \rightarrow E \vdash. \qquad d_1 = \{num, op\} \qquad (1)$$
$$E \rightarrow num \qquad d_2 = \{num\} \qquad (2)$$
$$\rightarrow op\ E\ E\ . \qquad d_3 = \{op\} \qquad (3)$$

It is seen that the director sets for productions (2) and (3) are found first, and that for production (1) is derived by taking the union of the director sets of productions (2) and (3).

In order to calculate the director sets in more general cases, we need to define certain relations on grammars. A non-terminal A is said to be **nullable** if there is a derivation which derives the empty string from A, i.e.

$$A =>^* \varepsilon.$$

A production, $A \rightarrow \alpha$, is said to be nullable if every symbol in the string α is nullable.

A comparison between the above definition of nullable and the definition of terminating in Section 6.4.4 hints at the algorithmic means to be used in the evaluation of this relation.

7.3.2 *FIRST* of a string

If α is a string of terminal and non-terminal symbols, then the productions of the grammar define a language of strings which may be derived from α. We define the set of first symbols in the non-empty strings derived from α as $FIRST(\alpha)$. In symbols

$$FIRST(\alpha) = \{a : a \in \Sigma \quad \text{and} \quad \alpha =>^* aw \text{ for some } w \in \Sigma^*\}.$$

It should be noted that $FIRST(\alpha)$ does not include ε even if α happens to be nullable, since ε does not belong to the alphabet Σ. Further, it should be noted that although the language $L(\alpha)$ may be infinite the set $FIRST(\alpha)$ is finite, since it has a cardinality which is at most equal to that of the finite alphabet Σ.

The calculation of *FIRST* must take into account the possibility of nullable symbols in the string α. Suppose that $\alpha = WXYZ \ldots$, where W, X, Y, Z are all non-terminal symbols. The set $FIRST(\alpha)$ includes all of the symbols of $FIRST(W)$, since anything which may begin a string derived from W may also be the first symbol of a string derived from α. However, if it is the case that W is nullable, then all of the symbols of $FIRST(X)$ must be included, since a derivation starting from α might begin by deriving ε from W, thus leaving the first terminal derived from X as the first symbol of the final string. Similarly, if W and X are both nullable, then the symbols of $FIRST(Y)$ must also be included in $FIRST(\alpha)$, and so on.

In general

$$FIRST(X_1 \ X_2 \ X_3 \ldots) = \underset{\{i: \ X_j \text{ is } nullable \text{ for all } j < i \ \}}{\bigcup} FIRST(X_i)$$

In this equation the notation indicates that the iterated union is to be

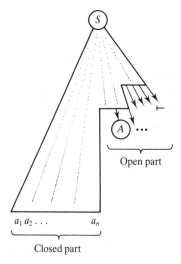

Figure 7.2 Partially completed parse for leftmost derivation, showing open and closed parts.

taken over all the *FIRST*(X_i) such that all the X_j which appear earlier in the string are nullable.

The *FIRST* sets unfortunately do not always provide all of the information required in order to check the LL(1) condition, because of the possibility that the whole of a production right-hand-side might be nullable. Where this is the case, we must consider the starting symbols of all of the strings which might legitimately follow the nullable non-terminal in a sentential form.

7.3.3 *FOLLOW* of a non-terminal symbol

Figure 7.2 diagramatically represents the situation partway through a leftmost derivation of a sentence. The derivation has produced a sentential form where A is the first non-terminal symbol. We call all the symbols to the left of A the **closed part** of the parse, while the right-hand part of the frontier, beginning with the A, is called the **open part** since its final embodiment in the terminal alphabet is yet to be seen. We are interested in finding all the terminal symbols which may begin strings which are derived from the open part, in the event that the symbol A derives the empty string and is thereby erased.

The set *FOLLOW*(A), where A is any non-terminal symbol, is the set comprised of every terminal symbol which may be the first symbol in a string derived from any substring which follows A in any sentential form.

Thus if $\alpha A\beta$ is a sentential form, then $FIRST(\beta)$ is included in $FOLLOW(A)$. Note carefully that the argument of $FOLLOW$ is a non-terminal symbol, while $FIRST$ is defined for strings from the vocabulary.

The above definition of $FOLLOW$ is not of great use in the computation of the set, since it is defined in terms of a possibly infinite set of strings which may be derived from the open parts which can follow a given symbol in a sentential form. We therefore adopt an approach which uses the finite production set to direct the search.

Suppose we examine the right-hand sides of every production of the grammar which contains an embedded A symbol. A typical production might be

$$B \rightarrow \alpha A\beta$$

where $A,B \in N$ and $\alpha,\beta \in V^*$. Clearly, if the production is useful, then $\alpha A\beta$ may appear embedded in a sentential form, and hence $FIRST(\beta)$ is included in $FOLLOW(A)$. Further, if it should be the case that β is nullable or is the null string, then $FOLLOW(B)$ is also included in $FOLLOW(A)$, since anything which follows the B ends up following the A if the β happens to be erased. The calculation of $FOLLOW$ sets may thus involve the solution of a set of simultaneous set-equations involving both $FIRST$ and $FOLLOW$.

As an example, we treat a grammar of regular expressions. This grammar is shown in Figure 7.3, which also shows the $FIRST$ set for each production right-hand-side.

$$\Sigma = \{a, \varnothing, \varepsilon, (,), |, *, \vdash\}$$
$$N = \{S,E,E_1,T,T_2,F,C,P\}$$

Since this grammar defines a meta-language, it is necessary to adopt the conventions mentioned earlier regarding the use of the same symbols both as meta-symbols of the grammar and also as symbols of the terminal alphabet. Thus 'ε' is the terminal symbol *epsilon* as it is used in a regular expression, while ε without quotes indicates an empty production. The grammar in Figure 7.3 has been augmented by the introduction of an explicit *stopper* symbol, $\vdash$, to ensure that no $FOLLOW$ set may be empty.

The nullable relation is easily found for this grammar, since the only right-hand sides which are nullable turn out to be those that are actually empty. Similarly, the $FIRST$ sets are easily found by first writing down the sets for those cases where the starting symbol is explicit, and then taking unions of these sets to form the $FIRST$ sets for productions which start with non-terminal symbols.

There are only three nullable productions in this grammar, so only three $FOLLOW$ sets are required in order to form the director sets and thus test the LL(1) condition. The three are $FOLLOW(C)$, $FOLLOW(T_1)$, and $FOLLOW(E_1)$.

We consider $FOLLOW(C)$ first. C occurs in the right-hand side of

	Production	Nullable	FIRST(rhs)
(1)	$S \to E\vdash$.	no	$\{(,a,\varnothing,\varepsilon\}$
(2)	$E \to TE_1$	no	$\{(,a,\varnothing,\varepsilon\}$
(3)	$E_1 \to \varepsilon$	yes	$\{\}$
(4)	$\to '|' E$.	no	$\{|\}$
(5)	$T \to FT_1$.	no	$\{(,a,\varnothing,\varepsilon\}$
(6)	$T_1 \to \varepsilon$	yes	$\{\}$
(7)	$\to T$.	no	$\{(,a,\varnothing,\varepsilon\}$
(8)	$F \to PC$.	no	$\{(,a,\varnothing,\varepsilon\}$
(9)	$C \to \varepsilon$	yes	$\{\}$
(10)	$\to '*'$.	no	$\{*\}$
(11)	$P \to '('E')'$	no	$\{(\}$
(12)	$\to a$	no	$\{a\}$
(13)	$\to '\varnothing'$	no	$\{\varnothing\}$
(14)	$\to '\varepsilon'$.	no	$\{\varepsilon\}$

Figure 7.3   Grammar for regular expression language.

only one production, (8), where it is the last symbol in the string. From this production we conclude that *FOLLOW(F)* is included in *FOLLOW-(C)*, since any symbol which follows an *F* may also follow a *C* if production (8) is used to replace the *F*. Furthermore, since production (8) is the only production in which *C* appears, *FOLLOW(F)* is the only contributor to the set *FOLLOW(C)*, and so the two sets are actually equal:

$$FOLLOW(C) = FOLLOW(F)$$

The symbol *F* occurs in just one production right-hand-side, (5), so we may conclude that *FIRST(T_1)* is included in *FOLLOW(F)*. However, since T_1 is nullable we conclude that *FOLLOW(T)* is also a subset of *FOLLOW(F)*.

Similar considerations applied to the other nullable productions finally lead to the following set of equations.

$FOLLOW(C)$	$= FOLLOW(F)$	(i)
$FOLLOW(T_1)$	$= FOLLOW(T)$	(ii)
$FOLLOW(E_1)$	$= FOLLOW(E)$	(iii)
$FOLLOW(F)$	$= FIRST(T_1) \cup FOLLOW(T)$	(iv)
$FOLLOW(T)$	$= FIRST(E_1) \cup FOLLOW(E)$	(v)
$FOLLOW(E)$	$= \{\vdash,)\}$	(vi)

Equation (vi) requires some little explanation. Productions (1) and (11) provide literal elements for the *FOLLOW(E)* set, while (4) states that

	Production	Director set
(1)	$S \rightarrow E \vdash.$	$\{(,a,\varnothing,\varepsilon\}$
(2)	$E \rightarrow TE_1.$	$\{(,a,\varnothing,\varepsilon\}$
(3)	$E_1 \rightarrow \varepsilon$	$\{\vdash,)\}$
(4)	$\rightarrow \text{'|'} E.$	$\{|\}$
(5)	$T \rightarrow FT_1.$	$\{(,a,\varnothing,\varepsilon\}$
(6)	$T_1 \rightarrow \varepsilon$	$\{|,\vdash,)\}$
(7)	$\rightarrow T.$	$\{(,a,\varnothing,\varepsilon\}$
(8)	$F \rightarrow PC.$	$\{(,a,\varnothing,\varepsilon\}$
(9)	$C \rightarrow \varepsilon$	$\{(,a,\varnothing,\varepsilon,|,\vdash,)\}$
(10)	$\rightarrow \text{'*'}.$	$\{*\}$
(11)	$P \rightarrow \text{'('}E\text{')'}$	$\{(\}$
(12)	$\rightarrow a$	$\{a\}$
(13)	$\rightarrow \text{'}\varnothing\text{'}$	$\{\varnothing\}$
(14)	$\rightarrow \text{'}\varepsilon\text{'}.$	$\{\varepsilon\}$

Figure 7.4   Director sets for regular expression grammar.

$FOLLOW(E_1)$ is a subset of $FOLLOW(E)$. We therefore have a situation where the two $FOLLOW$ sets are each subsets of the other and hence are equal, as already noted in equation (iii). We may therefore conclude that the smallest set which satisfies the equations for $FOLLOW(E)$ and $FOLLOW(E_1)$ is just the literal set shown in equation (vi).

Back-substituting this result, and using the known values for the $FIRST$ sets, finally leads to the solutions

$$FOLLOW(E_1) = \{\vdash,)\}$$
$$FOLLOW(T_1 = \{|,\vdash,)\}$$
$$FOLLOW(C) = \{(,a,\varnothing,\varepsilon,|,\vdash,)\}$$

We may now write the director sets for each production of the grammar, using the rule that the director set is just $FIRST(rhs)$ if the production is not nullable, and is the union of $FIRST(rhs)$ and $FOLLOW(lhs)$ in the event that it *is* nullable. Figure 7.4 shows the final result.

Checking Figure 7.4, we see that the director sets for productions (6) and (7) are disjoint, as are those for (9) and (10), and also for (3) and (4). The director sets for the four productions for A, (11), (12), (13), and (14), are also pairwise disjoint, so we conclude that a single symbol lookahead is an infallible determinant of the correct choice of production for a predictive parser, and that the grammar is thus LL(1).

7.3.4 Grammar transformations

In Chapter 8 we consider an extended notation for grammars which leads to a somewhat more compact representation of grammars such as the above. However, it is usually necessary to expand the grammar out to a form similar to that in the last two figures in order to check the LL(1) condition.

Any language which possesses an LL(1) grammar is said to be an LL(1) language. Conversely, however, if a particular grammar proves not to have the LL(1) property, it does not necessarily imply that the language which the grammar defines is not LL(1). It may just be that of all the possible grammars which define the same language, we happen to have chosen one which does not have this property. It is normal to attempt to transform such a grammar so that it does meet the LL(1) condition, but still defines the same language.

Unfortunately, there is no algorithmic method of deciding whether or not a *language* is LL(1). The best we may do is to try a few standard transformations to see what happens. In practice, if a language resists efforts to find an LL(1) grammar then it is reasonable to assume that the language is not LL(1), and to then try some of the more powerful methods of Chapter 9.

The useful transformations to try on non-LL(1) grammars are those which eliminate left-recursion by replacing it with right-recursion, and those which use factoring of productions to remove common director set elements.

Consider the two productions, one of which is left-recursive

$$E \rightarrow T \qquad\qquad\qquad\qquad\qquad\qquad (1)$$
$$\rightarrow E \; '|' \; T. \qquad\qquad\qquad\qquad\qquad (2)$$

These two might occur in a grammar for a regular expression language. The two productions derive strings $\{T, T|T, T|T|T, \ldots\}$, i.e. sequences of one or more Ts separated by the alternation symbol '|'. Clearly, the left-recursive production may be replaced by an equivalent right-recursive one without changing the strings which may be derived.

$$E \rightarrow T \; '|' \; E. \qquad\qquad\qquad\qquad\qquad (2a)$$

It should be noted in passing that the two grammars result in quite different derivation trees, even though they derive the same strings. Figure 7.5 shows the corresponding trees for one particular case.

Since alternation is associative in a regular expression, in this case the differing way of associating pairs of terms in the derivation tree is of no particular consequence. However, in a more general setting care is needed with the semantic actions if left- and right-recursion have been interchanged.

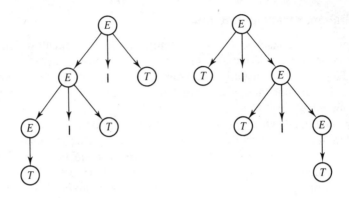

Figure 7.5 Derivation trees for the string '$T|T|T$', using left- and right-recursive
grammars.

A complete regular expression grammar which has no left-recursion
is:

$$E \rightarrow T \tag{1}$$
$$\rightarrow T \;'|'\; E. \tag{2}$$
$$T \rightarrow F \tag{3}$$
$$\rightarrow FT. \tag{4}$$
$$F \rightarrow P \tag{5}$$
$$\rightarrow P \;'*'. \tag{6}$$
$$P \rightarrow a \tag{7}$$
$$\rightarrow \;'\varnothing' \tag{8}$$
$$\rightarrow \;'\varepsilon' \tag{9}$$
$$\rightarrow \;'('\; E \;')'. \tag{10}$$

This grammar incorporates the conventional precedences. Closure has the
highest precedence followed by concatenation and then alternation.
However, this grammar is still not LL(1), as may be seen, for example,
by noting that productions (1) and (2) both include $FIRST(T)$ in their
director sets.

Non-LL(1) behaviour which is caused by two or more productions
starting with the same symbol may often be eliminated by a technique
which we call **left factorization**. The common part on the left of the
produced strings is factored out, leaving a **remainder** part for which a new
syntactic category and corresponding non-terminal symbol must be
defined.

The productions (1) and (2) may be factored by the introduction of a
new non-terminal symbol expression *remainder*, denoted R, leading to
the following new or modified productions.

$E \rightarrow TR.$
$R \rightarrow \varepsilon$
$ \rightarrow '|' \ E.$

This is the technique used to arrive at the grammar shown in Figure 7.3.

7.3.5 Showing that all regular languages are LL(1)

We may use the left-factorization technique to show that every language which has a regular grammar is also LL(1). Given a regular grammar, we augment it by the introduction of an explicit *stopper* symbol which marks the string-end. This is done by introducing a new non-terminal symbol T with just one production

$T \rightarrow \vdash.$

Every production of the original grammar which does not have a non-terminal on its right-hand side, $A \rightarrow a$, say, is replaced by the production $A \rightarrow aT$. Thus, the productions which terminated derivations in the original grammar do so explicitly in the augmented grammar by deriving T.

Since a (right-linear) regular grammar obviously cannot have any left recursion, and has no nullable productions, the only possible non-LL(1) feature which might occur is for groups of productions to start with the same terminal symbol. For example, suppose that we have three productions for the same non-terminal symbol which all start with the same symbol, a.

$A \rightarrow aB$
$ \rightarrow aC$
$ \rightarrow aT.$

For each of these productions the director set is just $\{a\}$. If we now introduce a new non-terminal K we may perform the left-factorization:

$A \rightarrow aK.$
$K \rightarrow B \mid C \mid T.$

Following this step, the right-hand sides of the original right-linear productions for B, C, and T are substituted for the three productions for symbol K. Of course, it is possible that this new group of productions for K will have common starting symbols. If this should be the case, then further left factorization is performed by inventing further new non-terminal symbols.

It is possible to see that this process of inventing new non-terminals will eventually terminate, since each new non-terminal may be expressed as an alternation of the original non-terminals, of which there is only a finite number. The set of new non-terminals is thus of bounded cardinality.

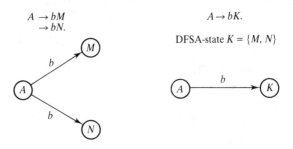

Figure 7.6   Left-factorization of a regular grammar.

It is crucial to this argument to note that, by construction, no production may ever share a starting symbol with T. If this were to be permitted, then an attempt at factorization of the pair of productions would lead to the introduction of a new non-terminal which would be nullable, and hence not right-linear. Since this situation is avoided, our factorization finally results in a new grammar which is not only LL(1), but also in the (right-linear) regular form.

The process of converting a regular grammar into an LL(1) grammar is formally equivalent to an NFSA to DFSA conversion. Recall that in forming an FSA from a regular grammar, each non-terminal symbol corresponds to an FSA state. It follows that two productions with the same starting symbol correspond to two transitions out of the same state with the same label. Thus overlapping starting symbols correspond to non-deterministic transitions, while each LL(1) production corresponds to a deterministic transition. The grouping of non-terminal symbols together in the factorization process corresponds to the grouping of NFSA states in the subset construction procedure. These correspondences are illustrated in Figure 7.6.

7.3.6   Relationship between language classes

The above constructive argument shows that every regular grammar defines a language which is LL(1). It is usually the case that there is a variety of different LL(1) grammars for any such language, some of which will not be right-linear. Some of the non-right-linear LL(1) grammars for a given regular language may be more compact and descriptive than a systematically constructed regular grammar, and may thus be a preferable basis for language definition. If an LL(1) recognizer is to be constructed for a language that just happens to be regular, then there is no reason to insist that the grammar be right-linear, because the recognizer may be implemented without a state diagram having to be constructed.

For example, the regular grammar for the real number language of

Chapter 4 is comparatively lengthy and not particularly descriptive. Since the language is regular, we may seek an LL(1) grammar secure in the knowledge that the task is possible. One such grammar is

> *number* → *OptSign digits OptFrac OptExp.*
> *OptSign* → ε
>   → '−'.
>   *digits* → *d rest.*
>   *rest* → ε
>   → *digits.*
> *OptFrac* → ε
>   → '.' *rest.*
> *OptExp* → ε
>   → 'E' *OptSign digits.*

This grammar is not regular, but it is quite descriptive, possibly as much so as the regular expression. Furthermore, it is LL(1), the proof of which is left to the reader.

It should be noted that the artifice of grammar augmentation has no special impact on the actual implementation of LL(1) parsers. In practice, every string recognizer must have some means of detecting the string end, whether by an explicit symbol or otherwise. In cases where the implementation is layered, it may be convenient to have the lower-level automaton recognize the string-end by whatever means are necessary, and to have it pass the symbol *stopper* to the upper level when it does so. This keeps the implementation of the upper level clean, by making the upper-level actions depend uniformly on the *symbol* rather than on a mixture of symbols and arbitrary conditionals. However, quite aside from convenience of implementation, the introduction of a stopper symbol is a necessary prerequisite to the testing of the LL(1) condition, so as to ensure that the *FOLLOW* set of every non-terminal symbol is well-defined.

We may now update the Venn diagram (Figure 6.11) which showed the relationship between various language classifications. The LL(1) languages are a proper subset of the context-free languages, while the regular languages are properly included in the LL(1) languages. The new version is shown in Figure 7.7.

7.3.7 Section checklist and summary definitions

1. Augmented grammar definition.
   - An augmented grammar is derived from an original grammar by the introduction of one new non-terminal, with a single production and an explicit stopper symbol.
   - The new non-terminal becomes the goal symbol of the augmented

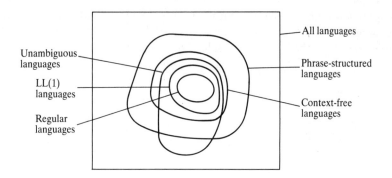

Figure 7.7   Venn diagram of language classes.

grammar, and has a production with right-hand side equal to the original goal symbol followed by an explicit stopper symbol.

2. Nullable symbol definition.

   - A symbol is nullable if it may derive the empty string.
   - The purpose of the augmentation of a grammar is to ensure that the *FOLLOW* set is defined for all non-terminals which might be nullable.

3. Definition of the *FIRST* set.

   - The set *FIRST*(α), where α is a string over V^*, is the set of all terminal symbols which might be the first symbol of a terminal symbol string derived from α.

4. Definition of the *FOLLOW* set.

   - The set *FOLLOW*(A), where A is a non-terminal symbol, is the set of all terminal symbols which may follow symbol A in a sentential form.
   - Equivalently, *FOLLOW*(A) is the union of the *FIRST* sets for all the open-part strings which may follow A in a partially completed parse tree.

5. Director set definition.

   - In the case that the production right-hand-side is not nullable, the director set of a production is the *FIRST* set of the production right-hand-side.
   - In the case that the production right-hand-side is nullable, the director set of a production is the union of the *FIRST* set of the right-hand side with the *FOLLOW* set of the left-hand-side symbol.

Exercises

7.1 The grammar shown in Section 7.1 for the reverse Polish string language is not LL(k). However, this does not imply that the language is not LL(k).

Show that the following grammar is LL(1), and informally show that it generates the reverse Polish string language.

$S \rightarrow num\ K\ \vdash.$

$K \rightarrow \varepsilon$

$\rightarrow num\ K\ op\ K.$

7.2 Consider the following right-linear regular grammar

$G \rightarrow aG \mid bG \mid aA.$

$A \rightarrow \vdash.$

Draw the NFSA for this language. Use left factorization to transform this grammar into an LL(1) grammar. Compare the resulting FSA with that formed by using the state subset procedure on the original NFSA.

7.3 Find the director sets for each production in the real number grammar in Section 7.3.7, and hence show that the grammar is LL(1).

7.4 In this chapter, an argument based on left factorization was used to show that any regular grammar is equivalent to an LL(1) grammar. It might be thought that the same reasoning could be applied to any grammar which has an explicit *FIRST* set, and has no empty productions.

The **Greibach normal form** of any grammar has productions in the form

$A \rightarrow a\beta,$

where $a \in \Sigma$, $A \in N$, and $\beta \in V^*$. It is known that any context-free language may be expressed in the Greibach normal form. Thus if it were possible to show that such a grammar may always be transformed into an LL(1) grammar it would imply that all context-free languages are LL(1). This is certainly not the case, so why does left factorization work for right-linear, but not Greibach normal form grammars?

In order to explore this question, try factorization of the following grammar, which generates odd-length palindromes over the alphabet $\Sigma = \{a,b\}$.

$G \rightarrow a \mid b \mid aGA \mid bGB.$

$A \rightarrow a.$

$B \rightarrow b.$

7.5 Using Figure 6.14 as a guide, derive an algorithm which computes the *nullable* attribute.

7.6 Show that if a clean grammar has a production $A \rightarrow \alpha A \beta$, where α is *nullable*, then the grammar is not LL(1). Further, show that if both α and β are *nullable* the grammar is ambiguous.

Further reading

Top-down parsing is a method of language recognition which had already been used intuitively by many writers of programming language compilers prior to the development of the theory set out in this chapter. The theory of LL(1) languages and their parsing automata was formulated by Lewis and Stearns (1968), and by Rosenkratz and Stearns (1970).

The method given in this chapter for checking the LL(1) condition and generating the director sets, is not the most efficient way of performing the task algorithmically. Methods suitable for machine implementation are given by Backhouse (1979) and, more recently, by Gough (1985).

Chapter 8 Implementing Top-down Parsers

8.1 Table-driven LL(1) push-down automata

The basic LL(1) push-down automaton has a stack, and a stack alphabet which is the union of the input alphabet and the non-terminal symbol set. An action table is indexed by the pair (*input symbol, stack-top symbol*). The possible actions are:

1. to replace the top-of-stack symbol by the right-hand side of an indicated production;
2. to pop the top-of-stack symbol and read a new input symbol;
3. to enter an error configuration.

The second action only occurs when a terminal symbol is on the top of the stack, so an obvious efficiency is to define the action table only for non-terminal stack-top symbols. The third action occurs either if the input symbol fails to match the stack-top terminal symbol, or if the lookup table indicates that no production of the current stack-top non-terminal is consistent with the current input symbol. Since by assumption the grammar from which the table is derived is LL(1), there is only a single choice of production for any (*input, stack-top*) pair.

An outline of an algorithm to control a table driven PDA is given in Figure 8.1.

Several points should be noted regarding this algorithm. First, the details of the procedures which *push* and *pop* on the PDA stack have been omitted, as have those of the procedures *GetSmbl*, which fetches the next input *symbol*, and *Error*, which clears the global Boolean variable *noErrors* and terminates the parse. The actual data structures necessary to store the production right-hand-sides and to implement the stack have also been omitted in the interests of brevity.

It is most important to note that only in the case of a symbol match between the stack-top and the input symbol is any input consumed. Thus the same input symbol may cause a whole cascade of non-terminal replacements, the symbol being finally replaced by the execution of another read operation only when a production starting with a terminal symbol is finally predicted.

The stack height may vary either upward or downward while any

```
    Relevant global declarations are:
type    StackSymbols = {. . . .};
        (* Tsmbls and Nsmbls are subranges of this type. *)
var     prodTable : array[Tsmbls,Nsmbls] of ProdIndex;

  procedure Parse(var result : BOOLEAN);
        var predicted : ProdIndex;
            symbol    : Tsmbls;

begin
    noErrors := TRUE;
    Push(GoalSymbol);
    GetSmbl(symbol);
    repeat
      if {topOfStack is a non-term} then begin
        predicted := prodTable[symbol,topOfStack];
        if predicted = errorProd then
          Error (* sets error flag, skips to string end. *)
        else begin
          PopStack;
          {push RHS of predicted onto stack };
          end
        end
      else if topOfStack = symbol then begin
        PopStack;
        GetSmbl(symbol);
        end
      else error;
    until symbol = stopper;
    result := noErrors and {stack is empty};
  end;
```

Figure 8.1   Table-driven LL(1) parser outline.

particular symbol is in the read position, since the prediction of a production with an empty right-hand side causes the popping of the stack but no subsequent replacement. It must be stressed that the meta-symbol ε is not a member of the stack alphabet, being neither a terminal nor a non-terminal symbol.

It may be seen from Figure 8.1 that the algorithm for controlling the PDA is sufficiently simple that, if necessary, an implementation in assembly language could be confidently contemplated. Since the algorithm uses no special facilities, such as recursive procedures or the like, it is readily implemented in FORTRAN or even BASIC. Of course, the

Stack top	*Input symbols*								
	a	$\varnothing$	ε	(	)	|	*	$\vdash$	
S	1	1	1	1	–	–	–	–	
E	2	2	2	2	–	–	–	–	
E	–	–	–	–	3	4	–	3	
T	5	5	5	5	–	–	–	–	*Predicted*
T	7	7	7	7	6	6	–	6	*production*
F	8	8	8	8	–	–	–	–	
C	9	9	9	9	9	9	10	9	
P	12	13	14	11	–	–	–	–	

Figure 8.2 Table for PDA to recognize the regular expression grammar of Section 7.3.

detailed design of the data structures does depend on the primitive data-structuring facilities available in the implementation language. None of the commonly used algorithmic languages provides a stack type, however, so this abstraction must be implemented, probably by a finite array and a stack-pointer index. Such an implementation introduces a new potential error condition, that of the stack overrunning the space allocated to the finite array into which it is mapped. This error condition must be explicitly tested for, particularly in run-time environments which do not support array-bounds checking. Any bounds violation should be reported by an explicit and meaningful diagnostic.

The techniques of sparse table compaction, as described in Chapter 3, may be used to reduce the space occupied by the production table. However, at least in the case of the small grammars considered here, the tables are typically less sparse than is the case for small FSA. As an example, the table for the PDA to recognize the LL(1) grammar of Section 7.3 is shown in Figure 8.2. This table should be carefully compared with that in Figure 7.4, in order to ensure that the way in which the director sets determine the lookup table is clearly understood.

8.1.1   Parsing the *WildOption* grammar of Section 4.4.3

We now consider a recognition task, complete with semantic actions, to illustrate some of the niceties involved. The grammar to be recognized is the *WildOption* meta-language of Section 4.4, i.e. the wildcard language for strings with optional substrings.

The grammar is shown in Figure 8.3, which includes the director sets.

Production index	Production	Director set
1	$W \rightarrow E$ eoln.	$\{a,*,\%,[,],eoln\}$
2	$E \rightarrow \varepsilon$	$\{],eoln\}$
3	$\rightarrow AE.$	$\{a,*,\%,[\}$
4	$A \rightarrow a$	$\{a\}$
5	$\rightarrow \, '*'$	$\{*\}$
6	$\rightarrow \, '\%'$	$\{\%\}$
7	$\rightarrow \, '['E']'.$	$\{[\}$

Figure 8.3 Grammar and director sets for the *WildOption* language of Section 4.4.

The alphabets in this grammar are:

$$\Sigma = \{ \, a, \, *, \, \%, \, [, \,], \, eoln \, \}$$
$$N = \{ \, W, \, E, \, A \, \}$$

where *a* designates any ordinary character.

The PDA production table is shown in Figure 8.4.

The semantic actions in this particular example are associated with input symbol recognition, and only parser actions which consume input by calling *GetSymbol* have an associated semantic action. Such a situation is not particularly unusual. However, in this example the semantic actions are simplified further because the action taken on the recognition of any particular input symbol does not depend on the context in which that symbol was found. In a more general situation, the incorporation of semantic actions may require more careful consideration, since they may be invoked by any parsing action, including those which consume no input, and may require access to subsidiary data beyond that provided by the parser itself. These more general considerations are touched on in Chapters 10 and 11.

It may be remembered from Section 4.4.3 that the data structure which is to be built by the semantic actions of the *WildOption* parser is a set of tables corresponding to a simple NFSA. Each state of the NFSA has an out-transition labelled by the character which we call advance-char, and which may be either an ordinary character, *a*, or a meta-symbol which matches any character. Every state has an optional self-loop, which, if present, is predicated on every character. Finally, every state has a list of ε-transitions, possibly empty, which lead to higher numbered states.

In general terms, the semantic actions work their way along the linear sequence of states. At any point during the table-building there is a

Stack-top	Input symbol						
non-term	*a*	*	%	[	]	*eoln*	
W	1	1	1	1	–	1	*Predicted*
E	3	3	3	3	2	2	*production*
A	4	5	6	7	–	–	

Figure 8.4 PDA table for the *WildOption* grammar.

current-state value, and the entries in the table for that state are filled in before the current-state ordinal is incremented. For example, the recognition of '*' causes the Boolean *selfLoop* to be set to *TRUE* for the current state. Recognition of an ordinary target alphabet symbol *a* causes the corresponding character to become the advance-char value for the current state, and the current-state value to be incremented. These actions, as described so far, are precisely those of the *WildScan* parser which was described in Section 5.2.2 for the regular meta-language without the option-brackets. We must now consider the consequences of the inclusion of the option-brackets, since it is the presence of these that make the language non-regular.

When devising semantic actions for the brackets, the key observation is to note that since option brackets may be nested, it is necessary to keep a working stack of incomplete ε-transitions. Whenever an option is opened, by the occurrence of a '[' symbol, the state number of the current state is pushed onto a 'semantic' stack. When the corresponding close symbol, ']', is detected, the semantic stack is popped. The state-number popped from the stack is that of the starting state for the ε-transition which implements the option, while the now current state is the end of that transition. Hence, the current state is added to the ε-list of the state whose identifying state-number was popped. These semantic actions are summarized in Figure 8.5.

A slight complication arises if a self-loop character appears as the first or last character inside an option bracket. The reason for this circumstance is discussed in the model solution to Exercise 4.11. In effect, it is necessary to detect two special cases. If the first character inside a bracket is an asterisk, then an ε-transition must be inserted to isolate the state from which the option-skipping ε-transition starts from the state which will have the self-loop. In this case, the final ε-list for the state will contain two states rather than just one. A similar change to the usual semantic action must be implemented if the last character with a bracketed string is an asterisk.

Symbol	Semantic action
a	Set advance-char of current state to *character*, increment state-ordinal.
'%'	Set advance-char to '%', increment state ordinal.
'*'	Set self-loop Boolean to *TRUE*.
'['	Push current state ordinal on semantic stack. If the next character is '*' then isolate state with ε-transition.
']'	If current state has a self-loop, then generate an ε-transition to isolate it, and update current state.
eoln	Mark end state, terminate parse.

Figure 8.5   Semantic actions for *WildOption*.

The steps involved in isolating a state are as follows.

procedure *IsolateState*; (* insert ε-transition *)
begin
    advanceChar[*currentState*] := *NUL*;
    {insert (*currentState* + 1) in ε-list of *currentState*};
    currentState := *currentState* + 1;
end;

We now trace the operation of this PDA as it parses a non-trivial string and concurrently builds the NFSA. The string which we consider is '*a**[[*b*[%]]*d*]'.

Figure 8.6 shows the configuration of the parse at each step. A state diagram corresponding to the partially built table is introduced at each step at which a semantic action is invoked. The derivation symbol between each stack representation is labelled by the production ordinal which has been used in that step.

A practical observation relating to the implementation of PDA, which like *WildOption* require stack structures for semantic actions, is that the two logical stacks, parser and semantic, may be interleaved on the one physical stack. In this case the current-state ordinal is pushed on the stack immediately before the right-hand side of production 7, as a side-effect of the prediction of that production. Whenever a ']' symbol is recognized the PDA stack is popped twice: the first time to delete the recognized terminal symbol, the second time to retrieve the associated state ordinal for the semantic action.

Note that the policy of mixing semantic and parser information on the same stack requires a deliberate circumvention of the type-checking performed by the compiler for strongly typed implementation languages such as Pascal. Logically the type of the stack element is a union of the vocabulary symbol-type with the semantic action selector type.

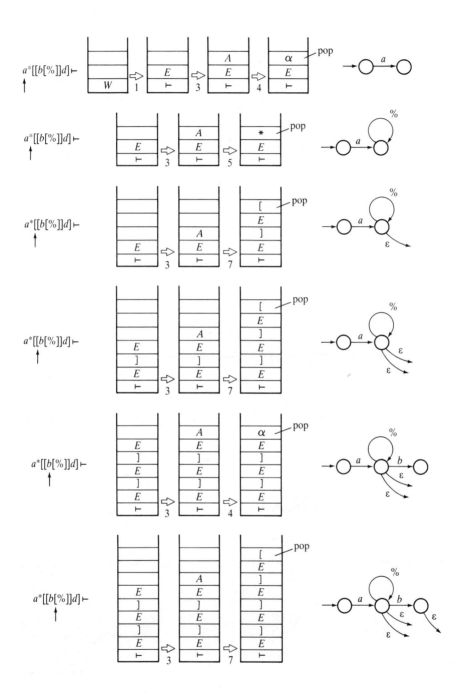

Figure 8.6   *cont. overleaf*

Figure 8.6 *cont.*

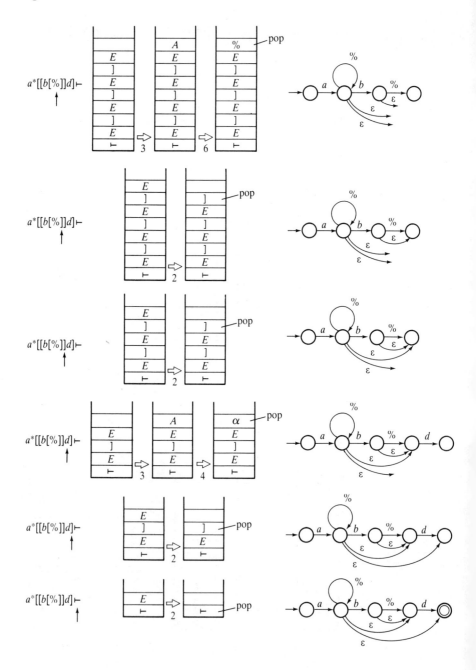

Figure 8.6 LL(1) PDA parsing a *WildOption* string.

Table-driven LL(1) parsers provide a straightforward method of implementing top-down parsing. However, the most widely used of the top-down methods, and the method which is advocated here for the recognition of all small languages, is directly programmed rather than table-driven. This method, called **recursive descent**, is flexible and has considerable intuitive appeal. It is the subject of the next section.

8.1.2 Section checklist and summary definitions

Table-driven LL(1) automata.

- Actions depend only on the current top-of-stack (TOS) symbol, and the next input symbol.
- If the TOS symbol is a terminal symbol, and matches the input symbol, the stack is popped and the next input symbol is read.
- If the TOS symbol is a non-terminal, the symbol is popped, and replaced by the right-hand-side production predicted to replace it.
- If the string ends, and the stack is empty, the string is accepted.

8.2 Recursive descent

Recursive descent is by far the most widely used method for parsing LL(1) languages. The method has a certain simplicity about it which makes the construction of the parsers relatively intuitive, and permits extremely flexible mechanisms for the incorporation of semantic actions and error recovery. In addition, the recursive descent method allows a convenient extension to the form of the grammars which may be used to define context-free languages. This extension often leads to a helpful compaction of the grammar. Recursive descent depends inherently on the use of an implementation language which supports recursive procedure calls, and is thus not directly suitable for implementation in older languages such as FORTRAN.

The basis of the recursive descent method is to associate a procedure with each syntactic category of the grammar. This procedure has the parsing subtask of recognizing those phrases which belong to the (sub)language derived from that syntactic category.

In general, each recognition procedure has as many branches as there are productions for that non-terminal symbol. The procedure chooses between the branches on the basis of the next input symbol. Since by assumption the grammar is LL(1), the next input symbol does uniquely determine which production is to be expected.

Each branch of a recognition procedure recognizes one production,

```
(* Production      Director-set
 S -> E stop       {num,op}
 E -> num          {num}
   -> op E E       {op}          *)

var symbol : SymbolType;

procedure ERecognize;
begin
  if symbol = num then (* E -> num *)
    GetSymbol; (* to get past num *)
  else if symbol = op then begin (* E -> op E E *)
    GetSymbol; (* to get past op *)
    ERecognize;
    ERecognize;
    end
  else error;
end; (* ERecognize *)

procedure SRecognize;
begin (* S -> E stop *)
  if (symbol = num) or (symbol = op) then begin
    ERecognize;
    if symbol = stop then (* do nothing *) else error;
    end (* then *)
  else error;
end; (* SRecognize *)

begin (* mainline code *)
  GetSymbol;
  SRecognize;
  { output result of parse }
end.
```

Figure 8.7   Skeleton of recursive descent parser for the Polish string grammar.

and does so by simply checking for the presence of a phrase corresponding to each vocabulary symbol on the right-hand side of the production. These checks are carried out by the procedure directly verifying the presence in the input stream of symbols matching the terminal symbols in the production, and by calling other procedures to recognize phrases corresponding to the non-terminal symbols. Because of this nested calling of procedures, if the underlying language is not regular then the possibility of direct or indirect recursive procedure calls cannot be avoided. This circumstance gives the method its name.

```
procedure KRecognize;
begin
   if {symbol in d-set for first production} then
      {recognize RHS of production #1}
   else if {symbol in d-set for second production} then
      {recognize RHS of production #2}

          .

          .
   else if {symbol in d-set for k-th production} then
      {recognize RHS of production #k}
   else error;
end;
```

Figure 8.8   Outline of general recognition procedure.

Figure 8.7 shows the procedures used to recognize the Polish string grammar of Section 7.1.1. These procedures have been commented to show their relationship to the productions which they implement, but have been simplified by omitting details of the error-handling mechanisms. The code of the procedures has been arranged in a systematic way to follow a set of rules for deriving procedures from productions.

The recognizer in Figure 8.7 adopts the convention that the first symbol of a phrase is fetched prior to the call of the procedure that recognizes it. This precondition is initialized by a first call to *GetSymbol* prior to the call of the procedure which recognizes the goal symbol, *SRecognize*. Note that input is only consumed by calls to *GetSymbol* following a successful matching of the current token symbol against the expected terminal symbol.

In cases where there is only a single production for any given non-terminal, as is the case for the non-terminal S in this example, it is possible to omit all prior checks on the input symbol. However, it may still be good practice to check that the input symbol is in the director set of the only production, since that policy leads to the earliest possible detection of errors.

The general rules for deriving recursive descent procedures from productions of an LL(1) grammar may be stated in terms of the steps of a top-down successive refinement design. Let us suppose that there are k different productions for a given non-terminal symbol K. The first outline of the procedure to recognize K is shown in Figure 8.8. This example uses successive **if**-statements, but **case** statements may be used instead.

The second step is to elaborate the right-hand-side recognition code for each production in its corresponding procedure branch. Each symbol in the right-hand side of the selected production gives rise to a single statement. If the symbol is a non-terminal, then the statement is a call to the procedure which recognizes that syntactic category. If the symbol is a terminal, however, then the statement simply checks for a symbol match. A typical statement would be:

> **if** *symbol* = *expectedSymbol* **then** (* is OK *)
>   *GetSymbol*
> **else** (* doesn't match, so . . . *)
>   *error*;

It is also possible to collect together all occurrences of the code which recognizes terminal symbols into a procedure traditionally called *Check*. This procedure would have a formal parameter corresponding to the expected symbol, and possibly also another selecting an error-recovery action.

It is important that consistent conventions be adopted in the interface between the lower-level procedure *GetSymbol* and the nested procedure calls within the parser. The most flexible convention is to insist that the next input symbol has already been read into the variable *symbol* before any procedure is called. Thus each procedure must return with the *GetSymbol* procedure, having already read the first symbol which does not belong to the recognized phrase. This allows director-set membership to be tested before the call of any nested procedure, and implies that no recursive descent procedure ever starts with a call to the symbol-reading procedure.

A common question raised in connection with recursive descent recognizers concerns the correct handling of the scope of the symbol variable *symbol*. It is undoubtedly best to keep the interface between the levels of the recognizer as clean as possible by treating the lower level as an abstract data object. This object provides access to the value of an encapsulated state variable, the current symbol, and also provides a parameterless procedure which calls for the lower-level recognizer to move to the next symbol. Since Pascal does not provide an encapsulation construct to allow such an abstraction to be implemented in a secure manner, it is necessary to declare the symbol variable so that it is of sufficiently global scope to be visible throughout the bodies of all of the recursive descent procedures. Additionally, the following rules should be complied with:

1. recursive descent procedures should treat the *symbol* variable as if it were read-only;
2. the *symbol* value should only be modified by calls to the parameterless procedure *GetSymbol*.

The final step in the development of a recursive descent parser is to consider how error detection is to be propagated from procedure to procedure, and to include semantic actions, if required. We will consider these questions again after discussing the extended or regular right-part grammars, but it is helpful at this stage to first consider a complete example.

8.2.1 Recursive descent and the *WildOption* language

Figure 8.9 is the complete set of procedures for a recursive descent recognizer for the *WildOption* language discussed in Section 4.4, and for which a table-driven LL(1) parser was developed in the previous section. In this figure it is assumed that a lower level recognizes the symbols of the scalar type *SymbolType*.

It will be seen that the main body of code is in the procedure *ARecognize*, which also holds the majority of the semantic actions. It will also be noted that within the procedure *ERecognize* a test on the director-set of the production $E \rightarrow AE$ is unnecessary, since the procedure *ARecognize* catches all wrong symbols with its second-last line. Obviously, an alternative would be to test for membership of the director set in *ERecognize*, and to omit the final **else** in *ARecognize*.

Comparing the procedures of Figure 8.9 with the table-driven PDA implementation discussed earlier raises an interesting point. The working stack which was necessary to correctly handle the semantic actions required by option brackets is missing in Figure 8.9. Instead, the variable *state* is declared local to *ARecognize*, so that each activation of *ARecognize* has its own, distinct instance of the variable. If the procedure calls are recursive, then each procedure has its own variable, which becomes visible again as the execution control path returns through the dynamic chain of procedure returns.

What has happened here is that the run-time stack for local variables, provided by every programming language which supports recursive procedures, has implicitly provided the equivalent of the semantic stack of the table-driven PDA. Similarly, the procedure return-stack of the programming language's run-time system provides the facility to nest non-terminal recognition which is provided in a PDA by the automaton's stack.

A small but significant point relating to the implementation of recursive descent parsers in the Pascal language is illustrated by this example. Most Pascal compilers demand that the defining occurrence of an identifier textually precede any used occurrence (except for the special case of pointer variables). This leads to a paradox, since *ERecognize* and *ARecognize* call each other, and they cannot both occur first. One of the two must therefore be declared **forward**, and the declaration of *ParseWildOption*, which calls both of the procedures, must occur last of all.

An alternative to the use of forward declarations, which may

```
type SymbolType = (stop,star,any,LSqr,RSqr,ordinary);
var symbol : SymbolType;

procedure ParseWildOption; (* W -> E stop *)
begin
  ERecognize;
  if symbol = stop
    then { mark endstate}
    else Error := TRUE;
end; (* ParseWildOption *)

procedure ERecognize;
begin
  if symbol in [stop,RSqr] then (* E -> empty *)
  else begin (* director set is checked in ARecognize *)
    ARecognize;
    ERecognize;
    end;
end; (* ERecognize *)

procedure ARecognize;
  var state : StateType; (* start state of e-transition *)
begin
  if symbol in [ordinary,any] then begin (* A -> a | '%'. *)
    AdvanceChar[CurrentState] := ch; (* actual char *)
    currentState := currentState + 1;
    GetSymbol;
    end
  else if symbol = star then begin (* A -> '*' *)
    SelfLoop[currentState] := TRUE;
    GetSymbol;
    end
  else if symbol = LSqr then begin (* A -> '['E']' *)
    state := currentState;
    GetSymbol;
    if symbol = star then IsolateState;
    ERecognize;
    if symbol = Rsqr then begin
      if SelfLoop[currentState] then IsolateState;
      {add currentState to e-list of state}
      GetSymbol;
      end
    else Error := TRUE;
    end
  else Error := TRUE;
end; (* ARecognize *)
```

Figure 8.9   Recursive descent procedures for *WildOption*.

sometimes be used, is to lexically nest the procedures. In this particular example *ARecognize* could be nested within *ERecognize*. The choice between the two methods is usually a matter of style. However, it is possible to devise programs for which there is no possible nesting to provide correct identifier visibility, and forward declarations must be used.

8.2.2 Regular right-part grammars

This section introduces a notation for extended grammars, which achieve a compactness of expression and are directly exploitable by recursive descent parsers. An alternative name for this class of extended grammars is the **regular right-part** (RRP) grammars. In effect, the permissible form of the right-hand sides of productions is extended to correspond to regular expressions over the vocabulary.

There are two new constructs which are used in the productions of extended grammars: **optionality** and **closure**. These terms have precisely the same meaning in this context as they have when used in the context of regular expressions. In this case, however, the meta-symbols which are conventionally used to indicate closure are different.

Closure is indicated by enclosing the optionally repeated substring in curly bracket meta-symbols '{' and '}'. A substring within closure brackets may be repeated zero, one or many times. Optionality is indicated by enclosing the optional substring in square bracket meta-symbols, '[' and ']'. A substring within option brackets may occur exactly zero times, or once.

Each production using one or other of these constructions corresponds to more than one production of the equivalent CFG. For example the production $E \rightarrow P$ ['**' P] produces the same strings as the two CFG productions

$$E \rightarrow P \mid P \;'**'\; P.$$

Similarly, the production $E \rightarrow T \{ \;'+'\; T \}$ produces the same sentential forms as the infinite set of context-free productions

$$E \rightarrow T \mid T \;'+'\; T \mid T \;'+'\; T \;'+'\; T \mid \; \dots$$

Of course, no CFG may contain such an infinite set, but must instead model the situation by incorporating a recursive production such as $E \rightarrow T \mid E \;'+'\; T$. The effect of the closure is thus to replace a recursive production by an iteration.

The implementation of such extended grammars still requires that the language be LL(1). Since the methods given in Chapter 7 for checking the LL(1) condition were stated in terms of context-free (non-extended) grammars it is usually necessary to transform an extended grammar into

```
procedure KRecognize; (* K -> α{β}γ *)
begin
  {recognize string α};
  while symbol in FIRST(β) do
    {recognize string β};
  {recognize string γ};
end;
```

Figure 8.10   Procedure outline to recognize a closure construct.

an equivalent CFG in order to form the director sets. This transformation may be performed in a completely mechanical fashion.

Consider a typical production using the closure construct

$$K \rightarrow \alpha\{\beta\}\gamma.$$

where α, β, γ all belong to V^*. An equivalent set of CFG productions is

$$K \rightarrow \alpha M \gamma.$$
$$M \rightarrow \varepsilon \mid \beta M.$$

where the new non-terminal, M, has been invented to stand in place of the closure in the original production. Note that the repeated β phrases in the language, which in the example are derived by the right-recursive production for M, might just as well be generated by left-recursion, as in the productions

$$M \rightarrow \varepsilon \mid M\beta.$$

The two alternative CFGs derive the same strings, but only the first form is useful for a recursive descent parser, because of the general prohibition on left-recursion if the grammar is to be LL(1).

In passing, we may also note that the substring β must not be nullable, since that would imply that there were two different ways of deriving an empty string from the symbol M, making the overall grammar ambiguous.

The director set of the production $M \rightarrow \varepsilon$ is $FOLLOW(M)$, while that of the production $M \rightarrow \beta M$ is $FIRST(\beta)$. Therefore, in order that the LL(1) condition applies to these two productions for M, we must have

$$FIRST(\beta) \cap FOLLOW(M) = \{\}$$

with β not nullable, and where $\{\}$ is the empty set. In terms of the original, extended production, this condition is

$$FIRST(\beta) \cap FIRST(\gamma.FOLLOW(K)) = \{\}$$

```
procedure BRecognize; (* B -> α[β]γ *)
begin
   {recognize string α};
   if symbol in FIRST(β) then
      {recognize string β};
   {recognize string γ};
end;
```

Figure 8.11   Procedure outline to recognize option construct.

where once again β may not be nullable. In this last equation, the *FIRST* function has been extended to apply not just to a string but to the product language of γ and *FOLLOW(K)*. In the case that γ is not nullable, this reduces to the simpler form

$$FIRST(β) \cap FIRST(γ) = \{\}$$

In the common case of **tail iteration**, where the closure is the last factor in the production, the factor γ in our typical production is absent, so the production becomes $K \rightarrow α\{β\}$. This production is LL(1), provided that, with β not nullable,

$$FIRST(β) \cap FOLLOW(K) = \{\}$$

A typical production using the optionality construct is

$$B \rightarrow α[β]γ$$

where α,β,γ all belong to V^*. In this case the equivalent CFG construct is

$$B \rightarrow αQγ.$$
$$Q \rightarrow ε \mid β.$$

where Q is a new non-terminal symbol. The productions for Q will be LL(1) if, with β not nullable,

$$FIRST(β) \cap FIRST(γ.FOLLOW(B)) = \{\}$$

The special cases here are the same as for the closure example.

Let us now suppose that the LL(1) condition is met for the typical production including a closure construct. In other words, we are assuming that the director sets for the two productions of the newly invented non-terminal M are disjoint. The original, extended grammar production may now be recognized directly by means of the recursive descent procedure skeleton in Figure 8.10.

Notice that the failure of the LL(1) condition would correspond to a situation in Figure 8.10, where it would be impossible to know when to

```
procedure ERecognize; (* E -> β{β} *)
begin
   repeat
      {recognize string β}
   until symbol in FOLLOW(E);
end;
```

Figure 8.12 Procedure outline to recognize positive closure.

terminate the **while** loop, because the same symbol could either start the γ-string, or be the first symbol of another β-string.

The example of a typical production with an option construct may be directly implemented by the code outlined in Figure 8.11. In this case we have assumed that the director sets for the two productions of the introduced non-terminal symbol Q are disjoint.

There are certain other standard forms which may be used to implement the recognition of extended grammars. For example, a production with a positive closure

$$E \rightarrow \beta\{\beta\}$$

for which the LL(1) condition is

$$FIRST(\beta) \cap FOLLOW(E) = \{\}$$

with β not nullable, may be recognized by the code outline in Figure 8.12.

The correspondence between the right-hand sides of the productions in extended grammars and regular expressions may be noted. If we also permitted the introduction of an alternative construct, then the correspondence would be complete. It is possible to do so, but for most of what follows we restrict the use of alternation to non-nested occurrences corresponding to alternative productions. The details of this final extension are left to the exercises and are sketched out in the model answer. In any case, we refer to these extended grammars in which the production right-hand sides are (possibly restricted forms of) regular expressions as regular right-part (RRP) grammars.

As a comparison of the relative compactness of the CFG and RRP formulations of the same language, consider the following extended LL(1) form of the meta-grammar for regular expressions.

$$S \rightarrow E \vdash.$$
$$E \rightarrow T \ \{'|' \ T \ \}.$$
$$T \rightarrow F \ \{ \ F \ \}.$$
$$F \rightarrow P \ ['*'].$$
$$P \rightarrow \ '(' \ E \ ')' \ | \ '\emptyset' \ | \ '\varepsilon' \ | \ a.$$

```
type SymbolType = (plus,minus,mult,divide,number,stopper,bad);
var  symbol : SymbolType;
     ch:     : CHAR;
     value   : REAL; (* used if smbl is a number *)

  procedure GetSymbol; (* lexical scanner *)
  begin (* assert: ch is last of old symbol *)
    if EOLN then symbol := stopper
    else begin (* discard last char, and any blanks *)
      repeat Read(ch)
      until (ch ⟨⟩ ' ') or EOLN; (* or both! *)
      if ch = ' ' then symbol := stopper
      else (* even if eoln is true *)
        if ch in ['0'..'9'] then ScanNumber;
        else if ch in ['+','−','*','/'] then
          case ch of
            '+' : symbol := plus;
            .

            .

          end;
        end (* else if *)
      else symbol := bad;
    end; (* if not eoln *)
  end;
```

Figure 8.13   Lower level of expression evaluators.

This grammar should be compared with Figure 7.3, from which it was derived. The number of productions has been reduced from 14 to 8.

8.2.3 Semantic actions and RRP grammars

We now must consider the influence of the extended grammar constructs on the task of embedding semantic actions within the recursive descent procedures. As an example we take a typical right-recursive production in an arithmetic expression grammar

$$expr \rightarrow term \ \{ \ addop \ term \ \}.$$

This production corresponds to the context-free productions

$$expr \rightarrow term \ rest.$$
$$rest \ \rightarrow \varepsilon$$
$$\rightarrow addop \ term \ rest.$$

In each case it may be assumed that $addop \rightarrow$ '+' | '−'.

```
procedure RRPExpression(var Evalue : REAL);
  (* Exp -> Term { addop Term } *)
  var   Tvalue,Total : REAL;
      IsPlus : BOOLEAN;
begin
  Term(Total); (* first call to Term initializes Total *)
  while symbol in [plus,minus] do begin
    IsPlus := (symbol = plus);
    GetSymbol;
    Term(Tvalue);
    if IsPlus then Total := Total+Tvalue
          else Total := Total-Tvalue;
  end; (* while *)
  Evalue := Total;
end;
```

Figure 8.14   Evaluating an expression, RRP production.

We look at several different versions of procedures which not only parse the strings conforming to the above production, but also evaluate the expression. In each case we shall assume that a lower-level recognizer defines certain types, and provides the procedure *GetSymbol*. The code of the lower level is given in Figure 8.13.

The first version of the evaluator directly implements the RRP production. It is assumed that the procedure *Term* returns the *REAL* value of the term which it has recognized in its **var** parameter. Figure 8.14 gives the code.

The semantic actions for the RRP production are very straightforward. The terms are evaluated from left to right, within the **while** loop, and the result accumulated in the local variable *Total*. Note that this variable must be local, as *RRPExpression* may be recursively called from the factor-recognizing procedure if the expression has parentheses. The technique of using a Boolean variable temporarily to remember whether the *addop* was '+' or '−' is familiar from the real number recognizers of Chapter 3.

Figure 8.15 implements the standard CFG version of the expression production. In this case the implementation of the semantic action is a little tricky. Since it is required that the value of each term be added or subtracted from the running total as the recognition procedure proceeds, the total is passed to the subsidiary procedure where it is updated. If the procedure *CFGExpression* itself was to perform the arithmetic operation on the result returned by procedure *Rest*, the effect would be evaluation from right to left.

```
procedure CFGExpression(var Evalue : REAL);
  var Rval : REAL

    (* can nest procedure instead of 'forward' decl. *)
    procedure Rest (var Rvalue : REAL);
      var Tval : REAL; IsPlus : BOOLEAN;
    begin (* Rest-> addop Term Rest *)
      if symbol in [plus, minus] then begin
        IsPlus := (symbol = plus);
        GetSymbol;
        Term(Tval);
        if IsPlus then Rvalue := Rvalue + Tval
                else Rvalue := Rvalue - Tval;
        Rest(Rvalue) (* recursion *)
        end
      else (* must be empty production, Rest -> empty *)
    end;

  begin (* Exp -> Term Rest *)
    Term(Rval);
    Rest(Rval); (* pass total for updating *)
    Evalue :=Rval
  end;
```

Figure 8.15   Evaluating an expression, CFG version.

There are at least two other ways in which the expression production may be manipulated, each leading to a different style of semantic action incorporation. An alternative RRP production would be

expr → term [addop expr].

The CFG version of this production would be

expr → term remainder.
remainder → ε | addop expr.

Implementation of the first of these is shown in Figure 8.16, the corresponding code for the CFG version being left to the reader. In this third version, just for variety, the code for the addition and subtraction cases has been separated, and no Boolean *IsPlus* is needed.

It is left to the reader to check that the version given in Figure 8.16 evaluates from right to left. It is possible to modify this procedure to make it evaluate left-to-right, by using the **var** parameter to pass the accumulating total, as was done in Figure 8.15. In that case, any

```
procedure ExprV3(var Evalue : REAL);
  var Tvalue, Rvalue : REAL;
begin (* Exp -> Term [ addop Exp ] *)
  Term(Tvalue);
  if symbol = plus then begin
    GetSymbol;
    ExprV3(Rvalue);
    Evalue :=Tvalue + Rvalue;
    end
  else if symbol = minus then begin
    GetSymbol;
    ExprV3(Rvalue);
    Evalue :=Tvalue - Rvalue;
    end;
  else Evalue := Tvalue;
end;
```

Figure 8.16   Evaluating an expression, third version.

outermost call of the expression-recognition procedure must pass an initial total of zero for updating.

Such contortions with semantic actions are best avoided, however. The production form with the closure evaluates from left-to-right very naturally, while the version with the option evaluates from right-to-left with the obvious semantic actions shown in Figure 8.16. Recursive descent thus provides a natural way of providing either evaluation order without resorting to obscure trickery.

This particular example has been considered in some detail in order to demonstrate the inherent flexibility of the recursive descent method. It must be noted, however, that if the normal conventions of arithmetic are to apply, left-to-right evaluation of *terms* and *factors* is required, and the algorithm sketched in Figure 8.14 is the one to use. The most common conventions for ordering arithmetic operations demand that both addition and multiplying operations should be carried out from left to right, while exponentiation should be carried out right to left.

A suitable grammar for a recursive descent evaluator with the natural semantic actions would be

$$sentence \rightarrow expression \; stopper. \tag{1}$$
$$expression \rightarrow [addop] \; term \; \{ \; addop \; term \; \}. \tag{2}$$
$$term \rightarrow factor \; \{ \; mulop \; factor \; \}. \tag{3}$$
$$factor \rightarrow primary \; [\; '**' \; factor \;]. \tag{4}$$
$$primary \rightarrow '(' \; expression \; ')' \; | \; number. \tag{5}$$

$addop \rightarrow$ '+' |'−'.
$mulop \rightarrow$ '*' | '/'.

This grammar, which is LL(1), includes an optional unary sign on the first *term* in any expression. It is important to ensure that this sign operates on the first *term* only, and not on the value of the complete expression. However, note that this grammar naturally evaluates a string such as −3**2 as −(3**2) rather than (−3)**2. In some programming languages, such as Algol-68, the latter form would be considered correct and the grammar would thus have to be modified.

A rather more important point relates to the treatment of repeated exponentiation. The convention given above is probably the most widely used, but nevertheless it is much safer to avoid the problem of possible misunderstanding by only permitting a single exponentiation. This is the approach used in the language Ada. A suitable grammar modification would be to replace the production (4) by a production which allows a *factor* to be a single *primary*, with an optional exponent which is also a *primary*.

$$factor \rightarrow primary \ [\ '**' \ primary \ ] \tag{4a}$$

In this modified grammar, the string 2**3**2 would be rejected as illegal and parentheses would have to be used to select either 2**(3**2) or (2**3)**2, whichever was intended. Note that the original grammar would accept the unbracketed string and would evaluate it as 2**(3**2).

A complete recursive descent expression evaluator for the language of expressions given by the above grammar is included in the case study at the end of this chapter.

A more radical solution to the problem of the implicit conventions for evaluation order of non-associative operators, is to demand explicit parentheses in all cases. This solution is explored in Exercise 8.6.

8.2.4   Section checklist and summary definitions

1. Recursive descent definitions.
   - Each non-terminal symbol in the grammar has an associated procedure which recognizes all substrings belonging to that syntactic category.
   - Each recognition procedure selects a section of code which recognizes a particular production right-hand-side, the choice being determined by the director set to which the current input symbol belongs.
   - Each symbol of the selected production is recognized, in order, by direct symbol matching in the case of terminal symbols, and the

calling of the corresponding recursive descent procedure in the case of non-terminals.

2. Regular right-part (RRP) grammars.

   - RRP grammars have productions with right-hand sides which are regular expressions over the vocabulary V. In particular, closure and optionality constructs may be freely used.

   - The LL(1) condition is checked for an RRP grammar by transforming to an equivalent CFG. It is done by introducing new non-terminal symbols which replace each closure or option subexpression in an RRP production.

3. The closure construct.

   - The effect of using the closure construct in an RRP grammar, is to replace a recursive construct in the equivalent CFG.

   - The closure construct is recognized by code
     while {symbol in dir. set of closure} **do** . . .;

4. Optionality.

   - The option construct replaces a null production. It is recognized by code
     if {symbol in dir. set of option} **then** . . .;

** 8.3   Recursive finite-state automata

The production right-hand-sides in an extended grammar are regular expressions. There are certain notational differences, specifically the use of '{. . .}' instead of '(. . .)*'. Nevertheless, the right-hand sides of the productions are just regular expressions over the vocabulary, V, rather than over the terminal alphabet, Σ, as for ordinary regular expressions.

We may devise a recognition method which is based on this analogy, drawing on the power and familiarity of the FSA techniques to assist in the recognition of non-regular languages. The recognition power of this method is precisely that of recursive descent, to which it bears a strong isomorphism. One advantage of this method, compared to recursive descent, is that implementation in a language providing recursive procedures is not necessary, thus leading to natural implementations in FORTRAN. Furthermore, compacted table-driven implementations are possible, and are generally much more convenient than table-driven LL(1) PDA since they directly implement the extended grammars.

In overview, the method implements a *family* of FSA, one for each non-terminal symbol. Each FSA may be thought of as being defined by a state diagram, the transitions of which are labelled by either terminal or non-terminal symbols.

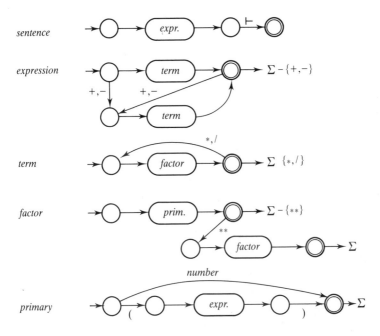

Figure 8.17   FSA family for expression recognition. Each FSA is a submachine.

For example, the extended arithmetic grammar given in Section 8.2.3 leads to the state diagram set in Figure 8.17. In this figure the various FSA have been formed from the production right-hand-sides, and converted to DFSA where necessary. A notational convenience is to write explicit symbols on terminal transitions in the usual fashion, but to show the 'procedure calls' to the FSA which recognize other non-terminals as though they were subexpressions of the regular expression.

The process of recognition proceeds by a standard state-updating loop so long as the selected transitions are labelled by terminal symbols. When a transition via a submachine is selected, the ordinal number of the next-state of the non-terminal transition is pushed onto a *state return-stack*, and the current state is replaced by the starting state of the selected submachine. Conversely, when a submachine completes recognition of a phrase belonging to its syntactic category, the state return-stack is popped, and the current state is replaced by the popped value.

It is important to note that the normal, terminal-symbol-labelled transitions cause an input symbol to be consumed by a call to the *GetSymbol* procedure, while neither a *push* nor a *pop* operation causes a further symbol to be read.

In order to clarify the connection between this mechanism and the LL(1) formalism, we consider the recognition of the productions of a

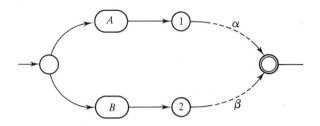

Figure 8.18   Submachine for typical production.

typical non-terminal symbol. Suppose non-terminal K has two productions

$K \rightarrow A\alpha \mid B\beta.$

where $A,B \in N$; $\alpha,\beta \in V^*$. The submachine which recognizes K is outlined in Figure 8.18.

In order that the submachine K should know which branch of the state diagram to follow from the start state, and hence which submachine to call, it is necessary that the director sets of the two productions $K \rightarrow A\alpha$ and $K \rightarrow B\beta$ should be disjoint, i.e. the LL(1) condition must hold. In this example, if the input symbol is an element of the director set of the first production, state 1 is pushed on the return stack and submachine A is called, while if the symbol is in the director set of the second production, state 2 is pushed and submachine B is called.

The task of each submachine, except for the one which recognizes the goal symbol, is to recognize a substring within a complete string. It is, therefore, necessary to use symbol lookahead to detect completion of the recognition of some phrases. However, by assumption the grammar is LL(1), so knowledge of the next symbol is always sufficient.

In Figure 8.17, for example, the submachine which recognizes the production

term → factor {('*'|'/') *factor*}.

can determine completion of its recognition because the *FIRST* set for the repeating substring, {*,/}, is disjoint from *FOLLOW*(*term*).

In principle, if any accept state of a submachine has an out-transition then it is possible to label the exit semi-transition with the *FOLLOW* set on which the exit is predicated. During the FSA interpretaton process, if the current state is an accept state and the input symbol is any member of the *FOLLOW* set, the stack is popped and a return is made. If the input symbol corresponds to a transition within the submachine, then interpretation proceeds as usual.

In practical terms it is never necessary to check for the presence of a symbol in the precise *FOLLOW* set in order to verify a termination condition. The reason is that the calling submachine will always detect any incorrect symbol by a failure of the symbol-match operation subsequent to the return. Thus it is only necessary to label an exit transition with a lookahead set consisting of the set difference of the alphabet Σ, and all those symbols which cause interpretation to stay within the same submachine.

The actual set *FOLLOW(term)*, for the grammar shown in Figure 8.17, may be verified as being $\{.,),+,-\}$, but instead of using this set the exit may as well be predicated on the set $\Sigma - \{*,/\}$ as shown in the figure.

If the exact *FOLLOW* set were to be used, then there would be three possible actions in the accept state:

1. stay within the *term* machine for symbols $\{*,/\}$;
2. pop the stack and return for symbols $\{.,),+,-\}$;
3. go to the error state for all other symbols.

On the other hand, if the submachine is implemented as shown in the diagram, then there are only two possibilities;

1. stay within the *term* machine for symbols $\{*,/\}$;
2. pop the stack for all other symbols.

If an invalid symbol causes a normal exit from the submachine, then the fact that the exit condition consumes no input will ensure that the erroneous symbol will still be in the symbol buffer, and will cause some later symbol match process to fail.

Similarly when choosing between several branches within a submachine one of the director-set membership tests may be omitted. In effect, one submachine call becomes the default action which is taken whenever the current symbol value fails the membership tests for the director sets of all other branches. This simplification still leads to a correct implementation, because any invalid symbol will be detected in the called submachine before any further input symbols are read.

The predication of the last branch on 'all other input symbols' leads to a structure for the component submachines which may be exploited to simplify table-driven implementations, as is shown below.

As a specific example of the use of the above reasoning, the expression submachine in Figure 8.17 would normally have the initial transitions chosen according to membership of the sets $\{+,-\}$, and $\{number,($\}$, where the last set is clearly the director set for the *term* machine. However, the same purpose may be achieved by using the sets $\{+,-\}$ and $\{all\ others\}$ (specifically $\Sigma - \{+,-\}$), since if the branch which calls for the recognition of *term* is selected by default when the input symbol is actually invalid, then the symbol will remain in the buffer until it is finally rejected by the submachine recognizing *primary*.

Apart from those changes necessitated by the existence of the submachine call and return actions, interpretation of such machines follows the methods of earlier chapters. In particular, state diagrams may

```
procedure RFSAInterpret(var accept:BOOLEAN);
  (* globals referenced include :
     type Actions = (noaction,call1,call2, . . .,callN,pop);
     var
          actionTable : array[StateType,SymbolType] of Actions;
          nextState   : array[StateType,SymbolType] of StateType;
          startState  : array[call1..callN] of StateType;
     function   PoppedState : StateType;
     function   EmptyStack : BOOLEAN;
     procedure Push(K : StateType);
     procedure InitializeStack;


  *)
  var    action : Actions;
         state, next : StateType;

begin
  InitializeStack;
  GetSymbol;
  state := start[goal];
  while symbol <> stopper do begin
    action := actionTable[state,symbol];
    next := nextState[state,symbol];
    if action = noaction then begin (* ordinary FSA step *)
      state := next;
      GetSymbol;
      end
    else if action = pop then
      state := PoppedState; (* note: no GetSymbol ! *)
    else begin (* must be call to submachine *)
      Push(next); (* push return state *)
      state := startState[action]; (* jump to new start *)
      end; (* again no GetSymbol *)
    end;(* while *)
  accept := (state in AcceptStates) and StackEmpty;
end;
```

Figure 8.19   Algorithm for recursive-FSA interpretation.

be manipulated by the NFSA-to-DFSA conversion technique, and the resulting DFSA minimized in the usual way. The standard caveat applies regarding the possibility of minimization making the insertion of semantic actions more difficult.

The table interpretation algorithm, equivalent to Figure 3.2 for normal FSA interpretation, is given in Figure 8.19.

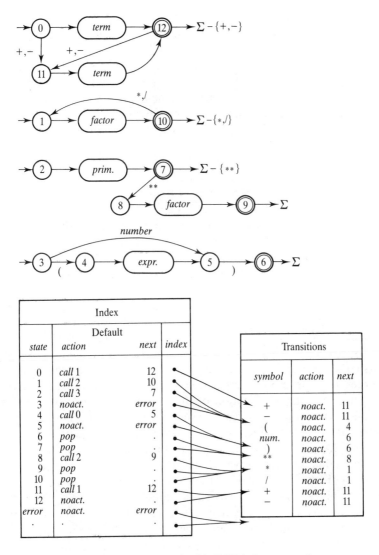

Figure 8.20   Compacted table RFSA for expressions.

As is the case for ordinary FSA, the recursive-FSA often possess highly redundant transition tables which may benefit from table compaction techniques. A small difference arises because very often the most common transition table entry, which is the one excluded in the compaction process, is not the *error* transition. To exemplify these considerations, the compacted table implementation of Figure 8.17 is given in Figure 8.20.

Several things should be noted about the data-structure in Figure

8.20. Firstly, no submachine is required for the goal symbol, since by assumption the string-end is determined by a calling main program. Secondly, to save space in the next state table, the default next state and action entries are held in the index array.

In Figure 8.20, for example, in the state diagram for *primary*, it will be seen that when in state 6, every lookahead symbol should be met with a *pop* action. Rather than have an entry repeated in the next state table for every possible symbol, *pop* becomes the default action if the next state table does not provide a symbol match. Clearly the next state table will be most compact when the transition indicated by the largest number of input symbols is used as the default. Sometimes, as in state 3, the error transition is the most common, and *error* is the default next state entry.

The technique of using a default next state entry in the index table may save execution time as well as data space. Although this technique is not treated in Chapter 3, it is applicable to FSA in general and not just to recursive machines.

Interpretation of the compacted recursive-FSA tables differs from the interpretation of uncompacted tables only in that a procedure *nextState* is used rather than an access to an array as was indicated in the algorithm of Figure 8.19. The procedure which accesses the compacted tables with default next state and action entries is shown in Figure 8.21.

It is usual for the recognizing automata to implement semantic actions concurrently with the recognition process, so the *action* entries in the tables may be more complicated than in the preceding figures. In particular, if the implementation of the semantic actions associated with grammar recognition using standard recursive descent techniques requires the use of local variables in the recognition procedures, then the recursive-FSA will require the use of a stack for the potentially multiple copies of semantic action variables. It is normal to interleave such variables with the return-stack values on the one physical stack.

In summary, the recursive-FSA method provides a table-driven parsing method with power equivalent to conventional recursive descent, but with some potential for greater compactness. However, this potential is obtained at the expense of somewhat greater difficulty in the incorporation of semantic actions, including the necessity of often having to program explicit semantic-stack structures.

8.3.1 Section checklist and summary definitions

1. Recursive finite state automata.

   - An RFSA consists a family of FSA, with transitions labelled by both terminal and non-terminal symbols. There is an FSA for each non-terminal in the grammar, which recognizes the language

```
(* Global declarations used include the following:–
var index : array[0..(maxState + 1)] of
             record
                defaultAction : Actions;
                defaultNext   : StateType;
                tableIndex    : 0..N;
             end;
var transitions : array[{however many}] of
             record
                symbol : SymbolType;
                action : Actions;
                next   : StateType;
             end;
   *)


procedure TableFetch;
   var I, limit   : INTEGER;
       found : BOOLEAN;


begin
   found := FALSE;
   I := index[state].tableIndex;
   limit := index[state+1].tableIndex;
   while (I < limit) and not found do
      if transitions[I].symbol = symbol then begin
         found := TRUE;
         action := table[I].action;
         next   := table[I].next;
         end
      else I := I+1;
   if not found then begin (* set to default values *)
      action := index[state].defaultAction;
      next   := index[state].defaultNext;
      end;
end;
```

Figure 8.21   Table lookup for compacted RFSA.

defined by the regular expression of production right-hand-sides for
that symbol.

- Terminal transitions are followed in the usual way, by reading the
  symbol and updating the state. Non-terminal transitions, however,
  are treated by pushing the successor state onto a state-return stack,
  and jumping to the start state of the appropriate FSA.

- When a substring is accepted, the state return stack is popped, and the FSA for that non-terminal symbol is exited.

2. RFSA and semantic actions.

- Some care in incorporating semantic actions is required, since there may be semantic actions associated with those moves of the machine, such as *call* and *return*, which consume no input.

8.4   The limits of LL(1) parsing

In this section we deal with a number of special topics relating to top-down parsing. Methods are introduced to deal with the occasional production which proves to be intractably non-LL(1), and with one of the strange quirks of recursive descent which allows the method to correctly parse certain ambiguous grammars.

8.4.1   Dealing with non-LL(1) features

There are two common circumstances in which a language resists attempts to find an LL(1) grammar. Firstly, there are cases where the grammar is not LL(1) because a small number of productions have overlapping director-sets, but are LL(k) for some value of $k > 1$. In such a case it would be possible to build an LL(k) parser, but this is almost never the correct method of attack. Since by assumption only a few productions require the longer lookahead, it is best to treat these special cases in an *ad hoc* manner.

Let us suppose, to be definite, that two productions share a common element a in their director-sets. That is

(i) $K \rightarrow \alpha, \quad d_\alpha = \{a, \ldots\}$
(ii) $\quad \rightarrow \beta, \quad d_\beta = \{a, \ldots\}$

where a is the common element, and, as usual, $\alpha, \beta \in V^*$. The procedure to recognize the non-terminal K is implemented much as any other recursive descent procedure, except that it incorporates a call to the *ad hoc* procedure 'lookahead' which examines as many new symbols of the input stream as are necessary to resolve the conflict. Figure 8.22 illustrates this mechanism.

This method should be used with some caution, and only then when absolutely necessary. It adds measurably to the complexity of the parser, but more especially to that of the lexical scanner, since it may necessitate the 'pushing back' of symbols onto the input stream after a long lookahead.

There are cases, however, where such *ad hoc* solutions are difficult to

```
procedure KRecognize;
  var FirstProd: BOOLEAN;

  procedure Lookahead(var result:BOOLEAN);
  begin { body of lookahead procedure } end;

begin
  if symbol = 'a' then begin (* ad hoc lookahead *)
    Lookahead(FirstProd);
    if FirstProd
      then {recognize prod #1}
      else {recognize prod #2}
    end
  else if symbol in {Rest of d1} then
    {recognize prod #1}
  else if symbol in {Rest of d2} then
    {recognize prod #2}
  else error:=TRUE;
end;
```

Figure 8.22 Procedure with *ad hoc* lookahead.

avoid. For example, in the parsing of the programming language
FORTRAN, almost arbitrarily long lookaheads are required in certain
pathological cases which may arise if keywords are also used as variable
identifiers. Such complicating features should, of course, be avoided in
the design of languages whenever possible, whether they be simple
command languages or programming languages.

The other circumstance in which attempts to find an LL(1) grammar
may fail, arises when prediction of the correct production requires the use
of non-syntactic information. Examples of this kind often appear in
programming languages. For example in Modula-2 the grammar fragment
which deals with the syntactic categories *qualident* (qualified identifier)
and *designator* is given by

$$qualident \rightarrow identifier \; \{'.' \; identifier\}.$$
$$designator \rightarrow qualident \; \{selector\}.$$
$$selector \rightarrow '.' \; identifier$$
$$\rightarrow '[' \; expressionList \; ']'$$
$$\rightarrow '^'.$$

This grammar is not LL(1) because the symbol '.' causes repetition of the
closure loop in *qualident*, and is also in *FIRST(selector)*. In practical
terms, the ambiguity arises because the character '.' is used between

module names and the identifiers which they qualify, and also between identifiers and record field names. The language Ada has a similar construct.

In such cases it is necessary to appeal to semantic tests to determine which production to choose. Often this is not a great overhead, since semantic tests must be carried out anyway, to test for those features in the language specification which are not described by context-free productions. In the example given above, checking in an identifier symbol table resolves the ambiguity by determining whether the identifier is a module name or some other class of identifier.

There are circumstances in which the second technique, use of semantic information, may be used as an alternative to an *ad hoc* lookahead. When either of the two methods will solve the uncertainty, semantic checking is usually to be preferred. This is because it leaves the lexical scanner unmodified, and may thus add less to the overall complexity. For example, consider a programming language compiler for a language which contains the two productions

$$statement \rightarrow assignment$$
$$\rightarrow procedureCall.$$

with the subgrammars

$$assignment \rightarrow variable ':=' expr.$$
$$variable \rightarrow identifier \{selector\}.$$
$$selector \rightarrow '[' expr \{',' expr \{ ']'$$
$$\rightarrow '.' identifier$$
$$\rightarrow '^'.$$
$$procedureCall \rightarrow identifier ['(' actualParameters ')'].$$

In this particular case the grammar is LL(2), since the second symbol of lookahead for the production *statement* → *assignment* belongs to the set $\{:=, [, ^, .\}$, while for the production *statement* → *procedureCall*, the second symbol belongs to a set which (for Pascal) is $\{(, ;, \text{'end'}, . . .\}$.

Notice in the above example that the purpose of the semantic test would be to determine whether the identifier was a procedure name or a variable name. If, as for some other languages, parentheses were used both for enclosing array indices and procedure parameters, then the grammar would not be LL(*k*) for any *k*, since an indefinitely long lookahead would be required to separate the two productions by purely syntactic means.

8.4.2 Ambiguous grammars and LL(1)

The limitations of top-down parsing have been emphasized, and we have explored some of the mechanisms which may be used to overcome these limitations. Nevertheless, there is a particular circumstance of some historical significance in which top-down parsers may be made to correctly parse non-LL(1) grammars.

A grammar is certainly ambiguous if it is possible to derive a sentential form in which two adjacent symbols are identical, non-terminal symbols which are both nullable and which also derive at least one non-empty terminal string. Starting from such a sentential form, the leftmost of the two non-terminals may produce the empty string, while the other derives some non-null terminal string. Alternatively, the rightmost of the repeated symbols may derive the empty string whilst the first derives the same terminal string as before, leading to the same final sentence.

The historical example of this ambiguity is the 'dangling else' problem of the programming language Algol 60. A simple grammar for the **if**-statement is

$$G \rightarrow statement \vdash.$$
$$statement \rightarrow ifStatement$$
$$\rightarrow otherStatement.$$
$$ifStatement \rightarrow \text{'if'} \; expr \; \text{'then'} \; statement \; elsepart.$$
$$elsepart \rightarrow \varepsilon$$
$$\rightarrow \text{'else'} \; statement.$$

This grammar is ambiguous, as is shown by the fact that the sentential form

if *con*1 **then if** *con*2 **then** *stat* **else** *stat* ⊢

has the two distinct derivation trees shown in Figure 8.23, where the non-terminal names have been abbreviated to their initial letters.

Loosely speaking, the ambiguity is not knowing with which '**then**' to associate the solitary '**else**'. As has been noted previously, an ambiguous grammar cannot be LL(1), and in this case the principle is demonstrated by the two productions for *elsepart* having director sets {**else**, ˆ} and {**else**}, respectively.

We may resolve this ambiguity by adding an extra *ad hoc* rule to the grammar, simply requiring that any '**else**' must be associated with the closest unpaired '**then**' to its left in the sentence. This is the usual interpretation of the **if-then-else** construction, and corresponds to the derivation of Figure 8.23(i). The effect of the extra rule may be described by context-free productions, one formulation being the grammar

$$G \rightarrow statement \vdash.$$
$$statement \rightarrow unbalancedIf$$
$$\rightarrow balancedStmt.$$
$$unbalancedIf \rightarrow \text{'if'} \; expr \; \text{'then'} \; statement$$
$$\rightarrow \text{'if'} \; expr \; \text{'then'} \; balancedStmt \; \text{'else'} \; unbalancedIf.$$
$$balancedStmt \rightarrow \text{'if'} \; expr \; \text{'then'} \; balancedStmt \; \text{'else'} \; balancedStmt$$
$$\rightarrow otherStatement.$$

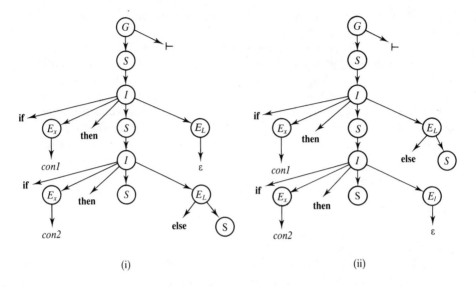

Figure 8.23   Example of the dangling **else** ambiguity.

Using this grammar, the parse tree for the same sentential form as used in Figure 8.23 is as shown in Figure 8.24. Unfortunately, this grammar is not LL(*k*) for any *k*, and no amount of left factorization will make it so. It is the more remarkable, then, that the original *ad hoc* disambiguating rule may be correctly implemented by an LL(1) parser. The key observation is that if the symbol 'else' is just arbitrarily deleted from the director set for the empty production in the original ambiguous grammar

elsepart → ε.

then the parser will never choose the empty production while any 'else' is the next symbol in the sentence. This simple strategy automatically associates each 'else' with the closest unpaired 'then', as required. It is interesting to observe that if the alternative disambiguating rule were to be chosen, so as to declare version (ii) of Figure 8.23 to be correct, then no such simple strategy is possible.

It is important to see that no such ambiguities arise if languages are designed so that all syntactic entities with significant substructures are explicitly delimited. In the case of programming languages, the simple expedient of starting if-statements with 'if' and ending them with 'end' (or 'fi') completely avoids the problem, both for the parser and for the human reader. This is the approach used in the language Ada.

The above method of arbitrary deletion of overlapping director-set elements, may be tried whenever an ambiguity shows itself as an overlap

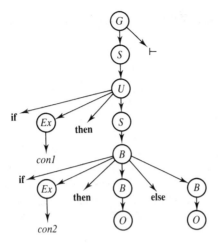

Figure 8.24 Derivation using unambiguous grammar.

between the director sets of a null and non-nullable production. However, in most cases of ambiguity, such as the ambiguous arithmetic grammar of Section 6.2, the method does not help.

In summary, the top-down methods of language recognition are both powerful and simple to implement. Although slightly less powerful than the bottom-up methods dealt with in Chapter 9, they are, nevertheless, adequate for most purposes. In particular, we advocate the use of recursive descent wherever possible, particularly for the non-specialist implementor of small languages.

8.4.3 Section checklist and summary definitions

1. Avoiding non-LL(1) grammar features.
   - The occasional production which is not LL(1) may be treated by implementing an *ad hoc* lookahead procedure, which is called to resolve the difficult cases.
   - The use of semantic information (from a symbol table, say) may often resolve clashes in the director sets.

2. Ambiguous grammars.
   - Certain ambiguous grammars can be correctly parsed by recursive descent parsers, by using non-CFG disambiguating rules to determine the parsing action. The ambiguous **if-then-else** grammar is prototypical.

8.5   Case study 2: An expression evaluator

8.5.1   Introduction and design

The problem addressed by this case study is that of implementing a recognizer for a language of arithmetic expressions. The expressions may contain numeric literals, and may also include identifiers which refer to symbolic values which are accessed via a symbol table. The recognizer is required to evaluate the submitted expression.

Such a recognizer is not a complete software tool, in that the code is not likely to be used as a complete program, but is a frequent component of many other contemporary programs. In the fragment of the implementation which is considered here, certain details are deliberately omitted, since they depend on the application in which the evaluator is embedded. In particular, the body of the low-level procedure *GetCh*, which fetches the next character for the scanner, is omitted. The details depend on whether the input is read from a file, obtained from a terminal, or obtained by indexing along a character array.

The type of symbol table organization and its corresponding lookup procedure have also been omitted, since they too depend on the application. In a conventional setting, with character-string identifiers, a symbol table similar to those discussed in Chapter 5 would be appropriate. In other circumstances, the identifier name-space may be of moderate cardinality and a table of descriptors indexed on identifier value might be used. Certainly, if names are single alphabetic characters, the character ordinal should be used to index into a 26-long table, rather than using a conventional lookup procedure. Such finite extent tables also occur in applications such as spreadsheets where identifiers select cell coordinates.

There has been much discussion of expression grammars throughout the preceding three chapters, so this example creates an opportunity to follow a design through to completion.

The grammar used here is a conventional arithmetic grammar, with left-to-right evaluation of repeated operators. It uses Ada syntax as a model for dealing with exponentiation, allowing only a single exponent unless explicit parentheses are used. The relevant production is

factor → *primary* ['*^*' *primary*].

Following the philosophy emphasized in the preceding chapters, the recognizer is implemented with two levels, and with as clean an interface between those levels as possible. The lexical level provides an abstract object, the current symbol value *symbol*, and a parameterless procedure *GetSymbol* which causes the value to be updated. The parser does not

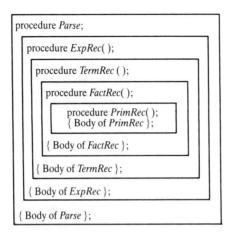

Figure 8.25   Outline of structure of parser.

interact with this object, except by reading the symbol value and by calling for the symbol update.

Two of the tokens, the lexical categories *number* and *ident* have lexical attributes associated with them. These attributes are also state variables of the lexical scanner, and are read from the scanner by the parser when the attributes are required for semantic actions. It is fundamental that the values which the variable *symbol* is assigned contain all the information required for recognition of string syntax. The lexical attributes are required only for the semantic actions.

An embedded real-number scanner accepts numeric literals of very free format, and is comparable with the scanner discussed in Chapter 3. Significant differences are that the version here is written as an **implicit state implementation** of the FSA. The effect is exactly that of a recursive descent procedure, but without recursion.

The real-number scanner contains an improved method for calculating the exponent factor for those standard Pascal implementations which do not supply an operator for exponentiation. The code calculates 10^n with a number of operations proportional to the number of significant bits of n. It does so by effectively finding the binary expansion of n.

The main purpose of the case study is to consider the parser construction. A fairly standard recursive descent skeleton has been adopted, in this case illustrating the use of procedure nesting to avoid the use of *FORWARD* declarations for the mutually recursive procedures. Figure 8.25 shows the overall structure.

The semantic actions are intertwined with the recognition actions, taking care that any semantic action which requires the use of lexical attribute information is executed before the *GetSymbol* procedure is called again. This is an important point, since the call of the scanner procedure may invalidate the attribute information by overwriting it.

In all cases, the recursive descent procedures respect the convention that the first symbol of the phrase to be recognized is already in the *symbol* variable before the procedure is called. All procedures, therefore, return to their caller with the input stream advanced one token past the recognized phrase. The lexical scanner adopts a similar convention, with the current value of the character variable *ch*, at the return of *GetSymbol*, being one position past the end of the token. Both of these preconditions are initialized by a procedure *InitScanner*. This procedure is called as the first action of the procedure *Parse*.

The question of error handling is somewhat glossed over here. A more detailed consideration of error handling for recursive descent parsers is given in Chapter 12. Since we are concerned here with only a single line of input the question of error recovery does not loom so large. What has been done in the example is to call one of a number of simple error-procedures whenever an error is detected. These procedures display a simple message and cause the expression evaluation to abort.

It turns out that the cleanest way of aborting execution of a standard Pascal program from inside a deeply nested and possibly recursively activated environment, is to use a **goto** to a (relatively) global label. This is one of the few circumstances where the use of **goto**s may be rationally defended as being 'structured'. Note carefully, however, that the target of the **goto** must be a position in the code in which no assertion regarding the outcome of the parse is in effect. In particular, the values returned by any functions or in any **var** parameters will be undefined.

Unfortunately, many microcomputer implementations of Pascal either forbid the use of **goto**s entirely, or only allow jumps to local (as opposed to relatively global) labels. This is understandable, since correct implementation of a **goto** from inside a recursive environment is actually quite hard to achieve, and has tripped-up several compiler implementors. Nevertheless, the question arises as to how the effect is to be achieved in cases where the language implementation forbids the mechanism used in the code given below. Some effort should be spent in order to see if the Pascal implementation which is to be used provides some exception-handling mechanism, or some other non-standard facility for abnormally terminating execution from deep inside a recursive environment. As a last resort, procedures may set a *BOOLEAN* flag which indicates the presence or otherwise of errors. In this case, the testing of flags after every procedure return clutters the code and hides the elegant simplicity of the recursive descent method.

8.5.2 Possible enhancements

An interesting extension, which is fairly easily incorporated, is to permit the use of a small number of unary functions, such as *SIN*, *COS* etc. in the expressions to be recognized. What is required is that the function names be in the symbol table, and that their associated descriptors contain a field which may be used to select the actual function to be executed when the name is recognized. This might be done by having an additional value in the *SymbolType* enumeration, *funcName* say, and an associated lexical attribute. The code required to recognize the non-terminal symbol *primary*, is modified by the additional production.

primary → . . . | *funcName* '(' *expression* ')'.

The relevant branch of code in procedure *PrimRec* might be as follows.

```
else if symbol = funcName then begin
    actual := {actual function selector}
    GetSymbol; (* read past name *)
    if symbol = Lbrac then begin
        GetSymbol; (* read past '(' *)
        ExpRec(val); (* evaluate argument *)
        val := {actual selected function, applied to val};
        if symbol = Rbrac then GetSymbol else BracError;
        end (* if symbol = Lbrac *)
    else Error; (* no '(' *)
    end (* symbol = funcName *)
```

8.5.3 An expression evaluator: The program

The following program contains an expression evaluator for expressions in an arithmetic grammar. The grammar also allows the four arithmetic operators and exponentiation, denoted by the caret symbol '^'. Expressions may contain identifiers and numeric literals. However, the code given here does not show the details of the symbol-table access mechanism.

The details of the input stream are hidden behind a procedure *GetCh*, which fetches the next character. This procedure also detects the input string termination, and passes a marker character to the lexical scanner, so that it can generate the *endSmbl* token. The details of the procedure are not given here, but for the standard file input might be as simple as

if EOLN **then** ch := EolMark **else** Read(ch).

```
PROGRAM ExpInt(input,output);

    const EolMark = {declare a control code . . . ASCII NUL maybe};
          Digits = ['0'..'9'];

    type SymbolType = (plus, minus, mult, divs, upArrow, Lbrac,
                        Rbrac, number, ident, errsmbl, endsmbl);

          DescPtr = ^ Descriptor;
          Descriptor = record
                          value : REAL;
                          {others as required . . . }
                       end;

    var  symbol    : SymbolType;        (* State variables of    *)
         numValue  : REAL;              (* the lexical scanner,  *)
         idDescr   : DescPtr;           (* read-only elsewhere.  *)

         ch : CHAR;                     (* Private to scanner.   *)


(* Lexical level of recognizer. Communicates with parser only
   via the symbol variable, and the two lexical attributes.      *)

procedure GetCh;
begin
  {details depend on input source}
end;

procedure ScanReal; (* free format number scanner *)
(* dd*['.' d*]['E' ['+'|'-']dd*] *)
(* returns value in numValue *)

  var total, power, coeff : REAL;
      negExp : BOOLEAN;
      expnt  : INTEGER;

  function OrdValue(digit : CHAR) : REAL;
  begin
    OrdValue := (ORD(digit) - ORD('0'))
  end; (* OrdValue *)

begin (* assert: first char is numeric *)
  symbol := number;
  total := OrdValue(ch); GetCh;
  while ch in Digits do begin
    total := total * 10.0 + OrdValue(ch); GetCh
    end;
```

```
    if ch = '.' then begin (* do fraction *)
      coeff := 0.1; GetCh;
      while ch in Digits do begin
        total := total + coeff * OrdValue(ch);
        coeff := coeff/10.0; GetCh
        end
      end; (* do fraction *)
    if (ch = 'E') or (ch = 'e') then begin (* do exponent *)
      GetCh;
      negExp := (ch = '-');
      if (ch = '+') or (ch = '-') then GetCh;
      if not(ch in Digits) then
        symbol := errsmbl (* return error symbol *)
      else begin (* ch is a digit *)
        expnt := ORD(ch) - ORD('0'); GetCh;
        while ch in Digits do begin
          expnt := expnt * 10 + ORD(ch) - ORD('0'); GetCh
          end; (* now calc. scale-factor *)
        if negExp then power := 0.1 else power := 10.0;
        if ODD(expnt) then total := total * power;
        expnt := expnt div 2;
        while expnt > 0 do begin
          power := power * power;
          if ODD(expnt) then total := total * power;
          expnt := expnt div 2
          end;
        end (* ch is a digit *)
      end; (* do exponent *)
    numValue := total
  end; (* ScanReal *)


procedure GetSymbol: (* lexical scanner *)

  var idString : {some string type} ;

  procedure GetIdent;
  begin (* assert: ch is alphabetic *)
    { details depend on lexical conventions}
  end;


  function Lookup : DescPtr;
  (* This procedure returns a pointer to the descriptor with identifier
     equal to idString. Returns nil if not found. *)
    begin
        { . . . }
    end;
```

Figure 8.26   *cont. overleaf*

Figure 8.26   *cont.*

```
begin
  (* assert: first char has already been read *)
  while ch = ' ' do GetCh;
  if ch in ['a'..'z', 'A'..'Z'] then begin
    GetIdent;
    idDescr := Lookup; (* seek in symbol table *)
    end
  else if ch in [EolMark,'+','-','*','/','(',')','^','0'..'9']
    then case ch of
      EolMark : symbol := endsmbl;
      '+' : begin symbol := plus;      GetCh end;
      '-' : begin symbol := minus;     GetCh end;
      '*' : begin symbol := mult;      GetCh end;
      '/' : begin symbol := divs;      GetCh end;
      '(' : begin symbol := Lbrac;     GetCh end;
      ')' : begin symbol := Rbrac;     GetCh end;
      '^' : begin symbol := upArrow;   GetCh end;
     '0','1','2','3','4','5','6','7','8','9'
          : ScanReal;
      end (* case *)
    else begin
    symbol := errsmbl;
    GetCh;
    end;
  (* assert: have read past end of symbol *)
end; (* GetSymbol *)

procedure InitScanner;
(*    This procedure initializes the input preconditions
      for scanner and parser. *)
begin
  GetCh;
  GetSymbol
end; (* InitScanner *)

(* end of lexical scanner procedures. *)

(* parser parser parser parser parser parser parser parser parser *)

(* Parser procedures:
   (i)  Error handling procedures;
   (ii) Recursive descent procedures. *)

procedure Parse;
  label 999; (* used for panic exit *)
  var result : REAL;

  (* error handling procedures: print message and take
     jump to a label declared in procedure Parse. *)
```

```
    procedure Error;
      begin
        WriteLn('Illegal expression.'); goto 999
      end;

    procedure BracError;
      begin
        WriteLn('Missing right brck.'); goto 999
      end;

    procedure SymError;
      begin
        WriteLn('Unknown Identifier.'); goto 999
      end;

    procedure EndError;
      begin
        WriteLn('Bad expression end.'); goto 999
      end;
```

(* Parser proc's: nested to avoid need for 'forward' declarations. *)
(* Precondition: GetSymbol has read past the end of previous phrase *)

```
procedure ExpRec(var val:REAL)
  var op     : SymbolType
    termval  : REAL

procedure TermRec(var val:REAL
  var op       : SymbolType;
      facval   : REAL;

  procedure FactRec(var val:REAL);
    var expval : REAL;

    procedure PrimRec(var val:REAL);
      begin (* primary -> ident | number | '(' exp ')' *)
        if symbol = number then begin
          val := numValue;
          GetSymbol;
        end
        else if symbol = ident then begin
          if idDescr = nil then SymError;
          val := idDescr^.value;
          GetSymbol;
        end (* symbol = ident *)
```

Figure 8.26   *cont. overleaf*

Figure 8.26   *cont.*

```
      else if symbol = Lbrac then begin
        GetSymbol; (* read past '(' *)
        ExpRec(val);
        if symbol = Rbrac then
          GetSymbol (* read past ')' *)
        else BracError;
        end (* symbol = Lbrac *)
      else Error;
    end; (* PrimRec *)

  begin (* factor -> primary ['^' primary] *),
    PrimRec(val);
    if symbol = upArrow then begin
      GetSymbol; (* get past '^' *)
      PrimRec(expval);
      val := exp(expval * ln(val));
      end;
  end; (* FactRec *)

  begin (* term -> factor (mulop factor)* *)
    FactRec(val);
    while symbol in [mult,divs] do begin
      op := symbol; GetSymbol;
      FactRec(facval);
      if op = mult then val := val * facval
                    else val := val / facval;
      end; (* while *)
  end; (* TermRec *)

begin (* exp = [addop] term (addop term)*. *)
  op := symbol; (* save for semantic action *)
  if symbol in [plus,minus] then GetSymbol;
  TermRec(val);
  if op = minus then val := - val; (* else nothing *)
  while symbol in [plus,minus] do begin
    op := symbol; GetSymbol;
    TermRec(termval);
    if op = plus
      then val := val + termval
      else val := val - termval;
    end (* while *);
end; (* ExpRec *)
```

```
    begin (* goal = exp endsmbl. *)
      InitScanner;
      ExpRec(result);
      if symbol = endsmbl then
        { use result . . . }
      else endError;
      999: ; (* just exits *)
    end; (* Parse *)

  begin (* mainline *)
    { . . . }
  end.
```

Figure 8.26   Expression evaluator code.

Exercises

8.1   Verify the director sets shown for the grammar in Figure 8.3.

8.2   Use the compacted sparse table technique with the default next-state mechanism, as described in Section 8.3, to compact the lookup table of the PDA for the **WildOption** grammar of Figures 8.3 and 8.4. Compare the operation of the standard compacted table version with the default next state version, paying attention both to space and time efficiency.

8.3   Implement the suggested extension to the case study.

8.4   The meta-grammar used in this book may be described in its own notation by the following grammar.

We suppose that any terminal or non-terminal identifier string of the target grammar is denoted *id*, and the lexical conventions allow symbols to be included within either kind of quote characters to form the lexical category *string*, denoted *str*.

$G \rightarrow$ *prod* {*prod*} *eof*.
prod $\rightarrow$ *id* '$\rightarrow$' *rhs* {'|' *rhs*}'.'.
  rhs $\rightarrow$ *tSeq* | 'ε'.
tSeq $\rightarrow$ *term* {*term*}.
term $\rightarrow$ *id* | *str* | '[' *tSeq* ']' | '{' *tSeq* '}'.

Show that this grammar is LL(1), but requires the use of the explicit fullstop at the end of each *prod* in order to meet this condition.

8.5   Consider the arithmetic grammar given below, in which multiply signs are implicit.

$G \rightarrow$ *expr* *eof*.
expr $\rightarrow$ [*addop*] *term* {*addop* *term*}.
term $\rightarrow$ *factor* {*mulop* *factor*}.

factor → *number* | '(' *expr* ')'.
addop → '+' | '−'.
mulop → '/' | ε.

Convert this grammar to the non-extended form, and derive the director sets in order to demonstrate the LL(1) property.

8.6 An alternative approach to the specification of expression grammars is used in the parallel programming language Occam. In this approach only element sequences linked by the same associative operator are permitted. Other operators must use parentheses. Thus '2/(2/2)' and '2*2*2' are both legal but '2/2/2' is not. An arithmetic subset of the grammar is

$\quad$ *expr* → ['−'] *prim* | *prim OP prim* | *prim* { *ASSOCOP prim* }.
$\quad$ *prim* → *number* | *variable* | '(' *expr* ')'.
ASSOCOP → '+' | '*'.
$\quad\quad$ *OP* → '+' | '*' | '−' | '/'.

The grammar as stated is not LL(1) (it is even ambiguous), and does not enforce the rule that only repetitions of the same associative operator are permitted in an unparenthesized phrase. Use factorization to transform the grammar into an LL(1) form, and also implement the above rule.

8.7 The following is an LL(1) extended (RRP) grammar for regular expressions.

$\quad$ *G* → *expr* ⊢. $\quad\quad\quad\quad$ Σ = {⊢,|,*,(,),*smbl*,∅,ε}
$\quad$ *expr* → *term* {'|' *term*}.
$\quad$ *term* → *factor* {*factor*}.
$\quad$ *factor* → *primary* ['*'].
primary → '(' *expr* ')' | *smbl* | '∅' | 'ε'.

Using the data structure devised for your answer to Exercise 4.8, work out how to insert table-building semantic actions into a recursive descent parser for this grammar.

8.8 Prove that any regular language may be recognized by a 'recursive descent' parser, without actually requiring any recursive procedure calls.

8.9 Suppose that the form of permitted productions in our meta-grammar is extended so as to permit alternation within right-hand sides (as well as between them). A typical production using this construct might be

A → α(β|γ)δ.

where α,β,γ,δ ∈ *V**. Deduce the conditions which must apply if this production is to correspond to those of an LL(1) CFG.

Further reading

The idea of recursive descent may be traced back at least as far as Conway (1963), and has become widely known and popular as a method of recognizing programming languages because of the wide distribution of the source code of a Pascal compiler which used the method (Wirth, 1971).

Mixed method parsers, which use an operator-precedence parsing algorithm for expression analysis and recursive descent for the rest of the syntax, are quite common in programming language compilers. However, as shown in this chapter, it is possible to control evaluation order of expressions in recursive descent, and hence to use recursive descent for the whole task.

Recursive FSA are not well covered in the standard compiler construction texts, although they did rank a mention in the unrevised first edition of Barrett and Couch's *Compiler Construction* (1979).

Chapter 9　**Bottom-up Parsing**

9.1　Introduction to bottom-up parsing

The class of languages which may be deterministically parsed bottom-up is greater than, and properly includes, the languages which may be parsed using the top-down methods. Unfortunately, the bottom-up parsing techniques require a little more effort to understand initially, since they are rather less intuitive than is recursive descent, for example. Furthermore, the construction of the better types of bottom-up parsers is too complicated to perform by hand, except for the most simple grammars. Nevertheless, the study of the bottom-up parsers is important for at least two reasons. Firstly, the existence of well-tested software tools which can automatically construct parsers from input grammars, makes the complexity of the method irrelevant to some extent. Secondly, the wider class of languages which may be accepted gives important flexibility to the language designer.

In this chapter we give a general overview of the bottom-up methods, concentrating on the detail of the so-called LR family of parsers, which produces a rightmost parse of a sentence during a left-to-right scan of an input string.

The object of the bottom-up parse is to start with the input string, which is, of course, a string of terminal symbols, and step-by-step to replace phrases by non-terminal symbols until finally the whole sentence is reduced to just the goal symbol S. The parse proceeds during a single left-to-right scan of the input string, and substring replacement takes place as soon as the phrase is recognized. If only correct replacements are made, as specified by the grammar, and provided that the initial string is a sentence in the language, then all the intermediate strings resulting during the parsing process will be sentential forms. Any one of the intermediate sentential forms arising during a parse may be thought of as consisting of two parts. The left-part is the partially reduced resultant of that part of the input string scanned so far, while the right-part is the remainder of the original input string.

The intermediate strings resulting from the bottom-up parsing of a string in the Polish expression language of Section 7.1.1 are shown here in Figure 9.1. The sample string is the same one as was used to demonstrate the LL(1) parsing method, so Figure 9.1 should be carefully compared and contrasted with Figure 7.1. For completeness, the form of the implicit trees are included in the figure.

One of the consequences of the immediate replacement of the recognized phrases, is that the non-terminal symbols are substituted at the right-hand end of what we have called the left-part of the sentential form. Now, the left-part is a string from the vocabulary, V, while the right-part contains only terminal symbols. It follows, therefore, that each newly substituted non-terminal symbol must be the rightmost non-terminal in the whole sentential form. This observation shows that the successive steps in the bottom-up parse are just the sentential forms of a rightmost derivation of the sentence. They are produced in reverse sequence however, so that the goal symbol is the ending point of the parse, rather than the starting point of the derivation process.

Since the method uses a left-to-right scan, and retraces the steps of a rightmost derivation, all parsers of this kind are called **LR parsers**. Notice that the actual replacement of a production right-hand-side by the non-terminal symbol does not take place until after all symbols of the right-hand side have been recognized. Contrast this situation with the top-down methods, where the production must be predicted in advance.

In practice, the parsing process is implemented by a push-down automaton, in which the stack holds information about what we have called the left-part of the sentential form. The operation of the automaton is as follows. Initially the stack is empty, and as input symbols are read, they are pushed (shifted) onto the stack. Whenever a substring replacement is to take place, the recognized substring is popped off the stack, and the substituted non-terminal symbol is pushed in its place.

A PDA move which transfers an input symbol onto the stack is called a **shift move**, while a move which substitutes a non-terminal symbol for a substring on the top of the stack is called a **reduce move**. Notice, however, that the use of the term 'reduce' is not to be taken too literally. When a reduction step uses a production rule, $A \to \alpha$ say, the number of symbols removed from the stack is $|\alpha|$, the length of the production right-hand-side, while exactly one symbol, A, is subsequently pushed onto the stack in its place. Since production right-hand-sides may be 0, 1, or more symbols long, the 'reduction' may increase the depth of the stack, leave it unchanged, or reduce it, respectively. After parsing a sentence, the final configuration of the automaton has the input string exhausted and the stack contains exactly one symbol, the goal symbol S.

The critical question, which we have glossed over so far, is to determine how the need for a reduce step is to be recognized. An allied problem is to characterize those properties of CFGs which permit an automaton to perform such recognition deterministically. Clearly, an inability to recognize the uniquely correct move for the PDA to make at

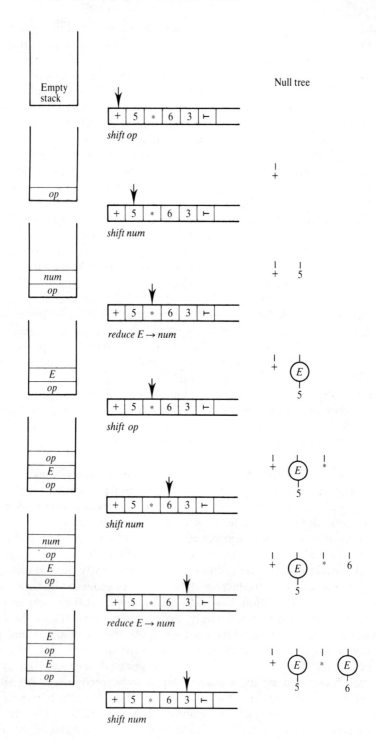

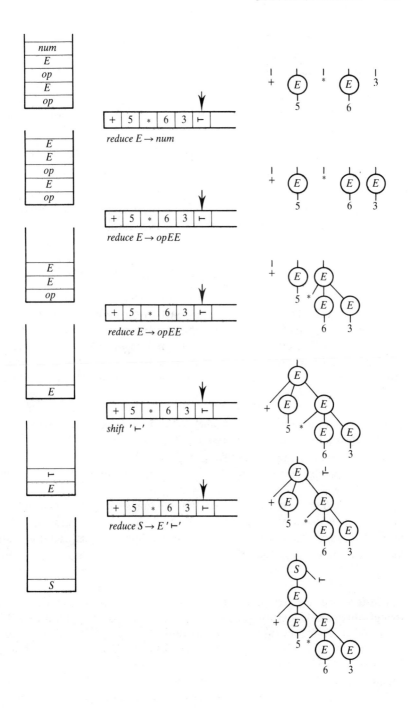

Figure 9.1 Bottom-up parsing of a Polish notation expression.

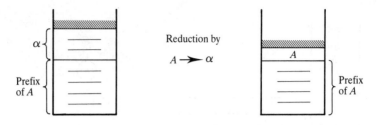

Figure 9.2   Parser stack before and after reduction.

some point during a parse would lead to the usual kind of backtracking system, with all of the inefficiency which that implies.

9.1.1   Recognizing viable prefixes of non-terminals

The whole viability of the LR family of parsers depends on a single, surprising result. The language of left-part strings, whose presence on the stack of a PDA indicates the possibility of a particular reduce step, is regular. The PDA controller, therefore, is just a finite state machine.

To be definite, suppose we wish to derive a rule which defines the language of permissible stack contents at a point at which the production

$$A \rightarrow \alpha$$

may be used in a reduce step. Clearly, the stack must have the string α at the top, but may have some other symbols below that. We call the string of symbols which appear below the production right-hand-side on the stack, the **prefix** of the symbol A. The situation might be as shown in Figure 9.2.

We are led then to consider the language of prefixes which may precede the non-terminal A in a sentential form. Suppose that we call this prefix language P_A. Now consider some production which contains an A in its right-hand side, for example

$$B \rightarrow \alpha A \beta$$

where α and β are strings from the vocabulary V. We conclude that any string which may legitimately precede a B may be turned into a legal prefix of A by following it by the string α.

Notice that here we are arguing backwards. We are not saying that any $\alpha A \beta$ string on the top of the stack may be replaced by a B. Instead, because of the context-free property, we are noting that any B symbol which appears in a sentential form may be replaced by $\alpha A \beta$. We argue, in effect, that if a symbol B may appear with that particular left-context, then the same prefix, followed by string α, is one of the possible prefixes of symbol A.

In terms of the languages involved, the set of strings of the product language formed from the prefix language of P_B and the string α is a subset of the prefix language P_A. In symbols

$$P_B\alpha \subseteq P_A$$

where P_B is defined consistently as the prefix language for the non-terminal symbol B.

This last set relation is equivalent to a production of a grammar defining P_A. Instead of saying 'a valid prefix of B followed by the string α is a valid prefix of A', we may equally say 'the syntactic category *prefix of A* may be replaced by the category *prefix of B*, followed by the string α'. In more familiar terms this is just the left-linear production

$$P_A \to P_B\alpha.$$

There will be as many productions for P_A as there are occurrences of the symbol A on the right of the productions of our original grammar. The (sub)languages of permissible prefixes, or **viable prefixes**, as we shall call them, are thus each defined by a finite set of left-linear productions, which therefore define a regular language.

In this regular grammar, the Ps are the non-terminal symbols, and strings from the original vocabulary, V, form the terminal symbols. We need not be concerned that the alphabet of the regular grammar might be unbounded. Although the alphabet is comprised of strings from the vocabulary of the original grammar, the finite number and bounded length of the original CFG productions provide that only a finite number of left-linear productions will be generated for the prefix-recognizing grammar. Hence, the corresponding prefix-recognizing automaton will have only a finite number of states.

In the case of the Polish string language of Chapter 7, the grammar is

$$
\begin{array}{ll}
S \to E \vdash. & N = \{S,E\} \\
E \to num & \Sigma = \{num,op,\vdash\} \\
\quad \to op\ E\ E.
\end{array}
$$

The productions of the prefix language for P are

$$
\begin{array}{l}
P_E \to P_S\varepsilon \\
\quad \to P_E\ op \\
\quad \to P_E\ op\ E.
\end{array}
$$

In this case we have padded the first production for P_E, which is derived from the first production of the original grammar, with an empty string ε, so as to fit it into the left-linear mould. Although ε is not a symbol of the underlying vocabulary, V, it does belong to V^*, and thus qualifies for use

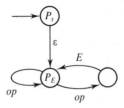

Figure 9.3   Viable prefix recognizer for the Polish string language.

as a 'terminal' symbol of the left-linear grammar which defines the viable prefixes.

It is not necessary to write any productions for the viable prefixes of the goal symbol, since for any context-free language the prefix language of the goal symbol is necessarily just the empty string. That is, in all cases we must have $P_S = \{\varepsilon\}$.

The correspondence between left-linear grammars and the equivalent NFSA is explored in the model solution to Exercise 6.7. It is wise to review this solution before continuing, if this has not been done.

The left-linear productions define a regular language which corresponds to some non-deterministic state diagram. In practice we do not actually need to form the regular grammar, since it is a simple matter to construct a non-deterministic state diagram directly from the productions of the original grammar. The process is performed as follows: A state is defined for each prefix syntactic category, with the start state corresponding to the prefix of the goal symbol. To every occurrence of a non-terminal symbol, A, on the right of a production, $B \rightarrow \alpha A \beta$ say, there is a transition labelled α, leading from P_B to P_A. For example, the state diagram for the Polish string language is given in Figure 9.3. Notice that this figure corresponds to a non-deterministic FSA.

If it should happen that the string α, in the production $B \rightarrow \alpha A \beta$, has a length greater than one, then there is a sequence of states leading from state P_B to P_A which spells out the symbols of the string α.

9.1.2 Recognizing the left context of a reduction move

Having defined the viable prefix languages for each of the non-terminal symbols in our original grammar, we may now proceed to recognize the stack contents corresponding to the complete left-context of each *reduce* move in our parser. As indicated in Figure 9.2, the stack content for a reduction

$$A \rightarrow \gamma$$

Figure 9.4   Left-context recognizer for production $A \to \gamma$.

is any viable prefix of A, followed by the string γ. We may recognize this language by a state machine formed by augmenting the state diagram of the prefix recognizer, according to the schema indicated in Figure 9.4. A chain of states, corresponding to the symbols of γ, lead from the prefix-recognizing state to a left-context-recognizing state. Each state which corresponds to the recognition of the left-context of a production has an exit transition added, indicated here by a double-headed arrow. Such exit transitions are labelled by the production for which the corresponding state indicates the left-context.

The above process has been carried out for the Polish string language prefix-recognizer, and results in the left-context recognizing automaton of Figure 9.5. This NFSA may be made deterministic in the usual way, using the subset construction procedure of Chapter 4, resulting in the DFSA of Figure 9.6.

The state diagram in Figure 9.6 completely defines the actions of a PDA in parsing the Polish string language, so we will briefly explore this example in some detail.

At the start of the parsing process, the PDA controller, as defined by the DFSA of Figure 9.6, is in the start state, and the stack is empty. The machine proceeds to read terminal symbols from the input string, and to shift them onto the stack. The state of the finite control is updated at each step, so that the controller is in the state corresponding to the stack contents. The parser is able to perform a *reduce* move when the DFSA reaches a state with an exit transition labelled by some production. The right-hand side of that production, which is necessarily on the top of the

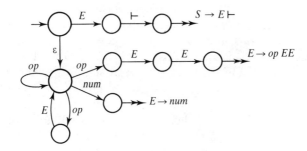

Figure 9.5   Characteristic NFSA for the Polish string language.

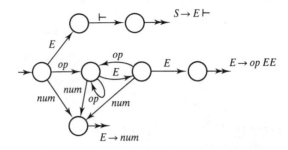

Figure 9.6   Characteristic DFSA for the Polish string language.

stack, is popped off and replaced by the left-hand-side non-terminal symbol.

After such a reduce move, it is necessary to re-establish the correct state of the DFSA based on the newly modified stack configuration. In principle this may be done by beginning in the start state and reading the stack from bottom to top, but in practice this is unnecessary. The practical method of re-establishing the FSA state is to retrace the transition path corresponding to the production right-hand-side as the symbols are popped from the stack during the reduce step. This process moves the FSA back to some **backup** state. The final, re-entry state is then established by the transition, indicated by the left-hand-side non-terminal symbol, which leads out of the *backup* state.

It is crucial to notice that the stack must contain the actual path information if the FSA is to be backed-up in the manner described. For example, in Figure 9.6, if a reduction move $E \rightarrow num$ is indicated, then there are three possible states to back-up to. The problem is neatly solved by pushing the state ordinals onto the stack, rather than the transition symbols as previously indicated.

The left-context recognizing DFSA, which is formed by the method outlined above, is called the **characteristic machine** for the context-free grammar.

The state diagram of the characteristic machine of a grammar may be thought of as one component of the two-part PDA controller. So long as the parser action is *shift*, the input string is read, and the state updated exactly as for any other FSA, except for the action of pushing the previous state ordinal onto the stack at each step. However, when the condition for any *reduce* action is met, the action of the machine is to abandon normal FSA interpretation, and to pass control to the reduction controller. The reduction controller performs the stack adjustments, and then restarts the FSA in the required re-entry state.

The transitions between states of the characteristic machine, the *shift edges*, are ordinary transitions. The *exit transitions*, on the other hand,

```
begin
   state := start;
   InitializeEmptyStack;
   GetSymbol;
   repeat (* until symbol = endSymbol *)
      action := PdaAction[state,symbol]; (* lookup in table *)
      if action = shift
         then begin (* normal FSA move *)
            Push(state); (* save path info. *)
            state := nextState[state,symbol];
            if symbol <> endSymbol then GetSymbol;
            end
         else (* adjust stack and establish re-entry state *)
            {reduce by indicated production};
   until symbol = endSymbol;
   Accept := not error and (topOfStackSmbl = goalSmbl);
end;
```

Figure 9.7   LR parser, outline of FSA interpreter part.

correspond to control jumps, and are labelled by the production which corresponds to the particular reduce action which is to be performed. This particular view of the parsing algorithm leads to the code in Figure 9.7. The details of the *reduce* procedure are omitted so as to stress the similarity with an ordinary FSA interpretation algorithm.

Note carefully that inside the **repeat** loop there is a *GetSymbol* action in only one of the two branches of the **if**. This observation emphasizes the possibility that a whole cascade of reductions may take place, without the consumption of any symbols of the input string.

The details of the reduce action, elided from Figure 9.7, are shown in Figure 9.8, in the form of a procedure. The diagram in Figure 9.8 is the reduce action as it appears on the relevant fragment of the state diagram of the characteristic machine.

Note carefully the special treatment of empty productions in this algorithm. In a sense the treatment is consistent, since if the production right-hand-side length $|\gamma|$ is zero, then we must pop (-1) symbols, i.e. push!

In the fragment of the characteristic machine shown in Figure 9.8, we say that the exit transition, $A \to \gamma$, *looks back at* the A transition out of state p. In the general case, a reduce exit may *look back at* a number of alternative transitions. In any particular instance of such a reduction step, the lookback transition which is chosen must correspond to the actual path by which the reducing state was entered. This is why it is necessary

```
(* procedure 'reduce by indicated production' *)
begin
   LhsSmbl := {LHS symbol of indicated production};
   RhsLength := {RHS length of indicated production};
   if RhsLength = 0 (* empty production *)
      then Push(state)
      else (* trace back state path *)
         {Pop (RhsLength − 1) state ordinals from the stack};
   (* now establish re-entry state *)
   state := nextState[topOfStackState,LhsSmbl];
end;
```

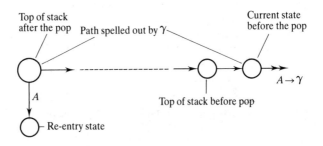

Top of stack after the pop   Path spelled out by γ Current state before the pop

A

Top of stack before pop

$A \rightarrow \gamma$

Re-entry state

Figure 9.8   Details of the reduce action.

to stack the state ordinals. In the characteristic machine of Figure 9.6, for example, it may be seen that the reduce exit, $E \rightarrow num$, looks back at the E transitions out of states 0, 3, and 4. The reader should check that this point is understood.

9.1.3   Conflicts in the characteristic machine

We are always able to convert any left-context recognizing NFSA into a deterministic characteristic machine by the usual methods. Unfortunately, forming a deterministic characteristic FSA does not, in itself, guarantee a deterministic parser. The potential difficulty is that, while the PDA control may always have a deterministic transition function, it may have a non-deterministic action function.

During the NFSA to DFSA conversion, states are merged as demanded by the subset construction process. If it should happen that a particular state ends up with exit transitions which are labelled by two or more distinct productions, then it is not clear which of these reductions is to be invoked in any particular case. Such an ambiguity is called a *reduce–reduce* **conflict**. Similarly, a state of the characteristic machine may possess an exit transition which is labelled by some production, but also has one or more out-transitions which are labelled by terminal symbols. In this case it is not clear whether a *shift* or a *reduce* should be performed when the state is entered, so we say that a ***shift–reduce* conflict** exists. In general, any state which has either a *reduce–reduce* or a *shift–reduce* conflict, or both, is said to be **inconsistent**, or **inadequate**.

If the characteristic machine of some grammar has no inadequate states, then the parser which it defines is said to have the LR(0) property. For example, the machine of Figure 9.6 has no inadequate states, demonstrating that the Polish string language is LR(0), as well as being LL(1). It is an exercise for this chapter to show that the Reverse Polish expression grammar, despite failing the LL(1) test, is nevertheless LR(0). In general, left recursion causes no particular problems for LR parsers. The zero index in the name LR(0) indicates that no symbol lookahead is required for parsers of this class.

It is important to note that when a grammar fails to be LR(0), the characteristic machine still has the correct parsing action included among the actions attached to the states. In other words, the LR(0) parser is always 'correct' in the sense that it indicates a correct action in each state. The problem is that when there is a choice of action indicated by the LR(0) machine, the one action which is correct in any particular instance must be selected by other means. The various mechanisms which be tried in order to resolve these conflicts are discussed in Sections 9.2 and 9.3.

9.1.4   Section checklist and summary definitions

1. The name 'LR'.
   - Any parser from the LR-family reconstructs a rightmost parse tree for a sentence in a single left-to-right scan of the input.

2. Bottom-up parsing and PDA.
   - At intermediate points of the parse, a forest of subtrees has been formed which derives the terminal symbols of the left-hand end of the sentence: the symbols already encountered.
   - The root symbols of the subtrees are the stack symbols of the LR PDA at that point in the parse.

3. Moves of an LR automaton.
   - A *shift* move of an LR automaton consists of reading an input symbol, and pushing (shifting) it onto the stack.
   - A *reduce* move of an LR automaton consists of popping the symbols of a production right-hand-side from the stack, replacing them by the left-hand-side symbol of the selected production.

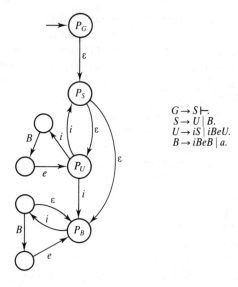

$$G \rightarrow S \vdash.$$
$$S \rightarrow U \mid B.$$
$$U \rightarrow iS \mid iBeU.$$
$$B \rightarrow iBeB \mid a.$$

Figure 9.9   Prefix recognizer for the **if-then-else** grammar.

4. Recognition of reduce contexts.
   - The languages of stack-content strings, which indicate reduction by particular productions of a grammar, are regular.
   - The recognition of reduction left-contexts may be carried out by an FSA called the characteristic machine of the grammar.
   - The characteristic machine of a grammar is also called the LR(0) FSA for the grammar.

5. The LR(0) property.
   - If some state of a characteristic machine has two or more reductions we say the state has a *reduce–reduce* conflict.
   - If some state of a characteristic machine has a reduce exit, as well as one or more shift transitions, we say the state has a *shift–reduce* conflict.
   - Any state which has a conflict is said to be inconsistent, or (synonomously) inadequate.
   - A grammar which has a characteristic machine with no inconsistent states is said to be LR(0).

6. The LR(0) machine is correct.
   - Every *shift* and *reduce* action indicated by a characteristic machine is correct for some sentence in the language.

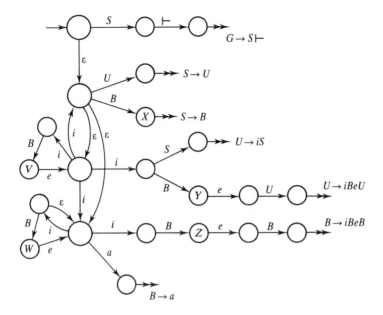

Figure 9.10 Characteristic NFSA for the **if-then-else** grammar.

- If a state of an LR(0) automaton is inadequate, then one of the indicated actions is correct, but we must find out which one by other means.

9.2 LR parsing with symbol lookahead

This section, and the next, explores the possibilities for resolving the conflicts in inadequate states of the characteristic machine by symbol lookahead. The starting point for these methods is the construction of the characteristic machine for the grammar.

The unambiguous **if-then-else** grammar discussed in Section 8.4.2 is used as a first example of these techniques. The state diagram for the prefix recognizer is shown in Figure 9.9, while the complete characteristic NFSA is shown in Figure 9.10.[†] In this grammar the structure due to other statements, or to the expression sublanguage has been suppressed by, in effect, pretending that the syntactic categories whose structure we wish to suppress are simply terminal symbols of the grammar. For example, it is assumed that **if** *expression* **then** may be replaced by a single

---

† In the model solutions to the exercises for this chapter, an alternative method is given for forming the NFSA directly from the grammar. This typically leads to a slightly less laborious subset construction procedure.

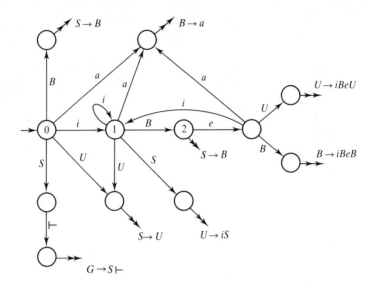

Figure 9.11   Characteristic DFSA for the **if-then-else** grammar.

symbol, i, while all other statements are represented by a. Finally, the symbol **else** has been abbreviated to e.

Recall that, in these NFSA, the transitions which are labelled by terminal or non-terminal symbols correspond to the action of reading the corresponding symbol, and, in effect, shifting it onto the stack. The exit transitions do not cause a symbol-reading action, and thus might consistently be thought of as being labelled by an epsilon. The actual label, associated with each exit transition in the state diagram, indicates the particular production associated with the reduce action of that exit.

The NFSA of Figure 9.10 may be made deterministic by the usual subset construction procedure. The resulting DFSA is shown in Figure 9.11.

The characteristic machine for this grammar is 'almost' LR(0). The only inconsistent state is state 2, which has a *shift–reduce* conflict. This inconsistent state arises, in the DFSA, from the merging of the states labelled V, W, X, Y, and Z in the NFSA of Figure 9.10. Note that if the characteristic machine were LR(0), then the parsing action would depend on the state only. If this were the case, an implementation based on a table-lookup would only require a one-dimensional array for the action function *PdaAction*.

Since a table-driven automaton requires a two-dimensional table to store the next state function, it seems a natural step to see if using a two-dimensional table indexed on the (*state*, *symbol*) pair might also resolve the conflicts in the inconsistent states of the characteristic machine.

Consider the conflict involved in state 2 of Figure 9.11. The choices for possible actions are to *shift*, which might be correct if the next symbol happens to be an e, or to *reduce* using the production $S \rightarrow B$. These two alternative actions may be distinguished, provided that the next symbols which may follow a reduction by $S \rightarrow B$ in state 2, do not include the symbol e.

9.2.1 Using the *FOLLOW* set

In Chapter 7 we defined the *FOLLOW* set of a non-terminal symbol. Clearly, in terms of the definition of *FOLLOW* (Section 7.3.7), if the next input symbol is not in *FOLLOW(S)*, then the reduction $S \rightarrow B$ cannot be valid. In fact, for this example, the relevant *FOLLOW* set is given by $FOLLOW(S) = \{\vdash\}$. Since the symbol e is not included in the *FOLLOW* set, we deduce that the correct action in state 2 may be determined as follows. If the next symbol (the lookahead) is e, then a shift action is consistent. Conversely, if the next symbol is $\vdash$ then it is consistent to reduce by the production $S \rightarrow B$. Finally, in the event that the next symbol is neither of these, we may immediately conclude that the input string is invalid.

The use of the *FOLLOW* sets is often sufficient to resolve the conflicts of inconsistent states. If this is so, then since the *FOLLOW* sets are easily generated, this is a simple solution to the problem. In the case that this stratagem resolves all of the conflicts in the characteristic machine of a particular grammar, then we say that the grammar is **simple LR(1)**. Since we are almost always interested in the case of a single symbol lookahead, we will often drop the index and refer to these grammars as being SLR.

9.2.2 An SLR grammar for regular expressions

We now pursue a somewhat more substantial example to further illustrate the SLR technique. A grammar which defines the language of regular expressions is

$S \rightarrow E\vdash.$
$E \rightarrow T \mid T'|'E.$
$T \rightarrow F \mid FT.$
$F \rightarrow a \mid F'*' \mid '(' E ')'.$

where a denotes an identifier symbol. Note that this grammar is not LL(1), although it may be made LL(1) by left factorization of the groups of productions for the non-terminals, E and T, and the introduction of a new non-terminal to eliminate the left recursion in non-terminal symbol

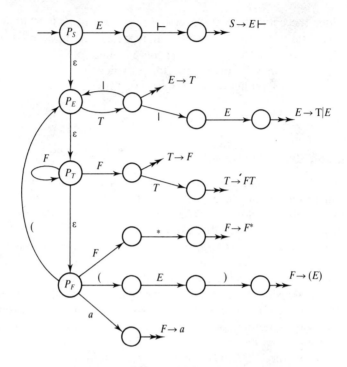

Figure 9.12   NFSA for regular expression grammar.

F. Such an equivalent LL(1) grammar has already been seen, in Figure 7.3.

The NFSA which recognizes the production left-contexts of the given grammar is shown in Figure 9.12.

When the subset construction process is applied to the NFSA of Figure 9.12, the characteristic machine of Figure 9.13 results.

In this characteristic machine, two *shift–reduce* conflicts exist. State 1 is inconsistent, since it may be exited by a normal transition corresponding to the shifting of any of the symbols *, (or a. Alternatively, the reduce exit indicates a reduction by the production $T \rightarrow F$. Similarly, state 2 is inconsistent, since it may be left either by the shifting of a |, or a reduction by the production $E \rightarrow T$.

The *FOLLOW* sets are easily derived from the grammar.

$FOLLOW(E) = \{\vdash, ')'\}$,
$FOLLOW(T) = FOLLOW(E) \cup \{'|'\}$
$\qquad = \{\vdash, ')', '|'\}$

In state 1, the terminal shift-set, $\{*,(,a\}$, is disjoint from $FOLLOW(T)$, so the SLR method resolves the conflict. To be specific, in state 1, if the lookahead terminal symbol belongs to $\{\vdash,),|\}$, then *reduce* is the correct action. Conversely, if the lookahead symbol does not belong to

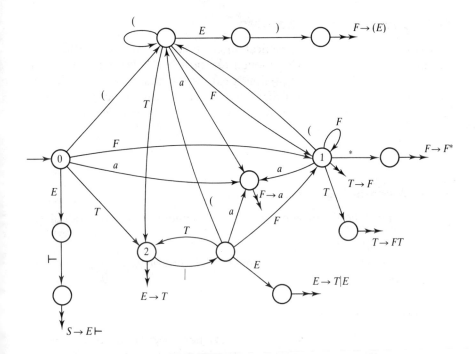

Figure 9.13   Characteristic DFSA for regular expression grammar.

FOLLOW(*T*), then the correct action is *shift*. In state 2, similarly, the SLR method is successful in resolving the conflict, since the *shift* and *FOLLOW* sets, {|} and {⊢,)}, are disjoint. In this particular case, an invalid string might have a lookahead symbol which belongs to neither set. This third possibility may be thought of as specifying a *shift* action, with a transition which leads straight to an error state.

9.2.3   Section checklist and summary definitions

1. Symbol lookahead parsers.
   - LR-family parsers may attempt to resolve the conflicts of inconsistent states by looking ahead at symbols of the input string.

2. Simple LR parsers.
   - If, in some state of a characteristic machine, the action to reduce by some production, $A \rightarrow \gamma$, is correct, then the next input symbol must necessarily belong to the set *FOLLOW*(*A*).
   - If the use of *FOLLOW* sets resolves the non-determinism of the action function in every inconsistent state, we say that the grammar is simple-LR(1), or SLR.

9.3 Lookahead LR parsers

Almost no grammars of practical interest are LR(0), while the SLR technique is almost powerful enough for most of the languages in which we are interested. For example, most expression grammars are SLR, and most constructs of modern programming languages may be described by SLR grammars. However, there are occasional problems, as we will now see.

9.3.1 A non-SLR grammar example

Consider the following fragment of a programming language grammar.

> *Goal* → *Statement* ';'.
> *Statement* → *ProcCall* | *Variable* '=' *Expression*.
> *ProcCall* → *identifier*.
> *Variable* → *identifier*.
> *Expression* → . . . .

We have assumed, for simplicity, that there are no array indices or procedure parameters. Furthermore, although we do not show this explicitly, we will assume that the substructure of expressions involves infix operators.

The grammar fragment has a characteristic machine as shown in Figure 9.14. As usual, the names of all of the symbols in the figure have been abbreviated to their initial letters. Note that state 1 has a *reduce–reduce* conflict.

We may easily calculate that *FOLLOW(ProcCall)* = {;}. Unfortunately, even without the details of the expression subgrammar, it is easy to see that the final symbol of an infix expression may be a variable, and hence the *FOLLOW* set for the syntactic category *Variable* also includes the semicolon symbol. We must conclude here that the *FOLLOW* sets for the left-hand-side symbols involved in the two reductions do not resolve the conflict. In effect, the SLR method has proved to be too weak.

The failure of the SLR method does not mean that a single-symbol lookahead is insufficient to resolve the conflict. Rather, it implies that the *FOLLOW* set is too general a mechanism to narrow down the set of possible symbols which may appear after a particular reduction.

In particular, the *FOLLOW* set takes no account of the actual context in which the particular reduction appears. In this example, it is obvious that the only valid symbol which may follow a variable at the beginning of a statement is an equals sign, '='. The troublesome symbol ';' can only follow a variable when it occurs as part of an expression, but never when it is part of the left-hand side of an assignment. Intuitively, it

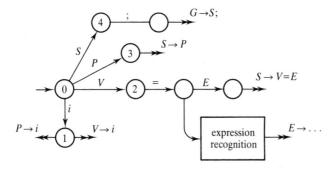

Figure 9.14 Characteristic machine for statement grammar.

may be seen that a lookahead of '=' indicates a valid reduction by the production of $V \rightarrow i$, while a lookahead of ';' indicates a reduction by the production of $P \rightarrow i$.

9.3.2 Forming the lookahead set of a reduction

There is a more powerful tool to resolve conflicts of the kind in the last example, that is, a separate *FOLLOW* set for each exit transition of the characteristic machine. We call such a set the **lookahead set** of that particular reduction. The calculation of the lookahead sets may be performed directly from the characteristic machine. We informally introduce the concepts involved in this calculation here, and defer discussion of the algorithmic means of forming these sets to the references.

If the method to be described resolves all of the conflicts of all the inconsistent states in the characteristic machine, then we say that the grammar is **lookahead LR(1)**, or LALR for short. A parser which is based on a characteristic machine which has been made deterministic by this method is called an **LALR parser**.

Referring to Figure 9.14 once more, we wish to deduce the consequences of choosing a particular reduction in state 1. Suppose, first, that we choose the exit marked $V \rightarrow i$ from state 1, which leads to the machine being re-entered via the V transition out of state 0. We may uniquely identify this transition as $(0,V)$, and we say that the exit under consideration **looks back** at transition $(0,V)$. The $(0,V)$ transition, in turn, leads to state 2, from which a symbol '=' may be shifted. We will say that the equals symbol is **readable** from the transition $(0,V)$. We conclude that the lookahead set which results from taking the $V \rightarrow i$ exit out of state 1 is given by

$$lookahead(1, V \rightarrow i) = \{=\}.$$

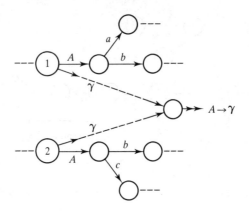

Figure 9.15   Example of a lookahead set construction.

In cases where an exit action *looks back at* several transitions, each of which *reads* one or more symbols, the *lookahead* set is the union of the sets of symbols which are readable from each transition. Figure 9.15 illustrates just such a typical situation.

In Figure 9.15, the reduction $A \rightarrow \gamma$ looks back at two transitions: $(1,A)$ and $(2,A)$. From $(1,A)$ the read set is $\{a,b\}$, while from $(2,A)$ the read set is $\{b,c\}$. It follows that the lookahead set for the reduction is $\{a,b,c\}$.

Consideration of the other reduction involved in the conflict in Figure 9.14, illustrates another important point. The exit $(1, P \rightarrow i)$ looks back at transition $(0,P)$, but $(0,P)$ does not directly read any symbol. However, having followed the transition $(0,P)$, the machine enters state 3. From state 3, another reduction exit may be taken. This new reduce exit, $(3, S \rightarrow P)$, in turn, *looks back at* transition $(0,S)$, which then *reads* a symbol ';'. We say that the transition $(0,P)$ *includes* the transition $(0,S)$, since any set of symbols readable from $(0,S)$ is included in the symbols readable from $(0,P)$.

Summarizing the above argument, we conclude that the lookahead set of the reduction $(1, P \rightarrow i)$ is just $\{;\}$, since that exit *looks back at* $(0,P)$, which *includes* $(0,S)$, which *reads* ';'.

A more general case of the *includes* relation is illustrated in Figure 9.16. Here, transition $(2,A)$ includes $(3,B)$.

In general, the lookahead set of any particular reduction is the set of all symbols which may be shifted next by the characteristic machine if the reduction is performed, allowing for the possibility of a cascade of consequent reductions. In practice, the algorithmic determination of these sets must also take into account the possibility of reductions by nullable symbols. This possibility affects the way in which both the *read* set and the *includes* relation are computed, as illustrated in Figure 9.17.

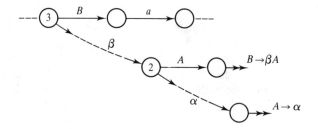

Figure 9.16 A more general lookahead calculation. Transition $(2,A)$ includes $(3,B)$.

In the figure, transition $(2,A)$ includes the transition $(3,B)$, since starting from transition $(2,A)$, the reduction $(1, \ B \to \alpha A Y)$ may be reached without shifting any new terminal symbols. Similarly, transition $(3,B)$ *reads* the symbol b, since the intervening non-terminal transition may be traversed without consuming any input-string terminal symbols.

It may seem curious, at first sight, that we have explained the generation of lookahead sets in terms of relations between transitions, rather than states. It is possible to provide a development based on states, which turns out to be not quite as general (or as powerful) as the full LALR method. The flaws of this *not-quite*-LALR method are explained in DeRemer and Penello (1982).

Discussion of the reasoning involved in calculating the LALR lookaheads has lead us far afield from our specific example. Let us now summarize what we found along the way. State 1 of Figure 9.14 has a *reduce–reduce* conflict. The reduce exit $P \to i$ has an LALR lookahead of $\{;\}$, while the reduce exit $V \to i$ has an LALR lookahead set $\{=\}$. The LALR technique has thus resolved the conflict, and we say that the grammar is LALR.

The LALR parsers are the most widely used bottom-up parsers at the present time. They appear to strike an ideal balance between the power

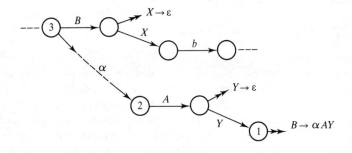

Figure 9.17 Example of symbol erasure.

of the underlying method, and the complexity of its implementation. In practice, the bottom-up parsers are often simplified by modifications to the CFG, which reduces the total number of non-terminal symbols and productions. This is often done in such a way that the modified grammar is ambiguous. Separate disambiguating rules must then be applied by the parser, so as to produce a deterministic machine. These techniques are discussed in Section 9.5.

9.3.3 Section checklist and summary definitions

1. Lookahead LR parsers.
   - An LALR (lookahead-LR) parser has a set of lookahead symbols attached to each reduce exit of the characteristic machine.
   - The lookahead sets for each reduction are computed from the characteristic machine. In general, each set is a subset of the *FOLLOW* set used for the same purpose in SLR parsers.
   - Where the use of the lookahead set resolves the non-determinism of the action function in every inconsistent state, we say that the grammar is LALR.

2. Computing the LALR sets.
   - The lookahead set of a reduction is the set of all terminal symbols which may be read from states reached after performing the reduction under consideration, but without consuming any further input symbols.
   - States may be reached directly, as re-entry states of the reduction, or indirectly, by a chain of consequent reductions following the prescribed reduction, without interspersed *shift* moves.

9.4 Other bottom-up parsers

9.4.1 The canonical LR(*k*) parsers

We now consider the extension of the LR method to the so-called **canonical LR(*k*) parsers**. There is some discussion of the LR(1) case.

The SLR and LALR parsers are essentially LR(0) automata which attempt to use symbol lookahead to resolve conflicts in inadequate states. It is possible, as an alternative, to specify an automaton which has separate states to take into account the right context of any particular production rule. If such an automaton takes into account *k* symbols of right context, we call it a **canonical LR(*k*) automaton**.

Let us suppose that we have a CFG, augmented, if necessary, with an extra production to ensure that a k-symbol lookahead exists for every non-terminal symbol. Such an augmenting production might be

$$G \rightarrow S \underbrace{\vdash \vdash \vdash \ldots \vdash.}_{k\text{-symbols}}$$

where G is a new goal symbol.

We wish to derive the relationship between the viable prefix languages of the various non-terminal symbols, in the presence of prescribed length-k right contexts. In particular, suppose that the goal symbol, G, has a rightmost derivation of some sentential form

$$G =>^+ \alpha A u v$$

where α is a string from V^*, A is the rightmost non-terminal, and the length of the terminal symbol string, u, is k. We refer to the complete string, uv, as the *right-context* of A, and to u as the length-k right-context of A. Note that, since this is a rightmost derivation, the right context is a terminal string, while the left context is a string from the vocabulary. We say that the prefix string, α, belongs to the language 'prefix of A with length-k right-context u'. This language is denoted here by $P_{A,u}$.

In order to reason about the relationships between the various P prefix languages, we define k-symbol extensions of the *FIRST* and *FOLLOW* sets which were introduced in Chapter 7. $FIRST_k(\beta)$ is the language of all length-k prefixes of the terminal strings which may be derived from a string β. In symbols

$$FIRST_k(\beta) = \{u : \beta =>^* uv, \text{ where } v \in \Sigma^*, \text{ and } u \in \Sigma^k\}$$

Similarly, $FOLLOW_k(A$, for any non-terminal symbol A, is the set of all length-k terminal strings which may follow symbol A in a sentential form. In symbols,

$$FOLLOW_k(A) = \{u : \text{there exist } \alpha,v \text{ such that } G =>^* \alpha A u v, \text{ where } \alpha \in V^*, u \in \Sigma^k, v \in \Sigma^*, \text{ and } G \text{ is the goal symbol}\}$$

The first k symbols of any right-context string of a non-terminal symbol A, must thus belong to $FOLLOW_k(A)$, and we are led to consider the prefix languages $P_{A,u}$ for each symbol A for every string u in $FOLLOW_k(A)$.

The viable prefix languages are related to each other in ways which may be directly determined from the productions of the grammar. For example, consider a typical production, $A \rightarrow \alpha B \beta$, where A and B are non-terminals, and α and β are (possibly empty) strings from the vocabulary V.

Let us suppose that the string u belongs to $FOLLOW_k(A)$, so that a

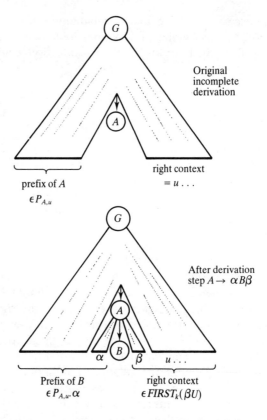

Figure 9.18   Prefix relationship with prescribed right-context.

prefix language, $P_{A,u}$, is defined. If the production $A \rightarrow \alpha B\beta$ is used to replace A in a sentential form in which the A has right-context u, then the prefix of B is the original prefix of A followed by string α, while the right-context will belong to $FIRST_k(\beta u)$. These steps are illustrated in Figure 9.18.

We may conclude from the production $A \rightarrow \alpha B\beta$ that the prefix languages are related by set relations equivalent to the left-linear productions

$$P_{B,w} \rightarrow P_{A,u}\alpha$$

for every w such that $w \in FIRST_k(\beta u)$. Note that the $FIRST_k$ set cannot be empty, since the string itself, u, is of length k.

Once again, as in the LR(0) case, we have identified the prefix languages as the syntactic categories of a regular language, in which the terminal symbols are strings from the vocabulary of our underlying CFG. Each left-linear production corresponds, as before, to a transition chain

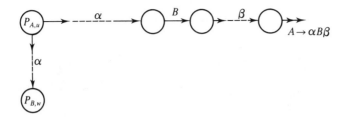

Figure 9.19   NFSA transitions arising from a typical production.

in some non-deterministic state diagram. Furthermore, since any finite grammar may only have a finite number of strings, such as u, the state diagram will be finite. The prefix languages are, therefore, regular, and the recognizing automaton is an FSA.

We may augment this prefix-recognizing FSA with 'side-chains', corresponding to the right-hand sides of productions, so that it recognizes the complete left-context of a particular reduction. The method is entirely analogous to that which we used for the LR(0) case, although the number of states tends to be rather greater. The resulting NFSA may be made deterministic, and is the controller state machine for a push-down automaton which we call the **canonical LR(k) automaton** for the grammar.

Figure 9.19 illustrates a fragment of a canonical NFSA, relevant to one particular production. Note that the reduction already has its lookahead prescribed, since the transition path starts from a prefix state with that prescribed right-context.

After the canonical NFSA has been transformed into a DFSA, we may immediately check the LR(k) condition. In the subset construction procedure, states will be merged which have distinct reductions and out-transitions. The grammar is LR(k) if no state has reductions and shift-transitions which have common elements in their length-k lookaheads.

In this case no elaborate lookahead calculation is required, since the lookahead strings are explicitly generated by the procedure which forms the NFSA. However, the enormously increased number of prefix states in the NFSA makes generation of the DFSA extremely difficult, even for the case of a single symbol lookahead, the LR(1) case.

9.4.2   A canonical LR(1) example grammar

We will work through an example of the derivation of the state diagram of a canonical LR(1) automaton for a very simple grammar. The grammar is as follows:

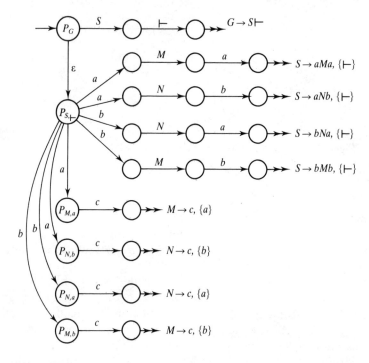

Figure 9.20   Canonical NFSA for a very simple grammar.

$G \to S\vdash.$
$S \to aMa \mid aNb \mid bNa \mid bMb.$
$M \to c.$
$N \to c.$

The canonical NFSA is illustrated in Figure 9.20. Each reduction is labelled by the corresponding production, and the lookahead set is given in brackets { }.

The $FOLLOW_1$ sets are

$FOLLOW_1(S) = \{\vdash\},$
$FOLLOW_1(M) = \{a,b\},$
$FOLLOW_1(N) = \{a,b\},$

so that we have a total of five prefix states to consider.

The left-linear productions for the prefix categories are, with the corresponding CFG production in parentheses,

$P_{S,\vdash} \to P_G\vdash$ $(G \to S\vdash).$
$P_{M,a} \to P_{S,\vdash}a$ $(S \to aMa).$
$P_{N,b} \to P_{S,\vdash}a$ $(S \to aNb).$
$P_{N,a} \to P_{S,\vdash}b$ $(S \to bNa).$
$P_{M,b} \to P_{S,\vdash}b$ $(S \to bMb).$

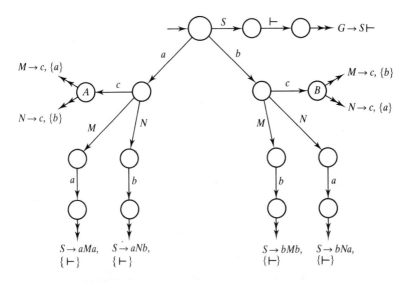

Figure 9.21   Canonical DFSA for a very simple grammar.

The corresponding DFSA is shown in Figure 9.21. It may be noted that this DFSA has no conflicts, since the two reduce actions in each of the states labelled A and B have distinct right-contexts. The grammar is thus LR(1).

This particular example is of special interest, as it is one of a very few examples of very simple grammars which are LR(1), but not LALR. The characteristic LR(0) machine for this grammar is shown in Figure 9.22.

Comparing this diagram with Figure 9.21 shows that a single state, C, in the characteristic machine, corresponds to the two distinct states, A and B, in the canonical LR(1) automaton. Furthermore, the single state C, has a *reduce–reduce* conflict which is not resolved by the LALR method. Both of the reductions out of state C in Figure 9.22 have an LALR lookahead set of $\{a,b\}$, as may be easily verified.

It is typical that the LALR automaton has a single state which corresponds to several distinct states in the canonical-LR(1) automaton. In fact, there is an alternative way of deriving the LALR machine, which starts with the LR(1) machine and then proceeds to merge states which are equivalent in the usual FSA sense. The problem is that occasionally states are merged which need to be kept separate in order to avoid the introduction of new conflicts.

Further investigation of the intricacies of this particular example, and its variations, is left to the exercises.

Use of the canonical LR method is somewhat hampered by the size of the resulting parser tables. Quite apart from the explosive increase in the number of NFSA states, as compared to the characteristic LR(0) machine, the size of the final DFSA may also be bigger by very large

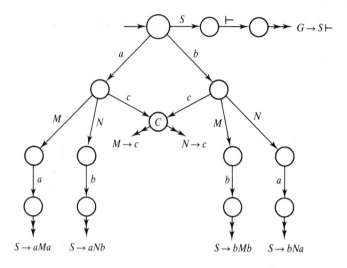

Figure 9.22   Characteristic LR(0) DFSA for a very simple grammar.

factors. For the grammars of many programming languages, the size of the LR(1) parser tables would exceed the primary memory of most small computers.

Some techniques have been developed to reduce the size of the LR(1) automata, without surrendering any of the power of the method. In effect, it is necessary to find conditions under which it is possible to merge states without introducing conflicts of the kind demonstrated in the example of Figures 9.21 and 9.22. However, it appears that in practice the number of grammar constructs which lead to LR(1) but not LALR properties is very small. The LALR method is thus likely to remain fashionable, particularly when used in conjunction with the ambiguity-resolving tricks which we discuss below.

9.4.3   Other shift–reduce parsers

Historically, a number of other kinds of bottom-up parsers have been devised and have become popular. Most of these have operated by making the *shift* or *reduce* decision based on 'precedence' relations between the symbols of the grammar. The use of such precedence relations is very convenient for simple tasks, such as might arise in expression grammars, but does not easily handle more complex situations.

In an attempt to make precedence parsers more powerful, a variety of ornate extensions have been devised. These methods have little to recommend them over the LL and LR methods, but nevertheless form a fascinating study for the historically inclined.

Finally, it should be noted that all of the methods which have been discussed so far only prove successful for a limited class of unambiguous CFGs. However, there is one parsing method which works with an unrestricted CFG, and this is due to Earley. This algorithm, which is the best such known, parses strings of length n symbols in a time which is bounded by a multiple of n^2 if the grammar is unambiguous, and has a running-time bound which is proportional to n^3 in cases where the CFG is ambiguous.

Earley's algorithm has been used in situations in which the recognizer must be specified in advance for a grammar which may later be extended, or changed. For comparison, the running time bounds for the determin-istic parsing algorithms of this chapter are proportional to the string length, n.

9.4.4 Section checklist and summary definitions

Canonical LR(k) parsers.

- For any CFG, the language of viable prefixes of non-terminal symbols with prescribed right-context strings is regular.
- The FSA which recognizes the left-contexts of reductions with prescribed length-k right-context is called the canonical LR(k) automaton.
- If a canonical LR(k) automaton has no conflicts in the action function of any state, we say that the grammar is LR(k).

9.5 Bottom-up parsing of ambiguous grammars

It is fundamental that no LR automaton can parse an ambiguous grammar. If a grammar is ambiguous then there must be at least one stack configuration for which the action table specifies two or more 'correct' actions. Nevertheless, if a language is specified, partly by context-free productions and partly by *ad hoc* rules, the overall specification may be unambiguous, even if the context-free portion of the specification is ambiguous. We have already seen one example of this principle in Chapter 8, where the productions for one **if-then-else** grammar were ambiguous when considered on their own. In that case, the introduction of a supplementary rule made the grammar unambiguous and the parser deterministic. The rule was that the production

 elsePart → ε

should never be chosen while the next input symbol was '**else**'. This same

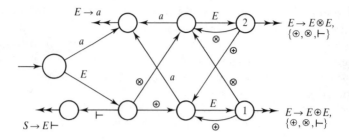

Figure 9.23 Characteristic machine for an ambiguous grammar.

disambiguating rule works for bottom-up parsers too, and forms the basis of one of the exercises for this chapter.

The technique of using an ambiguous grammar with separate precedence rules has been most widely applied to LALR parsers. However, the same technique is equally applicable to the SLR or canonical parsers of the preceding sections.

9.5.1 An ambiguous expression grammar

We consider a fairly general illustrative example of an expression grammar with two operations, which, to avoid preconceptions, we denote '$\oplus$' and '$\otimes$'. The grammar is

$S \rightarrow E\vdash.$
$E \rightarrow E{\oplus}E \mid E{\otimes}E \mid a.$

The ambiguity of this grammar expresses the fact that the productions do not define the left- or right-associativity of the operators, or their relative precedence. We will see, however, that separately stated rules of precedence may be used to resolve the ambiguity-induced conflicts in the parser.

The characteristic machine for the above grammar is shown in Figure 9.23. It will be seen that the states labelled 1 and 2 each have a *shift–reduce* conflict. The lookahead symbol sets for the reductions in state 1 and state 2 have been written below the productions. In each case the LALR lookahead set is identical to the *FOLLOW* set which would be used as SLR lookahead. The lookahead sets demonstrate that the grammar is neither LALR, nor SLR, and, because of the ambiguity, is not LR(k) for any value of k.

Taking state 1 as an example, and supposing that the next input symbol is $\oplus$, there are two possible actions: reduce by $E \rightarrow E{\oplus}E$, or *shift*. The *reduce* choice corresponds to choosing to operate on the two E expressions already encountered, before taking account of the next

State	*a*	$\oplus$	$\otimes$	$\vdash$
		Lookahead symbol		
1	*error*	*shift* $\oplus$	*shift* $\otimes$	*reduce* by $E \rightarrow E \oplus E$
2	*error*	*reduce* by $E \rightarrow E \otimes E$	*reduce* by $E \rightarrow E \otimes E$	*reduce* by $E \rightarrow E \otimes E$
3	. . .			

Figure 9.24 Partial action table for a disambiguated automaton.

operator. This implies left-associativity for the $\oplus$ operator, and hence left-to-right evaluation order. The *shift* choice in state 1, conversely, would correspond to evaluating from right to left. Similarly, and still in state 1, if the next symbol is $\otimes$, then the *reduce* choice corresponds to giving the $\oplus$ operator a higher precedence than $\otimes$, while the *shift* choice gives $\otimes$ the higher precedence.

9.5.2 Disambiguating the characteristic machine

For any given set of disambiguating rules, we may modify the action table of the parser so as to enforce the required associativity and precedence. As an example, the relevant fragment of the action table is shown in Figure 9.24, for the particular choice: $\otimes$ has precedence over $\oplus$; $\otimes$ associates on the left; while $\oplus$ associates on the right. Other possibilities are explored in the exercises.

Another way of looking at the effect of the disambiguating rules is to treat them as causing the deletion of symbols from the lookahead sets or *reduce* exits of the characteristic machine. For the rules chosen above, the lookahead set of the *reduce* exit in state 1 is just $\{\vdash\}$, while the lookahead set for the reduction in state 2 is $\{\oplus, \otimes, \vdash\}$. In the case of state 2, since it is required that the *reduce* action is always chosen, the shift transition out of state 2 may be deleted, leading to the final lookahead automaton shown in Figure 9.25. This figure should be compared with Figure 9.23.

It is an interesting observation that the same language may be specified by an unambiguous grammar which gives the same precedence and associativity to the operators as does the automaton in Figure 9.25. One such grammar is given by the set of productions

$S \rightarrow E\vdash$.
$E \rightarrow T \mid T \oplus E$.
$T \rightarrow a \mid T \otimes a$.

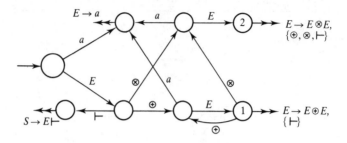

Figure 9.25   Disambiguated parsing automaton.

The resulting characteristic automaton, shown in Figure 9.26, is of comparable complexity to the disambiguated machine in Figure 9.25. Rather surprisingly, although the two automata ascribe the same abstract 'meaning' to any expression, the automata are far from isomorphic.

The great advantage of the method of using ambiguous grammars with separate disambiguating rules, is that this mechanism may be a more natural way of specifying the required syntax of a language than the exclusive use of unambiguous context-free productions.

9.5.3   Section checklist and summary definitions

1. Resolving conflicts in inconsistent states.
   - The conflicts in inconsistent states of an LR-family automaton may arise either because the grammar is not of the required class, or because the grammar is ambiguous, and hence is not LR(k) for any choice of k.
   - Conflicts in inconsistent states may be resolved by non-CFG rules which simply state a preference for one parser action over another, i.e. a precedence rule.

2. Disambiguated automata.
   - When the action function of an LR-family automaton is modified by *ad hoc* disambiguating rules, we call the resulting parser a disambiguated LR parser.
   - A disambiguated LR parser may be quite different to an LR parser for an unambiguous grammar for the same language.

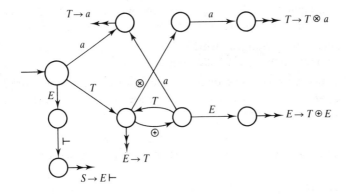

Figure 9.26 Automaton for an unambiguous grammar.

Exercises

9.1 Form the characteristic machine for the reverse Polish expression grammar

$S \rightarrow E\vdash.$
$E \rightarrow num \mid EE\ op.$

Hence show that the grammar is LR(0).

9.2 Form the characteristic machine for the grammar

$S \rightarrow E\vdash.$
$E \rightarrow T \mid T{\oplus}E.$
$T \rightarrow a \mid T{\otimes}a.$

Verify that Figure 9.26 is correct for this grammar, and that the grammar is SLR.

9.3 Show that the following grammar is LL(1), but not SLR.

$G \rightarrow S\vdash.$
$S \rightarrow AaAb \mid BbBa.$
$A \rightarrow \varepsilon.$
$B \rightarrow \varepsilon.$

Derive the LALR lookahead sets to show that the grammar is LALR.

9.4 The ambiguous **if-then-else** grammar of Section 8.4.2 is not SLR (or LR(k) for any k, for that matter). Derive the characteristic machine for this grammar, and show that the *shift–reduce* conflict may be resolved by an *ad hoc* rule which always *shifts*, if the next symbol is 'else'.

9.5 The ambiguous arithmetic grammar of Section 9.5 may be disambiguated in about ten different ways. Figure 9.25 shows the resulting lookahead automaton for just one of these choices.

Deduce the changes which are necessary in Figure 9.24 to implement each of the following choices:

a) $\otimes$ takes precedence over $\oplus$, and both evaluate left-to-right.

b) $\otimes$ and $\oplus$ have the same precedence, and evaluation is right-to-left in both cases.

9.6   The 'LR(1) but not LALR grammar' of Section 9.4 may be easily modified to make it LALR. The modified grammar is:

$G \rightarrow S\vdash.$
$S \rightarrow aMa \mid aNb \mid bNa \mid bMb.$
$M \rightarrow N.$
$N \rightarrow C.$

Form the LR(0) automaton for this grammar, and calculate the LALR lookahead sets.

9.7   It was shown in Chapter 6 that every non-empty regular language which does not include the empty string has a right-linear grammar which is also LL(1). Show that any such grammar is also LR(0).

Can you also prove this result holds for the left-linear grammars which arise from deterministic FSA?

[*Hint*: Consider the form of the viable-prefix recognizing NFSA which arise from the grammars corresponding to deterministic FSA. Hence consider the limitations on the state mergers which will take place when applying the subset construction procedure to such NFSA.]

Further reading

There are two different ways of introducing the LR parsers and we have made use of just one of these. The alternative to using the left-linear prefix grammars is to introduce the notion of an **item grammar**. Each mechanism leads to the same automaton for any given grammar, and both approaches were originally devised by Knuth (1965). The SLR and LALR methods are due to DeRemer (1971), Lalonde (1971) and Anderson *et al.* (1973). Various methods of reducing the size of canonical LR(*k*) parser tables are considered by Pager (1979).

The various varieties of precedence parsers are treated in detail in Aho and Ullman (1972), and most of the older compiler construction texts. Earley's parsing algorithm was first published in 1970, but has been recently reprinted in a special issue of *Communications of the ACM* (Earley, 1983).

The most efficient known method for computing the LALR lookaheads from the characteristic machine of a grammar is due to DeRemer and Pennello (1982), whose notation is the basis of the description in Section 9.3.

Various software tools are available which construct bottom-up parsers from grammar specifications. The *yacc* tool of UNIX is the most widely available of these (Johnson, 1975), but programs exist which also produce practical LR(1) parsers (Finn, 1985).

Chapter 10   **Semantic Actions and Tree-building**

10.1   Building a derivation tree

The semantic actions which are associated with the recognition of a string in any particular language are specific to that language, and require the most diligent attention in the construction of any language recognizer. The techniques of parser construction treated in this book make the construction of correct recognizers for the various classes of language relatively straightforward. We may be reasonably confident that our recognizers do indeed accept valid strings, but this, by itself, is no guarantee that actions other than the simple act of acceptance or rejection will be correct.

In order to be able to treat the incorporation of semantic actions in a systematic way it is clearly necessary to be able to specify the 'meaning' of each sentence in the language by some suitable formalism. There are a number of such formalisms, mostly aimed at the definition of the meaning of sentences in programming languages, but none of them is yet developed to the point where it makes the incorporation of semantic actions an entirely routine matter.

We will assume in what follows that the 'meaning' of any sentence in the particular language is understood by the constructor of the software tool, and that this meaning may be described in terms of operations which are performed on the various entities defined in the grammar's vocabulary. In particular, we will assume that the semantic actions may be unambiguously defined in terms of the derivation tree of a sentence. This is a very general situation, since the derivation tree lays bare the structure of any sentence in the language in a very direct way. In Chapter 11 we will look at alternative methods which do not require the construction of an explicit tree structure, and thus avoid some of the overheads of the methods of this chapter.

By defining the meaning or desired effect of a sentence in a language in terms of processing carried out on an explicit tree we usefully split the incorporation of semantic actions into two parts. The parser produces an explicit tree as a byproduct of the recognition process, and a separate tree-walking automaton then visits the nodes of the tree in whatever order is required to produce the desired final effect.

Both of the methods of recognition of context-free languages which we have considered, top-down and bottom-up, implicitly reconstruct a derivation tree for each sentence which they recognize. Parts of this implicit tree, or perhaps frontiers of the partially constructed tree, are represented on the parser stack, with data corresponding to various subtrees being formed and discarded during the recognition process. It is now our aim to make this tree explicit, as a first example of the way in which such structures may be constructed by a parser. It is stressed, however, that in practice a complete derivation tree is almost never constructed, since the data-structures treated in the later sections of this chapter are more efficient, and may carry equivalent information.

10.1.1   Tree-building and recursive descent

We consider the case of top-down parsers first, using recursive descent as an example. Our aim is to construct the tree by creating a node for each invocation of a non-terminal recognizing procedure. Thus the first action of the automaton after predicting a particular production is to create a node for that production, possessing as many child-links as there are right-hand-side symbols in the production. As the symbols of the right-hand side are recognized, the corresponding nodes are linked to the parent node.

This general principle holds good for parsers which are based on non-extended grammars, but if we are to make use of the full power of the recursive descent method we need to be able to handle production right-hand-sides with closure and optionality constructs, leading to the consideration of tree structures with nodes which may possess a variable number of offspring. We do this by introducing a sequence construct into our tree structures, so that instead of a node having a variable number of children of the same type, it will have a single child of **sequence** type, the sequence, in turn, being represented by a list of nodes. Figure 10.1 illustrates the data structure which we would expect to construct for a production which has a closure construct.

There are, of course, many different ways of representing trees. However, in order to make the considerations concrete, we will consider a particular implementation mechanism for the tree structures. We will suppose that the explicit tree is to be represented by a linked data structure built up of nodes which are dynamically allocated space by the use of the Pascal standard procedure *NEW*(). We will declare a separate record type for every symbol in the vocabulary, using an instance of that type for the node which represents any occurrence of the corresponding symbol. We shall also need a few additional housekeeping node-types, which will be used for the construction of the list structures which represent sequences.

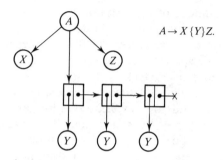

Figure 10.1   Production with closure and corresponding data structure showing the list structure.

Each record type which corresponds to a non-terminal symbol will have fields which are pointers to the nodes which form the offspring of that node. It follows that, where a particular non-terminal symbol has several possible expansions, there should be separate record variants corresponding to the different right-hand sides.

In most applications the records which form the nodes will require fields which correspond to other, semantic information. For example, in a programming language an identifier node would probably need at least one additional field which indicated the position of the identifier name in a symbol table. Where such additional fields exist in the records we call them **attributes**.

We will assume that the sequence constructs are accessed by a single pointer to the head of a list. The list will consist of a sequence of nodes, singly linked, each of which have offspring corresponding to the list elements. The final element in the list will have a next link which is **nil**, while in the case that the whole list is empty, the pointer which would normally point to the first element of the list will have the value **nil**.

In general, every recursive descent procedure will have a **var** parameter which will be a pointer to the root of the subtree corresponding to the phrase recognized by that procedure. Each procedure which is called will thus return a pointer to its subtree, and the subtrees will be linked within the calling procedure.

At this point it is best to consider a specific example. Figure 10.2 shows the data types necessary to represent the tree-fragments which arise from the production $A \rightarrow X\{Y\}Z$, an example of which was shown in Figure 10.1.

In order to create the tree from the elements defined in Figure 10.2 with the least possible disruption to the simplicity of the basic recursive descent schema, it is wise to define a set of tree-handling procedures. First, we need a set of procedures which creates the various node types,

```
type   (* first the node pointers *)
          APtr = ^ ANode;
          XPtr = ^ XNode;
          YPtr = ^ YNode;
          ZPtr = ^ ZNode;

       (* now the sequence elements *)

          YSeqPtr = ^ YSeqElement;

          YSeqElement = record
                               Y    : YPtr;
                               next : YseqPtr;
                            end;

       (* now the node types themselves *)

          Anode = record   (* A -> X{Y}Z. *)
                      X     : XPtr;
                      YSeq : YseqPtr;
                      Z     : ZPtr;
                   end;
          . . .
```

Figure 10.2   Type declaration for derivation tree.

and also other procedures which manipulate the sequence construct. Figure 10.3 shows the code for our typical production, where it is assumed that suitable procedures have been defined.

It will be seen that the incorporation of the tree-building actions creates little change to the outline of the recognition procedure. However, it is fair to point out that, in practice, it would be sensible to create a temporary sequence object within the procedure which is more elaborate than the single pointer *node^.YSeq* used in Figure 10.3. An additional pointer to the tail of the sequence will make the linkage of nodes within the loop much more efficient.

10.1.2   Building derivation trees bottom-up

If a derivation-tree fragment for this same production example is to be constructed using a bottom-up parser, a number of immediate differences arise. In the first place, the semantic actions can only be attached to

```
procedure ARecognize(var node : APtr);
  var element : YSeqPtr;
begin
  CreateANode(node);
  XRecognize(node^.X);
  InitializeEmptySequence(node^.YSeq)
  while symbol in DSet do begin
    CreateElementAndLink(element,node^.YSeq);
    YRecognize(element^.Y);
    end;
  ZRecognize(node^.Z);
end;
```

Figure 10.3   Recursive descent procedure with tree-building actions.

reductions in the LR automaton, and, since the bottom-up methods only deal with non-extended grammars, the derivation trees will have no sequence constructs.

We give a brief outline of the necessary semantic actions for an LR parser for this same example. We will assume that, as the parsing automaton interprets the FSA which recognizes the valid prefixes of each production, it pushes semantic information onto a 'semantic stack', as well as using the PDA stack for the state ordinals which are required for the normal operation of the parser. The data which are required to be on the semantic stack are the pointers to the roots of the subtrees of the recognized phrases. Thus, whenever a reduction is to be made a new node is created and the root nodes of the child subtrees are reclaimed from the semantic stack as the path of the production right-hand-side is retraced. These subtrees are attached to the newly created node, and a pointer to this new node pushed onto the semantic stack as the re-entry state is established. In practice, it is common to interleave semantic information with the parser state-ordinals on the same stack. However, we avoid such considerations here, in the interests of clarity.

Figure 10.4 shows a fragment of the characteristic machine for the fragment of the CFG which corresponds to the regular right-part production $A \rightarrow X\{Y\}Z$. In this case, the choice has been made to replace the iteration implied by the closure by a left-recursion. Each of the reductions shown in the figure has an attached action, which describes the tree-manipulation steps associated with that reduction.

It is seen that the creation of a derivation tree using either bottom-up or top-down parsers is relatively straightforward provided that appropriate node record structures are defined, and that appropriate tree structuring primitives are created. Despite this simplicity, a full derivation

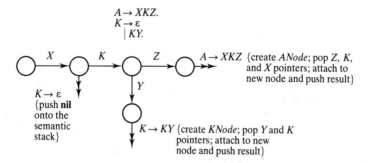

Figure 10.4 Fragment of LR automaton showing tree-building steps associated with reductions.

tree is usually wasteful of both space and time, since it often contains nodes corresponding to syntactic categories which have been invented merely to force the grammar into the particular mould demanded by the parser technology. Expression grammars of all types demonstrate this phenomenon very clearly, since they invariably contain numerous syntactic entities whose purpose is to enforce particular interpretations on strings with respect to associativity and precedence of operators.

As an example, in a straightforward regular expression grammar, the derivation trees for the simple expression $(a|b)^*c$, which would be constructed by a recursive descent or by an LR parser, are shown in Figure 10.5 (i) and (ii) respectively.

10.1.3 Section checklist and summary definitions

1. Building derivation trees.
   - Complete derivation trees are easily constructed either by bottom-up or top-down parsers.
   - For every vocabulary symbol a node-record type is declared. In the case of non-terminal nodes, the record contains sufficient pointer fields to link the child subtrees.
   - Where a non-terminal symbol has several different right-hand-side expansions, a variant record is defined with one variant for each distinct right-hand side.
   - In cases where a symbol has no attributes, no node record need be defined, instead, the presence of the node may be indicated by the value of a (non-pointer) field in the parent node.

2. Recursive descent.
   - Each recursive descent procedure creates a new node corresponding

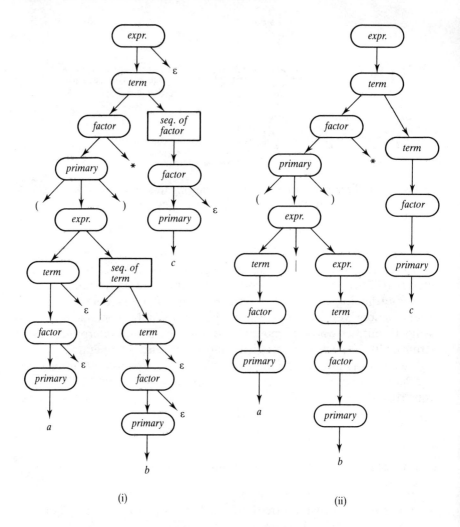

Figure 10.5   Derivation trees for the regular expression '$(a|b)*c$'.
(i) Tree arising from recursive descent parser.
(ii) Tree arising from bottom-up LR parser.

to the syntactic category which it recognizes. It calls subsidiary procedures in order to recognize other non-terminal symbols in the usual way.

- Each procedure returns a pointer to its newly created node. This node is the root of the derivation tree of the recognized phrase. The calling procedure links these nodes as children of its own node.

3. Bottom-up parsing.

- LR-family parsers build derivation trees by creating a semantic stack. This stack may be separate, or may be interleaved with the parser stack.

- The semantic stack holds, at any instant, pointers to the root nodes of the trees of the recognized phrases. When a reduction step is about to be performed, the top of the stack holds pointers to the right-hand-side symbol's trees.

- The tree-building action associated with a parser reduction step consists of creating a new node corresponding to the reduction symbol. The root pointers of the subtrees are then popped from the stack, attached to the new node, and the pointer to the new node is then pushed back onto the stack.

10.2 Abstract syntax trees

The 'meaning' of the string $(a|b)^*c$, derivation trees for which were shown in Figure 10.5, may be more succinctly described by the tree structure in Figure 10.6. In this diagram no distinction is made between the various kinds of subexpression phrases such as *expressions*, *terms*, *factors*, and *primaries*. The tree represents the relationship between the phrases, rather than the syntactic category to which each belongs. Note that the presence of various terminal symbols which may be necessary in the original string, in order to allow the string to be parsed, are omitted from the tree since they have no attributes and thus carry no information. For example, the fact that the atoms a and b are in alternation implies that in the original sentence they must have been separated by the solid vertical bar symbol. There is, therefore, no need to explicitly represent the bar symbol in the tree.

We call a structure such as Figure 10.6 an **abstract syntax tree** (AST). Abstract syntax trees are an attractive way of representing strings in a language since they make explicit the structure of the string in a particularly economical way. For many languages the AST of a string comes as close as we can get to a canonical form which summarizes the meaning of the string.

It is possible to define ASTs by formal means, specifically by an abstract grammar. Abstract grammars are a little different to the string grammars which we have dealt with so far, since they define tree-like structures rather than strings. However, despite the differences, understanding these grammars is not difficult, and the form of abstract grammar that we will use here is particularly simple.

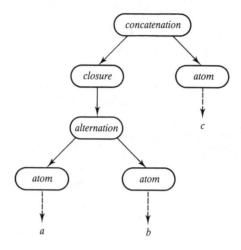

Figure 10.6   Abstract syntax tree for $(a|b)^*c$.

10.2.1   Interface definition language (IDL)

The formalism which we will use for defining abstract grammars essentially deals with three kinds of entities: nodes, node-classes, and attributes. We define the entities of the abstract grammar by means of a BNF-like notation called **interface description language** (IDL), best known for its use in the formal description of the common intermediate form for the programming language Ada. Actually we shall use a rather informal subset of the IDL notation.

Node classes, which here will have names which are always capitalized, are defined by means of an alternation. The alternation defines the various nodes which belong to the class. For our regular expression grammar we may thus define the node-class *EXP* by the IDL production

$$EXP ::= alternation \mid closure \mid concatenation \mid atom ;$$

This production states that there are four different members of the expression class, with the designations shown. The bar symbol has its usual meaning, while '::=' and ';' are other meta-symbols.

Each of these node types must be defined in terms of the type and designation of each of its components, including any subtree nodes that the node may have. Other components will be **attributes** of the node, which might be lexical or semantic attributes such as references to object descriptors in a symbol table. Traditionally, in IDL all such node components are called attributes, even though it may be argued that the use of the term for the subtrees of a node is somewhat inappropriate. In

$$ASTdef \rightarrow \textbf{'structure'}\ identifier$$
$$\textbf{'root'}\ classname\ \textbf{'is'}$$
$$\{\ ClassDef\ |\ NodeDef\ \}$$
$$\textbf{'end'}.$$
$$ClassDef \rightarrow classname\ '::='\ nodename\ \{\ '|'\ nodename\ \}';'.$$
$$NodeDef \rightarrow nodename\ '=>'\ [\ AttributeDef\{\ ','\ AttributeDef\ \}]';'.$$
$$AttributeDef \rightarrow attributename\ ':'\ Class\ .$$
$$Class \rightarrow classname\ |\ \textbf{'seqOf'}\ classname\ |\ externalType\ .$$
$$classname \rightarrow identifier.$$
$$nodename \rightarrow identifier.$$
$$attributename \rightarrow identifier.$$

Figure 10.7   BNF definition of syntax of IDL subset.

IDL the node components which determine the actual tree structure are called structural attributes, and have types which are defined by specifying the node-class to which the root-node of the particular subtree belongs. Non-structural nodes may have types which are externally defined types, but may also be references to other tree nodes. It is important to see that an attributed-AST is only a tree when the structural components are considered. When the other attributes are considered, there may be a directed graph structure superimposed on the tree. For example, in an AST which represents programs in a Pascal-like language, every node which represents a used occurrence of a particular identifier might have a semantic attribute which references the same defining occurrence of the object.

The so-called structural attributes which define the tree structure will have names prefixed by $as\_$, while attributes which have to do with the semantics of the tree or the lexical structure of the original string are prefixed by $sm\_$ or $lx\_$ respectively. In general, lexical attributes correspond to additional information which a lower-level automaton obtains as a side-effect of symbol recognition. On the other hand, semantic attributes are often not evaluated during the recognition of the sentence, but have their values assigned by the tree-walking automaton after parsing is complete. Semantic or lexical attributes may have types which are defined in the underlying implementation, such as *BOOLEAN*, *INTEGER*, and string types, for example.

Attributes, as well as being defined as belonging to a particular node-class, may also be defined in terms of a sequence constructor, **seqOf** node-class.

Nodes are defined by a node definition which lists the attributes and their respective types. In the case of the abstract syntax for the regular

```
structure regular expression
root EXP is

    EXP ::= concatenation | alternation | closure | atom ;

    concatenation=> as_factors        : seqOf EXP;
        alternation =>  as_alternatives : seqOf EXP;
            closure =>  as_expression  : EXP;
                atom=> lx_string       : IdentType;
end
```

Figure 10.8   Complete IDL for regular expression ASTs.

expression grammar the node definitions are as follows.

$$concatenation \Rightarrow as\_factors : \textbf{seqOf } EXP;$$
$$alternation \Rightarrow as\_alternatives : \textbf{seqOf } EXP;$$
$$closure \Rightarrow as\_expression : EXP;$$
$$atom \Rightarrow lx\_string : IdentType; \text{ — an external type}$$

In each case these nodes have only a single attribute, but in general nodes may have many attributes.

A BNF description of the subset of IDL used in this chapter is given in Figure 10.7, while Figure 10.8 gives the complete IDL of the tree structure for the regular expression language.

The literal strings such as '::=' and '=>' in Figure 10.7 are meta-symbols of IDL, as are the reserved words '**structure**', '**seqOf**', and so on. We do not specify the lexical conventions here, except to note that character case is significant, and that comments start with a double hyphen and are terminated by a line-break.

10.2.2 Implementation of abstract syntax trees

The whole point in specifying the form of an abstract syntax tree by means of an abstract grammar is to be able to consider the creation and manipulation of the tree separately from consideration of the actual data-structures used to represent the trees. Nevertheless, at least one method of implementation will be considered, so that it is possible to consider the mechanisms of the tree-building in some detail.

In Pascal, the most obvious method of implementing ASTs is to use pointers and linked structures. If this is done we obtain the following correspondence. Each node-class is implemented by a record type, with as many variants as there are members of the node-class. Each of these record variants will have as many fields as there are attributes for the corresponding node. Those attributes which are of some external type will be implemented by a record field defined as having that type, while attributes which are node- or tree-valued will correspond to fields which are pointers to the record type which implements the corresponding node-class.

Apart from these generalities, any implementation of an abstract grammar must also decide on the method of implementation of the sequence construct. One relatively straightforward method is to construct the sequence as a singly or doubly linked list of list-element nodes. In our example we will define a list-element record type, with a singly linked structure. The sequence type is implemented by a record which directly points to its first child-node, with a second pointer to the list element of the next node in the sequence. Sequences will not be constructed unless they will contain at least two nodes.

In some cases it may be possible to save storage space by representing lists as elements in contiguous positions in a one dimensional pointer array; however, some care is needed, since such an implementation may prove awkward to construct correctly if it is possible that a second list needs to be constructed midway through the construction of a first list. Such is the case for the regular expression grammar, for example, where an alternation list may need to be constructed when the parser is only part-way through the construction of a concatenation list.

A concrete implementation of the abstract syntax of the regular expression grammar could be as follows.

```
type   NodeType  = (concatenation, alternation, closure, atom);
       ExpPtr    = ^ ExpNode; (* any subexpression *)
       ListPtr   = ^ ListElement;

       SeqOfExp  = record
                       first : ExpPtr;
                       rest  : ListPtr;
                   end;

       ExpNode   = record case tag : NodeType of
                       concatenation,
                       alternation : ( seq  : SeqOfExp );
                       closure     : ( expr : ExpPtr );
                       atom        : ( name : IdentType);
                   end;

       ListElement = record
                       expr : ExpPtr;
                       next : ListPtr
                   end;
```

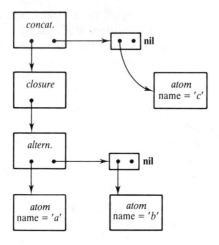

Figure 10.9   Implementation of AST for $(a|b)^*c$.

Note carefully that two nodes share the same variant structure, and thus have the same names for corresponding fields. This sharing facilitates the use of the same list manipulation procedures in each case, despite the rule of Pascal which prohibits the use of the same field names for different variants of the same record type. It should also be noted that the type used for the name field of the atom variant must have distinguished values to indicate the empty string and the empty language.

The linked data-structure, which is constructed in this implementation for the same string as was shown in Figures 10.5 and 10.6, is shown in Figure 10.9.

10.2.3   Building the AST top-down

We will now look in detail at the means by which an AST may be constructed by a recursive descent parser. Firstly, however, it should be reiterated that the parser still recognizes the conventional context-free string-grammar; the abstract grammar of the AST only affects the way in which the semantic actions are inserted into the code.

We wish to be able to build the AST by means of calls to utility procedures which create the new nodes, and link the list elements together as required. The creation procedures are very straightforward, essentially translating directly into calls to *NEW*, but the list manipulation procedures are a little more complex.

We will assume that every procedure which potentially constructs a sequence will have a list-access record as a local variable. This record will have a field which points to the list header node, and another which

```
type ListAccess = record
                      head : ExpPtr;
                      tail  : ListPtr
                  end;

procedure AddElement(var list : ListAccess;
                              ptr : ExpPtr (* new expr.*));
   var socket : ListPtr; (* new list element *)
begin
   NEW(socket); (* create new list element *)
   socket^.expr := ptr; (* plug sub-expr. in *)
   socket^.next := nil; (* mark as last in list *)
   (* now link element and update list status *)
   if list.tail = nil (* => exp is first of rest *)
     then list.head^.seq.rest := socket
     else list.tail^.next := socket;
   list.tail := socket
end;

procedure CreateConcatenation(var list : ListAccess;
                              firstEXP : ExpPtr);
begin
   NEW(list.head,concatenation);
   list.head^.tag := concatenation;
   list.head^.seq.first := firstEXP;
   list.head^.seq.rest := nil;
   list.tail := nil
end;
```

Figure 10.10   Typical utility procedure for tree-building parser.

accesses the list element which is currently last in the sequence. Thus each end of the list may be rapidly accessed and if any recursion occurs, the list access records do not become invalid.

With the definitions given above for the regular expression grammar, Figure 10.10 shows the relevant code for the list manipulation procedure, and for one of the *create* procedures. Note that the node-creation procedure also links in the first expression subtree. Since a recursive descent parser recognizes the phrases of any closure construct in the underlying grammar in left-to-right order, the list elements are always inserted at the tail of the list.

Figure 10.11 shows the list data structure after the initial call to *CreateConcatenation*, after the first call to *AddElement*, and after subsequent calls to *AddElement*.

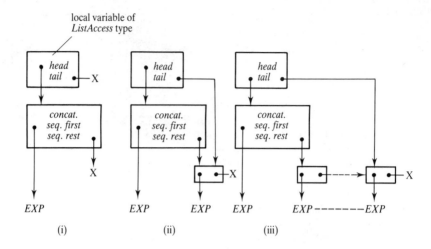

Figure 10.11   List data structures.
(i) After creation of header.
(ii) After addition of next element.
(iii) After addition of several elements.

The critical question which must be answered for any AST-building automaton is how the parser is to create nodes as side-effects of symbol recognition, given that the one-to-one correspondence between nodes and vocabulary symbols has been deliberately broken in the definition of the abstract syntax. In particular, for our example language, what is the relationship between the node-class *EXP* and the syntactic categories *expression*, *term*, *factor*, and *primary*?

For the regular expression language, all of the subexpression categories are potential members of the *EXP* class. The object of defining the AST is to avoid the appearance of intermediate nodes in the tree-representation which have only a single child and have no semantic content. Thus a *term* which derives only a single *factor* does not lead to the creation of a node in the AST. This is so because the semantic meaning of a *term* which consists of a single *factor* is the same as that of the solitary *factor*.

On the other hand, if a *factor* derives a terminal string which is the closure of a single *atom*, then even though the closure node has a single child, the node cannot be flattened out of the AST. This is so, since the presence of the node registers the semantic fact that a closure operation is to be performed on the subexpression. Clearly the meaning of a closure of a subexpression is different to that of the original expression.

The recursive descent procedures for building the AST differ from those which build a derivation tree in that it is possible to have a procedure return without creating a new node. A typical procedure which

```
procedure ExprRecognize(var ptr : ExpPtr);
  var TermList : ListAccess;
      Term : ExpPtr;
begin
  TermRecognize(Term); (* the first term *)
  if symbol <> bar then (* single term, no new node *)
    ptr := Term
  else begin
    CreateAlternation(TermList,Term);
    while symbol = bar do begin
      GetSymbol; (* get past bar *)
      TermRecognize(Term);
      AddElement(TermList,Term)
      end; (* now return the whole list *)
    ptr := TermList.head
    end;
end;

procedure TermRecognize(var ptr : ExpPtr);
  var Factlist : ListAccess;
      Factor : ExpPtr;
begin
  FactRecognize(Factor); (* first factor *)
  if not(symbol in FactStarters) then ptr := Factor
  else begin
    CreateConcatenation(FactList,Factor);
    while symbol in FactStarters do begin
      FactRecognize(Factor);
      AddElement(FactList,Factor)
      end; (* now return list *)
    ptr := FactList.head
    end (* else *)
end;

procedure FactRecognize(var ptr : ExpPtr);
  var Primary : ExpPtr;
begin
  PrimRecognize(Primary);
  if symbol = star then begin (* closure *)
    CreateClosure(ptr); (* = NEW(ptr,closure) *)
    Attach(ptr,Primary); (* Primary is child node *)
    GetSymbol;
    end
  else ptr := Primary (* no new node, just pass pointer *)
end;
```

Figure 10.12   *cont. overleaf*

Figure 10.12   *cont.*

```
procedure PrimRecognize(var ptr : ExpPtr);
begin
  if symbol = ident then begin
    CreateAtom(ptr);
    { copy lexical info. to ptr^ };
    GetSymbol;
    end;
  else if symbol = Lbrac then begin
    GetSymbol; (* get past '(' *)
    ExprRecognize(ptr); (* no new node, just pass param.*)
    if symbol = Rbrac then GetSymbol (* get past ')' *)
    else error
  else error
end;
```

Figure 10.12   Recursive descent procedures to build AST.

has a control path which avoids the creation of a new node will take the pointer returned by its own subordinate procedure and pass it unchanged back up the tree. For example, an expression-recognizing procedure which finds only a single term will return the pointer returned by the *TermRecognize* procedure as its own result.

A complete set of procedures for building the AST for the regular expression grammar illustrates most of the considerations, and are given in Figure 10.12. These procedures make use of the types defined earlier for implementation of the tree abstraction.

10.2.4   Building the AST bottom-up

We now consider the building of an equivalent AST for the regular expression language using a bottom-up parser. One immediate difference is that the LR grammar will necessarily not contain the sequence constructs which we wish to build into the tree structure. Indeed the sequences of *terms* and *factors* in the language may be described either by left- or right-recursive productions. The grammar turns out to be SLR in either case, but the nature of the semantic actions is somewhat different in each case.

Firstly, it must be decided how the structural information for the subtrees is to be held while the parsing proceeds. We will assume that a semantic stack holds pointers to the root nodes of all the subtrees of the partially constructed AST. This mechanism is the same as that which was

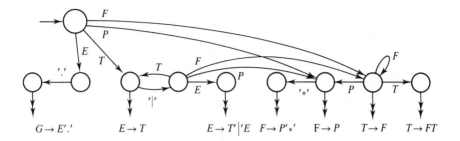

Figure 10.13   Fragment of characteristic machine with right-recursive productions.

suggested for derivation tree construction in Section 10.1. Every non-terminal symbol on the parser stack will have a corresponding pointer on the semantic stack, but terminal symbols on the parser stack in general will not. Indeed, the *atom* symbol is the only terminal which needs to be represented on the semantic stack, presumably by a pointer to a name table, or perhaps just by an identifier ordinal.

The key observation is that whenever a reduce action takes place in which only one subtree is replaced from the stack, then no new node will be created unless the semantic meaning of the new subexpression is different to the meaning of the replaced tree. Thus when a reduction is made by a unit production such as *term → factor*, the previous pointer to the *factor* subtree simply remains on the stack as the pointer to the root of the *term* subtree.

Let us assume that the specific syntax for the grammar is right recursive, being given by

>   *goal → expression '.'.*
> *expression → term | term '|' expression.*
>   *term → factor | factor term.*
>   *factor → primary | primary '*' .*
>   *primary → atom | '(' expression ')' .*

This grammar is very similar to the grammar treated in Chapter 9, the characteristic machine for which was shown in Figures 9.12 and 9.13. The fragment of the characteristic machine which arises from the first four production groups is shown in Figure 10.13.

The principles involved in creating the AST for this language, using a parser based on the complete characteristic machine of which Figure 10.13 is a part, may be demonstrated by treating the four reductions on the right of the figure.

Firstly, whenever an *atom* is read by the parser, an appropriate attribute is pushed onto the semantic stack. No other shift move causes any such semantic action.

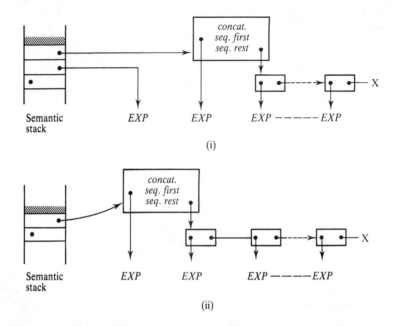

Figure 10.14 Data structure (i) before and (ii) after linking *factor* and *term* nodes.

Dealing first with the reduction which uses the production *factor* → *primary* '*', it is apparent that the top of the semantic stack will be a pointer to the root node of the subtree which corresponds to the *primary*. The shifting of the closure symbol '*' does not cause any change to the semantic stack. The correct semantic action associated with the reduction is thus to create a closure node and link the popped primary subtree to it, pushing the pointer to the closure node back on the stack as the root of the recognized *factor*. The code might be

```
procedure MakeClosure;
    var dummy : ExpPtr;
begin
    NEW(dummy,closure); (* create closure *)
    dummy^.tag   := closure;
    dummy^.expr := popOfStack;
    push(dummy);
end;
```

The standard procedure *NEW* instantiates an expression node of the nominated variant, and the stack operations apply to the semantic stack rather than to the parser stack.

The next reduction, that by *factor* → *primary*, is even simpler. The

```
procedure LinkFactorAndTerm; (* 'params' are on stack *)
  var term, factor : ExpPtr;
      list : ListAccess;
begin
  term := popOfStack;
  factor := popOfStack;
  if term^.tag = concatenation then begin
    LinkFactorToTermSeq(factor,term);
    push(term)
    end (* term is concat. *)
  else begin (* must create concat. node *)
    CreateConcatenation(list,factor);
    AddElement(list,term);
    push(list.head)
    end;
end;
```

Figure 10.15   Semantic action for production *term* → *factor term*.

pointer to the root of the *primary* subtree is on the top of the stack, and simply remains there as the pointer to the root of the *factor* subtree. There is, therefore, no semantic action at all. Similarly, the reduction by the production *term* → *factor* has no associated semantic action, since the required pointer is already in the correct place on the stack.

The reduction by the production *term* → *factor term* is the most complex that we consider here. The top element of the semantic stack will be a pointer to the root of the *term* subtree, while the next element on the stack will be a pointer to the root of the *factor* subtree. The correct semantic action is to link these two subexpression trees to a concatenation node. However, the actions vary according to whether the *term* node is already a concatenation, or is some other node variant. If the root node of the *term* subtree is already a concatenation node, then we would wish to link the new *factor* subtree to the head of the concatenation list. If the *term* is of some other variant, then we must create a new concatenation node, and link both *factor* and *term* to it.

Figure 10.14 shows the data structure before and after the semantic action, in the case that the root of the *term* subtree is already a concatenation node. The code to effect these actions is shown in Figure 10.15. The list-manipulation process for an alternation sequence is entirely analogous to the method shown for the concatenation.

A slightly different situation arises for the same language when the repetitive structure is modelled by means of left-recursive productions. The difference is that as new elements are recognized they must be added

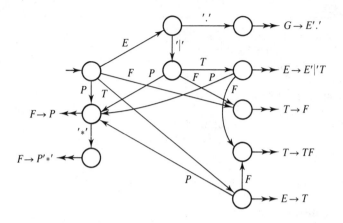

Figure 10.16   Fragment of characteristic machine grammar with left recursion.

to the right of the list structure which implements the sequence construct.

Consider the following grammar which generates the same regular expression language as the previous example.

>   *goal* → *expression* '.' .
> *expression* → *term* | *expression* '|' *term* .
>   *term* → *factor* | *term factor* .
>   *factor* → *primary* | *primary* '*' .
>   *primary* → *atom* | '(' *expression* ')' .

The fragment of the characteristic machine equivalent to Figure 10.13 is shown in Figure 10.16. All of the grammatical structure below the level of *primary* has once again been omitted in the interests of clarity. Again, it may be seen that the so-called unit productions, where one syntactic category replaces another, require no semantic action.

The productions with semantic actions which must add list elements to the tail of the lists, require somewhat different implementation than does the recursive descent parser. In a recursive descent parser there is a procedure invocation which is current during the whole of each sequence construction. A local variable of that procedure (of type *ListAccess* in our example) may conveniently hold pointers to each end of the sequence, allowing easy access to either end. In the bottom-up case no such procedure environment exists. Between any two reduction actions which link sequence elements, a pointer to the node simply sits on the semantic stack. In order to make an insertion at the right-hand end of the sequence, it is thus necessary to either walk down the list to its tail, or to modify the record structure so that the concatenation and alternation records themselves possess the required pointer. These considerations affect the way that the tree-building abstractions are obtained, but do not affect the manner in which the semantic actions invoke these procedures.

In summary, it may be stated that the building of an abstract syntax tree is hardly more difficult than the direct creation of a derivation tree. The advantages are all with the more compact form, and the more direct representation of the structure of sentences of the language make the design of the tree-walking automaton much simpler. Furthermore, the effort required to create a description of the form of the AST, in terms of IDL or otherwise, is well repaid in the assistance which such a description gives in the correct implementation of both the tree-builder and the tree-walker.

In the next section the design of tree-walking automata is briefly touched on. Although such a topic is necessarily closely involved with the semantics of the particular language for which the tree has been created, we deal with several different examples which all operate on ASTs for the regular expression language. These examples illustrate many of the considerations which commonly arise in the design of software tools based on such automata.

10.2.4   Section checklist and summary definitions

1. Abstract syntax trees.

   - An AST is a tree which represents the interrelationships between syntactic entities in a sentence.

   - An AST usually has far fewer nodes than the derivation tree for the same sentence.

   - ASTs may be defined by formal means, such as IDL, and then implemented in a variety of ways.

   - For record-and-pointer implementations of ASTs defined by IDL, each node-class corresponds to a record type, with as many record variants as there are node-types in the class. Structural attributes of the AST correspond to pointers to subtrees, although some very simple nodes may be included inline in the parent node.

2. Building syntax trees.

   - When building an AST not every recognized vocabulary symbol gives rise to a node on the tree, but only those which have either some substructure or some special semantic significance.

   - Recursive descent recognizers may build ASTs based on dynamic data-structures by causing each procedure to return a pointer to the root of the tree representing the recognized syntactic category. This pointer may be to a newly created node, or may be the same pointer returned by some subordinate procedure call.

   - Recognizers based on shift–reduce parsers may build ASTs based on dynamic data-structures by maintaining a stack of pointers to the roots of the subtrees which represent the phrases reduced at that point in the parse. When a reduction step is performed the stack may be left unchanged, or pointers may be popped and attached to a new node with a pointer to that new node being pushed back on the stack.

10.3   Tree-walking automata

We will consider several different tree-walking automata which operate on the ASTs produced by any of the parsers of the last section. It is important to note that all of these parsers will produce identical trees for any given string in the language. The differences between the three grammars which were used simply reflects the different parsing methods, and has little to do with the 'meaning' of the strings. In the case of regular expressions, the AST represents both concatenation and alternation by means of a sequence construct, despite the fact that the underlying grammars for the CFG-based parsers do not have sequence constructs. A nicely dual situation occurs for arithmetic grammars where, typically, expressions with binary operators are represented by binary trees even in cases where the parsing grammar contains a sequence construct. The difference is that, for example, the alternatives of an alternation really are a sequence, whereas the binary operators of an arithmetic grammar really do take just two operands.

10.3.1   A recursive tree-walker

We will assume that the objective of the language recognizer is to create an output file which details the contents of a compacted NFSA transition table, corresponding to the regular expression accepted as input. The desired file format is to consist of a sequence of lists, with each list detailing all the transitions out of one of the states. The (*symbol, next state*) pairs corresponding to ordinary transitions are to be listed first, followed by the *next state* ordinals corresponding to any ε-transitions. The lists are to be given in order of state ordinal, but with no particular ordering of the transitions within a list. It is intended that the subsequent reading of the output file should allow the direct creation of the compacted NFSA data structure described in the model answer to Exercise 4.8.

A formal grammar for the file format is

> *NFSAfile* → *headsmbl* { *statelist* } *eof.*
> *statelist* → *StateOrdinal translist epsilonlist endsmbl.*
> *translist* → *trsmbl* { *SymbolOrdinal StateOrdinal* }.
> *epsilonlist* → *epsmbl* { *StateOrdinal* }.

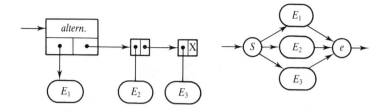

Figure 10.17   AST with alternation, and corresponding NFSA.

$SymbolOrdinal \rightarrow number.$
$StateOrdinal \rightarrow number.$

In this grammar the alphabet is

$\Sigma = \{number, headsmbl, trsmbl, epsmbl, endsmbl, eof\}.$

The difficulty in the creation of the output file is that any simple recursive tree-walking automaton will not discover all of the transitions out of any given state all at once. Rather, the transitions belonging to different states will be discovered in an interleaved fashion.

There are basically two approaches which may be utilized to resolve such difficulties. The transitions may either be held in some intermediate data-structure, which will enable subsequent output in correct order, or a more complex tree-walking algorithm may be devised. We will consider each approach, in turn.

Let us assume that we start by assigning state numbers to the *start* and *accept* states. At the outset it is not known how many states will be required, so we will assume that state numbers will be assigned in sequence, as required, by a procedure *GetStateOrd*. The algorithmic insight which is required to solve the problem is to notice the relationship between the *start* and *end* states of any expression, and the *start* and *end* states of its constituent subexpressions.

If the subexpressions are part of an alternation, then each of the subexpressions inherits the same *start* and *end* states as its parent node on the AST (see Figure 10.17).

In the case of a closure, the *start* and *end* states of the subexpression are the same state: a newly assigned state which is distinct from the *start* and *end* states of its parent on the tree. The *start* state must be linked to this new state by an empty transition, with another empty transition leading from the new state to the parent *end* state (see Figure 10.18).

Finally, in the case of a concatenation at least one new state must be created. The first subexpression must lead from the *start* state of the parent to a newly assigned state, while the final subexpression of the concatenation must lead from a newly assigned state to the parent *end*

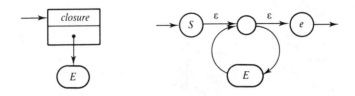

Figure 10.18   AST with closure node, and corresponding NFSA.

state. If there are more than two subexpressions then they must spell out paths between newly assigned nodes (see Figure 10.19).

In order to permit grouping of all the transitions out of a particular state, we will first assume that, at the time of each state's creation, a pair of lists is set up for the transitions belonging to that state. One list will hold the normal transitions, while the other will list the target states of any empty transitions. As transitions are discovered, they are linked to the appropriate list. The list insertions will be performed by a pair of procedures which insert empty transitions and normal transitions, respectively. The procedures will have headings

procedure *InsertEpsilon(start,finish : StateNumber)*;

procedure *InsertTransition(start,finish   : StateNumber;*
                      symbol   : SymbolType);

Once these lists have been set up, it is a simple matter to produce the required output. The lists are scanned in turn, and the appropriate ordinals and symbols are written to the file as each scan proceeds. The state assigning procedure will have a heading

procedure *GetStateOrd(var newstate : StateNumber)*;

and will be initialized to take account of the fact that the *start* and *accept* states are assigned numbers before the tree-walking starts at the root of the tree.

The tree-walking will proceed by means of calls to a procedure *encode*, which will be passed the starting and ending states of the subexpression for which it has to emit transitions. In the event that the subexpression is just a single atom, an appropriate transition will be emitted. In all other cases the *encode* procedure is called recursively for each child node in turn. The code for this procedure is shown in Figure 10.20. The whole encoding process will be started by a call to the *encode* procedure, with the starting and ending states equal to the assigned *start* and *accept* states of the automaton, and with the designated node being the root of the tree.

There are several things to be noted about the code of this procedure. Firstly, the code for the atom variant must finally take account

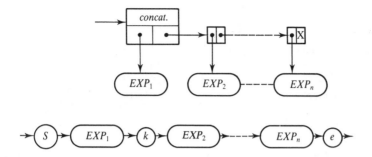

Figure 10.19   AST with concatenation, and corresponding NSFA.

of the fact that the atom may actually be either an empty string meta-symbol, or the empty language symbol. If the atom corresponds to the empty string, then an epsilon transition must be added to the appropriate list, rather than a normal transition. Conversely, if the atom belongs to the empty language symbol, then no transition at all is required. These special cases are disposed of first, with the entry of an ordinary transition resulting otherwise.

The code for the concatenation case is a little intricate. Both the first and last elements in the concatenation must be treated separately, because they each use one of the formal parameters as one actual parameter for the recursive call. The intermediate elements, which only pass newly assigned state ordinals as parameters, are handled by a loop structure.

10.3.2   A more complicated tree-walker

We will now explore the possibility of devising a tree-walker which visits the nodes in such an order that the required output file may be written directly, without the formation of the intermediate list structure.

First, we define a relation on the nodes of our ASTs which seeks to characterize the property that leads to transitions sharing a particular starting state. The relation is called *costarts*, and may be computed using the following rules.

1. The child nodes of an alternation *costart* with each other, and with their parent node.
2. Only the first child node of a concatenation *costarts* with its parent node.
3. The child node of a closure does not *costart* with its parent.

If a node has a child with which it does not *costart*, then that child must have a newly assigned state as its starting state. This non-costarting child

```
procedure encode(InState,OutState : StateNumber;
                          node : ExpPtr);
  var new1, new2 : StateNumber;
      element : ListPtr;
begin
  case node^.tag of
    atom:
      if node^.name = epsilon then
        InsertEpsilon(Instate,Outstate)
      else if node^.name = phi then (* no transition *)
      else InsertTransition(Instate,Outstate,node^.name);
    closure: begin
      GetStateOrd(new1); (* create new state *)
      InsertEpsilon(InState,new1);
      InsertEpsilon(new1,OutState);
      encode(new1,new1,node^.expr) (* self-loop *)
      end;
    alternation: begin (* for every child do . . . *)
      encode(InState,OutState,node^.seq.first);
      element := node^.seq.rest;
      repeat (* Assert: at least one more in list *)
        encode(InState,OutState,element^.expr);
        element := element^.next;
      until element = nil;
      end;
    concatenation: begin
      GetStateOrd(new1); (* first sub-expr.*)
      encode(Instate,new1,node^.seq.first);
      element := node^.seq.rest;
      while element^.next<>nil do begin
        (* intermediate nodes of concat.*)
        GetStateOrd(new2);
        encode(new1,new2,element^.expr);
        element := element^.next;
        new1 := new2
        end;
      (* postcondition: element^ is list end *)
      encode(new1,OutState,element^.expr);
      end;
  end (* case *)
end;
```

Figure 10.20   Tree-walking procedure.

will, therefore, be the root node of a subtree of nodes. In this subtree, in turn, some nodes may *costart* with their relative root-node, and will have the newly assigned state as the starting state of the new *costart* group.

We may now define a recursive tree-walking procedure which visits just those nodes of a tree which *costart* with the root node, thus emitting only those transitions which start at the *start* state. This is an important subgoal, even although ultimately we must also cater for the transitions out of all the other states. The method to be described walks the tree, visiting all the nodes of a group which *costart*. Whenever a node is visited which has a child node with which it does not *costart*, then state numbers are assigned for the *start* and *end* states of that child. The non-costarting child node is not visited, however; instead, the state-number information, together with a pointer to the node, is placed in a pending queue.

When all of the nodes in the current costarting group have been visited, then information on another subtree is retrieved from the queue. The node which is retrieved from the queue is previously unvisited, and will be the root node of the next *costart* group, with starting and ending states as previously determined. Since the state ordinals are allocated (and hence queued) in order, the transition groups determined by the tree-walker will appear in groups in the same order.

The only remaining complexity has to do with the treatment of empty transitions, since we wish for these to be emitted separately. Firstly, the tree-walker will cause the generation of all of the transitions in a particular *costart* set without any regard to whether the transitions are normal or empty. It is, therefore, necessary to create a temporary list of the epsilon transitions belonging to a particular *costart* set, and to output these after all the normal transitions have been emitted. Using this list is a great deal more efficient than the method in Figure 10.20, since in the present case only one list is in existence at any one time. The algorithm in Figure 10.20, on the other hand, created two lists for every state in the automaton.

The emission of the final epsilon transition for the standard implementation of a closure is also a slight difficulty, since when the child node and its costarting nodes are visited, the required *end* state of the empty transition is no longer known. This problem arises because the target state of the empty transition belongs to the parent node, and not to the child. The difficulty is easily overcome, however, by adopting the convention that a special marker element is pushed on the queue. This marker will indicate the *start* and *end* states of the empty transition, but will have a **nil** valued pointer to distinguish it from other queue elements. The queue element immediately following such a special marker will indicate the root node of the *costart* group, as well as the shared *start* and *end* state of the subexpression on which the closure operates.

Whenever the tree-walking automaton fetches a queue element which is one of the special epsilon transition marker elements it will enter the

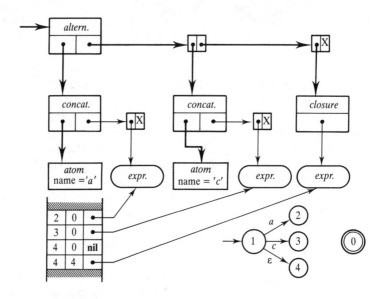

Figure 10.21   Partially walked AST, showing transitions and the *costart* root node queue. The heavy lines show the paths walked so far.

appropriate transition in the epsilon list, and then immediately fetch the next queue element, which will indicate the root of the associated *costart* group.

Figure 10.21 shows the contents of the queue after the walking of the first *costart* group of an AST. This example shows that several new states have been allocated ordinals and their respective *costart* root nodes queued. The example also includes a closure to illustrate the use of the special queue-marker. The partially constructed state diagram corresponding to the emitted transitions is also shown in the figure.

The tree-walking procedure consists of two parts. A recursive procedure, *covisit*, visits all of the nodes in any *costart* set and emits all of the transitions belonging to a particular relative *start* state. Whenever this procedure calls for the assigning of a new state ordinal, it also adds an element to the queue, specifying the information needed to restart the procedure for the *costart* group associated with the newly assigned state. Another procedure, *TranslateTree*, controls the overall tree-walking process. It removes elements from the queue one by one, passing the relevant parameters to a call of *covisit*. Before it does so, however, it checks to see if the retrieved element is a special marker, indicating an epsilon transition, or simply indicates the root of a normal *costart* set. The code for these procedures is shown in Figures 10.22 and 10.23.

Both parts of the tree-walking code make use of certain utility procedures. These do such things as enqueue and dequeue elements,

```
procedure covisit(InState,OutState : StateNumber;
                            node : ExpPtr);
   var new1, new2 : StateNumber;
       element : ListPtr;
begin
   case node^.tag of
     atom:
       if node^.name = epsilon then
          InsertEpsilon(InState,OutState)
       else if node^.name = phi then (* no transition *)
       else emit(InState,OutState,node^.name);
     closure: begin
       GetStateOrd(new1); (* create new state *)
       InsertEpsilonTrans(InState,new1);
       enqueue(new1,new1,nil); (* mark for final epsilon *)
       enqueue(new1,new1,node^.expr); (* now the EXP node *)
       end;
     alternation: begin (* for every child do . . . *)
       covisit(InState,OutState,node^.seq.first);
       element := node^.seq.rest;
       repeat (* Assert: at least one more in list *)
          covisit(InState,Outstate,element^.expr);
          element := element^.next
       until element = nil;
       end;
     concatenation: begin
       GetStateOrd(new1); (* first sub-expr.*)
       covisit(InState,new1,node^.seq.first);
       element := node^.seq.rest;
       while element^.next<>nil do begin
          (* other nodes: enqueue but do not visit *)
          GetStateOrd(new2);
          enqueue(new1,new2,element^.expr);
          element := element^.next;
          new1 := new2
          end;
       (* postcondition: element^ is list end *)
       enqueue(new1,OutState,element^.expr)
       end;
   end (* case *)
end;
```

Figure 10.22   Code of the procedure which visits nodes of a costart set.

```
procedure TranslateTree;                              /
  var start, accept, instate, outstate : StateNumber;
      ptr : ExpPtr;
begin
  InitializeQueue;
  EmitFileHeader;
  GetStateOrd(accept);
  GetStateOrd(start);
  enqueue(start,accept,root);
  while {queue not empty} do begin
    dequeue(instate,outstate,ptr);
    InitializeEpsilonList;
    if ptr = nil then begin (* special case *)
      InsertEpsilon(instate,outstate);
      dequeue(instate,outstate,ptr)
      end;
    covisit(instate,outstate,ptr);
    (* non-empties for this state now finished *)
    EmitEpsilonList;
    EmitEndSmbl
    end; (* of this costart group *)
  EmitFileTrailer;
  end;
```

Figure 10.23   Procedure to directly translate a regular expression AST into an output file.

insert epsilon transitions in the output list, and emit symbols to the output file. The details of these procedures are straightforward and are not given here.

The code of Figure 10.22 should be compared with that of Figure 10.20. It will be seen that a remarkable degree of similarity exists. The significant difference is that for child nodes which do not belong to the costart group currently under consideration, the parameters passed to the *enqueue* procedure are those which in the previous example would have been passed to a recursive call of *encode*.

In this procedure, the transitions corresponding to non-empty symbols are emitted directly to the output file, while the epsilon transitions are queued up for later output under the control of the procedure *TranslateTree*.

Many of the implementation details of the code of the translator procedure have been abstracted away by the use of procedures with names which indicate the general purpose of their operation. These omissions should cause little difficulty.

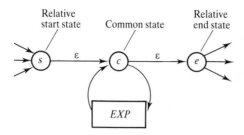

Figure 10.24 Fragment of state diagram for closure node.

10.3.3 The minimal-epsilon tree-walker

Both of the tree-walking automata which we have considered so far, have the production of output as their purpose. However, tree-walking may also be used for the evaluation of semantic attributes of the AST nodes. We shall now pursue a simple example of this type of tree-walking automaton.

We consider a computation which evaluates an attribute which may be used to limit the number of states in the NFSA state-diagram produced from a regular expression AST. The major source of additional states is the presence of unnecessary epsilon transitions arising from the simple encoding of the closure construct. It is possible to define a pair of Boolean valued semantic attributes for the *closure* variant of the *EXP* node-class. These attributes will indicate the necessity or otherwise of the two epsilon transitions. The *encode* procedure may then take account of this information when walking the tree.

The IDL fragment defining the closure node will now read

> *closure* => *as_expression*   : *EXP*,
>   *sm_input*_epsilon : *BOOLEAN*, (* true=>necessary *)
>   *sm_output*_epsilon : *BOOLEAN*; (* true=>necessary *)

These new attributes must be evaluated after the tree has been constructed, using reasoning equivalent to that which was employed for the manual methods described in Section 4.2.3.

Once again it is helpful, although not absolutely essential, to define relations on the nodes to clarify the situation. Consider the state diagram fragment arising from a closure node, as illustrated in Figure 10.24. It may be seen that the input-side epsilon transition may be removed, by merging the states marked s and c, provided that the relative start state, s, of the closure does not possess multiple out-edges. Similarly, the output-side epsilon transition may be safely removed by merging its two end states, marked c and e, provided that the relative end state of the closure e does not possess other in-edges.

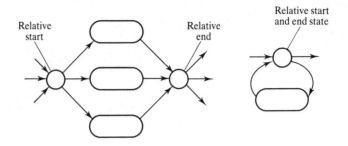

Figure 10.25   The semantic attributes *startHasOtherOutEdges* and *endHasOtherInEdges* are true for the offspring of all alternation and closure nodes.

We are led, therefore, to consider a pair of semantic attributes of each node in the AST,

sm_startHasOtherOutEdges : *BOOLEAN*,
sm_endHasOtherInEdges : *BOOLEAN*;

We might actually evaluate these attributes at every node, and store them in the node records. However, in this particular case we may avoid storing the attributes, since the values may be propagated downward from the root of the tree, as parameters of the recursive tree-walking procedures. Here the values are used to assign correct values to the *. . . epsilon* attributes of any closure nodes which are encountered along the walk. Note that it is the *epsilon* attributes which are the objective of our tree-walk, and it is these attributes which are to be inserted into the tree nodes for later use. The attributes which relate to the number of *out* and *in* edges are only needed during the attribute evaluation, and since they are not required later, need not be stored in the tree.

In similar cases, where a semantic attribute is evaluated from information passed down the tree from ancestor nodes, we say that the attribute is **inherited**.

The relationship between these semantic attributes for adjoining nodes of the tree is easily deduced. Figure 10.25 illustrates that the two attributes are both *TRUE* for every child of an alternation node, and for the child of a closure node. Note that the state with the self-loop in a closure is both the *start* and *end* state of the subexpression recognizer.

The situation with a concatenation node is somewhat more complex. The attribute *startHasOtherOutEdges* for the first child node will be equal to the same attribute for the parent node. Similarly, for the last child node in a concatenation, the attribute *endHasOtherInEdges* will be directly inherited from the parent node. The attributes for every intermediate node in a concatenation will take the value *FALSE*, unless

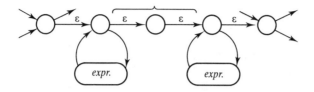

Figure 10.26   If two closures adjoin in a concatenation only one of the bracketed epsilon transitions may be removed.

the neighbouring node is a closure which has the adjoining epsilon transition removed. Clearly, if two adjacent nodes in a concatenation are both closures, then only one of the two adjoining epsilon transitions may be removed. Figure 10.26 illustrates this point.

We adopt the convention that, when a choice exists, the epsilon transition which leads toward a closure will be removed in preference to the out-transition of its left sibling. In this case, the test which must be performed during the scanning of the nodes of a concatenation is to see if the following node is a closure.

Figure 10.27 illustrates the state diagrams which would arise after processing a particular AST before and after use of the *propagate* procedure. Figure 10.28 is the attributed AST corresponding to the processed version of the AST in Figure 10.27.

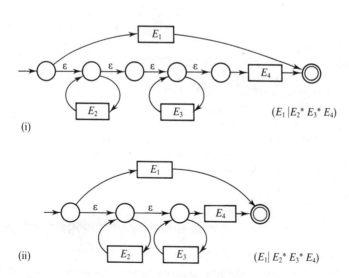

Figure 10.27   State diagrams (i) before and (ii) after evaluation of the
... *epsilon* attributes.

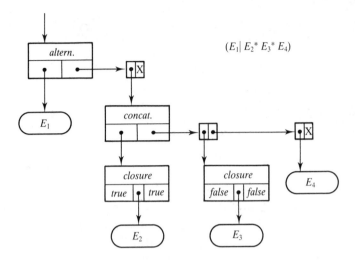

Figure 10.28   Attributed tree for the regular expression in Figure 10.27.

The code for a tree-walking procedure which propagates the node edge attributes through the tree, and assigns values to the . . . *epsilon* attributes of the closure trees is shown in Figure 10.29. Note that in this code, when dealing with the intermediate nodes of a concatenation, the attribute *endHasOtherInEdges* is set equal to *TRUE* if the next factor of the concatenation is a closure, and *FALSE* otherwise. This is because, according to our chosen convention, the inward epsilon transition of every closure in a concatenation after the first is always removed.

The consequent modifications to the *encode* or *covisit* procedures to take account of the additional attributes are left for the exercises.

In Chapter 11 we will be pursuing the possibility of producing output from a parser without the building of either an explicit derivation tree, or an AST. When these simpler methods are practicable they are generally to be preferred. But in cases where the connection between the desired output and the initial input-string format is indirect, as is the case for the example which we have treated in this chapter, then tree building methods are generally necessary.

10.3.4   Section checklist and summary definitions

1. Using tree-walking automata to produce output.
   - The standard recursive tree-walking algorithms may be used to emit output from an AST in various node orders.
   - When the required order of node visits in the tree does not

```
procedure propagate(StartHasOtherOutEdges,
                    EndHasOtherInEdges : BOOLEAN;
                                node : ExpPtr );
   var element : ListPtr;
begin
  case node^.tag of
    atom: (* no action *) ;
    closure: with node^ do begin
      inputEpsilon := StartHasOtherOutEdges ;
      outputEpsilon := EndHasOtherInEdges ;
      propagate(TRUE,TRUE,expr)
      end;
    alternation: begin (* for every child do . . . *)
      propagate(TRUE,TRUE,node^.seq.first);
      element := node^.seq.rest;
      repeat (* Assert: at least one more in list *)
        propagate(TRUE,TRUE,element^.expr);
        element := element^.next
      until element = nil
      end;
    concatenation: begin
      propagate(StartHasOtherOutEdges,
                (node^.seq.rest^.tag = closure),
                (* TRUE if next in concat is a closure *)
                node^.seq.first);
      element := node^.seq.rest;
      while element^.next <> nil do begin
        (* intermediate nodes of concat.*)
        propagate(FALSE,
                  (element^.next^.tag = closure),
                  element^.expr);
        element := element^.next;
        end;
      (* postcondition: element^ is list end *)
      propagate(FALSE,EndHasOtherInEdges,element^.expr)
      end;
  end (* case *)
end;
```

Figure 10.29 Recursive procedure which evaluates the attributes which indicate the necessity of the two epsilon transitions for a closure node.

correspond to any of the standard tree walks, then a special algorithm may be constructed.

2. Using tree-walks to evaluate semantic attributes.

- A semantic attribute of a particular node may be evaluated from information held in the ancestor nodes of that node. In such cases we call the attribute an inherited attribute.

- A semantic attribute of a particular node may be evaluated from information held in descendant nodes of that node. In such cases we call the attribute a synthesized attribute.

- For a recursive tree automaton, attribute information may be passed as parameters of the tree-walking procedure. Inherited attributes are evaluated from value parameters, while synthesized attributes make use of information propagated up the tree as the **var** parameters of returning procedures.

10.4   Software tools based on abstract syntax trees

There are a number of types of software tools which are most easily constructed using internal data-structures based on ASTs. The use of such trees, in some form, has become almost standard for the construction of programming language compilers, at least for the newer languages, such as Ada, or when it is necessary to perform a substantial analysis of the program structure to decide on the applicability of various optimization techniques. Since these considerations lie somewhat outside the objectives of this book, we shall consider some allied, but distinct, applications which are indicative of the uses of these techniques.

10.4.1   The DIANA intermediate form for Ada programs

Because of the intended application of Ada, and the way in which the language was designed, defined, and debated, it was the object of an enormous scrutiny prior to its general usage. It was understood at an early stage that the success of the language in increasing both the productivity of programmers and the quality of software products, would depend to a great extent on the degree to which the programming environment supplied and supported software tools capable of operating on Ada program scripts. The possible tools include such things as program formatters ('pretty-printers'), cross-reference generators, syntax-directed editors, and the like. An example of one of the more unusual tools which was considered was a 'domino stopper' which would determine which other packages, if any, would require recompilation when a given change was made to a particular package specification.

What many of these tools had in common, was a requirement to be able to gain ready access to semantic information which is implicit in the source code of an Ada program. Normally this information would be available to a software tool only after a process of syntactic and semantic analysis equivalent to that which a compiler performs during compilation. The question naturally arose, therefore, as to whether or not it was possible for many tools to share in the results of the semantic analysis which a single tool, usually the compiler, would perform. What was needed, in effect, was a standard representation for Ada programs, containing much more explicit information than the source script, but still free of the narrow machine dependencies of the object code which the compiler produces as its final output.

Because of the general nature of the requirements of the tools which had been suggested, and the need to provide for tools which had not even been thought of, it was necessary to provide an extremely flexible form. The result was a specification for an attributed AST. The name coined for the data type was DIANA, which is an acronym for Descriptive Intermediate Attributed Notation for Ada, and it combined the features of previous notations which had been developed at Carnegie-Mellon and Karlsruhe universities. The form was defined using the IDL notation described earlier in Section 10.2.1.

One of the important requirements for the form was the need to provide for the reconstruction of the source text from the tree. This is clearly necessary for pretty-printers, and also for many other tools. The point is that the user of a tool should be able to work in terms of the source text, without ever having to be aware of its method of internal representation, let alone the implementation of that representation. Tree-walking automata which reconstruct (source) strings from syntax trees are sometimes called **unparsers**.

The requirement for source reconstructability has a number of interesting consequences. In general, it is necessary for the tree to contain attributes which do not contribute to the 'meaning' of the program. There are two simple illustrations of this. Firstly, if there are symbol synonyms which, in our terms, the lower-level recognizer would normally hide from the parser, then the actual source representation of the particular synonym used must be stored in the tree. This involves the storage of an otherwise unnecessary lexical attribute. For example, the actual source representation of a numeric literal must be held, along with its actual value. Only the *value* of the number is important to the program's meaning, but it would be a little disconcerting for the programmer who has some valid reason for specifying a numeric literal in hexadecimal notation to have it reconstructed in decimal.

Furthermore, when there are syntactically superfluous symbols, such as unnecessary parentheses or leading plus signs in expressions, then these redundant symbols too must be explicitly represented in the tree.

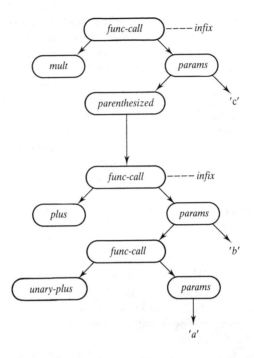

Figure 10.30   DIANA fragment for the expression '$(+a+b)*c$'.

This design decision makes the trees a little less compact, but still leads to a representation which is very much more efficient than the complete derivation tree. Figure 10.30 shows an example of a DIANA fragment for an expression with redundant symbols. Note the use of the explicit parenthesized node.

The semantic attributes, which are not shown in Figure 10.30, include such things as a reference in each variable node to the applicable defining occurrence of that object, and to its type descriptor. The form of the tree may look a little unfamiliar, as a result of the Ada rule that all operators are to be treated as applications of special (infix) functions.

It must be stressed that the DIANA definition does not specify a means of implementation of the trees which it specifies. The definition is that of an abstract data type, which may, indeed must, be implemented in many different ways. It is probable that in many cases the DIANA trees would be represented by pointer and record structures in computer memory. However, the structures must also be able to be saved and retrieved from secondary storage in order to be shared between the various tools. For secondary storage, some kind of 'flattened' representation is required, which may be simply parsed back into the more readily navigable form, when necessary. Furthermore, there is a great deal of freedom in the method by which the attributes are represented within a particular node. In some cases it might be convenient to actually hold the value of an attribute within a node, while in other cases it would be more economical to use an attribute representation which is a reference to a shared object outside the tree. Such implementation decisions do not modify the abstract meaning of a particular tree, nor do they change its conformance with the DIANA specification. The only impact that they have is on the ease with which the representations may be passed between tools which have different implementation structures.

It is too early yet to say to what extent the DIANA form will be adopted. Certainly the ideas which it incorporates have been extremely influential in the way in which the design of software tools is now being approached. However, there are certain difficulties which should not be underestimated. It appears that the DIANA representation of any given Ada program consumes an amount of computer memory which exceeds that of the original source code by a factor of about three. This necessitates, for many applications, the storage of much of the tree in secondary memory, and the implementation of some kind of 'demand paging' for subtrees. Furthermore, for compilers which attempt to provide very rapid compilation, it appears that the time and space overheads of building a DIANA representation rather than a compiler-specific intermediate structure are quite significant.

10.4.2 Syntax-directed editors

One of the most interesting applications of ASTs is in the construction of syntax-directed editors. These are editors for a particular programming language, which are able to determine the syntactic correctness or otherwise of a program text during its creation. The most influential of the early experiments in this field were those by Teitelbaum and Reps (1981) at Cornell University.

Syntax-directed editors provide for the display and manipulation of partially completed programs, and in some cases for the visible execution of program fragments. The essential feature of such systems is provision for the display of placeholders which correspond to unelaborated structures. In our terms, these placeholders are simply visible representations of non-terminal symbols of the grammar. At any instant, the program is internally represented by an AST, and the user has a window onto some part of the frontier of the tree. The frontier contains vocabulary symbols, and the user is able to select these for elaboration. The whole process of syntax-directed editing may be viewed as a user-directed process of program derivation. The user chooses which non-terminal is to be elaborated next, moves the cursor to indicate the relevant placeholder and selects a production by which to expand it.

Basically, there are two ways in which the elaboration of placeholders may be specified. Parser-based systems take the specified input string and attempt to build a subtree which has a root which matches the placeholder. Of course, it is normal to not complete an elaboration at one time, so the input string will usually not be a complete sentence in the language of the indicated non-terminal. Clearly, for placeholders which correspond to LL(1) productions, it is only necessary to input a single symbol to specify the particular production which will be used for elaboration.

It is possible to view parser-based syntax-directed editors as implementing a uniquely different type of error recovery. The user, by specifying the placeholder which is about to be elaborated, specifies a goal symbol for the parsing step which follows. The parser selects a production in the normal predictive parser fashion, and proceeds to recognize the phrase. If the complete phrase is present, then elaboration of the placeholder is complete. If on the other hand an incomplete phrase is submitted, then the parse will terminate in what would normally be considered an error state. However, in this case the fact that the syntax tree for the placeholder has been left incomplete is not an error. It is exactly what is required, since the dangling links of the open part of the parse-tree are exactly where new placeholders will appear on the screen.

The other method of expanding placeholders which has been implemented for syntax-directed editors is the insertion of templates by command. In this variation the user specifies a particular expansion, either by means of a characteristic command sequence, or by selection from a menu. The command selects a particular production and a subtree for that production is grafted to the tree at the position of the placeholder. In terms of the flat (as opposed to tree-like) view of the partially elaborated program which the user sees, the placeholder is replaced by a template which contains both language symbols and other placeholders. There is still a need, however, for some kind of rudimentary parser for low-level structures such as expressions. One of the advantages of insertion by command is that it is possible for commands to perform operations other than elaboration. For example, a single command might turn a **repeat** into a **while** loop, and modify the test condition appropriately.

There are interesting problems which arise in the implementation of such schemes, whether parser or command-based. Firstly, it is usual to try to shield the user from the full detail of the grammar, as well as from the actual underlying tree representation. As with the case of DIANA-based tools, the naive user should be able to understand what is happening in terms of the visible interface of the tool, in this case text on a screen. One of the problems, however, is how the tool is to treat grammar features which are ambiguous in the simplified form presented to users. Consider, once again, the dangling **else** problem of Pascal. We have seen that both

```
if <condition>
then
    if <condition>
    then
        <statement>
        <elsePart>
    <elsePart>;
. . .
```

Figure 10.31 Fragment of syntax-directed editor display.

top-down and bottom-up parsers can cope with this ambiguity by using simple disambiguating rules during a left-to-right scan of a source text. What, however, of the situation in an editor, where the input phrases may be elaborated in an entirely arbitrary order? Consider the situation where a program fragment contains a nested **if** statement, as in Figure 10.31.

In principle, the user should be able to select any placeholder, the outer *elsePart* say, and expand it at will. The problem is, if the outer *elsePart* is expanded by the production *elsePart* → **else** *statement*, then the inner *elsePart* no longer has the option of being elaborated by the empty production. The expansion of the outer *elsePart* must then cause the inner one also to expand to **else** *statement*. Conversely, the erasure of the inner *elsePart*, i.e. the elaboration *elsePart* → ε, must also cause the erasure of the outer *elsePart*. This particular problem may be avoided in editors which perform insertion by command, since a separate command may be implemented for insertion of a balanced or an unbalanced if-statement. The system is then able to check that the chosen expansion is valid without having to modify the tree otherwise, and may provide a quite separate command for transforming between the two forms.

There are many other fascinating and important issues involved in the design of syntax-directed editors. One of the important questions is the extent to which the editor should temporarily allow a partially elaborated program to be incorrect syntactically or semantically. Most such editors allow semantic errors such as undeclared identifiers to be entered, and give, at most, a friendly warning. There are also interesting questions regarding the best way of implementing major tree-surgery, corresponding to the 'cut and paste' operations which ordinary text editors provide.

10.4.3 Section checklist and summary definitions

- Software tools which perform manipulations of data which depend on attributes that are only computed with difficulty may usefully employ internal representations of data which are based on attributed ASTs.

- Where several different tools require access to the attributes of a particular input script, it may be convenient to share the tree representation. One tool must transform the input into the syntax-tree form, and possibly evaluate some attributes. The AST may then be passed as input to other tools.

**10.5   Attribute grammars

Attribute grammars provide a formal method for specifying the semantics of sentences in languages which are defined by CFGs. As we have seen, syntax trees may possess attributes which are not properties of the context-free syntax, and require separate processing on the constructed tree. In the case of language recognizers which construct explicit syntax trees it is usual to store such **semantic attributes** within the tree nodes. In Chapter 11 there is some discussion of an alternative mechanism, applicable to those recognizers whose semantic actions are sufficiently simple that attributes may be computed from information which is passed along as temporary data within the parser itself.

Attribute grammars give a theoretical basis for the computation of semantic attributes, and assist in the semi-automatic production of semantic analysers. In time, the automatic production of semantic analysers from attribute grammars may become as commonplace as the production of table-driven parsers from CFGs is at present.

An **attribute grammar** (AG) consists of a set of context-free productions each of which has an associated set of **rules** expressed in the form of **semantic functions**. The AG associates a finite set of attributes with each grammar symbol. The semantic functions specify the way in which the attributes of particular symbols are to be evaluated from the attributes of other symbols *in the same production*.

The AG specifies the semantic attributes of any sentence in terms of purely local properties. Attribute values only depend on the attributes of neighbouring nodes in the tree. In effect, the semantic properties of a language are reduced to stepwise computations in exactly the same way as the productions of a CFG reduce the syntax of a language to computations which are performed one production at a time.

In what follows we shall adopt the notation that an attribute named A say, which belongs to a symbol X, will be denoted $X.A$ by analogy with the *dot* notation which Pascal uses for field selection within records. If an

$$
\begin{array}{lll}
Goal & \rightarrow Exp \vdash. & Goal.value \ := Exp.value \\[4pt]
Exp & \rightarrow Term & Exp.value \ := Term.value, \\
& \rightarrow Exp \ '+' \ Term. & Exp_1.value \ := Exp_2.value + Term.value. \\[4pt]
Term & \rightarrow Fact & Term.value \ := Fact.value, \\
& \rightarrow Term \ '*' \ Fact. & Term_1.value := Term_2.value * Fact.value. \\[4pt]
Fact & \rightarrow number & Fact.value \ := number.value, \\
& \rightarrow '(' \ Exp \ ')'. & Fact.value \ := Exp.value.
\end{array}
$$

Figure 10.32   *value* attributes for real expressions.

explicit tree representation of a sentence happens to use Pascal records as tree nodes, then the analogy is exact.

As a first example, we shall look at a formal method of specifying the *value* attribute of the non-terminal symbols in a language of real-valued expressions. The attribute grammar is shown in Figure 10.32.

It should be noted that, in the case of productions which have multiple symbols with the same name, the occurrences are given subscript numbers in the attribute rules. The numbering is simply left-to-right within the production. Note also that the quoted occurrences of arithmetic operators in the productions refer to the *symbols* for addition and multiplication within the sentences. Within the *rules* + and * refer to actual arithmetic operations carried out during evaluation of the value attributes.

In the case of this example grammar there is only one rule per production, and the rules all specify evaluation of attributes of non-terminal symbols. However, *terminal* symbols may have attributes as well. In the case of the terminal symbol *number* this is clear, but in the case of more complicated arithmetics even the operator symbols might have semantic attributes. For example, in Pascal every '+' operator has a semantic attribute which specifies whether the operator denotes an integer or real operation (or perhaps even denotes a set union).

10.5.1 Inherited and synthesized attributes.

Let us suppose that we have a typical production, $X \rightarrow \alpha B \beta$, where α and β refer, as usual, to strings from the vocabulary. Any attribute rule such as

$$X.A := f(\text{attributes of } B, \alpha \text{ and } \beta)$$

where f is some arbitrary function of its arguments, is said to specify a

synthesized attribute of X. In effect, the attribute value for X is computed from information in the subtree derived from X. Conversely, if a semantic equation specifies a value for a right-hand-side symbol, say

$$B.A := f(\text{attributes of } X, \alpha \text{ and } \beta),$$

then $B.A$ is said to be an **inherited attribute**. The inherited attributes of a symbol are thus computed from information held in the environment of the symbol in the derivation tree.

Finally, we may define **intrinsic attributes** of symbols as being those which are independent of the syntactic context. What was previously referred to as *lexical* attributes fall into this category, since their values are determined by a lower-level recognizer, rather than being computed by some semantic function within the parser or semantic analyser. The *value* attribute for the symbol *number* in the example of the last section is just such an intrinsic attribute.

The appearance of intrinsic attributes is actually a consequence of the separation of language rules into *lexical* and *syntactic* grammars. An alternative point of view is to consider intrinsic attributes as being synthesized attributes of the lower-level grammar. In the case of the *value* attribute for numbers, the attribute value is synthesized from the positional and value attributes of the digits of the string which denotes the number.

It may be noted that the example grammar of the last section contained synthesized attributes only, so that all information flowed *up* the tree, from the intrinsic attributes of the leaves to the final value of the root. In general, however, AGs have a mixture of both inherited and synthesized attributes which must be computed, so that information flows both up and down the tree.

Many attribute grammar formalisms allow for the rules to include **condition** equations as well as ordinary semantic functions. Conditions are Boolean-valued functions of attributes of the symbols in a production. Such conditions may be thought of as evaluating a special synthesized attribute *correct*, which must have the value *true* for every node if the sentence is semantically valid.

The process of tree attribution consists of calculating consistent attribute values for all the nodes, in some order. An attribute which has a value is said to be **available**, while an attribute which is defined by some semantic function is said to be **ready for evaluation** when all of the arguments of the function are available. At the outset of the process only the intrinsic attributes are available. These are used to evaluate other attributes, which are then used for other attributes, and so on, until all attributes are available.

The attribution process, however, cannot be successfully carried out for arbitrary attribute grammars. For example, an attribute must not circularly depend on its own value, or it will never become ready for

```
procedure XRecognize({information for inherited attributes};
                     var {information for synthesized attributes of the
                          parent, and inherited attributes of the later
                          siblings.}                                      );
begin
  {evaluate inherited attributes from value parameters};
  {recognize RHS of the production };
  {evaluate synthesized attributes and var parameters};
end;
```

Figure 10.33 Schema for recognition of *L*-attributed grammar.

evaluation. Furthermore, if the attribution is not only to be possible but also efficient, then it is usual to require further restrictions in the manner in which attributes may depend on each other.

10.5.2 The *L*-attributed grammars

An attribute grammar is said to be **L-attributed** if the semantic functions are restricted in such a way that the tree may be fully attributed in a single depth-first, left-to-right walk of the syntax tree. In effect, this restriction imposes the following rules.

1. An inherited attribute of a node may depend on an inherited attribute of its parent in the tree.
2. An inherited attribute of a node may depend on synthesized attributes of its *left* siblings in the tree.
3. The synthesized attributes of a node may depend arbitrarily on the attributes of its child nodes.

The point in imposing these rules is to ensure that, as the traversal of the tree proceeds, all required attributes are available. For a recursive tree-walker, each node is visited only once, and every attribute is evaluated before the traversal finally leaves the node. The above rules ensure that attributes can only depend on nodes which have already been visited.

An important consequence of having an *L*-attributed grammar is that the tree is able to be fully attributed concurrently with the tree-building actions of a top-down parser. The depth-first, left-to-right scan of the tree is exactly the order in which the nodes are created, so that they may be immediately attributed.

The combination of recursive descent parsers with *L*-attributed grammars provides a particularly clear example of the way in which such a grammar is used. Inherited attributes are computed from parameters which are passed as *value* parameters of the recognition procedures. Synthesized attributes, on the other hand, depend on information which is returned in **var** parameters of subsidiary procedures. Figure 10.33 is a schema for such a recognition (and attribution) procedure.

In effect, inherited attributes are ready for evaluation at node-creation time, while synthesized attributes are ready for evaluation as soon as all the subtrees of the node have been constructed.

Finally, it should be noted that sometimes the overall semantic action required of a language recognizer may be construed as the evaluation of some synthesized attribute of the root node. One such example is evaluation of the *value* of an expression. In such cases, if the grammar is *L*-attributed, an explicit tree need never be built. Node attributes then exist only as local variables of the recognition procedures of the parser. When a procedure returns, the attributes of the corresponding symbol may be safely discarded. According to the definition of the *L*-attributed property, the node will never be visited again, and any unevaluated attributes of other nodes which depend on the discarded values may be computed from the **var** parameters which are returned by the procedure.

10.5.3   Multiple tree passes

The condition that a grammar be *L*-attributed is far too restrictive in a great number of applications. It is then necessary to build an explicit tree, and to make multiple passes over the nodes. It is possible to invent hierarchies of AGs which permit complete attribution of all possible trees with some predetermined number, k, of passes over the tree. This may be thought of as in some sense equivalent to the classification of CFGs into various classes which may be parsed with k symbols of lookahead. We shall not pursue the details here, however.

The case study at the end of Chapter 8 demonstrated the way in which attributes as simple as the *value* of an arithmetic expression may be evaluated concurrently with a parse of the string. That example was particularly simple since the grammar contains only synthesized attributes and was therefore *L*-attributed. In order to treat a more difficult example we shall once again consider the problem of converting from a regular expression to an NFSA, formulating the solution in attribute grammar terms. As we shall see, this tree cannot be built and attributed concurrently.

We shall adopt a formalism in which the expressions, terms, and factors of the grammar all possess two integer attributes *start* and *finish* which hold the state ordinals which are the starting and ending states of that (sub)expression in the corresponding state diagram. As discussed in Section 10.3, these attributes may be determined by a tree-walking automaton which traverses the syntax tree after it is built. We shall

Production	Rules	
$term \rightarrow factor$	$factor.start \quad := term.start$	(1)
	$factor.finish \quad := term.finish$	(2)
$term \rightarrow term\ factor$	$term_2.start \quad := term_1.start$	(3)
	$factor.finish \quad := term_1.finish$	(4)
	$term_2.finish \quad := NewState$	(5)
	$factor.start \quad := term_2.finish$	(6)
$factor \rightarrow primary$	$primary.start \ := factor.start$	(7)
	$primary.finish := factor.finish$	(8)
$factor \rightarrow primary\ {}^{\prime *\prime}$	$primary.start \ := NewState$	(9)
	$primary.finish := primary.start$	(10)

Figure 10.34   Attribute grammar for NFSA state-number attributes.

consider only the two most difficult of the attribute evaluations, those for concatenations and closures.

A fragment of a grammar suitable for a bottom-up parsing of regular expressions is given by the following productions.

$term \rightarrow factor \mid term\ factor$.
$factor \rightarrow primary \mid primary\ {}^{\prime *\prime}$.

An attribute grammar which allows for the computation of the *start* and *finish* attribute for each node of the derivation tree is given in Figure 10.34. Note that in this figure, as usual, where there are multiple occurrences of the same symbol in a production, the occurrences are numbered from left to right. The function *NewState* is presumed to allocate a new state ordinal whenever that is required.

Rules 1 and 2, and rules 7 and 8 are **copy rules**. They reflect that a term consisting of a single factor does not have any semantic effect on the corresponding state machine. Rules 3 to 5, on the other hand, determine that when a term consists of a term concatenated with a factor, the starting state of the child-term and the finishing state of the factor are exactly those of the parent-term. The final state of the child-term and the first state of the factor are both given by some new state ordinal allocated by the function *NewState*. Finally, rules 9 and 10 reflect the fact that the starting and ending states of a subexpression which is the child of a closure node are equal to each other, but are distinct from the starting and ending states of the closure node. Figures 10.17, 10.18, and 10.19 illustrate each of these cases.

In this particular grammar, *all* attributes are inherited, and only

Production	Rules		
term → *factor* *rest*.	*factor.start*	:= *term.start*	(1)
	factor.finish	:= *rest.start*	(2)
	rest.finish	:= *term.finish*	(3)
rest → ε	*rest.start*	:= *rest.finish*	(4)
rest → *factor* *rest*.	*factor.start*	:= *NewState*	(5)
	factor.finish	:= *rest₂.start*	(6)
	rest₂.finish	:= *rest₁.finish*	(7)
	rest₁.start	:= *factor.start*	(8)
factor → *primary* *optStar*.	*primary.start* :=	**if** *optStar.null* **then** *factor.start* **else** *NewState* **end**;	(9)
	primary.finish :=	**if** *optStar.null* **then** *factor.finish* **else** *primary.start* **end**;	(10)
optStar → ε	*optStar.null*	:= TRUE	(11)
optStar → '*'.	*optStar.null*	:= FALSE	(12)

Figure 10.35   Attribute grammar fragment for top-down grammar.

depend on attributes of the parent or the left sibling. The grammar is thus *L*-attributed. Unfortunately, the grammar is unsuitable for top-down parsing; since it contains left recursive productions, the attribution cannot be performed concurrently with a recursive descent parse.

An alternative grammar fragment which is suitable for top-down parsing would be the following.

> *term* → *factor* *rest*.
> *rest* → ε | *factor* *rest*.
> *factor* → *primary* *optStar*.
> *optStar* → ε | '*'.

This is a CFG form equivalent to the RRP productions

> *term* → *factor* {factor}.
> *factor* → *primary* ['*'].

Dealing first with the attributes for the *factor* production, it is clear that the inherited attributes for the *primary* must depend on whether or not the optional asterisk symbol follows. If the asterisk is absent, then the

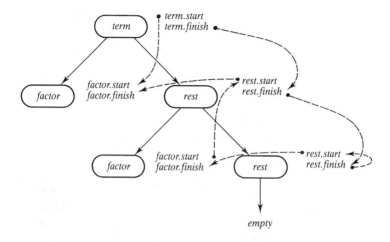

Figure 10.36   Attribute dependencies in a simple tree example.

attributes of the *primary* are simply copied from the *factor*. When the asterisk is present, however, the attributes of the primary are both equal to some new state ordinal which needs to be allocated. A possible way to incorporate these rules into attribute functions is to define a Boolean-valued, synthesized attribute of the symbol *optStar*, named *optStar.null*. In this case, the *primary* attributes are determined by a conditional function.

In the case of the *term* productions, it is possible to define an attribute *rest.null* and use a conditional function for the inherited attributes of the *factor*. However, it also is possible to define the attribute functions in other ways. Figure 10.35 shows one such attribute grammar fragment.

The way in which information flows around a tree in the process of attribution, using the grammar in Figure 10.35, is different to all of the examples treated so far. For the first production, rule 2 evaluates an inherited attribute for *factor.finish*. However, this attribute depends on *rest.start*, which is seen from rules 4 and 8 to be a synthesized attribute. When *rest* is erased by the second production, the value *rest.start* is (indirectly) copied from the *finish* attribute of its parent in the tree. In contrast, when the *rest* symbol is not erased, the synthesized attribute *rest.start* is a newly allocated value. Figure 10.36 shows the attribute dependencies in a typical, simple tree example.

In this figure a dotted line from one attribute to another implies that the second attribute depends on the value of the first. In effect, the *finish* attribute ripples down the right-hand edge of the concatenation subtree, until the erased *rest* is found. This symbol synthesizes a *start* value which percolates back up the tree causing new state ordinals to be allocated along the way. This particular attribution may be performed in a single, depth-first tree traversal which proceeds from *right* to *left*.

This example has been deliberately chosen to illustrate the impossibility of concurrent parsing and attribution for some languages. In this example, if we try to build the tree bottom-up, the attributes are all inherited. This means that, during parsing, the attributes for each newly constructed node depend on the attributes of parts of the tree not yet constructed. Once the tree has been completely constructed we may completely attribute it in a single depth-first, left-to-right traversal.

By contrast, if we try to construct the tree top-down, nodes which belong to concatenations and closures have attributes which depend on synthesized attributes of nodes which are further to the *right* in the tree. Since in this case the nodes are constructed left-to-right, these attributes are not available when needed. In each case, the difficulty arises because of the impossibility of knowing that a particular factor of a concatenation is the last until *after* it has been parsed.

In the case of traversal of the AST, it is possible to attribute the nodes of a concatenation sequence in a single left-to-right scan. This is possible because the sequence is completely constructed *before* the traversal is made. The test condition in the **while** loop of Figure 10.20 shows one way of doing this.

Finally, it may be noted that the difficulty with closures does not arise in the case of regular right-part grammars, because the presence of a closure is announced *in advance* by the left brace symbol. However, the problem with concatenations remains unaltered.

10.5.4   Section checklist and summary definitions

- Attribute grammars are a method of formally specifying the semantics of languages in terms of the underlying CFG.

- An attribute grammar defines attributes for each grammar symbol, and defines semantic functions which determine how particular attributes are computed from the attributes of other symbols which appear in the same CFG production.

- If an attribute has been evaluated it is said to be available. When every argument of a semantic function is available the attribute which it defines is said to be ready for evaluation.

- If a semantic function of a production computes an attribute of the left-hand-side symbols in terms of attributes of the right-hand-side symbols, then the attribute is said to be synthesized. Information for synthesized attributes thus flows *up* the derivation tree.

- If a semantic function of a production computes an attribute of a right-hand-side symbol, then that attribute is said to be inherited.

Information for inherited attributes thus flows into a node from its parent and siblings on the derivation tree.

- Attributes of symbols which are determined by a lower-level recognizer are said to be intrinsic. Intrinsic attributes are synthesized attributes of the lower-level grammar.

- A grammar is said to be *L*-attributed provided the inherited attributes of every production obey certain restrictions. The inherited attributes of a symbol in a production may depend on inherited attributes of the LHS symbol of the production, or on any attribute of the symbols which are further left in the production RHS. They may not depend on synthesized attributes of the LHS symbol, or on attributes of symbols which are further to the right in the production RHS.

- If a grammar is *L*-attributed, then it may be completely attributed during a single, depth-first, left-to-right traversal of the derivation tree. In particular, it may be completely attributed during parsing by a top-down parser.

- Many language features of interest cannot be defined by attribute grammars in such a way that trees may be attributed during parsing. In these cases one or more separate traversals of the tree may be required.

Exercises

10.1 A simple hierarchical index is to be implemented as an AST. The index provides for items and sub-items, with each item possessing a list of page numbers corresponding to the used occurrences of the indexed term. A possible IDL definition is as follows.

> **structure** *Index*
> **root** *ILIST* **is**
>
> ILIST ::= list;   — only one node of this class
> list => asItems : **seqOf** *ITEM*;
>
> *ITEM* ::= item;   — only one node of this class
> *item* => lxItemName : *string*,   — an external type
>   asOccurList : **seqOf** *INTEGER*,   — page numbers
>   asSubItems : **seqOf** *SUBITEM*;   — possibly empty
>
> *SUBITEM* ::= subItem;   — only one node of this class
> *subItem* => lxItemName   : *string*,   — external type
>   asOccurList   : **seqOf** *INTEGER*;— page numbers
> **end**.

Draw a diagram of the structure of the tree representing an index which includes the following entries.

aardvark : 25, 147.

. . .

Pascal
   Blaise : 17, 38;
   language : 17, 54, 108.

. . .

zymurgy : 78.

10.2 Write a procedure outline for a tree-walker for the trees defined by the IDL of Exercise 10.1, and which produces output in the indented format indicated in the exercise. This is a simple example of an *unparser*.

10.3 Devise an IDL definition for ASTs to represent strings in a (forward) Polish expression language. The grammar is

   goal → *expr* '='.
   expr → *atom* | *binop expr expr* | *monop expr*.
  binop → *sub* | *add* | *mul* | *div*.
  monop → *negate*.
   atom → *number* | *ident*.

[*Hint*: Note that the operators have no attributes other than their designating tag.]

10.4 Write Pascal declarations which implement the IDL in your answer to Exercise 10.3, and write a recursive descent AST builder for this language.

10.5 Two of the statements in a simplified programming language have the following grammar.

   statement → *assignment* | *increment*.
  assignment → *variable* ':=' *expression*.
   increment → '*INC*' '(' *variable* ',' *expression* ')'.
  expression → ['−'] *term* {'+' *term* }.
    term → *variable* | *constant*.

The *INC* function increments the designated *variable* by the value of the *expression*.

Create an IDL definition of AST type for this grammar fragment. You may assume that each variable node has a semantic attribute which 'points' to the descriptor for that variable, and that every constant node has a semantic attribute which accesses the value of the constant.

10.6 Suppose that, in the grammar of Exercise 10.3, the *INC* operation may be performed more efficiently than a simple assignment which performs the same task, so that it is desirable to transform the tree to the *INC* form whenever that is possible.

Design a procedure which obtains a tree-to-tree transformation to obtain the more efficient form whenever possible.

10.7   Write the code for a syntax-directed tool which reads the output file produced by the tree-walking procedures of Section 10.3, and creates an NFSA data structure along the lines of the model solution to Exercise 4.8.

10.8   Modify the *encode* procedure of Figure 10.20, so that it makes use of the semantic attributes evaluated by the procedure in Figure 10.29.

Further reading

Tree-building is one of the standard ways in which programming language compilers represent the structure of a program during translation. Many of the standard compiler construction texts give more detail on this topic. One example which deals in detail with the use of attribute grammars to formally define the syntax and so-called static semantics of programming languages is by Waite and Goos (1984).

The defining document for the interface description language, IDL, of which we have used a subset, is by Nestor *et al.* (1981), while the use of IDL to define the standard intermediate forms for software tools which operate on Ada programs is detailed in *The DIANA Reference Manual* (Evans *et al.*, 1983).

A more advanced treatment of attributed trees and attribute grammars is provided in *GAG: A practical compiler generator* (Kastens *et al.*, 1982), and in *Generating language-based environments* (Reps, 1982), which address compilers and syntax-directed editors respectively.

Chapter 11 Syntax-directed Translation

11.1 Simple translation

For many of the tasks for which language recognizers are used, the semantic actions may be thought of as the emission of an ordered sequence of output symbols belonging to some output alphabet. Of course, in many cases the required output quite literally is a string, or perhaps a file. It is then often helpful to consider the whole task of language recognition as being an input-string to output-string transformation, which we call 'string to string translation', or when the context is clear, just 'translation'.

In some cases the relationship between the input and output strings is highly indirect, as is the relationship between a regular expression and its representation as a file specifying the transitions of a compacted FSA table. In other cases, such as the translation of a simple algorithm from BASIC to FORTRAN, the relationship is immediately apparent, even if the implementation of the translator itself is non-trivial.

In the previous chapter we saw how the emission of output may be performed after the construction of some kind of explicit tree representation of a sentence. The complete sentence is then parsed before any output is produced, often leading to the creation of very large data structures. **Syntax-directed translation** is the name given to a group of techniques which allows output to be generated incrementally during the parsing process, thus avoiding the construction of auxiliary data structures to represent the completely parsed sentence.

The derivation of a sentence in a language specified by a CFG consists of a number of elementary replacement steps each corresponding to a production of the grammar. The introduction of syntactic categories allows us to deal with component sublanguages as single, named entities, even though in many cases these sublanguages are infinite. In syntax-directed translation we would like to adopt the same level of abstraction, and deal with the component sublanguages of output substrings as single entities.

In its simplest form, a syntax-directed translation scheme associates an output substring with each phrase of the CFG. There may be variations in the ordering of the symbols between the input and output substrings in a translation, but there is still a recognizable correspondence between the two.

Consider, for example, the translation of an algebraic expression from the normal infix-operator form to reverse Polish notation. In the input language we may have two substrings which each belong to the syntactic category *term* combined together by an addition operator. In the corresponding output string there will be substrings corresponding to the two component *terms*, followed by an addition operator. The derivation

$$expression \implies term_1 \; '+' \; term_2$$

expresses the idea that an expression may be composed of two substrings of the syntactic category *term*, separated by an addition operator. Similarly, the translation of this production

$$expression \implies term_1 \; term_2 \; 'add'$$

expresses the idea that the output is comprised of two substrings each of which is the translation of the syntactic category *term* in the input string, with the two followed by an addition symbol. In this particular example, the order of the substrings in the input happens to be the same as the order of the corresponding translations in the output, but such is not always the case.

Notice that we may write 'output substring corresponding to a *term*' with the same facility as we write 'input substring belonging to the syntactic category *term*'. Only if there is this correspondence can we hope to find a simple translation scheme.

In order to formalize what follows, we suppose that we have an input (source) alphabet Σ, and an output (target) alphabet Δ. We will further assume that the language is defined by a CFG which introduces a set of syntactic categories, the non-terminal alphabet, N, and a set of productions. We express the relationship between the derivation rules for the input strings and the emission of output strings by associating a translation string with each production right-hand-side. Just as the right-hand side of each production is a string from the vocabulary $(\Sigma \cup N)$, so the translation is a string from the union of the output alphabet and the non-terminal alphabet, $(N \cup \Delta)$. Notice carefully that although we will use the same non-terminal symbols in both productions and translations, the meaning is subtly different. In a production a non-terminal symbol stands in place of some substring from the input alphabet, while in a translation the same symbol will stand in place of a corresponding substring from the output alphabet.

We now associate a translation string with every production of the grammar. The convention which we will follow is that the translation string is separated from the production right-hand-side by a comma. Such an augmented grammar is called a **syntax-directed translation scheme** (SDTS).

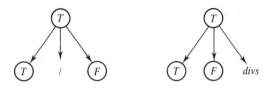

Figure 11.1   Corresponding derivation steps in an SDTS.

An SDTS for an infix to reverse Polish expression translator is

goal	→ *expr* $'='$,	*expr* $'end'$.	(1)
expr	→ *term*,	*term*	(2)
	→ $'+'$ *term*,	*term*	(3)
	→ $'-'$ *term*,	*term* $'negate'$	(4)
	→ *expr* $'+'$ *term*,	*expr* *term* $'add'$	(5)
	→ *expr* $'-'$ *term*,	*expr* *term* $'sub'$.	(6)
term	→ *fact*,	*fact*	(7)
	→ *term* $'*'$ *fact*,	*term* *fact* $'mult'$	(8)
	→ *term* $'/'$ *fact*,	*term* *fact* $'divs'$.	(9)
fact	→ *atom*,	*atom*	(10)
	→ $'('$ *expr* $')'$,	*expr*.	(11)

In this example, the input alphabet is $\{atom,+,-,*,/,(,),=\}$, and the output alphabet is $\{atom,negate,add,sub,mult,divs,end\}$. Using this notation, the production right-hand-side string and the translation string share the same left-hand-side non-terminal symbol. A typical production, (9) say, may be thought of as stating 'A *term* in the source language may be a (substring corresponding to the syntactic category−) *term* followed by a divide symbol followed by a (substring corresponding to the syntactic category−) *factor*'. The translation part of the rule then states 'The translation of a *term* may be a (target alphabet substring which is the translation of a−) *term*, followed by a (target alphabet substring which is the translation of a−) *factor*, followed by the symbol *divs*'.

Note carefully that in the translation strings a minus sign in the source language translates into a *negate* or *sub* depending on the context, reflecting that in the output language unary and binary operations are distinguished.

In cases where some syntactic category is repeated in a production right-hand-side, we introduce subscript indices on the non-terminal symbols. This ensures that it is clear which occurrence of the symbol in the translation string corresponds to each occurrence in the production. For example, a production might appear in an SDTS as

$$A \rightarrow aB_1bB_2, \qquad B_1B_2x.$$

The two parts of each rule of an SDTS may be thought of as supplying

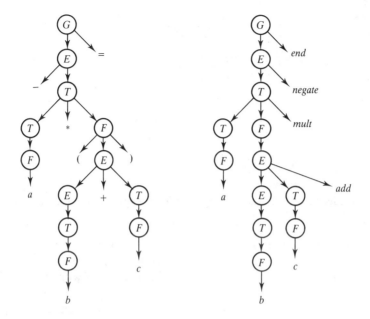

Figure 11.2 Corresponding trees generated by an SDTS.

replacement rules for the simultaneous derivation of corresponding sentences in the source and target languages. The replacement subtrees for production (9) in each language are shown in Figure 11.1.

Any derivation of a sentence in the source language will lead to the derivation of an equivalent sentence in the target language, with the two completed strings being given by the frontiers of the two final trees. An example of equivalent trees derived by this method are shown in Figure 11.2, for the equivalent strings '$-a*(b+c)=$', and '*a b c add mult negate end*'.

Of course, our real interest is not in deriving corresponding sentences in the two languages, but in producing a translation of the source sentence as a byproduct of the parsing process.

It may be noted in passing that in the example the task of translating between the two languages is easily performed by the methods of the previous chapter. First an AST is formed, getting rid of the parentheses and many of the unit-length replacements in the derivation tree. This tree is then walked in postorder, with a simple one-to-one translation between node designations and output alphabet symbols producing the output. The AST for the example in Figure 11.2 is shown in Figure 11.3.

Let us assume a situation in which the completion of the recognition of the right-hand side of a production also leads to the completion of the output of symbols corresponding to that particular expansion of the

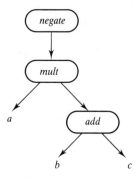

Figure 11.3   Abstract syntax tree for the expression in Figure 11.2.

left-hand-side symbol. If the recognized symbol is in turn part of the right-hand side of another production, then another component of that new construct has been translated. This idea can only work provided that the non-terminal symbols in the translation part of each rule appear in exactly the same order as the corresponding symbols in the right-hand side of the production part of the rule. Only when this is the case can the output for some construct be emitted without waiting to see the context in which it appears further up the implicit derivation tree. Consider, for example, an SDTS with a rule

$$A \rightarrow BC, \qquad CB.$$

Here the recognition of the symbol B cannot lead to the emission of output, since according to the translation part of the rule the 'B-output' must follow the 'C-output', but the C-part of the input string has not even been encountered at that point of the parse. Clearly, in such cases some data structure must be created to hold sufficient information to allow the out-of-order output to be deferred until the appropriate time.

In all cases where an SDTS has rules in which the translation part of the rule has non-terminal symbols occurring in exactly the same order as the corresponding symbols in the production right-hand-side, then we say that the SDTS is **simple**.

In the next two sections we investigate the incorporation of semantic actions in top-down and bottom-up parsers so as to implement syntax-directed translation for a simple-SDTS.

11.1.1   Section checklist and summary definitions

Syntax-directed translation schemes (SDTS).

- An SDTS consists of a CFG in which every production right-hand-side (RHS) has an associated translation string.

- In cases where a non-terminal symbol appears more than once in a production RHS, each occurrence is given a unique subscript index, and the corresponding occurrence in the translation string is identified with the same index.
- If Σ, N, and Δ, respectively, denote the input, non-terminal, and output alphabets, then each production RHS is a string from $(\Sigma \cup N)^*$, while every translation is a string from $(N \cup \Delta)^*$.
- An SDTS is said to be simple if the non-terminal symbols in the translation string occur in the same order as the corresponding occurrences in the production RHS.

11.2 Simple-SDTS and recursive descent

The first consideration in implementing a simple-SDTS by recursive descent must be to ensure that the grammar is in a suitable form for the parsing method, that is, that the regular right-part grammar obeys the LL(1) condition.

The possibility of using an RRP grammar requires a slight extension to the notation introduced in the last section. Firstly, the repetitive structure implied by the closure construct must be reflected in the translation rules. Optional elements in the grammar must also find their expression in the translation rules. We adopt the convention that curly brackets are used in the translation string to enclose the translation elements corresponding to closure constructs in the production right-hand-sides. Similarly, square brackets are used to indicate the translation elements which correspond to an optional element in the production part of a rule. In general, we use subscript non-terminal occurrences enclosed within closure meta-symbols, so that the corresponding occurrence in the translation string may be identified.

An extended-LL(1) simple-SDTS for the infix to reverse Polish translator using the described conventions is as follows.

Production	Translation
$goal \rightarrow expr \ '='.$	$expr \ 'end'$
$expr \rightarrow [addop] \ term_1 \ \{addop \ term_n\}.$	$term_1 \ ['negate'] \ \{term_n addop\}$
$term \rightarrow fact_1 \ \{mulop \ fact_n\}.$	$fact_1 \ \{fact_n mulop\}$
$fact \rightarrow atom$	$atom$
$\rightarrow \ '(' \ expr \ ')'.$	$expr$

In this grammar we have presumed that the lexical symbols '+' and '−' are both counted as *addops*, with a similar convention for the multiplying operators. In the translation strings the unary minus will translate into a *negate* symbol in the output, while a unary plus will translate into the null string.

We may now embed the emission of output symbols into the code of a perfectly straightforward recursive descent parser. Figure 11.4 shows example code. We assume the existence of the usual procedure *GetSymbol* which fetches the next input symbol into the scanner state variable *symbol*, and a utility procedure *Emit* which causes the emission of any designated symbol of the output alphabet. *Emit* has a heading

> **procedure** *Emit*(*sy* : *OutSymbolType*);

where *OutSymbolType* is some enumerated type specifying the target alphabet Δ.

In the specification of the translation which Figure 11.4 provides, we deliberately glossed over one small point. The question is, do the symbols *addop* and *mulop* refer to terminal symbols or non-terminal symbols?

If we take the view that *addop* is a non-terminal, then it will be necessary to introduce a few new rules into the SDTS to translate the new non-terminal productions. It will be necessary also to modify one of the previous rules to take account of the fact that the addition symbols have two distinct contexts. The new and modified rules might be as follows.

Production	Translation
expr → [*unary*] *term*$_1$ {*addop*$_n$ *term*$_n$}.	*term*$_1$ [*unary*] {*term*$_n$ *addop*$_n$}
unary → *plus*	ε
→ *minus*.	*negate*
addop → *plus*	*add*
→ *minus*.	*sub*

The trouble is that if we view *addop* as being a syntactic category then the translation scheme is no longer simple, since the strings corresponding to *term*$_n$ and *addop*$_n$ are reversed in the output, as are those for *unary* and *term*$_1$.

It was remarked in the last section that if an SDTS was not simple, then data structures might need to be created to hold information regarding the deferred output. It is possible to view the variable *op* which stores the operator symbol in the procedure *ExprTranslate* as being just this data structure.

11.2.1 Deferring output for non-simple translations

Since we have already discovered simple means to reverse the order of output for the *term* and *operator* translations for the previous example, it hardly seems worth while pursuing alternative mechanisms to achieve the same end. However, another technique which is more general in its applicability will be demonstrated.

A general technique to circumvent a non-simple translation rule in an SDTS is to divert the output of the troublesome non-terminal to some kind of buffer area in which the output may be queued. The procedure

```
procedure ExprTranslate;
  var op : SymbolType;
begin
  if symbol in addops then begin
    op := symbol;
    GetSymbol;
    TermTranslate;
    if op = minus then Emit(negate) (* else nothing *)
    end
  else TermTranslate;
  while symbol in addops do begin
    op := symbol;
    GetSymbol;
    TermTranslate;
    if op = minus then Emit(sub)
    else Emit(add))
    end (* while *)
end;

procedure TermTranslate;
  var op : SymbolType;
begin
  FactTranslate;
  while symbol in mulops do begin
    op := symbol;
    GetSymbol;
    FactTranslate;
    if op = star then Emit(mult)
    else Emit(divs)
    end (* while *)
end;

procedure FactTranslate;
begin
  if symbol = atom then begin
    { copy lexical attribute to output };
    GetSymbol;
    end
  else if symbol = open then begin
    GetSymbol; (* get past '(' *)
    ExprTranslate;
    if symbol = close then GetSymbol
    else error('missing right parenthesis')
    end
  else error('illegal factor')
end;
```

Figure 11.4 Procedures for recursive descent translator.

```
procedure ExprTranslate (var destE : Destination);
  var OutQueue : Destination;
      (* in this case 'queue' is a single symbol *)

      procedure UnaryTranslate(var destU : Destination);
      begin
        if symbol = plus then GetSymbol (* no emit *)
        else begin
          GetSymbol;
          Emit(destU,negate);
          end
      end;

      procedure AddopTranslate(var destA : Destination);
        (* similar to UnaryTranslate *)

begin
  InitializeEmptyQueue(OutQueue);
  if symbol in addops then begin
    UnaryTranslate(OutQueue); (* save output *)
    TermTranslate(destE); (* immediate output *)
    EmitQueue(OutQueue); (* emit saved output *)
    end
  else TermTranslate;
  while symbol in addops do begin
    AddopTranslate(OutQueue); (* save output *)
    TermTranslate(destE); (* immediate output *)
    EmitQueue(OutQueue); (* emit saved output *)
    end (* while *)
end;
```

Figure 11.5   SDTS procedure with output deferral.

Emit is modified so that it is able to switch its output to this queue, and there must be a dequeueing procedure to copy the deferred symbols to the output stream at the appropriate time. Figure 11.5 shows the code of the *ExprTranslate* procedure, modified to work this way. Each recursive descent procedure is passed an actual parameter indicating the actual destination for its direct output. The *Emit* procedure has a corresponding destination procedure.

Of course, the code in Figure 11.5 is unnecessarily complicated. There is no need to form a queue structure and switch the output of the *Emit* procedure, since it is known that the deferred output is always just a single symbol. However, the code given is important as an example, since it demonstrates the technique which must be used if the extent of the deferred output is not known in advance. It is also important to note that, in the general case, the possibility of recursion necessitates that the deferred output queues are kept as local variables of the translation procedures. What appears to be direct output within some procedure may, in fact, be output to the queue of the procedure which invoked it.

However, an alternative interpretation of the code in Figure 11.4, is just to view *addop* as being a single terminal symbol with two variants (or perhaps a Boolean-valued lexical attribute). In this view the storing of the local variable *op* corresponds to simply remembering which variant was encountered. Whichever interpretation is taken of the division between the lexical and syntactic grammars, it is clear that the embedding of the translation actions within the recursive descent parser has not particularly increased the complexity of the code beyond that of the bare recognizer.

The translation example which we have used here is particularly simple, but nevertheless demonstrates the major principles. An example of slightly greater complexity is treated in Section 11.4.

11.2.2 Section checklist and summary definitions

1. Simple-SDTS and recursive descent.
   - The incorporation of simple-SDTS actions into a recursive descent parser, involves the introduction of statements into the body of each recognition procedure, which call for the emission of symbols belonging to the output alphabet Δ.
   - On the successful return of each recognition procedure, an input language substring has been parsed and a corresponding output substring emitted.

2. Deferred output.
   - Difficulties caused by non-simple translation rules may be circumvented by implementing a system in which output from certain recognition procedures is buffered and emitted at some appropriate later stage.

11.3 Simple-SDTS and bottom-up parsing

11.3.1 Postfix translations

The incorporation of semantic actions which emit translation strings into an LR parser needs separate consideration, since it turns out to be somewhat different to the case of recursive descent.

The chief difference arises because a production is not recognized until the whole of the right-hand side has been parsed. If the parser is to emit code corresponding to right-hand-side non-terminal symbols as they are recognized, then any emitted output which belongs to the production as a whole, rather than to the components, must appear at the end of the output. Consider the rule

$$expr \rightarrow expr \; '+' \; term, \qquad expr \; term \; 'add'.$$

By the time the LR automaton enters the state which indicates reduction by the given production, the output corresponding to the components *expr* and *term* have already been emitted. If recognition of the completed production calls for the emission of any symbol of the output alphabet in any position other than the end, then it will be too late. In the given case there is no problem, since the symbol '*add*' is emitted at the end of the translation string.

The general condition which must apply to translation rules, if they are to be readily implemented by an LR parser, is that any output alphabet symbols of the translation part of the rules must appear after all of the non-terminal symbols. The general form of each rule must be

$$A \rightarrow \underbrace{uBvC \ldots Dw,}_{\text{any symbols from } V} \qquad \underbrace{BC \ldots Dx.}_{\substack{\text{non-terminal} \\ \text{symbols only}}}$$

where A, B, C, D, all belong to N; u, v, w all belong to Σ^*, and x is some string from Δ^*. Note that B, C, and D must appear in the correct order in the translation string (i.e. the condition that the SDTS be *simple*), and that the terminal symbols from Δ must all appear at the end.

If the translation scheme obeys the above conditions, we say that the translation is **postfix**. Note, however, that the use of the term postfix in this connection does not necessarily have to do with postfix operators such as occur with reverse Polish expressions, although it is a fact that reverse Polish expression grammars do lead to postfix, simple-SDTS.

A left-recursive, postfix simple-SDTS for the infix to reverse Polish translator was given previously, and is repeated here.

goal	$\rightarrow expr \; '=',$	*expr* '*end*'.	(1)
expr	$\rightarrow term,$	*term*	(2)
	$\rightarrow \; '+' \; term,$	*term*	(3)
	$\rightarrow \; '-' \; term,$	*term* '*negate*'	(4)
	$\rightarrow expr \; '+' \; term,$	*expr term* '*add*'	(5)
	$\rightarrow expr \; '-' \; term,$	*expr term* '*sub*'.	(6)
term	$\rightarrow fact,$	*fact*	(7)
	$\rightarrow term \; '*' \; fact,$	*term fact* '*mult*'	(8)
	$\rightarrow term \; '/' \; fact,$	*term fact* '*divs*'.	(9)

$$fact \rightarrow atom, \qquad atom \qquad\qquad (10)$$
$$\rightarrow \text{'(' } expr \text{ ')'}, \qquad expr. \qquad\qquad (11)$$

It will be seen that the semantic actions associated with the reduction actions of the parser are very few in number. For many reductions all of the required output has been generated before the reduce action is initiated. Productions (2),(3),(7),(10) and (11) are in this situation, while the others require the emission of a single symbol to complete the output.

However, in order to make a comparison between the ease with which simple-SDTS may be implemented using top-down and bottom-up parsers, it is necessary to investigate the extent to which the insistence upon postfix translation rules is a real restriction.

11.3.2 Dealing with non-postfix constructions

On the face of it, it would seem that the top-down methods have a clear advantage for simple-SDTS, since it is possible to emit output symbols at any time during the recognition of a production right-hand-side, and not just at the end, as implied by the restriction to postfix translations. What is not clear, however, is whether or not this apparent advantage of the top-down methods outweighs the greater applicability of the LR methods. Furthermore, it is often possible to evade the restriction to postfix translation by means of transformations of the grammar.

Let us consider a typical situation in which a translation rule calls for emission of non-postfix output, a production

$$A \rightarrow aBC, \qquad BxCz.$$

where A, B, $C \in N$; $a \in \Sigma$; and x, $z \in \Delta$. A recursive descent parser will have a procedure with a structure along the following lines,

```
procedure ATranslate;
begin
  case symbol of
      . . .
    a: begin
        GetSymbol; (* get past 'a' *)
        BTranslate;
        Emit(x);
        CTranslate;
        Emit(z)
      end;
      . . .
  end; (* case *)
end; (* ATranslate *)
```

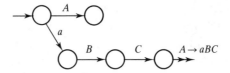

Figure 11.6 Fragment of LR characteristic machine.

For the bottom-up method, the fragment of the characteristic machine which recognizes this production will be as shown in Figure 11.6.

Since the C-output will have already been emitted by the time that the reduction state is entered in this machine, it too late to do anything about the x symbol.

However, consider a transformation of the grammar which introduces a new, null non-terminal K, and for which recognition of the K causes an x to be emitted.

$A \rightarrow aBKC,$ $BKCz.$
$K \rightarrow \varepsilon,$ $x.$

The fragment of the characteristic machine will now be as shown in Figure 11.7. The restriction to postfix translation has been complied with, by the artifice of making the emission of the required intermediate symbol a semantic action of the recognition of the newly invented, null non-terminal K. Note that the translation string for K trivially obeys the postfix restriction.

What is not at all clear, from a casual inspection of Figures 11.6 and 11.7, is that the characteristic machine for the modified grammar will be LALR, or even LR(1) for that matter. The LALR lookahead of the symbol-erasure reduction, $K \rightarrow \varepsilon$, will be all of the symbols of $FIRST(C)$, presuming for simplicity that C is not also nullable. What, however, if there are other terminal or non-terminal transitions out of the same state, which share some of the same terminal symbols in their $FIRST$ sets? Such a circumstance will have no effect on the machine fragment shown in Figure 11.6, but will lead to a fatal *shift–reduce* conflict in Figure 11.7.

Fortunately, a classic theoretical result dispells any doubts which might linger regarding the possibility of the introduction of new non-terminals as *hooks* on which to hang symbol emission actions. In effect, Brosgol (1974) showed that if the construct is LL(1), then it is always possible to introduce a marker symbol on which to attach the emission action, without causing a conflict of the type which we have hinted at. Arguing in reverse, we may state that if the introduction of the marker symbol is not possible, then the language construct is not LL(1) either.

It should also be noted that it is often possible to attach the required emission action to a terminal transition rather than to null reduction. In

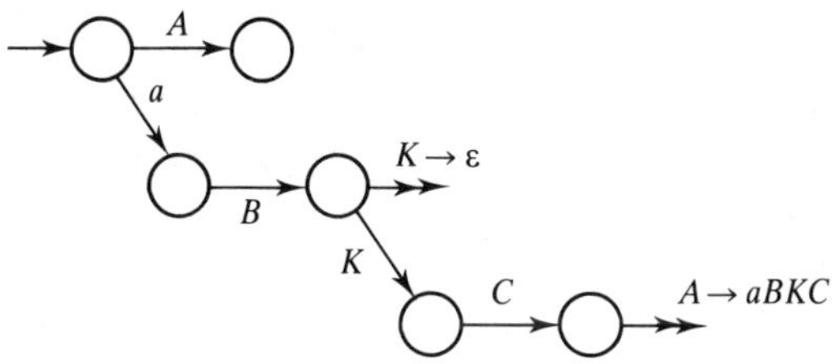

Figure 11.7 Characteristic machine with nullable symbol.

essence, the method requires the introduction of a unit production which derives the terminal symbol, and the required semantic action is attached to the corresponding reduction. If, in the previous example, the translation of production $A \to aBC$ was required to start with an explicit output string, xBC say, then a new non-terminal, K, may be introduced with a single production $K \to a$. This production will have a translation x. The connection between the possible conflicts in the prefix state and the LL(1) condition for this example, are explored in Exercise 11.1.

We must, therefore, conclude that the restriction to postfix translations for bottom-up translators does not cause any real disadvantage compared to top-down methods, except for the additional work involved in transforming the grammar by introducing suitable marker symbols. Since it is usually the case that the grammar will also need modification to comply with the extended-LL(1) restrictions required by a recursive descent parser, there is little basis for strong preference either way.

11.3.3 Section checklist and summary definitions

- Bottom-up translation by a simple-SDTS is only possible if the translation strings obey the postfix condition.
- An SDTS translation is said to be postfix if and only if no emission of output symbols is required until the reduction takes place. This implies that all translation strings must have all output symbols at the right-hand end of the string.
- In cases of non-postfix translations, it is necessary to insert nullable non-terminal symbols into the production right-hand-sides. The emission of output symbols can then be attached to the reduction of the new symbol to the empty string, ε.
- The introduction of nullable non-terminal symbols will never lead to a parser conflict if the language construct is LL(1). Therefore, if a recursive descent parser may implement a particular translation rule, then an LR family parser may also do so.

11.4   More general syntax-directed translation

In more general situations, syntax-directed translation is more complicated than has been indicated by the examples so far. Certainly the
possibility of output substrings needing to be emitted out of order
requires attention, as does circumventing the restriction to postfix
translations for bottom-up parsers. Quite apart from these considerations,
however, it is very often the case that the output code depends on
contextual information beyond that given by the syntactic rules. The
symbols to be emitted in any particular case may depend on semantic
information which needs to be computed along with the parse.

In the vast majority of cases of syntax-directed translation, it is
necessary to perform semantic actions other than the simple emission of
output. We have only looked at the two extremes of a possible spectrum.
At one extreme, the building of an AST provides for the summarization
of all of the information contained in the original source language string,
but does not directly provide any output. At the other extreme, we have
discussed syntax-directed translations in which the only effect of
recognition is the emission of an output string. Furthermore, for these
translation schemes there has always been a unique correspondence
between the syntactic entities and the output substrings into which they
translate.

In practice, it is very common to have to combine the emission of
output with the building of subsidiary data-structures. In many cases the
exact output to be emitted for any given syntactic construct depends on
other, semantic information regarding the string which has been
recognized. A typical example of this arises in the translation of
arithmetic expressions in those languages which have arithmetic operands
of different numerical types, such as integers and real numbers. In such
cases the arithmetic operators are said to be overloaded, since, for
example, the same multiply symbol '*', is used to specify both integer and
real-number multiplication. The emitted output, then, depends on the
numerical type of the operands, an attribute which is not immediately
available from the syntactic form of the expression.

11.4.1   A conditional, top-down, SDTS translation

We will explore a very simple example which illustrates some of these
points. The object is a reverse translation from (forward) Polish
expressions into normal infix form. The complexity arises because we
wish to emit parentheses only when it is absolutely necessary to do so.
The dual problem, that of translating into infix form from reverse Polish,
turns out to be much more difficult, and is not at all suitable for syntax-
directed translation, as we shall see.

```
procedure ExprTranslate(NeedParenthIfSum : BOOLEAN);
begin
  case symbol of
    atomsmbl: begin
                Emit(atom);
                GetSymbol;
              end;
    starsmbl: begin
                GetSymbol;
                ExprTranslate(TRUE);
                Emit(multiply);
                ExprTranslate(TRUE)
              end;
    plussmbl: begin
                GetSymbol;
                if NeedParenthIfSum then Emit(open);
                ExprTranslate(FALSE);
                Emit(add);
                ExprTranslate(FALSE);
                if NeedParenthIfSum then Emit(close)
              end
  end (* case *)
end;
```

Figure 11.8   Translation to infix form, top-down version.

The CFG which we will use is given by

$G \to E\vdash.$
$E \to a \mid '*' \, EE \mid '+' \, EE.$

The conditions under which it is necessary to emit parentheses for a subexpression are easily deduced. In the syntax tree, if an addition node is the child of a multiply node, then parentheses are necessary. Parentheses are not needed in any other case, provided it is permissible to use the associative laws for multiplication and addition. This does mean that an expression such as '$a*(b*c)$' which leads to the Polish string '$*a*bc$' will translate back into the infix string '$a*b*c$' without any parentheses.

If it is necessary to ensure that the translation leads to an infix string with exactly the same evaluation order as the Polish string from which it was translated then a more complex set of rules is required. Working out the details of these rules is left to the exercises.

If an explicit tree were to be built, it would be simple to emit the correct output, by defining a Boolean-valued attribute at each node 'need

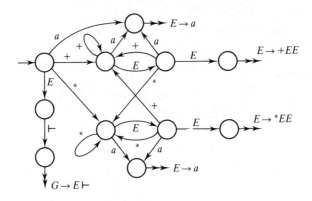

Figure 11.9 Characteristic machine for Polish expression grammar (unmodified).

parentheses if a sum'. This attribute would be computed from information inherited from the parent node. The attribute has the value *true* if the parent is a product node, and is false otherwise. With the introduction of a conditional form of translation, the SDTS for the grammar is

$$G \rightarrow E\vdash, \qquad\qquad E'.' \ .$$
$$E \rightarrow a, \qquad\qquad a$$
$$\rightarrow \ '*'E_1 E_2, \qquad E_1'*'E_2$$
$$\rightarrow \ '+'E_1 E_2, \qquad \textbf{if } \textit{NeedParenthIfSum} \textbf{ then}$$
$$\qquad\qquad '('E_1'+'E_2')'$$
$$\textbf{else}$$
$$\qquad\qquad E_1'+'E_2$$
$$\textbf{endif.}$$

It is not necessary to build an explicit tree in order to make use of this attribute, since it is an inherited attribute determined by the parent node. In the case of a recursive descent parser, the attribute may be passed as a Boolean value-mode parameter to each recursive call of the expression-recognition procedure. Suitable code is shown in Figure 11.8. This code is very simple, and very little need be said about it. However, what of an LR parser to perform the same task?

11.4.2 A conditional, bottom-up SDTS translation

In Chapter 9 it was noted, in passing, that both forward and reverse Polish string grammars were LR(0). The characteristic machine for the grammar given above is shown in Figure 11.9. In this figure the state for the reduction $E \rightarrow a$, is split into two to reduce the clutter.

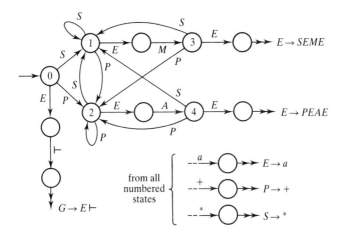

Figure 11.10   Characteristic machine for modified grammar.

It is clear that the SDTS given for the translation to infix form does not meet the postfix condition and hence cannot be used directly in a bottom-up recognizer. However, the grammar is LL(1), so we may be encouraged to try insertion of null non-terminal symbols into the grammar as hooks for the symbol emission actions.

A suitable grammar modification leads to the following SDTS.

$G \rightarrow E\vdash$, $E'.'$.
$E \rightarrow a$, a
$\quad \rightarrow SE_1ME_2$, E_1ME_2
$\quad \rightarrow PE_1AE_2$,   **if** *NeedParenthIfSum* **then**
                                         $\quad PE_1AE_2')'$
                                         else PE_1AE_2
                                         endif.
$M \rightarrow \varepsilon$, $'*'$.
$A \rightarrow \varepsilon$, $'+'$.
$S \rightarrow '*'$,   (* no output *)
$P \rightarrow '+'$,   **if** *NeedParenthIfSum* **then**
                                         $\quad '('$
                                         endif.

This scheme emits the same output strings as the previous grammar, but has translations which are postfix as well as being simple. Note that new non-terminals, M and A, have been invented to signify the emission of the *multiply* and *add* output symbols, respectively. Emission of a left parenthesis is attached to a non-null non-terminal, a new symbol P which derives the initial plus sign. The characteristic machine for this new grammar is shown in Figure 11.10.

Productions	Semantic action on completion
$G \rightarrow E\vdash$,	$Emit('.')$;
$E \rightarrow a$,	$Emit(a)$;
$ \rightarrow SE_1ME_2$,	$PopOpStack$;
$ \rightarrow PE_1AE_2$,	$PopOpStack$; **if** $StackTop = '*'$ **then** $Emit(')')$ **endif**;
$M \rightarrow \varepsilon$,	$Emit('*')$;
$A \rightarrow \varepsilon$,	$Emit('+')$;
$S \rightarrow '*'$,	$PushOp('*')$;
$P \rightarrow '+'$,	**if** $StackTop = '*'$ **then** $Emit('(')$ **endif**; $PushOp('+')$;

Figure 11.11   Semantic actions for modified grammar.

It may be seen that in this particular machine all the reductions appear on distinct states which have no shift actions. Therefore, in this case (and quite unusually) the recognizer is LR(0). We must now find some method of propagating the information required to decide when a parenthesis is to be emitted. Unlike the case with recursive descent, there are no parameters which may be used to pass attribute information to and fro, and the predicate must be evaluated from the parser stack, or a new data-structure devised for the purpose.

The most straightforward way to keep track of whether or not the current reduction has an immediate parent node on the implicit parse tree which corresponds to a multiplication operation is to keep a semantic stack of the operators which have been encountered. Whenever an operator symbol announces the start of a sum or product, then the corresponding symbol is pushed on the operator stack. On completion of the recognition of the production, the operator is popped back off.

The necessity for emitting a left parenthesis may be gauged by whether or not the operator currently on the top of the semantic operator stack is a *multiply*. The corresponding condition for the emission of a right parenthesis on completion of the recognition of the addition production depends on whether or not the popping of the *plus* sign associated with the completed production exposes a *multiply* operator on the top of the stack. Note, however, that the operator stack must be initialized with a *bottom* symbol, so that querying the value of the stacktop of an empty stack is not an error.

Figure 11.11 shows the complete set of semantic actions corresponding to each reduction action. This table should be compared with the

SDTS for the modified grammar shown above, from which it was derived. This example is typical of practical syntax-directed translations. Once the translation strings have been transformed into a conditional postfix form, then semantic actions may be devised which not only emit the postfix symbols, but also perform whatever updating of the data structure is necessary to support the condition evaluation. The table lookup procedure of the LR automaton then, not only retrieves the appropriate shift or reduce action, but also returns a datum which is used to select the semantic action.

11.4.3 An unsuitable grammar for syntax-directed translation

As a final example, or perhaps counter-example, we consider an apparently simple translation scheme which is unsuitable for syntax-directed translation.

The task of translating from *reverse* Polish expressions to minimally parenthesized infix expressions appears to be no more difficult than the case last considered. An SDTS might be as follows.

$$G \rightarrow E\vdash, \qquad E'.'.$$
$$E \rightarrow a, \qquad a$$
$$\rightarrow E_1E_2,'*', \qquad E_1'*'E_2$$
$$\rightarrow E_1E_2, \qquad \textbf{if } NeedParenthIfSum \textbf{ then}$$
$$\qquad\qquad\qquad\qquad '('E_1'+'E_2')'$$
$$\qquad\qquad\qquad \textbf{else } E_1'+'E_2$$
$$\qquad\qquad\qquad \textbf{endif}.$$

This SDTS is simple, and the grammar was shown to be LR(0) in the solution to Exercise 9.1. A bottom-up recognizer would seem to be indicated, if only the translations could be put into the postfix form. Introduction of erasable non-terminal symbols, as in the previous example, but in this case named L, M, and A, now leads to the following SDTS.

$$G \rightarrow E\vdash, \qquad E'.'.$$
$$E \rightarrow a, \qquad a$$
$$\rightarrow E_1ME_2,'*', \qquad E_1ME_2$$
$$\rightarrow LE_1AE_2'+', \qquad \textbf{if } NeedParenthIfSum \textbf{ then}$$
$$\qquad\qquad\qquad\qquad LE_1AE_2')'$$
$$\qquad\qquad\qquad \textbf{else } E_1AE_2$$
$$\qquad\qquad\qquad \textbf{endif}.$$
$$M \rightarrow \varepsilon, \qquad '*' .$$
$$A \rightarrow \varepsilon, \qquad '+'.$$
$$L \rightarrow \varepsilon, \qquad \textbf{if } NeedParenthIfSum \textbf{ then}$$
$$\qquad\qquad\qquad '('$$
$$\qquad\qquad\qquad \textbf{endif}.$$

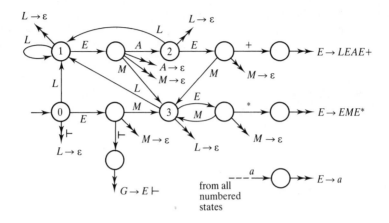

Figure 11.12   Characteristic machine for modified grammar.

The characteristic machine for the grammar is shown in Figure 11.12. As may be seen, there are *shift–reduce* conflicts for every occurrence of the reduction $L \rightarrow \varepsilon$, and there is a *reduce–reduce* conflict for the reductions $M \rightarrow \varepsilon$ and $A \rightarrow \varepsilon$. This comes as no surprise, since the grammar is not LL(1). In fact, a moment's consideration will show that when faced with a string '*atom atom atom . . . . . . * ⊢*' the emission of a correct infix operator as the second symbol of the translation may require an indefinitely long lookahead, since it may not be determined until the second last symbol in the input string has been read. This particular translation thus cannot be performed either by bottom-up or top-down methods without building data structures equivalent to the complete syntax tree.

11.4.4   Section checklist and summary definitions

1. Side-effects and attribute evaluation.
   - Many syntax-directed translation applications require that additional, semantic information be available to determine the correct output string. In such cases, it is necessary for the translator to evaluate semantic attributes as a side-effect of parsing. In general, it may be necessary to create data structures outside of the parser stack to hold data relating to these attributes.

2. Conditional translation.
   - The SDTS notation may be extended to allow for a conditional form of translation, where the output string associated with a particular production right-hand-side depends on the value of some

semantic attribute. These conditional forms may, in general, have multiple branches.

- The conditional SDTS notation indicates how the semantic attributes are used, by stating the translation string associated with each production for various values of appropriate attributes. However, a more general mechanism is required to specify how the attributes are generated and propagated, as well as how they determine the output strings.

- In the case of bottom-up SDTS, it is convenient to associate a single semantic action with each parser reduction, with the action including code for both conditional translation, when required, and attribute evaluation and propagation.

11.5 Case study 3: A simple pretty-printer

11.5.1 Introduction

There is a useful class of software tools which takes correct computer programs as input and creates output files containing the same program in some standard format. Such software tools are called **pretty-printers**. This section looks at the design of a simple pretty-printer for programs written in standard Pascal.

Since this is posed as an exercise in syntax-directed translation, it will be assumed that the input is a sequence of tokens which correspond to a sentence in the Pascal language. These tokens belong to an input alphabet consisting of exactly 60 symbols. These symbols are:

35 reserved words;
 3 lexical categories;
21 special symbols;
 1 pseudo-symbol *eofsy*.

Since the tool is to be implemented in Pascal, it is necessary to choose names for the tokens which do not clash with the reserved words. This is done by declaring an enumerated type for the alphabet which has names such as beginsy, endsy, varsy, for the reserved words **begin**, **end**, and **var**. The other tokens have descriptive alphabetic names. The declaration of the symbol type is shown in Figure 11.13.

The output alphabet will consist of the union of the input alphabet and the special formatting symbols newline and indenting spaces. Note that, unlike many tools which operate on Pascal source texts, no distinction need be made between numbers which are in real and integer format. Furthermore, in order to simplify the task, it will be assumed that

```
type   SymbolType = (
       (* error symbol *)
          err,
       (* keywords *)
          dosy,ifsy,insy,ofsy,orsy,tosy,andsy,endsy,nilsy,setsy,notsy,
          forsy,divsy,varsy,modsy,filesy,thensy,casesy,typesy,gotosy,
          withsy,elsesy,arraysy,beginsy,constsy,untilsy,whilesy,labelsy,
          packedsy,downtosy,recordsy,repeatsy,programsy,functionsy,
          proceduresy,
       (* special symbols *)
          plus,minus,star,slash,assigns,dot,comma,semicolon,colon,
          equal,noteq1,less,lesseql,greateql,greater,Lparent,Rparent,
          Lsquare,Rsquare,carat,dotdot,
       (* lexical categories *)
          number,ident,stringsy,
       (* end of file marker *)
          eofsy );
```

Figure 11.13   Symbol type for a Pascal pretty-printer.

any formatting spaces or newlines in the input are to be ignored, and that, for the present, comments should be ignored also.

In outline, the design will consist of a lexical scanner and a recursive descent parser which includes translation code. Since it is probable that the parser will be modified to recognize more details of the syntax than the first version, it is sensible to plan from the outset to construct a lexical scanner which recognizes the whole Pascal input alphabet. The parser may then be modified at will, without requiring the scanner to be modified to recognize any new tokens.

The code for the pretty-printer in the final form considered in this section runs to some 1000 lines of Pascal. Because of this bulk, the complete text is not listed, but rather, typical fragments are shown. In particular, the code of the lexical scanner is omitted. The scanner uses a perfect hash-function technique for recognizing reserved words, and is very much along the lines of the example code in Section 5.2. The grammar given in the *Pascal user manual and report* (Jensen and Wirth, 1974) is suitable for recursive descent parsing with only very minor modifications. In general we shall follow that reference in choosing names for the syntactic categories.

As a first example of the considerations which are involved in the design, we will consider a small subproblem, that of formatting compound statements. A typical SDTS which might be considered for the compound statement might be

$compound \rightarrow$ **'begin'** $statement_1$ {$';'$ $statement_n$} **'end'**,

> **'begin'**
> *newline indent statement$_1$*
> {$';'$ *newline indent statement$_n$*}
> *newline* **'end'**.

This translation indents the included statements, relative to the **begin** and **end** symbols, and places the semicolons which separate the statements on the same line as the preceding statement.

However, since compound statments may be nested, the emitted *indent* output in the translation scheme implies indentation relative to the current left margin, which must therefore be a local variable of the procedure. It is thus necessary to pass the required indent level as a value parameter to the procedure which recognizes the compound statement. In general, each recursive descent procedure will have a parameter, *mar*, which sets the left margin position for the recognized phrase. As the level of nesting increases, each procedure will pass an actual parameter to its subordinate procedures with value *mar + step*, where *step* is the indent-per-level constant. In the terminology of Chapter 10, the current margin of a statement is an inherited attribute, passed from calling to called procedures of the parser.

It will be assumed that utility procedures exist for the formatting actions of the parser procedures. In particular, a procedure *WriteGet-Symbol* writes the current symbol to the output stream, and calls for the lexical scanner to fetch the next symbol from the input stream.

As it turns out, it is convenient to separate the two actions of emitting a newline and emitting the spaces which indent the following structure, so that the two actions may be taken independently. The two procedures are called *NewLine* and *Margin*, where *Margin* has a formal parameter equal to the number of spaces required to reach the desired left margin. It is also convenient to adopt the convention that, at the call of each procedure which recognizes a statement, the output stream is already positioned somewhere on the correct line, but may require indenting to the correct margin position.

With these conventions, a first attempt at a procedure to recognize the compound statement might be as shown in Figure 11.14. The code for the recognition of statement sequences has been moved to a separate procedure, since it will also be used in the recognition of program and procedure blocks, and for the repeat statement.

Note that the code of Figure 11.14 does not attempt to output the formatting blanks for its subordinate statements, but merely provides for the emission of associated newlines. It does provide the formatting spaces for the output symbols which it directly emits, the beginning and ending

```
procedure StatSequence(mar : INTEGER);
begin
  (* statSequence -> statement {';' statement} *)
  Statement(mar);
  while symbol = semicolon do begin
    WriteGetSymbol;
    NewLine;
    Statement(mar);
    end;
end; (* assert: output position is at end of statement *)

procedure Compound(mar : INTEGER);
begin (* compound -> beginsy statSequence endsy. *)
  (* assert: current value of symbol = beginsy *)
  Margin(mar);
  WriteGetSymbol; (* beginsy *)
  NewLine;
  StatSequence(mar + step)
  NewLine; Margin(mar);
  WriteGetSymbol;
end; (* assert: output position is at end of endsy *)
```

Figure 11.14   Simple formatter for compound statements.

keywords. There are alternative conventions which might be adopted, but the important thing is that whichever convention is chosen it is enforced uniformly.

The chief problem with the code of Figure 11.14 is that a newline is invariably emitted before each statement is recognized, so that empty statements have a blank line allocated to them. The code will therefore format the perfectly legal compound statement **begin** $S1$; $S2$; **end** as

```
begin
  S1;
  S2;

end.
```

This is not incorrect, since there *is* an empty statement between the final semicolon and the end-symbol. However, the use of the extra semicolon is a very common idiom. Many teachers believe that less semicolon errors arise from adopting this convention than from adopting a policy of having no redundant semicolons. In effect, the choice is between having the occasional semicolon error when an additional statement is added immediately before an **end**, and having errors due to the odd erroneous

```
procedure RepeatRec(mar : INTEGER);
begin (* repeat -> repeatsy statSequence untilsy expression. *)
  Margin(mar);
  WriteGetSymbol; (* repeatsy *)
  if symbol in FirstStatement then NewLine;
  StatSequence(mar + step);
  NewLine; Margin(mar);
  WriteGetSymbol; (* untilsy *)
  Expression(mar + 6);
end; (* assert: position is at end of endsy *)
```

Figure 11.15   Formatting procedure for repeat statement with conditional
newline emission.

insertion of a semicolon before an **else**. In any case, it seems
unreasonable for a pretty-printer to emit a blank line whenever an empty
statement is encountered, unless it is policy to stamp out the use of such
extraneous semicolons.

In order to determine whether or not the next statement is empty, it
is only necessary to check whether the current symbol, presumed to be in
the director set for statement, is actually in *FIRST*(*statement*) or is in
FOLLOW(*statement*). Defining appropriate constant sets, the calls to
procedure *NewLine* in Figure 11.14 may be replaced by

if *symbol* **in** *FirstStatement* **then** *NewLine*;

corresponding to a conditional translation of the production for a
statement sequence.

Production: *statSequence → statement* {*';' statement* }.

Translation: *statement*
       {*';'*
        if *symbol* **in** *FIRST*(*statement*)
         then *Newline* **endif**;
       statement }.

Once again, it is stressed that the statement-translating procedures emit
any necessary indenting spaces, so that the translation is not only
conditional, but also involves the passing of an inherited *Margin* attribute
to the subordinate procedures.

The corresponding code for the procedure which recognizes the
repeat statement is shown in Figure 11.15.

Figure 11.15 directs attention to two potential problems. Firstly, what
happens if the program is erroneous, and the symbol which should be

until is not; and what happens if, say, the expression is too long to fit on one line. The code in Figure 11.15 simply prints out whichever token happens to be present in the input stream in the position in which **until** was expected. In contrast, the archetypal recursive descent procedure would check the actual symbol for correctness with code such as

> **if** *symbol* = *untilsy*
>   **then** *WriteGetSymbol*
>   **else** *Error*.

Since it is our aim to sensibly format correct programs, and not to usurp the error diagnosis task of a compiler, we will adopt a simple policy. At selected points in the parse, the program will simply skip over symbols, by copying them from input to output, looking for a symbol belonging to some prescribed set. If the input is free of errors, there will be no skip, since the very next symbol will be in the expected set. In either case, formatting will be recommenced when a symbol is found which belongs to the set. A procedure *ErrorSkip* implements this feature.

If a phrase which is normally written out on a single line is too long for that line, then it is sensible to fold the line so that continuation lines begin just inside the currently prevailing margin. It is a simple matter to check if the length of the next symbol will cause the right margin to be exceeded, and to emit a newline and appropriate indenting spaces as necessary. However, this requires that the current margin attribute be passed as a parameter to each call of the *WriteGetSymbol* procedure, and that the lexical scanner supply a symbol-length attribute for each symbol.

Another consideration at this stage might be the circumstances under which optional formatting symbols ought to be emitted. For example, which of the following translations should be used for an array declaration?

> Production: *array* → **'array'** *simpleType* **'of'** *type*.
>
> Translation (version 1):   **'array'** *simpleType* **'of'** *type*.
>
> Translation (version 2):   **'array'** *simpleType* **'of'**
>   *newline indent type*.

Ideally, the answer to this question would depend on how far across the page the *simpleType* extends, and how much space the *type* takes up.

Unfortunately, there is no way in which a *simple* syntax-directed translator can decide on this basis, since at the time that the decision must be made, the space required for the *type* is unknown. Nevertheless, an informed guess may be made on the basis of the information available. If an attribute *actualPos* is maintained, holding the current output position, then the column in which the *type* would start for translation 1 is known. Furthermore, it is plausible to suggest that if the *type* starts with an identifier symbol then it is probably quite short, since it is probably just a typename. It is then possible to invoke a utility procedure

FoldIf((*actualPos* > *halfway*) **and** (*symbol* <> *ident*),*mar* + *step*);

This mechanism is not foolproof of course. For example, the *type* might extend across many columns, even if it starts with an identifier (it might be a subrange declaration, say). However, the mechanism will get it right most of the time, and the automatic folding of the *WriteGetSymbol* procedure will ensure a plausible format is produced even for the exceptional cases.

A final preliminary decision concerns the extent to which the detailed structure of phrases which are unimportant, from the point of view of formatting, may be glossed over by simply copying symbols from input to output streams. Some syntactic categories, such as *expression* in Figure 11.15, have no formatting associated with them, apart from any folding associated with the right margin. It is convenient in such cases to 'parse' such an expression by simply skipping symbols until an appropriate symbol from *FOLLOW*(*expression*) is found. Some care must be exercised, however, since using the complete *FOLLOW* set to stop the skipping would be erroneous. The complete set would include symbols such as the right parenthesis, which may follow a nested expression, but cannot occur following a valid expression at the outer level. The appropriate skip-halting set is

stoppers = *FOLLOW*(*statement*) + {'**of**','**do**','**to**','**then**','**downto**'}.

With this definition, the body of the procedure to recognize an expression becomes a call to the utility procedure *SkipTo*(*stoppers*).

As might be expected, such corner-cutting can greatly reduce the size of the recursive descent parser, but is not without its dangers. A classic example occurs in the parsing of those type declarations which are normally unformatted, i.e. those arising from the productions

type → *identifier* | *subrange* | *enumeration*.

It would appear at first sight that all three of these are handled by code within the type recognition procedure which goes something like

case *symbol* **of**
    ident, number, LParent : *SkipTo*([*semicolon*]);
        . . .

on the basis of the argument that 'all type declarations end with a semicolon'. But, is this true? What about the production

variant → *caseLabelList* ':' '(' *fieldList* ')'

in which any non-empty *fieldList* ends with *type*? In fact, *FOLLOW*(*type*) is the set {';', ')'}. A correct procedure which cuts this particular corner is given in the final code as procedure *FindTypeEnd*. This procedure contains an interesting echo of the solution to Exercise 6.8.

11.5.2 Implementation

The parser shown at the end of this section (Figure 11.17) implements all of the features discussed in the introduction. There is a full set of formatting utility procedures, which can easily be incorporated into the recursive descent code to implement the translation. These procedures are:

WriteGetSymbol: writes the current symbol and fetches the next;

Accept: emits the current symbol if it has the specified value;

NewLine: emits a line-break;

Margin: emits spaces until the actual position attribute is equal to or greater than the specified margin;

SkipTo: copies symbols to the output until a member of the specified set is encountered, folding at the current margin;

FoldIf: emits a line-break, indent sequence if the specified condition evaluates to true;

ErrorSkip: copies symbols to the output until a member of the specified set is found. No formatting.

The code of the parser is almost as readable as the STDS from which it was derived. It is a simple matter to modify the code to provide alternative formatting conventions, according to one's own ideas of preferred style. The code shown attempts to increase the density of the printed code, by trying to minimize the number of newlines which are emitted. For example, structured statements following a **then**-symbol or an **else**-symbol do not automatically start on a new line unless the actual indent position is already well across the page.

Certain economies have been taken in the parser, by using the same code to recognize several types of phrase. For example, the same procedure recognizes the main program, and any procedure or function declarations which are nested within it. The effect is just that although correct programs are treated correctly, certain incorrect programs will be formatted without any hint of trouble. Thus a procedure which incorrectly has a type name following its heading will be accepted just as if the initial keyword has been **function** rather than **procedure**. This particular choice is in accordance with the general philosophy that complete syntax checking is not one of the objectives of this particular program.

A more important difficulty is caused by the possibility of the word *forward* replacing the *block* part of a procedure declaration. The problem is that *forward* is a lexical anomaly. Elsewhere in a Pascal program it may be freely used as an identifier, but following a procedure heading it has special syntactic significance. *Forward* is best described as a **context-**

```
procedure ProgRecognize;

  function CheckForward : BOOLEAN;
    var    I : INTEGER;
  begin
    I := 1;
    while ((buffer[I] = LCforward[I]) or (buffer[I] =
          UCforward[I])) and (buffer[I] <> Mark) do
      I := I + 1;
    CheckForward := ((buffer[I] = LCforward[I]) or (buffer[I] =
                    UCforward[I]));
  end;

begin
  HeaderRec(indent);
  if symbol = ident
    then if CheckForward
      then begin
        Margin(indent);
        WriteGetSymbol(indent);
        end
      else
    else begin
      DeclaresRec(indent + Step);
      Block(indent);
      end;
  ErrorSkip([semicolon,dot]);
end;
```

Figure 11.16   Pretty-printer output, procedure *ProcRecognize*.

sensitive marker. It seems inappropriate to have the scanner recognize *forward* as a special token, since this would litter the code of the parser. Instead, if an identifier is the next symbol following a procedure heading, a special check is made to see if the identifier is 'forward' in upper-case, lower-case or any combination of cases. In many implementations a similar check for the context-sensitive marker *external* would be required in the same position.

As an example of the output of the program, a fragment of the output produced when the program processes its own source file is shown in Figure 11.16. The fragment is the formatted code of the procedure *ProgRecognize*. In this case the parameter *step* has been set to 3. Note especially the deletion of comments.

11.5.3 Possible enhancements

There are a number of areas in which the program, as given, might be usefully enhanced. Two such extensions are of immediate interest. Firstly, it would be useful to retain comments in the program, so as to aid the readability of the code. Also, it would be useful to have better control over the format in cases where there are several options.

The problem with retaining comments in the produced output is that there are so many different conventions for commenting programs that it is difficult to deal with all the possibilities sensibly. Comments may appear anywhere in a program that 'whitespace' is valid, they may, therefore, appear between any two symbols, but may not be embedded within a symbol.

Almost all commenting conventions distinguish between at least two different cases. First there are **formatting comments** which are often multi-line, and supply narrative at the start or end of significant program structures such as procedures. Then there are **embedded comments** which are usually short, and occur within or between statements and declarations. It is sensible to leave narrative comments as much unchanged as possible, but to ensure that the proximity of embedded comments and the objects to which they refer are as undisturbed as possible. Any restriction in the commenting conventions of the original input source code makes this task much simpler.

One widely used commenting convention insists that embedded comments are the last item in the line of code in which they appear. This case is relatively easy to handle within a pretty-printer structure by allowing the scanner to distinguish between two cases: comments which start on a new line, and those which do not. Comments which start on a new line are recognized by the fact that a line-break has been encountered in the input since the previous symbol was scanned. There are several design issues to be determined, however, even in this simplified case. Firstly, and of greatest importance, it must be decided whether the scanner is to handle the writing of comments to the output, or various comment fragments are to appear in the *SymbolType* declaration. The problem is that the scanner does not have sufficient knowledge to perform the task cleanly, since it has no knowledge of the parsing context. Conversely, the parser has the required contextual information, but can only deal with comments by, in effect, following every call to *WriteGetSymbol* by code which deals with all of the possible comment types which might have been discovered following the previous symbol. The choice is either to complicate the interface between scanner and parser, by making some parsing context available to the scanner, or to clutter the code of the parser. Some further aspects of these choices are explored in Exercise 11.5.

Finally, it should be clear that any seemingly intelligent formatting of a Pascal program requires access to information which is not available in a timely manner during a left-to-right scan of a source text. A really good job may be made of the task if the possible sizes of the formatted output for all structures is known before any output has to be produced. This is relatively easy to do if the source is available in the form of an abstract syntax tree. Unfortunately, it seems a little extreme to build a complete tree from a program text, just in order to format an output file prettily. If a syntax tree is being produced for other purposes perhaps, it is a relatively simple matter to make the tree available to a pretty-printer, which might then be considered to be an **unparser**.

```
program PrettyPrinter(input,output); (* kjg 1986 *)

(* Produces a formatted output file from a correct Pascal program.
This version ignores comments and does not perform a 100% syntax
check. *)

const   LineMax = 132;
        MarginR = 72;(* right margin *)
        limit   = 58;(* Fold margin *)
        halfway = 39;(* MarginR div 2 *)
        Step    = 3; (* indent step *)

        { other constants for scanner system };

type    SymbolType = ( err,
            (* keywords *)
                dosy,ifsy,insy,ofsy,orsy,tosy,andsy,endsy,nilsy,setsy,
                notsy,forsy,divsy,varsy,modsy,filesy,thensy,casesy,
                typesy,gotosy,withsy,elsesy,arraysy,beginsy,constsy,
                untilsy,whilesy,labelsy,packedsy,downtosy,recordsy,
                repeatsy,programsy,functionsy,proceduresy,
            (* special symbols *)
                plus,minus,star,slash,assigns,dot,comma,semicolon,
                colon,equal,noteql,less,lesseql,greateql,greater,
                Lparent,Rparent,Lsquare,Rsquare,carat,dotdot,
            (* lexical categories *)
                number,ident,stringsy,
            (* end of file marker *)
                eofsy);

        SymbolSet = set of SymbolType;

        { other scanner types };
```

Figure 11.17   *cont. overleaf*

Figure 11.17   *cont.*

```
var     buffer : LineType; (* scanner puts symbol here *)
        SymLen : 1..LineMax; (* length of last symbol *)
        actualPos : INTEGER; (* position in output line *)
        inFile, outFile : TEXT;
        LCforward, UCForward : packed array[1..8] of CHAR;
        (* upper and lower case 'forward' *)
  { scanner procedures are omitted };

procedure ParseInput; (* body is right at end *)

  const   DeclStarters = [labelsy,constsy,typesy,varsy,proceduresy,
                    functionsy];
          FirstStatement = [number,casesy,ident,forsy,beginsy,whilesy,
                    gotosy,repeatsy,withsy,ifsy];
          FollowStatement = [semicolon,endsy,untilsy,elsesy];
          ConstBegins = [ident,LParent,plus,minus,number,stringsy];
          Selectors = [LParent,Lsquare,carat,dot];

  procedure NewLine;
  begin
    WriteLn(outFile);
    actualPos := 0;
  end;

  procedure Margin(skip : INTEGER);
  begin
    skip := skip − actualPos;
    while skip > 0 do begin
      Write(outFile,SP);
      skip := skip − 1;
      actualPos := actualPos + 1;
      end;
  end; (* assert: actualPos >= skip *)

  procedure WriteGetSymbol(mar : INTEGER);
    var I : INTEGER; old : SymbolType;

    function SpaceRequired : BOOLEAN;
      const Always = [dosy .. proceduresy,plus .. assigns,
                    colon .. greater];
      begin (* should a space follow the last symbol? *)
        if symbol in [comma,semicolon,dot,RParent,Rsquare]
          then SpaceRequired := FALSE
          else SpaceRequired := (old in Always) or (symbol in Always)
      end; (* SpaceRequired *)
```

```
begin
  if (actualPos >= MarginR) or
    ((actualPos + SymLen + 1 >= MarginR) and (SymLen > 1))
    then begin
      NewLine;
      Margin(mar + 1)
      end;
  I := 1;
  actualPos := actualPos + SymLen;
  while buffer[I] <> Mark do begin
    Write(outFile,buffer[I]);
    I := I + 1;
    end;
  old := symbol;
  GetSymbol;
  if SpaceRequired then begin
      Write(outFile,SP);
      actualPos := actualPos + 1;
      end;
end; (* WriteGetSymbol *)

procedure Accept(sym : SymbolType;mar : INTEGER);
begin
  if symbol = sym then WriteGetSymbol(mar);
end;

procedure FoldIf(condition : BOOLEAN; mar : INTEGER);
begin
  if condition then begin
    NewLine;
    Margin(mar);
    end;
end;

procedure SkipTo(halt : SymbolSet; mar : INTEGER);
begin
  while not (symbol in (halt + [eofsy])) do
    WriteGetSymbol(mar);
end;

procedure ErrorSkip(halt : SymbolSet);
begin
  if not (symbol in halt) then begin
    NewLine;
    Write(outFile,'(* error skip *)');
    SkipTo(halt,0);
    end;
end;
```

cont. overleaf

Figure 11.17   *cont.*

```
procedure ProgRecognize(indent : INTEGER); FORWARD;
procedure Statement(mar : INTEGER); Forward;

procedure IdList(mar : INTEGER);
begin (* assert: margin already set and symbol = indent *)
  WriteGetSymbol(mar); (* ident *)
  while symbol = comma do begin
    WriteGetSymbol(mar); (* comma *)
    Accept(ident,mar);
    end;
end; (* IdList *)

procedure HeaderRec(mar : INTEGER);
begin
  Margin(mar;)
  WriteGetSymbol(mar); (* keyword *)
  Accept(ident,mar);
  if symbol = LParent then begin
    SkipTo([RParent],actualPos);
    WriteGetSymbol(mar + 8);
    end;
  SkipTo([semicolon],mar + 8); (* ': ident' maybe *)
  WriteGetSymbol(mar + 8);
  NewLine;
end; (* HeaderRec *)

procedure DeclaresRec(mar : INTEGER);
  var oldsy : SymbolType;
      local : INTEGER;

  procedure TypeRec(mar : INTEGER);

    procedure FieldListRec(mar : INTEGER);
      var fieldMargin : INTEGER;

      procedure RecordSection(mar : INTEGER);
      begin (* assert : actualPos = mar *)
        if symbol = ident then begin
          IdList(mar);
          Accept(colon,mar);
          FoldIf((actualPos − mar) > limit,mar + Step);
          TypeRec(actualPos);
          end; (* else RecordSection −> empty *)
      end; (* RecordSection *)
```

```
    procedure VariantRec(mar : INTEGER);
    begin
      if symbol in ConstBegins then begin
        Margin(mar);
        SkipTo([colon],mar);
        WriteGetSymbol(mar);
        FoldIf(actualPos > halfway,mar + Step);
        Accept(LParent,mar);
        FieldListRec(actualPos);
        Accept(RParent,mar);
        end;
    end; (* VariantRec *)

begin (* FieldListRec *)
  Margin(mar);
  RecordSection(mar); (* maybe empty *)
  while symbol = semicolon do begin
    WriteGetSymbol(mar); (* semicolon *)
    FoldIf(symbol in [ident,casesy],mar); (* i.e. if more *)
    RecordSection(mar); (* maybe empty *)
    end;
  if symbol = casesy then begin (* variant part *)
    (* assert: actualPos = mar *)
    WriteGetSymbol(mar); (* casesy *)
    SkipTo([ofsy],mar);
    WriteGetSymbol(mar); (* ofsy *)
    NewLine;
    VariantRec(mar + Step);
    while symbol = semicolon do begin
      WriteGetSymbol(mar + Step);
      NewLine;
      VariantRec(mar + Step);
      end;
    end; (* variant part *)
end; (* for a correct program, symbol in [endsy,RParent] *)

procedure FindTypeEnd(mar : INTEGER);
  var count : INTEGER;
begin (* assert: symbol in [ident,number,LParent] *)
  count := 0;
  repeat
    if symbol = LParent then count := count + 1
    else if symbol = RParent then count := count - 1;
    WriteGetSymbol(mar);
  until (symbol in [semicolon,RParent]) and (count = 0);
end; (* FindTypeEnd *)
```

cont. overleaf

Figure 11.17   *cont.*

```
begin (* TypeRec, assert: margin already set *)
  case symbol of
    ident,number,LParent : FindTypeEnd(mar);
    packedsy,filesy,setsy,arraysy : begin
      if symbol = packedsy then WriteGetSymbol(mar);
      WriteGetSymbol(mar); (* keyword *)
      if symbol = Lsquare then begin
        skipTo([Rsquare],actualPos);
        WriteGetSymbol(actualPos);
        end
      else if symbol = LParent then begin
        SkipTo([RParent],actualPos);
        WriteGetSymbol(actualPos);
        end;
      WriteGetSymbol(mar); (* ofsy *)
      FoldIf((actualPos > halfway) and
             (symbol <> ident),mar + Step);
      TypeRec(actualPos);
      end;
    carat : begin
      WriteGetSymbol(mar); (* '^' *)
      Accept(ident,mar);
      end;
    recordsy : begin
      WriteGetSymbol(mar);
      NewLine;
      FieldListRec(mar + Step);
      NewLine;
      Margin(mar);
      Accept(endsy,mar);
      end;
    end; (* case *)
  end; (* TypeRec: no newline *)

begin (* DeclaresRec *)
  local := mar + 8;
  while symbol in DeclStarters do begin
    Margin(mar);
    case symbol of
      labelsy : begin
        WriteGetSymbol(mar);
        SkipTo([semicolon],local);
        WriteGetSymbol(local);
        NewLine;
        end;
```

```
typesy : begin
  WriteGetSymbol(mar);
  while symbol = ident do begin
    Margin(local);
    WriteGetSymbol(local); (* ident *)
    WriteGetSymbol(local); (* equals *)
    FoldIf((actualPos > halfway) and
            (symbol <> ident), local + Step);
    TypeRec(actualPos);
    Accept(semicolon,mar);
    NewLine;
    end;
  end;
constsy : begin
  WriteGetSymbol(mar);
  while symbol = ident do begin
    Margin(local);
    SkipTo([semicolon],local);
    WriteGetSymbol(local);
    NewLine;
    end;
  end;
varsy : begin
  WriteGetSymbol(mar); (* varsy *)
  while symbol = ident do begin
    Margin(local);
    IdList(local);
    WriteGetSymbol(local); (* colon *)
    FoldIf((actualPos > halfway) and
            (symbol <> ident), local + Step);
    TypeRec(actualPos);
    Accept(semicolon,mar);
    NewLine;
    end;
  end;
proceduresy, functionsy : begin
  NewLine; (* blank line *)
  ProgRecognize(mar);
  Accept(semicolon,mar);
  NewLine;
  if symbol = beginsy then NewLine; (* again *)
  end;
  end; (* case *)
  SkipTo(DeclStarters + [beginsy],0); (* error recovery *)
  end; (* while *)
end; (* DeclaresRec, assert: actualPos = 0 *)
```

cont. overleaf

Figure 11.17   *cont.*

```
procedure ExpressionRec(mar : INTEGER);
  const    stoppers =
           FollowStatement + [ofsy,dosy,thensy,tosy,downtosy];
begin
  SkipTo(stoppers,mar);
end;

procedure StatSequence(mar : INTEGER);
begin
  Statement(mar);
  ErrorSkip(FollopStatement);
  while symbol = semicolon do begin
    WriteGetSymbol(mar);
    if symbol in FirstStatement then NewLine;
    Statement(mar);
    ErrorSkip(FollowStatement);
    end;
end; (* StatSequence *)

procedure Compound(mar : INTEGER);
begin
  Margin(mar);
  WriteGetSymbol(mar);
  if symbol in FirstStatement then NewLine;
  StatSequence(mar + Step);
  NewLine;
  Margin(mar + Step);
  Accept(endsy,mar);
end; (* Compound *)

procedure Block(mar : INTEGER);
begin
  Margin(mar);
  WriteGetSymbol(mar);
  if symbol in FirstStatement then NewLine;
  StatSequence(mar + Step);
  NewLine;
  Margin(mar);
  Accept(endsy,mar);
end; (* Block *)
```

```
procedure WhileRec(mar : INTEGER);
begin
  Margin(mar);
  WriteGetSymbol(mar);
  ExpressionRec(actualPos);
  Accept(dosy,mar);
  if symbol <> beginsy then begin
    FoldIf(actualPos > halfway,mar + Step);
    Statement(actualPos);
    end
  else Statement(mar);
end; (* WhileRec *)

procedure WithRec(mar : INTEGER);
begin
  Margin(mar);
  SkipTo([dosy],mar);
  WriteGetSymbol(mar); (* dosy *)
  if symbol <> beginsy then begin
    FoldIf(actualPos > halfway,mar + Step);
    Statement(actualPos);
    end
  else Statement(mar);
end; (* WithRec *)

procedure ForRec(mar : INTEGER);
begin
  Margin(mar);
  WriteGetSymbol(mar);
  Accept(ident,mar);
  Accept(assigns,mar);
  FoldIf(actualPos > limit,mar + Step);
  ExpressionRec(actualPos);
  WriteGetSymbol(mar + Step); (* tosy or downtosy *)
  FoldIf(actualPos > limit,mar + Step);
  ExpressionRec(actualPos);
  Accept(dosy,mar);
  if symbol <> beginsy then begin
    FoldIf(actualPos > halfway,mar + Step):
    Statement(actualPos);
    end
  else Statement(mar);
end; (* ForRec *)
```

cont. overleaf

Figure 11.17   *cont.*

```
procedure IfRec(mar : INTEGER);
  var local : INTEGER;
begin
  local := mar + Step;
  Margin(mar);
  WriteGetSymbol(mar);
  ExpressionRec(actualPos);
  NewLine;
  Margin(local);
  Accept(thensy,mar);
  if not (symbol in [beginsy,semicolon,ifsy,repeatsy,elsesy])
    then begin
      FoldIf(actualPos > halfway,local + Step);
      Statement(actualPos);
      end
    else Statement(local);
  if symbol = elsesy then begin
    NewLine;
    Margin(local);
    WriteGetSymbol(local);
    if not (symbol in [beginsy,semicolon,ifsy,repeatsy,elsesy])
      then begin
        FoldIf(actualPos > halfway,local + Step);
        Statement(actualPos);
        end
      else Statement(local);
    end;
end; (* IfRec *)

procedure RepeatRec(mar : INTEGER);
begin
  Margin(mar);
  WriteGetSymbol(mar); (* repeatsy *)
  NewLine;
  StatSequence(mar + Step);
  ErrorSkip([untilsy]);
  NewLine;
  Margin(mar);
  WriteGetSymbol(mar);
  ExpressionRec(actualPos);
end; (* RepeatRec *)
```

```
procedure CaseRec(mar : INTEGER);
  var localMargin : INTEGER;
begin
  Margin(mar);
  WriteGetSymbol(mar); (* casesy *)
  ExpressionRec(actualPos);
  Accept(ofsy,mar);
  NewLine;
  localMargin := mar + Step;
  while symbol in ConstBegins do begin
    Margin(localMargin);
    SkipTo([colon],localMargin);
    WriteGetSymbol(localMargin); (* colon *)
    FoldIf((actualPos > halfway) and (symbol
           <> beginsy), localMargin + Step);
    Statement(localMargin + Step);
    Accept(semicolon,mar); (* optional ';' *)
    NewLine;
    end;
  ErrorSkip([endsy]);
  Margin(mar + Step);
  WriteGetSymbol(mar);
end; (* CaseRec *)

procedure Statement(*mar : INTEGER*);
begin
  ErrorSkip(FirstStatement + FollowStatement);
  while symbol = number do begin
    WriteGetSymbol(0); (* numeric label *)
    WriteGetSymbol(0); (* colon symbol *)
    NewLine;
    end;
  Margin(mar);
  case symbol of
    ident : begin
      WriteGetSymbol(mar);
      if symbol in Selectors then
        SkipTo([assigns] + FollowStatement,actualPos);
      if symbol = assigns then begin
        WriteGetSymbol(mar + Step);
        FoldIf(actualPos > limit,mar + Step);
        ExpressionRec(actualPos);
        end;
      end;
```

cont. overleaf

Figure 11.17   *cont.*

```
      gotosy : begin
          WriteGetSymbol(mar);
          Accept(number,mar);
          end;
    beginsy  : Compound(mar);
    whilesy  : WhileRec(mar);
    ifsy     : IfRec(mar);
    withsy   : WithRec(mar);
    repeatsy : RepeatRec(mar);
    forsy    : ForRec(mar);
    casesy   : CaseRec(mar);
    end;
  end; (* Statement *)

procedure ProgRecognize(*indent : INTEGER*);

  function CheckForward : BOOLEAN;
    var I : INTEGER;
  begin
    I := 1;
    while ((buffer[I] = LCforward[I]) or
          (buffer[I] = UCforward[I])) and
          (buffer[I] <> Mark) do
      I := I + 1;
    CheckForward := ((buffer[I] = LCforward[I]) or
                      (buffer[I] = UCforward[I]));
  end;

begin (* prog -> header declares block *)
  HeaderRec(indent);
  if symbol = ident
    then if CheckForward
      then begin
        Margin(indent);
        WriteGetSymbol(indent);
        end
      else (* nothing *)
    else begin
      DeclaresRec(indent + Step);
      Block(indent);
      end;
  ErrorSkip([semicolon,dot]);
end; (* ProgRecognize *)
```

```
begin (* for all nested procedures, symbol must be already read *)
  InitScanner; (* establish parser precondition *)
  ErrorSkip([programsy,proceduresy]);
  NewLine;
  ProgRecognize(0);
  Accept(dot,0);
  NewLine;
  ErrorSkip([eofsy]);
  WriteLn('ended normally');
end; (* ParseInput *)

procedure CreateOutName;
  var I : INTEGER;
begin
  { creates outfile-name from input filename };
end;

begin (* main line *)
  (* file opening procedures may be system dependent *)
  Write('infile > '); ReadLn(filename);
  CreateOutName;
  WriteLn('outfile = ',outFilename);
  Open(inFile,filename, . . . );
  Open(outFile,outFilename, . . . );
  Reset(inFile);
  Rewrite(outFile);
  InitTables;

  ParseInput;

  Close(inFile);
  Close(outFile);
end.
```

Figure 11.17   Parser code for the Pascal pretty-printer.

Exercises

11.1   Consider the following syntax-directed translation scheme (SDTS) fragment.

$$A \rightarrow aBC, \quad xBCy$$
$$\mid \quad aD, \quad\quad Dz.$$

In this fragment,

$$A,B,C,D \in N, \quad a \in \Sigma, \text{ and } \quad x,y,z \in \Delta$$

Suppose that the non-postfix translation in the first production is avoided by the introduction of a new non-terminal K, with translation

$$K \to a, \qquad x.$$

Form the characteristic machine for the modified grammar fragment, and deduce the condition that there are no conflicts in the machine.

11.2 Repeat the previous problem, but for the case where a null non-terminal J is introduced as a marker for the emission of the x output.

11.3 An automaton is to be constructed which translates from Polish expressions to parenthesized infix form. However, unlike the example in Section 11.4, this translator is to ensure the same order of evaluation for the infix expression as implied by the original Polish form. Thus '++abc' and '+a+bc' should translate into 'a+b+c' and 'a+(b+c)', respectively. Devise an SDTS, based on Figure 11.8, with conditional translations which implement such a translation. For simplicity, assume that '+' and '*' are the only operators, and that in the infix form the operators are each left-associative and that multiplication has the higher precedence.

11.4 Repeat the previous problem for the case that there are all four arithmetic operators $\{+,-,^*,/\}$ augmented in the Polish source string by a *negate* operator which translates into a unary minus sign. Assume the usual precedence and evaluation order in the infix form.

11.5 Consider an extension to the pretty-printer which treats comments by defining several different kinds of comment fragment. Make sure that your mechanism allows for comments which are spread over several lines, but still allows the parser to check whether or not an embedded comment will fit on the current line.

Further reading

A more advanced treatment of syntax-directed translation, at least as it applies to the translation of programming languages, is given in Aho *et al.* (1986).

Chapter 12　**An Introduction to Error Recovery**

12.1　Models of error behaviour

For most of the situations considered in this book, the mere detection of an error, or the diagnosis of the nature and position of an error, is sufficient. There are situations, however, in which it is necessary to attempt some degree of error recovery so that syntactic checking of the remainder of the string may proceed. This is usually the case in translators for programming languages, where it is probable that more than one syntactic error exists in a program draft. It is essential to detect as many errors as possible at each presentation of a program to its translator, so that the total number of correction and submission cycles may be minimized.

In this chapter we consider the error detecting and recovery actions which are possible for the main kinds of parser which we have considered. It is important to bear in mind, however, that the totality of possible errors which may be detected includes errors other than those which the parser detects. Certain restrictions on the strings allowed in a language may be stated in forms other than the use of context-free grammars. In fact, as was pointed out in Chapter 6, there are certain commonly used rules, such as 'declaration before use for identifiers', which simply cannot be modelled by CFGs. In such cases we may describe the rules as being 'semantic', since they are only discovered during the evaluation of the semantic attributes of the sentence's representation. The handling of errors discovered during attribute evaluation is not a topic which we will explore here, although the need for accurate reporting of the nature and location of such errors is as great as for those discovered during parsing.

Generally speaking, whenever a string is found to be in error it may be assumed that the error is 'small' in some sense. The simplest kind of errors to consider are those in which perhaps only a single symbol is in error. We may consider three cases: a single symbol has been omitted, a single symbol has been erroneously included, or an incorrect symbol has been substituted for a correct one. We call these three kinds of errors **deletion**, **insertion**, and **substitution** errors, respectively.

If we take the Pascal programs as an example of sentences in a reasonably complex language, then it is possible to think of familiar examples of each type of error. A very common deletion error in Pascal programs is the omission of the semicolon between statements, particularly when the program has been edited to insert an additional statement between an earlier statement and an **end**. The most common syntax error in programs written by inexperienced Pascal programmers, is the insertion error which arises from the presence of an extra semicolon immediately preceding an **else**. A common substitution error in Pascal programs is the use of the colon in place of the equals sign in type and constant declarations.

In any given context it may be that one or other form of error predominates, but usually it is necessary to consider sensible recovery from errors of all three classes. It may also be necessary to consider errors in which several symbols are involved, for example, transposition errors in which two symbols occur in the wrong order.

Firstly, we must consider the error detection mechanism which operates in the two main classes of parser which we have described, including the effect of any short-cuts which have been used in the parser construction. Let us suppose that we have a particular syntactic category in the grammar, which has, say, three productions.

$$A \rightarrow \alpha \mid \beta \mid \gamma \ .$$

where A is a non-terminal symbol, and α, β, and γ are all strings from the closure of the vocabulary V. Now consider the recognition of the terminal symbol strings belonging to category A by means of a recursive descent parser. It is presumed that the three productions have distinct director-sets, d_1, d_2, and d_3, respectively.

It would be a common practice to call the procedure which recognizes the category A without first checking that the current symbol is in the union of the three director sets. As will be seen, no irreparable harm is done by such a choice.

A possible outline for the procedure which recognizes A might be

```
procedure Arecognize;
begin
  if symbol in d₁ then
    {recognize α}
  else if symbol in d₂ then
    {recognize β}
  else {recognize γ}
end;
```

Notice carefully that the procedure does not check that the actual symbol is in the director set of γ before calling for the recognition of this vocabulary string. The alternative and more careful implementation of the recognition would be to have the last two lines of the above procedure replaced by code such as

```
        .
        .
        .
    else if symbol in d₃ then
        {recognize γ}
    else {declare an error}
end;
```

In this second case it is clear that any errors are immediately notified, but what are the implications of the simplified form, as it affects error detection?

Firstly, it should be noted that if the procedure or procedures which call *Arecognize* check that the current terminal symbol is in the director set of *A* before the call, the **else** branch of the sequential test will never be exercised in the 'careful' version of the procedure. If this is the case, then the original version would be quite adequate. However, if such a test has not been made, then a non-terminal symbol-recognizing procedure corresponding to the first symbol of the string γ may in turn be called without any check being made that the current symbol is actually valid. We may thus have a whole cascade of calls to recognition procedures without the validity of the current symbol being checked. Clearly this situation cannot continue indefinitely, since the LL(1) assumption excludes the possibility of left-recursion.

Finally, therefore, even if the director set has not been checked, the parser must reach a configuration where the production right-hand-side which is to be recognized begins with a terminal symbol. At this point the code will read somewhat like

if *symbol* = *x* **then** *GetSymbol* **else** {report an error};

and the error will finally be detected.

Notice that although the detection of the erroneous symbol may have been deferred by several procedure calls, the error is still detected before another symbol has been read. Thus the position of the scanner's buffer variable in the input string is the same for both methods, and the error is detected as soon as it is known that the next symbol cannot possibly be a valid continuation of the syntactic structure recognized previously.

The deferral of error recognition, however, does have some implications for error diagnosis and reporting. Consider, for example, a typical expression grammar in which the procedures which recognize *expressions*, *terms*, and *factors* do not check director sets until it is absolutely necessary. If the first symbol in an expression is erroneous, then the fact will not be discovered until the procedure which recognizes *primary* fails to match the current symbol to any of the start symbols of its possible productions. Certainly the error will have been detected without reading any additional symbols, but the error message which the parser produces must reflect the fact that it is *expression* recognition which has failed, and not *primary* recognition.

Similar considerations apply in the case of bottom-up parsers if so-called default reductions are used. Default reductions are useful in reducing the size of parser tables for LR-style recognizers. What is involved is that, in any state involving one or more reductions, one of the reductions is taken as the default action in the case that the current symbol does not indicate either a shift, or one of the other reductions for the state. Thus all input symbols which are actually erroneous for that particular parser configuration will cause the default reduction to take place. Since a reduce action does not cause an input symbol to be shifted, the erroneous symbol will remain as the current symbol no matter how many such default reductions are cascaded. Ultimately, a state must be reached in which only shift actions are possible, and the error will then be detected without reading past the erroneous symbol, just as in the top-down case.

However, for bottom-up parsers, as for top-down methods, the diagnosis of and recovery from errors may be made significantly more difficult if the recognition of the error is deferred in this way. In the case of an LR parser, a sequence of stack symbols may have been removed by a cascade of default reductions, thereby obscuring the state of the automaton when the first opportunity to recognize the error occurred.

It will be stressed in the following sections that some compromise is usually appropriate in the trade-off between parser efficiency and ease of incorporation of error actions. The price of such a compromise is in the precision with which errors may be diagnosed and reported.

12.1.1   Section checklist and summary definitions

1. Simple error classification.
   - Most error recovery schemes are based on the assumption that the error is small, in the sense that it involves only a small number of symbols, perhaps only one.
   - Single-symbol errors can be classified simply as deletion, insertion, or substitution errors.
   - Deletion errors arise from the absence of some necessary symbol in a phrase.
   - Insertion errors arise from the introduction of an extraneous symbol into an otherwise correct phrase.
   - In a substitution error, an erroneous symbol has been substituted in place of the correct one.

2. The effect of omitting set membership tests.

- In recursive descent parsers, the omission of an explicit director set membership test for the last alternative of an alternation cannot lead to acceptance of an erroneous sentence.

- In LR parsers, the omission of the lookahead membership test for a single *reduce* action in each state cannot lead to acceptance of an erroneous sentence.

- In each class of parser, the omission of a symbol set-membership test may lead to deferral of the error reporting, and make production of a specific diagnostic message more difficult.

12.2   Simple error recovery by symbol skipping

In this section we consider a simple and well-tested approach to error recovery. We shall discuss the application of the principle to both top-down and bottom-up parsers, leaving more detailed consideration of the application of the principles to the later sections.

One of the simplest methods of error recovery is based on discarding the most recent part of the parse, and attempting a resynchronization by skipping input symbols. This method, sometimes called 'panic mode', is somewhat crude. However, it is very simple to implement, and has very few nasty surprises for the implementor.

So far as the method is based on theoretical principles at all, it can be justified since the error is probably localized in the vicinity of the point at which the parse failed. Whether the error configuration was triggered by one of the previous symbols, causing the parser to head off down a wrong path, or by the omission of a symbol at the failure point, is irrelevant to the corrective action. Recognition of one or more syntactic category is abandoned, and the parser placed in the configuration which would have arisen had the parsing subtask been successfully completed. Since, in general, not all of the symbols intended as part of the abandoned structure will have been read, the parser skips over zero or more input symbols until a symbol is found which might begin a valid phrase starting from the corrected configuration.

The method is particularly simple to implement in cases where there are significant substructures in the sentences of the language which start or end with characteristic 'key' symbols.

To take a rather simple example, consider the skeleton of an LR-family parser, shown in Figure 12.1. The submachines which recognize the subgrammars for categories A and B have been abstracted away, leaving just that part of the machine which recognizes the production $X \rightarrow AB$.

Consider the situation which arises when an error transition is

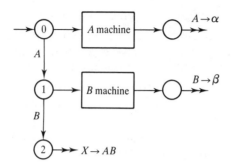

Figure 12.1   Simplified LR automaton.

indicated in the interior of the *A*-machine. It is assumed that the symbols of the input which caused entry into the *A*-machine, together with the input symbols about to be skipped, were all part of an erroneous attempt to spell out an *A* phrase.

The recovery action is to pop the parser stack until the relative start state 0 is reached, and then to advance the state to state 1, just as though an *A* substring had been completely recognized. In order to synchronize the restart, it is necessary to skip input symbols until a symbol is found which gives a shift transition out of state 1. If the recovery is successful then, in effect, the parse tree shown symbolically in Figure 12.2 has been constructed. In this figure, the dotted portions of the tree correspond to the inferred subtree and the skipped input symbols.

There is somewhat of a flavour of predictive parsing about such an error-recovery method, in that the real intent of the erroneous phrase is guessed at, and a suitable resynchronization point predicted. This connection becomes clear when the application of the same principle to a recursive descent parser is considered.

Figure 12.3 represents the state of a top-down parse equivalent to Figures 12.1 and 12.2 at the instant that the error becomes apparent. The procedure to recognize category *X* has called the procedure to recognize *A*, which has failed midway through its task. In this case the error-recovery is to skip input symbols until a suitable symbol is found, and to cause the *A*-recognition procedure to return. The attempted recognition of *B* then proceeds. The set of valid restart symbols will be related in some way to the relevant follow set, but may involve other symbols also.

Such a simple explanation glosses over several niceties. Firstly, the syntactic phrase which is to be discarded may not correspond to the actual procedure in which the locus of control resides at the point at which an error is detected. The error may very well be detected in a subordinate, nested procedure. Secondly, the discarded phrase need not be a complete procedure, but may be merely an inline section of code corresponding to

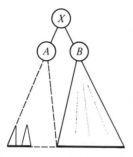

Figure 12.2 Rightmost parse tree with inferred subtree.

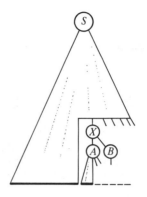

Figure 12.3 Top-down parser configuration at error.

an anonymous, non-recursive syntactic category.

Before the details of a specific example are considered, some general hints regarding the pitfalls in this simple strategy should be mentioned. If the assumption regarding the actual error location is incorrect then a whole cascade of subsequent spurious error reports may ensue. Furthermore, there may be semantic information in the skipped symbols, the absence of which leads to a variety of spurious semantic-error diagnostics. This phenomenon is familiar to the users of programming language compilers which recover from errors in the declaration part by skipping over symbols. Every beginning computer user will have been mystified by error messages which diagnose that a particular identifier is undeclared when the declaration is visibly present. Some degree of avoidance of such confusion is obtained by designing error messages which explicitly indicate the extent of symbol skipping.

12.2.1 Section checklist and summary definitions

- Error recovery by symbol-skipping attempts to abandon the parsing of some phrase, and to discard the input symbols corresponding to the abandoned phrase.
- In bottom-up parsers, the parsing automaton must be placed in a state corresponding to the successful recognition of the abandoned phrase. Corresponding input symbols must then be skipped and the automaton restarted.
- In recursive descent parsers, symbols are skipped, and the procedure corresponding to the abandoned phrase is exited, so that control may return to the statement which recognizes the following phrase.
- The choice of skip-halting set may either be based on the presence of

distinctive symbols in the starting set of the following phrase, or on distinctive ending symbols in the abandoned phrase. Sometimes a combination of both methods may be used.

12.3   Error recovery in recursive descent parsers

In this section we consider the symbol-skipping method of error recovery applied to recursive descent parsers. There are some general principles which are useful in the implementation of parsers which use this strategy, and these will be illustrated by means of simple examples.

It is assumed, in what follows, that there is a utility procedure *SkipTo*, which may be called from anywhere within the recursive descent parser. This procedure will have a value parameter which determines the set of symbols at which the skipping will halt. We shall call this the **skip-halting set**. In practice, it is usual for the procedure to have a second, message parameter, which causes the associated message to be inserted in the appropriate output stream. The procedure might be as follows.

> **procedure** *SkipTo*(*haltSet* : *SymbolSet*;
>   *message* : *MessageType*);
> **begin** (* assert: *haltSet* includes the *stopper* symbol *)
>   {insert message in output stream};
>   **while not** (*symbol* **in** *haltSet*) **do** *GetSymbol*;
> **end**; (* assert: current *symbol* is in *haltSet* *)

Note the asserted postcondition. Any reasoning about the error-recovery behaviour of the parser will depend on the use of this assertion. The postcondition obviously depends on the precondition that every halt set includes the end-of-input pseudo-symbol which the scanner emits when the end of input is detected.

In essence, the success of the whole symbol-skipping method depends on the possibility of choosing suitable skip-halting sets. There are several different possibilities which arise in different circumstances. Firstly, it may be that, for the grammar to be considered, the appropriate skip-halting set for a particular non-terminal symbol may be determined without regard for the context in which the phrase appears. In this case the various sets will be constants of the recognition procedures. Usually, however, a greater degree of discrimination in the choice of resynchronization point may be obtained by using a skip-halting set which depends on the particular context.

It will be recalled, in connection with the SLR and LALR parsing methods, that the *FOLLOW* set of a non-terminal symbol lumps together all possible symbols which may follow that non-terminal in a sentential form. It is possible, however, for separate lookahead sets to be associated with the various contexts in which a particular symbol may appear. This kind of separation of possible follow symbols is exactly what is required in this application also.

Each procedure of a recursive descent parser recognizes the context-free productions associated with one non-terminal. The normal parsing action of the procedure is, therefore, by definition, independent of the surrounding context. There is no reason, however, why the procedure should not make its error-recovery action dependent on a skip-halting set which has been passed to it as a parameter. The calling procedure is aware of the context, and thus can send the appropriate *halt* set as the actual parameter of the call.

As a general rule, each recursive descent procedure will take a *halt* set as a formal parameter. If it should turn out that a particular procedure always takes the same parametric set, then the parameter may be removed and replaced by a constant when the parser design is being fine-tuned and optimized. It is sensible, therefore, to adopt a uniform structure initially.

We will assume that each recognition procedure has a guaranteed postcondition. This condition will be either that the final symbol of the recognized phrase was correctly matched, or that the current symbol belongs to the *halt* set which it was passed as the actual parameter. Of course we expect that normally *both* conditions will be true, but we must be able to cope with each of the other possibilities. This condition suggests a way of relating the *halt* set which is passed to a procedure, and the sets which it in turn will pass to its own subordinate procedures. In the following examples many of the postconditions are explicitly spelled out to remind the reader, and the programmer, of the actual range of possible conditions which may exist at that point of the control flow.

12.3.1 First case: starting symbols are distinctive

As a simple first example, we shall consider error recovery within a procedure which recognizes a production $A \rightarrow BC$. We shall assume that there is some distinctive set of symbols, *CStarters*, which indicates the start of the phrase which corresponds to the non-terminal C. Figure 12.4 shows typical error-recovery code for this case.

It is typical practice to take the skip-halting set from the formal parameter, add extra symbols by a set union, and use the union as an actual parameter for a call to a subordinate procedure. The point in this choice is one of defensive programming. If there should be not only an error in the B phrase, but the characteristic symbols which start C are also omitted, then the choice of set as shown will ensure that the symbol skipping within the *BRecognize* procedure does not read past a potential resynchronization point at the end of the A phrase. Of course, the called procedures, *BRecognize* and *CRecognize*, may in turn supplement the set

```
procedure ARecognize(haltSet : SymbolSet);
  const CStarters = [ . . . ];
begin (* A -> BC *)
  BRecognize(haltSet + CStarters);
  (* assert: a match on last of B, or symbol
          is in (haltSet + Cstarters) *)
  CRecognize(haltSet);
end; (* assert: a match on last of C, or symbol is in haltSet *)
```

Figure 12.4   Set accumulation for error recovery.

with more symbols, adding extra symbols corresponding to marker symbols of significance within their own substructure. These new sets will then be passed to further subordinate procedures. The actual skip-halting set at any point in the recognition will, therefore, be the union of the resynchronization sets for every phrase which encloses the current input position.

It should be noted that the set union in Figure 12.4 implements the kind of context-sensitive lookahead set that was mentioned previously. It may very well be that the set $FOLLOW(B)$ includes many symbols which are not in the set *CStarters*. By making the choice of set supplement shown in the figure, we are selecting the expected symbols in the context of this particular production.

We would like to be able to have a stronger postcondition on exit from the procedure, such as 'either no errors in the phrase, or the symbol is in *haltSet*', but we cannot make any such assertion. The fact that the final action of the procedure was not an (indirect) return from procedure *SkipTo* only guarantees that, if there was an error detected, then the system has since successfully matched at least one symbol, and hence thinks itself resynchronized.

Inside recognition procedures which match terminal symbols, there will be code similar to the following, where we shall assume a version of procedure *SkipTo* which has a single parameter only.

```
procedure BRecognize(haltSet : SymbolSet);
begin
  . . .
  if symbol <> xxx then SkipTo(haltSet)
    else begin
    GetSymbol;
    . . .
    end;
end;
```

This code attempts to resynchronize after the end of the *B*-phrase if an error is detected. Of course, it is also possible for the *BRecognize* procedure to attempt to resynchronize within the current phrase, by using a set which includes additional symbols.

12.3.2   Alternative case: ending symbols are distinctive

Sometimes the starting symbols of the phrases which are expected to follow a particular phrase are insufficiently distinctive to be successfully used as a skip-halting set. This situation typically arises when *FOLLOW* for the particular symbol includes some symbol which is extremely common. We must then rely on finding some distinctive *ending* symbol of the current phrase, rather than trying to find the start of the following phrase.

Consider the following problem as an example. An error has occurred during the parsing of declarations in a program written in a Pascal-like language. Clearly it is no help skipping to the first symbol belonging to *FOLLOW*(*declaration*), since this will include the symbol *identifier* which occurs (almost) everywhere. It is obviously better to look for the semicolon which ends the erroneous declaration, and then try to resynchronize on the symbol following that.

This example is interesting, since it also illustrates another point. Clearly, using a skip-halting set consisting of just the expected semicolon would be rather dangerous, since the error might actually turn out to be a missing semicolon. To tackle this problem, we will define several different sets. There is the set of symbols which definitely do indicate the start of the next phrase, *markers* = {**var**, **procedure**, . . . }, say. This *marker* symbol set will be a subset of the *FOLLOW* set. Then there is a set of symbols which indicates the end of the current phrase, in this case just the set *enders* = {*semicolon*}. We will skip, therefore, until either a semicolon or marker symbol is found, and read one further character if the halting symbol is a semicolon.

Abstracting the general features of this example, we will assume that all of the recognition procedures which suffer such difficulties will have a pair of parameters, the normal halt set, which is the union of the lookahead sets of all enclosing phrases, and a set of distinctive markers which is the halt set minus the troublesome 'common' symbols of the enclosing phrases. The error-recovery strategy should ensure that the skip after an error never goes past a distinctive marker, and also ensures the normal postcondition. Let us consider the same production as in Figure 12.4, $A \rightarrow BC$. Once again we will assume that the set of all starting symbols for *C* is denoted *CStarters*, but that this set includes some symbols which commonly occur within the *B*-phrases. The set *CMarkers* is a subset of *CStarters*, but comprises just those symbols which are

```
procedure BRecognize(haltSet  : SymbolSet; (* all follow syms. *)
                        markers : SymbolSet);(* distinctive ones *)
   const BEnders = [ . . . ];
begin
   . . .
   if symbol <> xxx then begin
        SkipTo(markers + BEnders); (* find end *)
        SkipTo(haltSet); (* now find next start *)
        end
      else begin
        GetSymbol;
        . . .
        end;
end; (* assert: a match on last of B, or the symbol is in haltSet *)

procedure ARecognize(haltSet : SymbolSet);
   const CStarters = [ . . . ];
        CMarkers = [ . . . ];
begin (* A -> BC *)
   BRecognize(haltSet + CStarters, haltSet + CMarkers);
   CRecognize(haltSet);
end; (* assert: a match on last of C, or the symbol is in haltSet *)
```

Figure 12.5   A subordinate procedure with two set-parameters.

distinctive start symbols of a *C*-phrase. Figure 12.5 shows typical code for this case.

In Figure 12.5, when the procedure *BRecognize* detects an error, it seeks a distinctive symbol, either an end-marker of *B*, or a distinctive starter of a following phrase. If the halting symbol is a member of the set which marks the end of the *B*-phrase, one final symbol must be read. It is convenient to do this by another call to *SkipTo*, which will usually skip just the ending symbol, but also establishes the desired postcondition.

12.3.3 Error recovery within closures

It is worth looking carefully at the application of these techniques to recursive descent parsers which recognize grammars with closure constructs. In many applications, the use of closures makes it possible that very long input phrases may correspond to a single procedure call. It is, therefore, very important to provide for recovery *within* the production right-hand-sides, rather than abandoning the recognition of the whole phrase.

```
procedure ARecognize(haltSet : SymbolSet);
   const CStarters = [ . . . ];
begin
   BRecognize(haltSet + CStarters);
   (* assert: a match on last of B, or symbol is
            in (haltSet + CStarters) *)
   while symbol in CStarters do
      CRecognize(haltSet + CStarters);
   end; (* assert: a match on last B or C symbol,
               or the symbol is in haltSet *)
```

Figure 12.6 Recovery within a closure, first version.

We will consider a typical regular right-part production with a closure, and consider successive refinements of the error-recovery strategy. The production is $A \rightarrow B\{C\}$. Straightforward implementation of the techniques of this section leads to the first refinement shown in Figure 12.6.

One problem with the code of Figure 12.6 is that if an error occurs between the B-phrase and the first C-phrase, or between two C-phrases, then the procedure will return prematurely. What we would like to do is make repeated attempts at resynchronization within the closure. In order to achieve this we must check the symbol which is current when the **while** loop exits. If this symbol does not belong to the required halt set, then a further skip should be initiated, halting on either a *haltSet* or a *CStarter* symbol. If a *CStarter* symbol is found, then the **while** loop should be re-entered. Figure 12.7 shows one possible encoding.

In this figure, the **while** loop processes error-free sequences of C-phrases, while the enclosing **repeat** loop is responsible for the repeated resynchronization attempts. Some effort should be made to ensure understanding of the way in which the various tests and skips transform the assertions in this example.

Of course, it is possible that the recognition of a production with a closure may suffer from the same kinds of difficulty that were discussed in connection with Figure 12.5. In general, similar solutions should be sought, perhaps using two set-valued parameters, one which indicates the desired set of symbols for the exit assertion, and the other, a set of distinctive symbols to use for skip-halting within the closure loop.

```
procedure ARecognize(haltSet : SymbolSet);
  const CStarters = [ . . . ];
begin
  BRecognize(haltSet + CStarters);
  (* assert: a match on last of B, or symbol
           is in (haltSet + CStarters) *)
  repeat
    if not (symbol in (haltSet + CStarters)) then
      SkipTo(haltSet + CStarters);
      (* assert: symbol in (haltSet + CStarters) *)
    while symbol in CStarters do
      CRecognize(haltSet + CStarters);
  until symbol in haltSet;
end; (* assert: symbol in haltSet *)
```

Figure 12.7   Recovery within a closure, second version.

12.3.4 Section checklist and summary definitions

- A very flexible method for choosing skip-halting sets for recursive descent parsers involves passing the set as a parameter to each recognition procedure.

- In general, recursive descent procedures take the halt set in the formal parameter, and pass it on to any subordinate procedures after augmenting it by including any additional symbols indicated by the local context.

- In cases where it is the ending symbols of a phrase which are distinctive, rather than the starting symbols of the next phrase, the error recovery should skip to a symbol in the ending set, and then attempt to find a following symbol which belongs to the required starting set.

- If the starting symbols of a phrase include both distinctive and commonly occurring symbols, then it may be convenient to pass two parameters to the recognition procedure of the preceding phrase.

- Because of the very large number of symbols which may be involved in a single phrase which corresponds to a closure, it is important to attempt repeated error recovery within the procedure which recognizes such a construct.

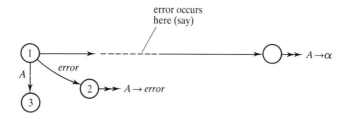

Figure 12.8 Parser fragment with error reduction.

12.4   Error recovery in bottom-up parsers

The principles of error recovery by symbol-skipping in bottom-up parsers are fairly straightforward. The only difficulty is that the error-recovery mechanisms must somehow be integrated into the operation of the parser-generator programs which create the tables for the parsing automaton.

A widely used method for specifying the points in the parsing at which error-recovery actions are attempted is to include special error productions in the grammar. In effect, these error productions define the syntactic units at the end of which resynchronization will be attempted. For example, if it is desired that errors which occur within phrases corresponding to some non-terminal symbol A should cause skipping to the end of the A-phrase, then the symbol A will be given an additional production

$A \rightarrow error$

where the name *error* is a new meta-symbol which refers, in effect, to a new non-terminal symbol with special properties. The presence of this production causes the prefix-of-A state to be tagged in the NFSA, and corresponding states in the DFSA to be similarly distinguished.

In the event that an error occurs during parsing, the state of the automaton is backed-up by popping the parser stack until one of the distinguished states is on the top of the stack. This state will have an out-transition on the special non-terminal symbol *error*, as shown in Figure 12.8. In the event that such an error-backup action is performed, either the parser itself or the semantic action attached to the *error* reduction must call for the skipping of input symbols until a symbol is found in the lookahead set of the reduction in the re-entry state, state 2.

Note that the symbol lookahead set of such a state may be calculated from the characteristic machine by the usual SLR or LALR methods. Use of the SLR lookahead would correspond to the strategy discussed in Section 12.3 for the case where the complete *FOLLOW* set is used as a skip-halting set. Use of the LALR lookahead corresponds to the case

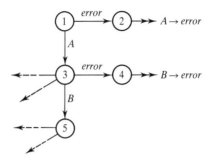

Figure 12.9   Machine fragment with cascaded error reductions.

where the skip-halting set takes account of the context in which the particular *A*-phrase has occurred. However, a small but important point to be borne in mind during the lookahead calculation is whether or not it may be appropriate to consider the error symbol itself to be nullable. Consider, for example, the characteristic machine fragment shown in Figure 12.9.

In calculating the LALR lookahead of the reduction (2, *A* → *error*), it will be seen that all of the *shift* transitions out of state 3 will be in the *read* set of transition (1,*A*) and hence will be in the lookahead. However, if *error* is considered to be nullable, then the transition (1,*A*) *includes* (3,*B*), so that the *shift* transitions out of state 5 are also in the lookahead. The lookahead set will thus contain symbols from both *FOLLOW(A)* and *FOLLOW(B)*, even if the symbol *B* is not otherwise nullable.

Let us suppose, with this machine fragment, that an error occurs while parsing an *A*-phrase, and that the symbol-skipping step in state 2 halts on a symbol which belongs to the *shift*-transitions out of state 5, but not those out of state 3. The next parser action will find no legal *shift* transition, and hence will declare another error. The machine will thus proceed to state 4, but will not skip any further symbols before performing the second error reduction, since the current symbol will already be in the lookahead set of the reduction. The effect of treating the *error* symbol as being nullable is thus to cause the skip-halting sets of enclosing phrases to be included in the accumulation of the lookahead set, much as was suggested as the standard technique for forming skip-halting sets for recursive descent parsers.

Just as for top-down parsers, the use of the lookahead set of a syntactic category as the skip-halting set may be insufficient, particularly if it is the *end* of one phrase which is distinctive, rather than the *beginning* of the next. It is possible to incorporate this possibility by permitting error productions to be specified in the form

A → *error a*

where *a* is the distinctive symbol which marks the end of the *A*-phrase. In this case, the symbol-skipping action should stop when the next symbol is an *a*, allowing the parsing machine to resume normal operation with a shift action. However, if this approach is adopted the effect of a missing *a* symbol must also be considered. In particular, it should be noted that, since the error transition does not lead to a state with a reduction, there is no hook on which to hang a user-written error-recovery action.

As an example of the possible behaviour of the parsing machine in the case where the lookahead set of a simple error production is not a distinctive skip-halting set, let us trace the behaviour of a machine which includes the fragment shown in Figure 12.8. We will assume that the lookahead set of the error reduction in state 2 includes terminal symbols which commonly occur within *A*-phrases. The symbol skipping action in state 2 will stop at the first symbol which is in the lookahead set, which we will assume, in the first instance, is a false synchronization. However, somewhere along the paths leading out of state 3 an error will occur, because of the lack of true resynchronization. The machine will, therefore, back up to state 1 again and re-enter state 2. Since at least one symbol will have been matched during the false start, the error action will skip to a new symbol which belongs to the lookahead. The error-recovery actions may thus include repeated false starts on the common symbols, until finally the symbol is found which really is the start of the following phrase. Because of the possibility of repeated false starts, it is often desirable to suppress error output messages following an initial error, until sufficient symbols have been successfully shifted to make it probable that resynchronization has actually been achieved.

12.4.1 Error recovery within a recursive production

As a final example of error recovery in bottom-up parsers, we will consider error recovery within a recursive production system corresponding to the closure discussed in Section 12.3.3.

Corresponding to the regular right-part production $A \rightarrow B\{C\}$, we have the following productions, where we assume that left-recursion has been chosen and that both *B* and *C* have been given simple error productions.

$A \rightarrow BK.$
$K \rightarrow \varepsilon$
   $| \ KC.$
$B \rightarrow \ldots | \ error.$
$C \rightarrow \ldots | \ error.$

The fragment of the characteristic machine corresponding to these productions is shown in Figure 12.10.

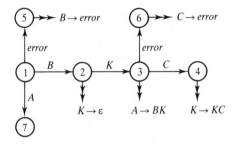

Figure 12.10   Characteristic fragment for a left-recursive production.

In this figure, the LALR lookahead sets of the two error reductions are the same, being equal to the union of $FIRST(C)$ and the follow set of the A transition out of state 1. In terms of the relations defined in Section 9.3, for the $B \rightarrow error$ reduction we have

$(5,B \rightarrow error)$ *looks back at* $(1,B)$, while
$(1,B)$ *reads* $FIRST(C)$, and
$(1,B)$ *includes* $(1,A)$.

Similarly, for the $C \rightarrow error$ reduction we have

$(6,C \rightarrow error)$ *looks back at* $(3,C)$,
$(3,C)$ *includes* $(2,K)$, and then
$(2,K)$ *reads* $FIRST(C)$, and
$(2,K)$ *includes* $(1,A)$.

In this example, after an error, the resynchronization will be attempted with a next symbol which is either a starter of a C-phrase, or is one of the expected followers of the A-phrase. The error-recovery action is thus comparable with that of the recursive descent code in Figure 12.7.

In general, the inclusion of error recovery in bottom-up parsers requires some care. Systems in which the symbol skipping action is explicitly specified by the user by way of a semantic action, rather than being determined by the parser-generator, are undoubtedly more flexible. However, they require the user to understand rather more about the characteristic machine. As an example, it may be seen that if the grammar fragment which lead to Figure 12.10 also included an error production for symbol A, then there would be a fatal *reduce–reduce* conflict in state 1, between the reductions $A \rightarrow error$ and $B \rightarrow error$.

12.4.2 Section checklist and summary definitions

- A simple method of incorporating error recovery into bottom-up parsers is to provide for the inclusion of error productions in the grammar.

- Error productions are usually specified in the form $A \rightarrow error$, where *error* is a new symbol which has special semantics associated with it.

- When a parsing automaton finds that no non-error action may be associated with the current input symbol, the state is backed up until a state is found which has a transition on the special symbol *error*. The symbol error is shifted and parsing continues.

- If a symbol-skipping action is to be associated with an error, then this may either be attached to the error reduction as part of the user-specified semantic action, or may be automatically placed by the parser-generator.

Exercises

12.1 Consider the design of recursive descent parser procedures to recognize the expression grammar used in case study 2 at the end of Chapter 8. Decide on skip-halting sets for the procedures in the case that the grammar is embedded in a Pascal-like programming language.

12.2 As pointed out in Section 8.4.2, a recursive descent parser is able to parse the ambiguous grammar

statement → *ifStatement* | *anyOtherStatement*.
ifStatement → **'if'** *expr* **'then'** *statement elsepart*.
    elsepart → ε | **'else'** *statement*.

Assuming the existence of the set $FOLLOW(statement)$ = {';', . . . }, write procedures for recognizing this grammar fragment, using symbol skipping for error recovery.

Consider the recovery action which your parser takes for each of the following single-symbol errors:

- 'then' is deleted;
- a misspelt 'then' is taken to be an identifier symbol; and hence a member of $FIRST(statement)$;
- an extra ')' appears before the 'then';
- a ';' is inserted between *statement* and 'else';
- 'else' is misspelt.

Further reading

A bibliography of error-recovery methods is given in Ciesinger (1979). An interesting early paper in this area, one of the first to discuss error recovery in relation to the underlying grammar, is that of Irons (1963). An early use of error productions was described by Wirth (1968), while discussion of error recovery in LALR parsers constructed using the UNIX tool *yacc* is given by Aho and Johnson (1974).

Chapter 13 **Final Words**

13.1 Choice of parsing method

The bottom-up parsing methods introduced in Chapter 9 are an important alternative to the top-down methods of Chapters 7 and 8. The choice between the methods is not all that straightforward, so some general guidelines are given here.

The grammars which are suitable for bottom-up parsing are, in many cases, more 'natural looking' than the grammars required for the top-down methods. The kind of grammar transformations which are necessary to make a grammar conform to the LL(1) condition, such as the removal of left-recursion and the application of left factorization, often make the grammar rather unwieldy. Furthermore, the freedom to modify evaluation order is rather more obvious in the case of the LR family of parsers, particularly if the 'ambiguous CFG with separate precedence rules' technique is used.

On the other hand, the actual parser construction for the recursive descent method is much more intuitive than the manipulation of characteristic automata. It must also be noted that, for languages which have closure constructs and optional syntactic entities, it is the regular right-part grammars accepted by recursive descent parsers which appear the more natural.

It may appear at first sight that the inclusion of semantic actions in bottom-up parsers presents rather greater difficulties than is the case for predictive methods such as recursive descent. After all, in a predictive parser the symbols are predicted in advance and checked off the list one by one as they are recognized. Individual semantic actions may thus be performed before and after each symbol is recognized, if necessary. On the other hand, a bottom-up parser does not announce the production to be used until the whole right-hand side has been recognized. Any semantic actions which are required by the production must thus be done all at once, and in retrospect. However, as was indicated in Chapter 11, the grammar used for parsing may be modified by the introduction of nullable symbols so as to achieve the same effect as that of predictive parsing.

For those languages which are sufficiently complex, the incorporation

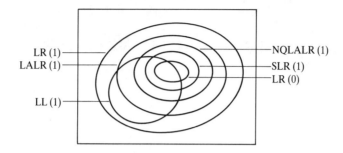

Figure 13.1   Venn diagram of grammar classes.

of error-recovery actions in parsers may also be an issue. This topic was introduced in Chapter 12, for both types of parser. Once again, the theoretical ability to incorporate error-recovery actions is similar between the two classes of parsing method, although the design process may very well prove simpler for predictive parsers. In particular, both classes of parser are capable of reporting an error as soon as the current input symbol could not possibly be a valid continuation of the part already scanned. In each case, an error is detected before a single additional input symbol is read.

For an LR-family parser, an erroneous symbol may trigger an incorrect reduction, or even a whole cascade of reductions. However, such reductions cannot lead to any state where the erroneous symbol will be shifted. The situation is analogous to that which arises in a recursive-descent parser, when a subsidiary procedure is called without a check being first made that the lookahead symbol is in the correct director-set. One or more such procedure calls may be made, but the error will finally be caught, since only a successful symbol match will result in a new symbol being read.

13.1.1 Comparison of different grammar classes

Theory has produced a number of interesting results regarding the comparative expressive powers of the various grammar subclasses which we have considered. The most important result shows that any LL(1) grammar is also LR(1), so that the most general method of bottom-up parsing with a single symbol of lookahead is more powerful than the equivalent top-down method.

The other members of the LR family of parsers form a hierarchy with strict inclusion, as shown in Figure 13.1. Any grammar which is LR(0) is also SLR(1), any SLR(1) grammar belongs to the 'not-quite-LALR(1)' category, and so on. In each case the set differences are non-empty.

Members of each of the difference sets have been demonstrated, either in the text or in the exercises for Chapter 9, except for the 'LALR but not NQLALR' case.

The relationship between the LL(1) grammars and the non-canonical parsers of the LR family is a little harder to pin down. Certainly there are LR(0) grammars which fail to be LL(1) for simple reasons, such as the presence of left recursion. On the other hand, it is relatively easy to find examples of grammars which are LL(1) but not SLR. One such example appears in Exercise 9.3. For some years it was believed that the the the LL(1) grammars were strictly included in the LALR category, but this has been proven not to be the case.

In Chapter 7 we saw that that every regular language has an LL(1) grammar, although some regular grammars may require left-factorization to make them LL(1). The model answers for Exercise 9.7 show that every regular *language* has a grammar which is also LR(0).

However, such a comparison of the inclusion or otherwise of the various grammar classes is a little misleading. Normally we are interested in the language constructs which may be parsed, rather than in the grammars. In practice, most of the language constructs of modern programming languages may be expressed either by means of LL(1) or LALR grammars. The grammars are perhaps different, but both are capable of defining the same languages. Some constructs, such as the need for left-to-right 'evaluation' do not fit easily into the LL(1) mould, although this is no difficulty for recursive descent parsers recognizing RRP grammars equivalent to an LL(1) grammar.

No matter which parsing method is used, there must be a willingness on the part of the analyst to modify the grammar until it fits the requirements of the chosen parsing method. If this is to be done with moderate to large languages, then it is important to have software tools which are capable of automatically checking conformance to the method. For large grammars it is simply too time-consuming (and too error-prone) to attempt such tests manually. The use of appropriate tools is discussed later in this chapter.

The relative sizes of the various parsers is an important considera-tion, particularly for the larger languages. SLR and LALR methods require exactly the same amount of space, which seems to be roughly comparable with the space required for an LL(1) parser for the same language. Recursive descent parsers, however, may occupy somewhat more space then LALR parsers, a factor of two being not uncommon.

In computing environments which use demand-paged virtual memory, the locality properties of the recursive descent parsers may be advantageous. The code for the group of procedures which are needed for any particular part of the overall parsing task will be a small fraction of the total, so that recursive descent parsers have a small and slowly varying working set. On the other hand, table-driven parsers frequently have a table access pattern which is apparently random, necessitating allocation of sufficient memory to enable the whole of the table to be resident at once, to avoid poor performance.

The popular choices for the parsers of programming languages at the present time are:

1. automatically constructed, table-driven LALR parsers, possibly with precedence rules added to resolve ambiguities in the CFG specification;
2. hand-programmed recursive descent parsers, possibly relying on access to semantic information to resolve the occasional non-LL(1) feature in the grammar.

Both methods have their advocates, and each method is capable of good performance, provided that sufficient care is taken in specifying the grammar, as well as in implementing it.

For the small languages used for command processing, and for interaction with application programs, there is a choice of several satisfactory methods. For such smaller tasks, however, it is believed that there should be a clear preference for recursive descent. This is partly because such parsers are easier for the non-specialist programmer to create correctly, but more particularly, because in such applications the parser is but one small part of a larger program. In such cases it would place an added burden on program maintenance if one module for a table-driven parser were to be embedded in an otherwise hand-written, high-level language program.

13.1.2 Theoretical limitation of the CFG mechanism

We shall now backtrack to consider an absolute limitation on the form of languages which may be described by CFGs. The result properly belongs back in Chapter 6, but would have seemed both artificial and difficult if introduced there. This result is the analogue, for CFGs, of the limitation on regular languages demonstrated by the pumping lemma.

We suppose that the grammar to be considered is finite, that is, it has only a finite number of productions, and that there is some maximum length which production right-hand-side strings do not exceed. We will further assume that the language which is generated is infinite, so that there are arbitrarily long strings in the language.

What will be proved is that there is a simple, repetitive pattern in the strings which may be derived using such a grammar. This pattern is certainly more complex than that demanded by the pumping lemma for regular languages, but nevertheless forms a useful criterion to prove that certain language features cannot be described by any CFG.

First, consider the form of the derivation tree for any string in the

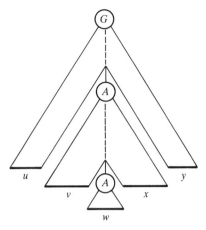

Figure 13.2   Derivation tree with a repeated A symbol on a path from the root to a leaf.

language defined by some (finite) grammar. Since the length of right-hand-side strings of productions is limited, the extent to which the tree may 'branch' at each level is also limited. We may thus safely conclude that for sufficiently long sentences the height of the tree becomes great enough to exceed the cardinality of the non-terminal alphabet, $|N|$. We shall now consider an example of such a tree.

It is not necessary to make the assumption that the grammar is unambiguous, but instead, we assume that of all derivation trees for the sentence in question, we choose a tree of minimal height. If the height of the tree is n, where $n > |N|$, then there is some path in the tree from root to leaf which passes through n nodes, each corresponding to some syntactic category. Since, by assumption, n exceeds the cardinality of the alphabet, there are more nodes then there are different categories, and hence at least one non-terminal symbol must appear twice on the path. Let us assume that A is such a repeated symbol. Figure 13.2 illustrates such a tree, and shows the 'highest' and 'lowest' occurrence of A on the selected path.

We label the substrings which are derived from the various nodes of the tree as shown in the figure. The complete sentence is $uvwxy$, where u, v etc. are strings from Σ^*. The string vwx is derived from the upper A symbol, while the w in the centre of this string is derived from the lower A.

Since we are assuming that the grammar is context free, we may freely prune the subtree at the lower A, and substitute a copy of the subtree derived from the upper A. Figure 13.3 illustrates the results of this tree-surgery. The derived sentence is now $uvvwxxy$. It is clear that we

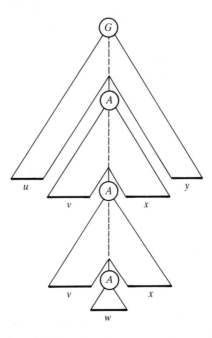

Figure 13.3   Derivation tree after substitution of the subtree derived from the upper *A* symbol.

might continue this process an arbitrary number of times, by repeatedly pruning the *w* subtree and grafting a *vwx* tree in its place.

We are led to the conclusion that every sufficiently long sentence in any language defined by a CFG has a pair of substrings, like *v* and *x* in the example, which may be repeated an arbitrary but equal number of times. We may thus 'pump-up' the sentence to any desired length.

Further consideration shows that the strings *v* and *x* cannot both be empty, since otherwise the upper *A* could be replaced by the lower one, without changing the sentence, thus reducing the height of the tree and contradicting the assumption that the tree was of minimal height.

The above argument may be made formal and precise, and is variously known as the '*uvwxy* theorem', and also sometimes as the 'pumping lemma for CFGs'. We shall be content with using it to prove one result, that the language $a^k b^k c^k$ cannot be context free.

For a grammar of any specified, finite size we may choose *k* sufficiently large so that the conditions of the theorem are met. We may, therefore, conclude that substrings equivalent to *v* and *x* must exist somewhere in this string. But where are they to be found? Clearly the *v* and the *x* cannot both consist of strings which use only one of the alphabet symbols, since in that case the pumping of the pair would upset

```
program A(input);
begin
  while true do (*nothing*)
end.

program B(input);
begin
  (*nothing*)
end.

program C(input);
  var I : integer;
begin
  I := 0;
  while not eof(input) do begin
    I := I + 1;
    readln(input);
    end;
  while I <> 10 do (*nothing*);
end.
```

Figure 13.4   Terminating and looping programs.

the balance of the number of *a*s, *b*s, and *c*s. We conclude, therefore, that at least one of the strings must contain two different members of the alphabet.

Let us assume that x is the substring that contains two different alphabet symbols, ' . . .*bc* . . .', say. Now, however, we note that if the string x is repeated we get *b*s and *c*s out of order. A similar conclusion is reached if we assume that v is the string with two different symbols, or if a different choice of the symbols is made.

Having exhaustively considered and rejected all possible positions for the pumpable pair of substrings, we must reluctantly conclude that no such CFG can exist, and thus the language is not context free.

13.1.3 Computability

This book has dealt almost exclusively with two particular classes of languages: the *regular* languages, which are recognized by finite state automata, and the *context-free* languages, which are recognized by pushdown automata. Each of these language classes have restrictions on the form of strings which may belong to the languages, as demonstrated by the pumping lemma and the '*uvwxy*' theorem.

```
program X(input);

    function WillLoop(P,D : Text) : boolean;
      . . .
    end;

begin
  if not WillLoop(input,input) then
    while true do (*loop forever*)
  (* else exit immediately *)
end.
```

Figure 13.5   The test program X.

There are also more general types of automata, which recognize wider classes of languages, and are less restricted in their form. What is not at all intuitively obvious is that there are languages which are perfectly well defined, but for which no algorithm can be given for deciding if a string belongs to the language.

The normal development of the theory of computability depends on defining a very general type of automaton and then demonstrating that certain languages cannot be recognized by such a machine. We shall adopt a rather more direct approach, by simply showing that one particular problem is unsolvable in principle.

Consider the execution of a possibly incorrect program, P, with input supplied from a text, D. This execution will either terminate, or will become caught in an endless loop. Since we consider a program which becomes caught in a loop to be erroneous, we would like to be able to devise a software tool which inspects a program text and a data file and determines whether the execution will succeed or loop. At first sight the problem would seem to be difficult, but not impossible. Consider the three programs in Figure 13.4. Program A loops on all inputs, program B terminates for all inputs, and program C terminates only for input files which are exactly 10 lines long.

Let us suppose, to be definite, that we have a function which is given a program text and a data file as parameters, and computes whether or not the program will loop on that input.

function *WillLoop(P,D : Text) : boolean*;

We shall prove that such a function cannot exist, or rather that if it exists it cannot always be correct.

We shall consider the special problem of determining whether or not a particular program will loop when it takes its own source file as input.

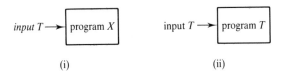

Figure 13.6   Machines with conjugate behaviour.

Clearly, if we can determine the result for an arbitrary input file we may determine the result for this special case. For example, we can deduce that program C will *not* loop when given its own text as input. We shall use the function *WillLoop* within another program, given in Figure 13.5.

Let us suppose that program T is used as input to program X. Now if program T does loop then *WillLoop* returns *true*, and program X exits correctly. However, if T terminates correctly then X will loop endlessly in the **while** loop. In effect, we have constructed the situation illustrated in Figure 13.6. For any program T, if machine (ii) halts then machine (i) loops, while if (ii) loops then (i) halts.

Since we have asserted that function *WillLoop* can correctly analyse *any* program, there is nothing to stop us applying file X as the input data for the program X. Figure 13.6 then becomes Figure 13.7.

As usual, machine (i) loops if and only if machine (ii) halts. However, this is impossible since (i) and (ii) are identical machines! We must conclude that function *WillLoop* cannot exist, since if it does we may use it to construct an impossible program which loops forever, if and only if it does not loop forever.

The above argument should not be taken to imply that it is not possible to write a program which analyses programs in order to detect errors which will lead to the program looping on certain inputs. What the example proves is that any such function must fail for some programs, either by returning a wrong answer or by going into a loop itself and thus never returning an answer. Both failure methods remove the paradox in Figure 13.7, either by allowing *both* machines to halt (by the function erroneously returning *true*), or by allowing both machines to loop (by the function erroneously returning *false*, or by not returning at all).

The set of all those programs which terminate when given their own source file as input is a well-defined language; we have even seen some examples in Figure 13.4. However, we have demonstrated that there can be no exact way of recognizing this language.

We must not despair in the face of such negative results, however. Instead, it is necessary to understand the effect of such a theoretical limitation. In the case of program analysis, we may construct a correct function which returns *false* if the program definitely will not loop, but will return *true* either if the program will loop or is too hard to analyse.

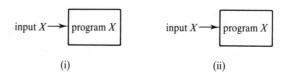

(i)   (ii)

Figure 13.7   The paradoxical situation.

We might call this function *MightLoop*. The reader may check that the use of *MightLoop* instead of *WillLoop* in program *X* avoids all traces of paradox.

13.1.3 Section checklist and summary definitions

1. Comparison of language classes.
   - The classes of grammars which may be parsed by LR-family automata form a hierarchy with strict inclusion.
   - If a grammar belongs to a particular class, then it necessarily belongs to every 'wider' class.
   - The hierarchy is: LR(1) (least restricted), LALR, NQLALR, SLR, LR(0) (most restricted).

2. Semantic action capability.
   - The abilities of top-down and bottom-up parsers to incorporate semantic actions are similar.

3. The '*uvwxy*' theorem.
   - Every sufficiently long sentence in a language defined by a CFG has a pair of substrings which may be repeated an arbitrary, but equal, number of times.
   - If the original sentence is *uvwxy*, where *u*, *v*, etc. are all terminal symbol strings, then the 'pumped' sentences would be *uvvwxxy*, *uvvvwxxxy* etc.
   - At least one of the strings, *v*, *x*, must be non-empty.

4. Computability.
   - There are languages which cannot be exactly recognized by any algorithm.

13.2   The meta-toolkit

This book has emphasized techniques of syntax-directed tool construction which may be implemented by hand, within a normal programming environment. Nevertheless, there are a number of tools which may assist in the production of such programs. Such a set of tools, intended for assistance in the production of other software tools, might be termed a **meta-toolkit**.

13.2.1   Tools for finite state automata

Many of the FSA which are met in practice are so small that it is hardly necessary to seek the assistance of automated methods. However, there are a number of tools which are helpful.

Consider the steps involved in implementing an FSA from a regular expression.

1. Convert the regular expression into an NFSA;
2. convert to a DFSA by the subset-construction procedure;
3. encode the DFSA transitions into a table or program.

Performing each of these steps automatically is not a difficult task. Most of the steps involved in the tool design have been treated as examples in the text.

In the case of implementation languages, such as ISO Pascal, it is very awkward to automate step 3, however. This is because of the absence of a facility to define constant arrays which might be used for a table-driven automaton. It is possible, of course, to produce a text file which may be included in a user-written program as the body of a table-initialization procedure. This is probably the best approach when a compacted lookup table is to be implemented. In this case the tool should certainly calculate the starting indices, and decide whether the error state should be used as the default next state, or whether the mechanism described in connection with the recursive finite state automata should be used.

Programmed implementation is often used when the number of states in the automaton is small. In this case, the output of the tool should be a DFSA transition table corresponding to the result of step 2 above. The program is then manually produced from the transition table, and semantic actions, if any, are incorporated as required.

In the case of table driven automata, the incorporation of semantic actions will require some editing of the table-initialization procedure suggested above. In languages such as Pascal, an ordinal value may be inserted into the table, and then used as a **case** selector in an omnibus semantic action procedure.

Of course, one of the most common situations in which FSA arise in practice is in the implementation of lexical scanners. In such cases, there is a whole family of FSA which recognizes the tokens of the next higher-level machine from substrings in the lower-level alphabet. The scanner must recognize the language of each of these tokens, and must also be able to find the end of each token within the continuing input string.

There are existing tools for the automatic production of lexical scanners, of which the most widely available is the *lex* tool under UNIX. This has been used in a very large variety of contexts, many of which are not obvious, in the sense that the underlying problem does not immediately appear to be one of lexical scanning. In addition, many people have found it to be a very useful tool for conventional purposes, such as the production of lexical scanners for programming language compilers.

Nevertheless, for conventional applications of lexical scanners, many people, including this author, prefer to construct scanners by hand. It seems that, for many applications, the mixture of a large number of single character tokens and a small number of lexical categories with considerable substructure, is most easily handled with a handwritten scanner. An example of the kind of special feature which may be taken into consideration in a manually constructed scanner, and which is quite difficult to treat in an automated fashion, is the recognition of nested comments used as an example in Exercise 6.8.

The point is that very often lexical grammars contain a minority of tokens the recognition of which is quite complex. Production of a tool capable of handling every conceivable variation of specification is therefore very difficult, and the effort usually unwarranted.

As was pointed out in Chapter 4, there are many different automata which recognize the same regular language, and in some circumstances the effort required to find the unique FSA with the minimum number of states is warranted. Fortunately, however, this is seldom the case for software automata.

An algorithm exists for finding the minimal automaton equivalent to a given FSA, due to Hopcroft (1971), but described rather more accessibly by Gries (1973). This algorithm is extremely interesting for the student of data structures and algorithm design. The running time of the program is bounded by a time proportional to $n*log(n)$, where n is the number of states in the original automaton. The more obvious approaches to the problem take times proportional to n^2 or even n^3.

The Hopcroft algorithm may be used as the basis of a meta-tool, but as remarked earlier, the number of states in the FSA is seldom a constraint in the implementation of regular languages.

13.3   Parser generation tools

Parser generation tools fall into two categories corresponding to the top-down and bottom-up methodologies. It is possible to construct tools which produce tables for table-driven LL(1) parsers, or for table-driven recursive-FSA parsers, and there are published examples of such tools. However, the predominant method of constructing top-down parsers is recursive descent.

13.3.1   Director set generation

For recursive descent parsing, the most valuable meta-tool is a director-set generator. The production of director sets by hand, for all but the smallest grammars, is a time-consuming and error-prone task. Access to an automatic generator is, therefore, a great advantage. The most efficient method of checking the LL(1) condition, and deriving director sets for a grammar, is due to Gough (1985).

An interesting design question is whether the tool should just produce director sets, or should generate all of the *FOLLOW* sets, whether needed or not. It has been pointed out (Dwyer, 1985) that using 'lazy evaluation' to construct only those *FOLLOW* sets which are actually required may lead to speed improvements for the algorithm. Nevertheless, a *FOLLOW* set, which is not strictly required for director-set generation, is occasionally used during the incorporation of error-recovery actions. It might be used, for example, as the basis of a skip-halting set for panic-mode error recovery.

13.3.2   *Yacc, and LR parser-construction tools*

The use of a meta-tool is a virtual necessity for constructing LR family parsers. The construction of bottom-up parsers without such a tool is simply not practicable.

The variation of the LR parsing theme used most in practical applications, is the LALR(1) method. Section 9.3 gives an outline of the LALR method described in terms which correspond to those used in DeRemer and Pennello's (1982) algorithm for generating the LALR lookaheads of a CFG, and thereby checking the LALR(1) condition. This algorithm is rather more efficient than that used in the most widely available parser-generators. It is the basis of a commercially available parser-generator system, the MetaWare™ translator writing system.

There have been a number of other LR family parser-generators described in the literature, but the most widely available and most widely used is the *yacc* tool of UNIX. The name is an acronym for 'yet another compiler-compiler'. This tool is of sufficent importance that almost a whole section is devoted to it.

Yacc accepts a description of a CFG as input, together with attached semantic actions. The output of the program is a file in the C programming language, which may then be compiled along with other files making up the language recognizer. *Yacc* has facilities for insertion of semantic actions, error recovery, and can use precedence rules to resolve parsing conflicts in ambiguous grammars.

The overall format of *yacc* input is given by the regular right-part (RRP) grammar production

$$input \rightarrow declarations \ '\%\%' \ rules \ ['\%\%' \ programs].$$

The declaration section contains the declarations of the terminal symbols of the grammar. In may also contain C language declarations for objects which are used in the semantic actions. Note that only terminal symbols are declared explicitly. Undeclared names which occur within the rules are taken to be non-terminal symbols. It follows that an error, such as the misspelling of a symbol name in the rules section, will show itself as an unreachable symbol or a non-terminating production, rather than as a specific undeclared-identifier diagnostic.

The list of rules is specified in a format which is generally similar to that described in Chapter 11 for syntax-directed translation schemes. The format may be described by the following RRP grammar fragment.

$$rules \rightarrow rule \ \{';' \ rule\} \ [';'].$$
$$rule \rightarrow lhs \ ':' \ rhs \ \{'|' \ rhs\} \ [action].$$
$$action \rightarrow '=' \ '\{' \ semantic\text{-}action\text{-}code \ '\}'.$$

Any number of rules may be given for each non-terminal symbol, but the first rule in the rules section must be for the goal symbol of the grammar.

Since a single semantic action is attached to all of the alternate right-hand sides making up a single rule, in practice, as many separate productions are required as there are distinct semantic actions. The left-hand side of each rule is a non-terminal symbol, while the right-hand sides are strings from the vocabulary. The production part of each rule, therefore, consists of one or more productions in a (non-extended) CFG.

13.3.3 Semantic actions in *yacc*

The action part of each rule, if present, is an arbitrary sequence of statements in the C language. These statements may call for the emission of output, as in the simple SDTSs discussed in Chapter 11, or may invoke tree-building actions, creating data structures for processing by later phases of the recognizer. However, there are a number of special facilities built into *yacc* which make the specification of such actions more convenient.

It must first be explained that C is an expression-oriented language, and that the execution of every statement has an associated expression value which it returns. In the case of *yacc*, it is possible to explicitly control the return value of a semantic action, so that the return value may be used as a component in the evaluation of other expressions. The return value may be assigned to be some numeric value, or perhaps to be a pointer to the root of some newly created tree structure.

Within an action, the special symbol $$ refers to the return value of the action. Similarly, the symbols $1, $2, etc. refer, respectively, to the return values of the first, second, etc. symbols of the right-hand side.

As an example, the rule

factor : Lparenthesis expression Rparenthesis = {$$ = $2};

expresses the fact that the value of a parenthesized expression is equal to the value of the enclosed expression. (Note that in language C, the equals sign is used to denote an assignment.)

If the actions return pointers as their values, then these values may be sent as actual parameters to subsequent node-creation procedures. The action which calls the node-creation procedure would then return a pointer to the newly created node as its own return value. A typical usage might be as follows.

term : term STAR factor = {$$ = *CreateMult*($1,$2)};

Finally, there is a useful facility, called **bundling**, which provides a mechanism for deferring output when a syntax-directed translation rule is not *simple*. A bundle may be a string of output characters, or a sequence of bundles. A bundle may be formed by 'bundling' together other bundles in any required order, with the composite bundle being finally emitted as output by the bundle-printing procedure *bprint*. The use of bundles is thus a ready-made mechanism for the kind of output reordering which was discussed in Section 11.2.1.

13.3.4 Ambiguous grammars and *yacc*

One of the features of the *yacc* interface, which is very useful for constructing parsers for expression languages, is a facility for automatically dealing with ambiguous grammars by means of separate disambiguating rules, as discussed in Section 9.5. This is especially useful for languages which, like the expression sublanguage for C itself, have a complex structure with many layers of precedence.

In effect, this facility allows very simple grammars to be chosen for structures such as expressions, and for rules of precedence and associativity to be separately stated. These rules are stated in the declarations section of the input. For example, to obtain the associativity and precedence used in the example in Section 9.5.2, the declarations should contain the lines

> %*right circlePlus*
> %*left   circleX*

where the token names *circlePlus* and *circleX* are chosen for the symbols ⊕ and ⊗, respectively. These declarations state that ⊕ associates on the right, and ⊗ on the left. The fact that the tokens appear on separate lines, with ⊕ first, specifies that ⊗ has the lower precedence.

13.3.5   Error recovery in *yacc*

The mechanisms which are built into *yacc* to provide for error recovery in the constructed parsers are similar, in general terms, to those discussed in Chapter 12. Productions may be specified in the rules section of a *yacc* input file which are of the form

> $A \rightarrow error \; \alpha$

where α is some (possibly null) string from the vocabulary.

In the event that no other parsing action is possible, a constructed parser will act as though it had seen the special symbol *error*, and will remove states from the stack until a state is reached from which such a 'symbol' may be shifted. In the event that a non-empty string, α, is specified, the parser will discard symbols until a symbol which may begin α is encountered.

As a practical heuristic which prevents cascades of error messages from accompanying repeated attempts at resynchronization, the parser remains in the special error state until it has correctly shifted three input symbols. When it is possible to detect resynchronization by other means, there is a facility for a user-specified semantic action to switch the parser back to normal operation.

The facilities which are provided in *yacc* for error recovery are thus rather rudimentary. In effect, these facilities provide 'hooks' onto which the user may attach error-recovery actions of greater or lesser complexity, as warranted by the particular application.

Further reading

The '*uvwxy*' theorem is discussed in Hopcroft and Ullman (1979), where it is used directly and indirectly to show that a number of different constructs do not correspond to CFGs. This reference is also a good starting point for a more formal discussion of computability.

The *yacc* tool is described by Johnson (1975), and is described in the documentation of most UNIX systems. An alternative approach to parser generation is described by Finn (1985).

Answers to Selected Exercises

Chapter 2

2.3 The most obvious of several solutions has the state diagram:

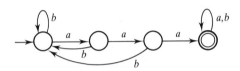

2.4 Using the same notation as for Figure 2.4, the state diagram is:

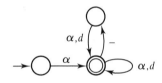

2.5 This question is hard! However, consider a system which answers the question of acceptability of a digit string by performing a long division. Clearly, only the final remainder is of importance, and the quotient digits may be discarded as they are produced.

At each step in the division an input-string digit is read in, and concatenated with the *remainder* from the previous step. A new quotient digit is calculated and discarded, and the resulting remainder saved for the next step.

We may, therefore, conclude that the information saved between steps is a remainder in the range 0 to 6, and hence exactly seven states suffice.

2.6 Given: a finite state diagram with each state labelled 'accept' or 'non-accept', and which includes an explicit error state. Now,

1. make a copy of the FSA, but have the *accept* labels with complementary values,

2. otherwise leave all transitions unchanged.

The original and copied FSA start in the same state, and, since the transitions are all the same, will end up in the same final state. Therefore, if one FSA is in an accept state the other will necessarily be in a non-accept state. Thus the FSA accept complementary languages.

It follows that any language accepted by an FSA has a complement language which is accepted by an FSA of equal (and hence finite) state cardinality. Therefore, the complement of any regular language is also regular.

2.7 $R = \{I, II, III, IV, V, VI, VII, VIII, IX\}$
$L = \{I, II, III\}$

Thus, from the definition,

$R/L = \{\varepsilon, I, II, V, VI, VII\}$

2.8 X is the set of all odd-length strings of 'x's. Now, since A is the finite language $\{a, xa\}$, it follows that the product language, P, is

$XA = \{xa, xxa, xxxa, xxxxa, \ldots\}$

i.e. the set of all strings $x^n a$, $n \geqslant 1$. However, from the definition of the quotient,

$Q = P/A = \{\varepsilon, x, xx, xxx, xxxx, \ldots\}$

i.e. the set of all strings x^n, $n \geqslant 0$. Since $Q = (XA)/A \neq X$, we conclude that the product and quotient are not exact inverses.

2.9 It is given that L_1 and L_2 are not disjoint, and hence there is at least one string which belongs to both languages. Suppose that s is such a string. Now s belongs to L_1, and s belongs to L_2. Therefore, from the definition, ε belongs to the quotient L_1/L_2.

Chapter 3

3.1 In Figure 3.9, change the first **case** statement to alter the target state of the 'I' transition out of state 3 from error to state 4, as shown in Figure 2.7.

```
case state of
    0,1,2,3,5,6,7 : State := State + 1;
    4,8,9,10      : State := error;
end;
```

3.2 The state diagram is as follows.

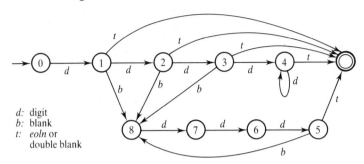

d: digit
b: blank
t: eoln or
    double blank

The code to implement the machine has the detection of termination as its only complication. It is possible to unravel the problem of separating single blanks from pairs by various means, but the cleanest method is to treat 'terminator' and 'blank' as separate symbols which are recognized by a lower-level procedure.

Suitable code might have the outline:

```
procedure GetNumber;
    var state : 0..9 (* 9 is error *)
        smbl : (digit,blank,term,illegal);

    procedure ReadSmbl; (* fetches smbl *)
        var ch : CHAR;
    begin
        if EOLN(input) then smbl := term (* no GET *)
        else begin
            READ(ch);
            if (ch in '0'..'9') then smbl := digit
            else if ch = ' ' then (* is it one or two? *)
                if input^ = ' ' then smbl := term else smbl := blank
            else smbl := illegal
        end; (* outer else *)
    end; (* ReadSmbl *)

begin
    GET(input); (* fetch first character *)
    state := 0; ReadSmbl;
    while smbl <> term do begin
        .

        .
        ReadSmbl;
    end;
    if state in [1..5] then . . .
end;
```

3.3   In a typical implementation of the **case** statement for small word-length computers, the **case** statement code carries out the following steps:

1. check **case** select variable against the known upper and lower bounds of the selection range;
2. use the **case** select variable as an index into a jump table;
3. execute the selected code;
4. unconditionally jump to the end of the statement code.

For inline code, the **case** statement thus has an overhead equivalent to two separate tests and jumps. If the **case** statement is entered via a trap dispatcher in the runtime support system then the overhead may be twice as great. Under those assumptions it would appear that a sequence of **if** tests will be faster if the mean number of tests to select the code is three or less.

In any event, if speed of execution is an issue, the most likely values should be tested for first in the **if . . . else if . .** case.

3.4   **procedure** *RDIGIT*(**var** *digvalue* : *INTEGER*; *I,V,X:CHAR*):
```
      const error = 6;
      var State : 0..6;
          value : 0..9;
begin
      State := 0;
      value := 0;
      while ch in [I,V,X] do begin
        if ch = I then
          case State of
            0,1,2,4 : begin
                           State := State + 1;
                           value := value + 1
                      end;
                  5 : begin
                           State := 2;
                           value := 7
                      end;
            3,error : State := error
          end
        else if ch = V then
          case State of
                  0 : begin
                           State := 4;
                           value := 5
                      end;
```

cont. overleaf

cont.

```
        1 : begin
                State := 3;
                value := 4
            end;
       2,3,4,5,error: State := error
     end
  else (* ch = X *)
     if State = 1 then begin
                State := 3;
                value := 9
            end
     else State := error;
     READ(ch);
   end (* while *);
   if State = error
     then OK := FALSE
     else digvalue := value;
end;
```

3.5   A suitable state diagram is

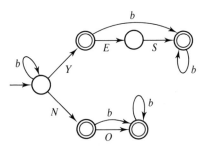

b: blank

The implementation must take care in testing for the termination condition if actual trailing spaces are to be separated from end-of-line conditions. The problem is simply that, in standard Pascal, when a *READ(ch)* procedure is followed immediately by a successful test for *EOLN*, the character *ch* is the character *before* the carriage-return and in general should be processed by the FSA before the interpretation is ended. A simple solution is to use the *EOLN* test to set a Boolean flag, which causes an exit from the interpretation loop after the last character is processed. A rather more elegant solution is to separate the Pascal *READ* into separate assignment and *GET* operations:

GET(*input*);
state := *start*;
while not *EOLN* **do begin**
   ch := *input*^;
   { process character *ch* };
   GET(*input*)
end; (* while *)

Some implementations of Pascal, notably UCSD, implement a file type *INTERACTIVE*, for which the order of assignment and *GET* in the built-in procedure *READ* are reversed from the order in the Pascal Report. For such systems the problem does not arise, since when a *READ*(ch) returns *EOLN* true, *ch* is the space corresponding to the carriage-return character.

3.6 Suppose we are given a Mealy machine with states named *A,B,C*, ... A transition function specifies the successor state for every (*state, symbol*) pair, and an action function is also defined for every pair.

We now construct a Moore machine equivalent to the given machine as follows. For every transition in the Mealy machine we define a state in the new machine. If the transition passed from state *I* to state *J* on symbol *a*, then we label the new state '*IaJ*'. Since this is to be a Moore machine we attach semantic actions to states rather than to transitions, so for state *IaJ* we attach the same action as was on the transition to which it corresponds. The start state is a special case: if *A* is the start state of the Mealy machine, then we label the start state of the new machine '*_aA*'.

For any state, *IaJ*, in the new machine, we attach in-transitions on symbol *a* from every state with a name that ends in an '*I*'. Suppose now that the old and new machines are each presented with the same string. By construction, if the original machine is in state *X*, then the new machine must be in a state with a name which ends in '*X*'. Furthermore, the semantic action which is executed by the new machine on entry to a state '*YbX*' is precisely that which the original machine would execute on leaving state *Y* by the *b*-transition. The two machines thus perform the same actions and are functionally equivalent in the sense that we have defined.

Chapter 4

4.1 The state diagram is as follows.

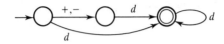

4.2 Using the notation d_+ = '1'..'9', $d = (0|d_+)$, a regular expression for the language is

$(d_+d^*|0) [.(d^*d_+|0)]$

There are many other, equivalent solutions!

4.3

Syntax diagram:

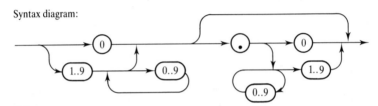

NFSA:

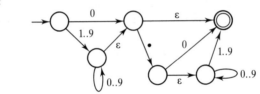

DFSA:

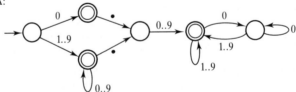

4.4

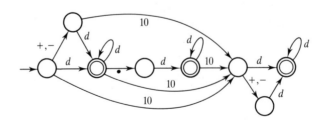

4.6 The regular expression is $(a|b)^*a(a|b)(a|b)(a|b)$. The corresponding NFSA is simple:

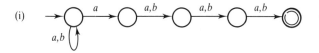

(i)

The DFSA, however, is much more complex, requiring 16 states. In general, the language which specifies the 'nth to last symbol' in a string will require 2^n states for its DFSA.

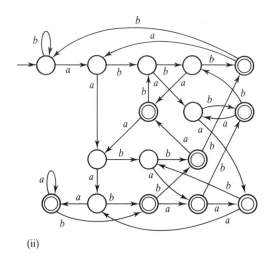

(ii)

4.7 A skeleton for such a program consists of a procedure which matches a single character. If successful, the procedure recursively calls itself until the accept state is found, causing a global flag to be set to true. If no match can be found on the remainder of the input string, then this is shown by the recursion returning with the flag still set to false. In this event, the procedure attempts a loop followed by an advance. If either this is not possible or the attempt fails anyway, the procedure returns with the flag still false. Note that when the state backtracks, the input must also be backed-up. In the following code, we assume that the input string exists in an array indexed $1..K$. It is possible also to perform the backtracking without using recursion.

This code utilizes the same data structure as the code in Figure 4.22, with which it should be compared. It is assumed that the input string is held in a character array *InString*.

```
function WILDSCAN : BOOLEAN;
  var flag : BOOLEAN;
      state : NfsaState;

  procedure MATCH(charnum : StringIndex;
                  present  : NfsaState);
  begin
    if InString[charnum] in ALPHABET then begin
      (* string has not ended, try to advance *)
      if (InString[charnum] = AdvanceChar[present])
        or (AdvanceChar[present] := '%') then
        (* try to match next char with next state *)
        MATCH(charnum + 1, present + 1);
      if not flag and SelfLoop[present] then
        (* advance has failed, try to loop instead *)
        MATCH(charnum + 1, present)
      end (* advance attempt *)
    else (* string has ended, check if in endstate *)
      if present = ENDNUM then flag := TRUE;
  end;

begin
  flag := FALSE;
  MATCH(1,0); (* start the search *)
  WILDSCAN := flag
end;
```

4.8 There are two essential differences in the storing and accessing of sparse NFSA tables as compared to the sparse DFSA tables discussed in Section 3.3. There may be empty transitions out of any state, and there may be several transitions on the same symbol from any state. The latter implies that the algorithm which searches the table must not stop when it finds a match on the particular input symbol, but must complete the scan of the list in case there are several matches. In general, there may be more than one ε-transition out of any state, so that each state must have a list of empty-successors.

One simple solution to the problem is to form three arrays: a *next state* array much as described in Section 3.3, an *ε-list* array, and an *index* array. The *index* array keeps two start indices for each state: *TransStart*, and *EpsilonStart*. The algorithm which builds the direct successor set for state N must scan the *next state* array from *index*[N].*TransStart* to *index*[$N+1$].*TransStart*. The ε-closure algorithm, on the other hand, will access the *ε-list* list array from the start point *index*[N].*EpsilonStart* through to *index*[$N+1$].*EpsilonStart*.

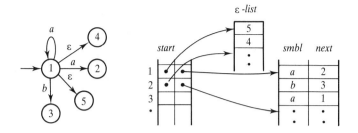

The detailed answer to the next question indicates that the only accesses to either the *next state* or ε-*list* structures require only the unordered lists implied by a '**for** *every* . . .' iteration.

4.9 The detail of the answer to this question will depend on your answer to 4.8. However, certain general observations are in order.

The concept involved in almost any algorithm for finding the ε-*closure* is first to find all the states which may be reached by a single empty transition, and then to add those which may be reached from the newly found elements of the set. A recursive algorithm seems attractive:

procedure *EpsilonClosure*(**var** *S* : *DfsaState*);

    procedure *DagClosure*(*node* : *NfsaState*);
    begin
      S := *S* + [*node*]; (* adds node to set *)
      for {every *EmptySuccessor* of *node*} **do**
        DagClosure(*EmptySuccessor*);
    end; (* DagClosure *)

begin
    for {every *state* in *S*} **do**
      DagClosure(*state*)
end; (* EpsilonClosure *)

This algorithm is very simple, even when the '**for**{every . . . }' bits are elaborated so as to fit the particular data structure. Unfortunately the procedure will loop forever if there is a cycle in the empty transitions. It works correctly if the empty transitions form a directed acyclic graph (DAG), hence the name.

A correct recursive algorithm would simply note whether or not a state was already in the closure in order to avoid recursing indefinitely. The code is:

procedure *EpsilonClosure*(**var** *S* : *DfsaState*);

```
    procedure GraphClosure(var s : DfsaState);
    begin
      S := S + [node]; (* adds node to set *)
      for {every EmptySuccessor of node} do
        if not (EmptySuccessor in S) then
          GraphClosure(EmptySuccessor);
    end; (* GraphClosure *)

begin
  for {every state in S} do
    GraphClosure(state)
end; (* EpsilonClosure *)
```

An iterative procedure along the lines suggested in the statement of the question is probably better, however.

procedure *EpsilonClosure*(**var** *S* : *DfsaState*);
  var *fringe* : *DfsaState*; (* = set of NfsaState *)

```
begin
  fringe := S;
  while fringe <> [] do begin
    {choose any state in the fringe};
    fringe := fringe − [state]; (* remove it *)
    for {every EmptySuccessor of state} do
      if not (EmptySuccessor in S) do begin
        S := S + [EmptySuccessor];
        fringe := fringe + [EmptySuccessor]
      end
  end
end; (* EpsilonClosure *)
```

It is easy to prove that this algorithm terminates correctly. A state may only be added to the fringe once, and one state is removed at each traversal of the **while** loop.

Since the order in which states are removed from the fringe is arbitrary, it may be convenient to keep the fringe as a stack rather than a set. In this case states are pushed on the fringe and the last-in state is always chosen first. Note that if the fringe is kept as a stack, then a depth-first traversal of the graph is obtained, while if the fringe is implemented as a first-in-first-out queue, then a breadth-first traversal is obtained.

An efficient data-structure for the *DfsaState* type might also be some structure other than a Pascal 'set'. The points to bear in mind, if a list structure is chosen, are that there must be efficient ways of performing the operation **for** {every state}, and evaluating the predicate **if** {state in S-list}.

4.10 The key change, which is required in order to allow multiple strings to be searched for concurrently, is to create an NFSA which has multiple start states and multiple accept states.

For the efficiency of the algorithm, it is important to keep the linear structure of the NFSA intact, so that the advance state is always (*presentState* + 1). This may be achieved by allocating states to the first string from 0 to n, say, and then for the second from $(n+1)$ up. The set of start states will thus include 0, $(n+1)$, etc. The string will be accepted if the intersection of the final state-set with the set of accept states is non-empty.

The simplest way of implementing an extension which allows the meta-characters '*' and '%' to be searched for, is to use an escape character mechanism. One character, say '\', is chosen so that whatever character follows the escape character is treated as a literal character, even if it is a meta-character. A literal backslash character is then specified by a double backslash pair '\\'. The modifications to Figure 4.22 for the BuildTable procedure are shown below.

```
type NfsaState = 0..K;
var  INPUTSET, ALPHABET : set of CHAR;
     AdvanceChar : array[NfsaState] of CHAR;
     SelfLoop     : array[NfsaState] of BOOLEAN;
     MatchAll     : array[NfsaState] of BOOLEAN; (* new *)
     ENDNUM    : NfsaState;

procedure BUILDTABLE; (* version with escape character '\' *)
   var inpt : CHAR; current : NfsaState;
begin
   current := 0; Read(inpt);
   SelfLoop[current] := FALSE;
   MatchAll[current] := FALSE;
   while inpt in INPUTSET do begin
     if inpt = '*' then SelfLoop[current] := TRUE
        else if inpt = '%' then MatchAll[current] := TRUE
        else begin
          if inpt = '\' then Read(inpt); (* get literal *)
          AdvanceChar[current] := inpt;
          current := current + 1;
          SelfLoop[current] := FALSE;
          MatchAll[current] : FALSE;
          end; (* else *)                          cont. overleaf
```

cont.

>   *Read(inpt)*;
>   **end**; (* while *)
>   *ENDNUM* := *current*; (* mark end state with NUL *)
>   *AdvanceChar[current]* := *CHR(0)*;
>   **end** (* BuildTable *);

Note the modification to the data structure by the introduction of the new Boolean *MatchAll*, since the occurrence of a literal percent character can no longer be used in the table to match all characters. In practice a check on the legality of the character following the escape character might be sensible.

4.11 In the case of the *Wildcard* language, the ε-transitions are never necessary, since the ordinary states in the straight line state chains have only a single in and out transition. The ε-transitions, therefore, necessarily meet the deletion conditions of Section 4.2.3.

The situation is quite different in the case of the *WildOption* language. Consider the NFSA arising from the string '*a[*b*]c*'.

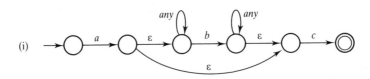

Clearly, neither of the ε-transitions may be removed without changing the language recognized. For example, if both transitions were to be deleted, the recognized language would become '*a*[b]*c*'. Careful consideration shows that the ε-transitions must be retained only when an asterisk is within an option bracket, is adjacent to one of the bracketing symbols, and also includes a non-'*' character. No problem arises, for example, for either of the strings '*a[b*c]d*' or '*a[*]b*', the NFSA for which are shown below.

4.12 The modified data structure for the NFSA does not contain a self-loop field for each state. Instead, a **set** of states which possess self-loops is created during building of the NFSA data structure. If this set is called *LoopSet*, then the set of all states in the present state which have self-loops may be found in a single set-intersection operation. Figure 4.21 then becomes as shown.

procedure *UpdateState*(**var** *present* : *DfsaState*; *ch* : *CHAR*);
(* Forms the successor state of *present* *)
  var *element* : *NfsaState*;
       next   : *DfsaState*;
begin
  next := *present* * *LoopSet*; (* set intersection *)
  for *element* := 0 **to** *ENDNUM* **do begin**
    if *element* **in** *present* **then begin**
      if (*AdvanceChar*[*element*] = *ch*) **or**
      (*AdvanceChar*[*element*] = '%')
        then *next* := *next* + [*element* + 1])
    end; (* outer if *)
  end; (* for *)
  present := *next*;
end; (* UpdateState *)

Note that in this case the code in the critical, inner loop has been effectively halved, with a significant speed gain.

4.13 The key concept involved in the improvement sought, is the inversion of the data structure, so that for every input character c a set *advance*[c] is formed. This set will contain all those states which include character c as a legal advance character. It is then possible to find every NFSA state which meets the criterion for advancement to the next state, by one set intersection operation.

The criterion for advancement from a state j on symbol c is

1. j is in the present state set;
2. j is in the set of states which have c as their advance character, *advance*[c].

All such states may be found by a single set intersection.

Having found the set of eligible states, the set of next states is obtained by including a state ($j+1$) for every state j in the eligible set.

With a bit-vector representation for Pascal sets, it is clear that all that is required is a single position shift of the eligible set. However, it is not possible to do this in a machine independent fashion, since some machines number bits left to right, while others number right to left. In any case, many machines will not have a suitable multiword shift operation if the set type is larger than one word.

Below is a skeleton of the code which might be used if the set happens to occupy the same space as an integer, and bit 0 is the least significant bit of the machine word. An undistinguished variant record is used to bypass the type checking of the compiler, so that an arithmetic operation (in this case a multiplication by 2) may be performed on the set variable to obtain the effect of a logical shift.

```
procedure UpdateState(var present : DfsaState; ch : CHAR);
(* Forms the successor state of present *)
    type TrickWord = record (* to bypass type checking *)
                        case BOOLEAN of
                            TRUE  : (state : set of NfsaState);
                            FALSE : (word : INTEGER);
                     end;
    var temp : TrickWord;
begin
    temp.state := present * advance[ch]; (* eligible states *)
    temp.word := temp.word * 2; (* shift . . . left maybe? *)
    present := present * LoopSet + temp.state;
end; (* UpdateState *)
```

If, in this example, the bits had been assumed to be numbered from left to right, then a **div** operation would be used, instead of the multiplication by 2, as in the given code. In a more realistic setting, with a large set type, the structure of the trickword might need to be more complex, and an assembly language routine might be required to give the multi-word shift.

Note, in any case, the total elimination of loops in the *UpdateState* procedure. Since almost all of the machine time is spent in this procedure, the order of speedup possible is extremely large.

Chapter 5

5.1 What is required is a new procedure *InsertIfNotPresent*, and a modified *Lookup* procedure.

In the example code below, it is assumed that the variable *top* still points to the first character of the new identifier, while a variable *newTop* points beyond the marker character which ends the new identifier.

With the same declarations as in Section 5.1, the procedures might be as follows. (Compare Figures 5.4 and 5.5.)

```
function Lookup(ix : Spellix; bk : Buckets) : DescPtr;
    (* returns Lookup = nil if not found *)
    var ptr    : DescPtr;
        found : BOOLEAN;
```

```
      function Compare(lexAtt,ix:Spellix) : BOOLEAN;
      begin
         {Compare the two strings starting at
          stringTable[ix] and stringTable[lexAtt] }
         end; (* Compare *)

begin
   found := FALSE;
   ptr := hashTable[bk];
   while not found and (ptr <> nil) do begin
      found := Compare(ptr^.spix,ix);
      if not found then ptr := ptr^.next;
   end; (* if not found then exit is with ptr = nil *)
   Lookup := ptr;
end; (* Lookup *);

procedure InsertIfNotPresent(var inserted : BOOLEAN);
   (* the ident. to test starts at stringTable[top] *)
   var desc : DescPtr;
       bkt  : Buckets;
begin (* test if string is already in table *)
   bkt := HASH(top);
   if Lookup(top,bkt) = nil then begin (* insert *)
      NEW(desc);
      with desc^ do begin (* link new descr. *)
         next := hashTable[bkt];
         spix : top;
         {assign other attributes}
      end; (* with *)
      hashTable[bkt] := desc;
      top := newTop; (* string already in table *)
      inserted := TRUE;
   end (* of insert *)
   else inserted := FALSE;
end (* Insert *);
```

5.2   The code for generating such a hash function will necessarily be machine dependent. In particular, it is necessary to treat the set as some kind of extended arithmetic type. The compiler must therefore be tricked into permitting these manipulations. As in the case of Exercise 4.12, we define a *Trickword*.

Let us suppose, to give a definite example, that the machine set type may extend over 16 8-bit bytes, i.e. a set of 0..127, and the integer size is 4 bytes. The hash function might be as follows.

```
type NFSAState = 0..127;
     DFSAState = set of NFSAState;

     Trickword =
       record
         case BOOLEAN of
           TRUE  : (subset : DFSAState);
           FALSE : (words : array[0..3] of INTEGER)
       end;
function HASH(s : Trickword) : Buckets;
   (* function is sent s.subset, but treats it as s.words *)
begin
   (* $T− turn off overflow traps *)
   HASH := (s.words[0]+s.words[1]+s.words[2]+s.words[3])
                 mod BucketMax;
   (* $T= restore overflow traps *)
end;
```

Of course, if the number of NFSA states exceeds the set size of the Pascal implementation, it will be necessary to have a more complicated trickword structure, with an array of sets as well as an array of arithmetic words.

5.3 A hash table system is required, which stores records containing fields with the factors I, J, and the number $I^3 + J^3$. The sum of cubes is used as the key attribute, with this number reduced modulo some prime as hash function.

The first few solutions are:

Number	I_1	J_1	I_2	J_2
1729	1	12	9	10
4104	2	16	9	15
13832	2	24	18	20
20683	10	27	19	24
32832	4	32	18	30
39312	2	34	15	33
40033	9	34	16	33
46683	3	36	27	30
64232	17	39	26	36

5.4 One possibility is to have two lists attached to each bucket. The first list holds spelling indices only, and no deletions are ever made from this list. The other list is the normal descriptor list which suffers insertions and deletions on block entry and exit, exactly as described in Section 5.3.

When an identifier has to be looked up, it is searched for first in the spelling index list. If the name was ever inserted into the list, it will still be present, since nothing is deleted from this list.

If the identifier is found in the spelling index list, the descriptor list is searched to see if the descriptor corresponding to that name is still visible. Note that the second search is potentially much faster than the first, since index comparisons are made, rather than string comparisons.

The real question is, does the space and time overhead involved in maintaining the two lists nullify the space saving due to string table sharing?

5.5 The following values of m and n result in a perfect hash function in the two cases, where m is restricted to being a power of 2. (Once again, these figures apply to the ASCII character set, and will differ for other character sets.)

Standard 35 keywords		With extra keywords	
m	n	m	n
32	164	32	165
64	147	64	151
128	161	128	176
256	–	256	–
512	158	512	158

Note that using lower-case characters for the keywords does not change the number of buckets that are required. In each case the hash function used was

$bucket := (ORD(id[1]) * m + ORD(id[length]) + length)$ **mod** n.

Chapter 6

6.1 The derivation trees are identical to Figures 6.3 and 6.4.

6.2 We choose *Command* as the goal symbol and *ComString* and *Term* as other syntactic categories. We also suppose that the atomic commands and integer repetition counts are recognized by some lower-level automaton, so we need not show the substructure here. The alphabets are

$\Sigma = \{'<', '>',$ *atom, repcount,* $'$$'\},$
$N = \{Command, ComString, Term\},$

and the grammar is

Command → *ComString* '$$'.
ComString → *Term*
            → *ComString Term*.
      Term → *atom*
            → *repcount* '<' *ComString* '>'.

It may be seen that the grammar does not correspond to a regular language, since nested angle brackets are possible.

6.3 The method given for DFSA works perfectly well for NFSA, for the case that there are no ε-transitions.

6.4 The clue to the solution to this problem is to see that there are two different kinds of string, a type-1 string and a type-2 string. A type-1 string consists of type-1 atoms which are either individual words or strings inside round brackets. Anything inside round brackets is a type-2 string, which consists of type-2 atoms, and so on.

Using

Σ = {(, [,),], W, ⊢},
N = {*Goal*, *String1*, *atom1*, *String2*, *atom2*},

the grammar is

  Goal → *String1* ⊢.
String1 → ε
         → *atom1 String1*.
  atom1 → '(' *String2* ')'
         → *W*.
String2 → ε
         → *atom2 String2*.
  atom2 → '[' *String1* ')'
         → *W*.

6.5 If the bottom of the stack is marked with the *bottom* symbol ⊥, and the end of string with the symbol ⊢, then the action table is

| | *Input symbol* | | | | | |
Stacktop	(	[	]	)	W	⊢
⊥	push (	error	error	error	–	accept
[	push (	error	pop	error	–	error
(	error	push [	error	pop	–	error

In the event that your grammar does not permit the empty string, it is most straightforward to use an additional state to note that at least one atom has been encountered.

6.6 The resulting grammar is not clean, and when it has its non-terminating productions removed there is no grammar left!

6.7 The comment at the end of Section 6.3 was to the effect that the label on each state of an FSA corresponding to a left-linear grammar indicated the syntactic category already recognized.

Starting from this point, we devise the following rules:

- associate each state except for the start state with a non-terminal label;
- for every transition, introduce one left-linear production;
- for a transition from state-A to state-B on symbol a, the production is $B \rightarrow Aa$;
- for a transition from the start state to state-X on symbol a, the production is $X \rightarrow a$.

As an example of this procedure, we apply the steps to the DFSA shown on the left in Figure 6.10.

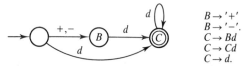

$$B \rightarrow '+'$$
$$B \rightarrow '-'.$$
$$C \rightarrow Bd$$
$$C \rightarrow Cd$$
$$C \rightarrow d.$$

The grammar turns out to rather simpler than the right-linear grammar corresponding to the same DFSA, as a result of not having to be concerned about live- and dead-end states.

6.8 Normally, it would be necessary to have a stack to keep track of the nesting level of symbols such as comment delimiters. However, in this case the stack alphabet, in effect, has only a single symbol, *open-comment*. We are thus able to dispense with the stack, and just keep a count of how many *open-comment* symbols have been read.

Typical code might be as follows.

```
procedure SkipComment;
  var nestingLevel : INTEGER;
begin (* assert: current ch is a '{' *)
  nestingLevel := 1;
  Read(ch);
  while nestingLevel <> 0 do begin
    if ch = '{' then
      nestingLevel := nestingLevel + 1
    else if ch = '}' then
      nestingLevel := nestingLevel −1;
    (* else do nothing *)
    Read(ch); (* read past one character *)
    end; (* while *)
end; (* assert: ch is one past the final '}' *)
```

The details of the algorithm are only slightly more complex in cases where the two-character comment delimiters are required. In that case the code might be as follows.

```
procedure SkipComment;
  var nestingLevel : INTEGER;
begin (* assert: ch is the '*' of an open comment *)
  nestingLevel := 1;
  Read(ch);
  while nestingLevel <> 0 do begin
    if (ch = '(') and (input^ = '*') then begin
      nestingLevel := nestingLevel + 1;
      Read(ch); (* get past '(' *)
    end
    else if (ch = '*') and (input^ = ')') then begin
      nestingLevel := nestingLevel -1;
      Read(ch); (* get past '*' *)
      end;
    (* else do nothing *)
    Read(ch); (* read past one character *)
    end; (* while *)
end; (* assert: ch is one past final close comment *)
```

Note the careful attention to the pre and postconditions in this version. There are many possible conventions, but in this code the guiding principle is that a new character must not be read until the current one is recognized, and once a character has been recognized it must be passed over before control is returned.

Chapter 7

7.1 It is easy to prove that the grammar is LL(1), after making the observation that the set $FOLLOW(K) = \{\vdash, op\}$ does not contain the symbol *num*.

To prove formally that the grammar does indeed generate the reverse Polish grammar is not a trivial matter. One method is to use induction on the length of derivation sequences, to show that the substitution of the third for the second production has the effect of inserting *num op* in the final sentence. A similar argument applied to the non-LL(1) grammar shows that this insertion is the final effect of increasing the derivation sequence length there also.

7.2 Introducing a new non-terminal symbol $K \rightarrow G|A$, we obtain the grammar

$$G \rightarrow aK \qquad \qquad \text{(i)}$$
$$ \rightarrow bG. \qquad \qquad \text{(ii)}$$
$$K \rightarrow aK \qquad \qquad \text{(iv)}$$
$$ \rightarrow bG \qquad \qquad \text{(v)}$$
$$ \rightarrow \vdash. \qquad \qquad \text{(vi)}$$

Production (i) replaces the first and third productions in the original grammar, while productions (iv) to (vi) are the right-linear forms of the productions $K \rightarrow G$ and $K \rightarrow A$.

Note that the symbol A is no longer reachable in the new grammar, since its only right-hand-side occurrence has been replaced by the new symbol K in the factorized production (i). The symbol A has thus been eliminated.

This is an important and sometimes overlooked point. The use of production factorization should always be followed by a check for useless productions, since the process may introduce these.

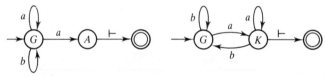

NFSA for original grammar.   DFSA for factored grammar.

The factored grammar leads to precisely the same DFSA as the subset construction, in which a DFSA state equivalent to K is formed by merging NFSA states G and A.

7.3 It is necessary to augment this grammar so that the empty productions will have well-defined lookaheads. We will suppose that an arbitrary end condition translates into the symbol *sep*.

Production	Director set
$G \rightarrow$ *number sep*.	$\{+,-,d\}$
number $\rightarrow$ *OptSign digits OptFrac OptExp*.	$\{+,-,d\}$
OptSign $\rightarrow \varepsilon$	$\{d\}$
$\rightarrow$ '+'	$\{+\}$
$\rightarrow$ '−'.	$\{-\}$
digits $\rightarrow$ *d rest*.	$\{d\}$
rest $\rightarrow \varepsilon$	$\{E,sep,.\}$
$\rightarrow$ *digits*.	$\{d\}$
OptFrac $\rightarrow \varepsilon$	$\{E,sep\}$
$\rightarrow$ '.' *rest*.	$\{.\}$
OptExp $\rightarrow \varepsilon$	$\{sep\}$
$\rightarrow$ 'E' *OptSign digits*.	$\{E\}$

7.4 The original grammar is not LL(1), and factoring the productions to remove the common starting symbols does not help, since one of the productions for each new non-terminal will be empty. These empty productions have director sets which clash with the other production of the same left-hand side. The trick of introducing a special symbol which derives the end symbol, essential to the method as used for right-linear grammars, does not work in this case. This is because the use of a production which derives a single terminal symbol does not terminate the derivation. There may be more than one non-terminal in the sentential form, unlike the case for a right-linear regular grammar.

Since we already know that the palindrome languages cannot be parsed at all with any finite lookahead by any deterministic method, it should come as no surprise that the LL(1) method will not work.

7.5 The solution is a simple rearrangement of the terminating test used in Figure 6.14. The essential difference is that the *suspectCount* field for each production right-hand-side is renamed *notNulCount*, and refers to the number of right-hand-side symbols which are not yet known to be nullable. As symbols are found to be nullable, the *notNulCount* field for every production which uses that symbol is decremented.

When a count reaches zero, the left-hand-side symbol of that production is declared to be nullable, and is placed on the fringe-stack so that the consequences of that symbol's nullability will be propagated.

Note that it is still necessary to check that the same non-terminal is not pushed twice. An ambiguous grammar could have several ways of deriving the empty string, and multiple insertions on the list would invalidate the algorithm by decrementing the counts more than once on behalf of the same non-terminal symbol occurrence.

```
procedure FormNullable;
type NTIndex   = 0..k;
     ProdIndex = 0..N;

     ProdInfo   = record
                      prodLHS : NTIndex;
                      notNulCount : INTEGER
                  end;

     NonTermInfo = record
                       nullable : BOOLEAN;
                       usedOccurrences : {List of ProdIndex}
                   end;
```

```
var  productions : array[ProdIndex] of ProdInfo;
     synCats     : array[NTIndex] of NonTermInfo;
     fringe      : {stack of NTIndex};
     deleteSmbl  : NTIndex;
     pIndex      : ProdIndex;

begin
   { read in the grammar, initializing the notNulCount field to
     indicate the total number of RHS symbols. Also, create a list of
     used occurrences of each NT symbol, and set every nullable
     field false.};

   (* initialize the fringe stack *)
   {set fringe to the empty stack};
   for pIndex := 0 to N do (* for every production *)
      with productions[pIndex] do
         if (notNulCount = 0) and
               not synCats[prodLHS].nullable
            then begin
            synCats[prodLHS].nullable := TRUE;
            {push prodLHS on fringe stack};
         end; (* if, with and for *)

   (* pop a terminating NT and decrement counts on its list *)
   while {fringe not empty} do begin
      delSymbol := {pop of fringe};
      for {every prodIndex pIndex on the list for delSymbol} do
         with productions[pIndex] do begin
            notNulCount := notNulCount - 1;
            if (notNulCount = 0) and
                  not synCats[prodLHS].nullable
               then begin
               synCats[prodLHS].nullable := TRUE;
               {push prodLHS on fringe stack};
               end (* if *)
            end (* with and for *)
   end; (* while *)
end;
```

Chapter 8

8.2 The table in Figure 8.4 is a production prediction table, rather than
a next state table, but an analogous technique may be used. The

table would be

Stacktop symbol	Default production	Table start		Symbol	Production
W	1	•		]	error
E	3	•			2
A	error	•		eoln	2
–	–	•		a	4
				*	5
				%	6
				[	7

The access procedure might be:

```
function PredictedProd(Top : StackSymbol;
                         smbl : InputSymbol) : ProdOrdinal;
  var found : BOOLEAN;
      current, endIndex : ListIndex;
begin
  found := FALSE;
  current := Index[Top].Start;
  endIndex := Index[SUCC(Top)].Start;
  while (current < endIndex) and not found do
    if smbl = ProdList[current].Symbol then
      found := TRUE;
    else current := current + 1;
  if found then
    PredictedProd := ProdList[current].Production
  else PredictedProd := Index[Top].DefaultProd
end;
```

This method will be slower than a complete, uncompacted table, but will occupy much less space.

8.4 The context-free grammar equivalent to the extended grammar in the question is as follows.

$$
\begin{array}{ll}
G \rightarrow prod\ pRest\ eof. & (1) \\
pRest \rightarrow \varepsilon & (2) \\
\quad \rightarrow prod\ pRest. & (3) \\
prod \rightarrow id\ '\rightarrow'\ rhs\ rhsRest\ '.'. & (4) \\
rhsRest \rightarrow \varepsilon & (5) \\
\quad \rightarrow\ '|'\ rhs\ rhsRest. & (6) \\
rhs \rightarrow tSeq & (7) \\
\quad \rightarrow\ '\varepsilon'. & (8) \\
tSeq \rightarrow term\ tRest. & (9) \\
tRest \rightarrow \varepsilon & (10) \\
\quad \rightarrow term\ tRest. & (11) \\
term \rightarrow id & (12)
\end{array}
$$

$$\to str \qquad\qquad\qquad (13)$$
$$\to '[' \; tSeq \; ']' \qquad\qquad (14)$$
$$\to '\{' \; tSeq \; '\}'. \qquad\qquad (15)$$

Equations for the *FOLLOW* sets are

$$FOLLOW(tRest) = FOLLOW(tSeq)$$
$$= FOLLOW(rhs) \cup \{']', '\}'\}$$
$$= FIRST(rhsRest) \cup FOLLOW(rhsRest) \cup \{']', '\}'\}$$
$$FOLLOW(rhsRest) = \{.\}$$
$$FOLLOW(pRest) = \{eof\},$$

leading to the following director sets.

Production	Nullable	First	Director set
(1)		$\{id\}$	$\{id\}$
(2)	true	$\{\}$	$\{eof,)\}$
(3)		$\{id\}$	$\{id\}$
(4)		$\{id\}$	$\{id\}$
(5)	true	$\{\}$	$\{.\}$
(6)		$\{|\}$	$\{|\}$
(7)		$\{id,str,\{,[\}$	$\{id,str,\{,[\}$
(8)		$\{\varepsilon\}$	$\{\varepsilon\}$
(9)		$\{id,str,\{,[\}$	$\{id,str,\{,[\}$
(10)	true	$\{\}$	$\{],\},|,.\}$
(11)		$\{id,str,\{,[\}$	$\{id,str,\{,[\}$
(12)		$\{id\}$	$\{id\}$
(13)		$\{str\}$	$\{str\}$
(14)		$\{[\}$	$\{[\}$
(15)		$\{\{\}$	$\{\{\}$

If the explicit '.' was not specified in the grammar, then *FOLLOW(rhsRest)* would be equal to *FOLLOW(prod)*, and hence include the symbol *id*. Since *FOLLOW(tRest)* would then include *id*, the director sets for the productions of *tRest* would then overlap and the grammar would not be LL(1).

In practical terms, if the explicit stop is left out, it is impossible to tell if an *id* symbol belongs to the current *rhs*, or is the left-hand side of a new *prod*. Note that without the stop, the grammar is LL(2), since a lookahead of $id \to$ indicates the start of a new *prod*.

8.5 The only productions which differ from the usual, explicit multiply grammar, is

$$term \to factor \; \{ \; mulop \; factor \; \}.$$
$$mulop \to \varepsilon \mid '/' \; .$$

These transform into CFG productions with the following director sets.

Production	Nullable	First	Director set
term→factor tRest.		{num,)}	{num,)}
tRest→ε	true	{}	{+,−,eof,)}
→mulop term.		{l,),num}	
mulop→εtrue	{}	{(,num}	
→'l'.		{l}	{l}

8.6 One factored grammar is given by

> expr → '−' prim | prim rest.
> prim → number | variable | '(' expr ')'.
> rest → ε | '−' prim | '/' prim |
>   '+' prim { '+' prim } | '*' prim { '*' prim }.

That this grammar is LL(1) may be seen by inspection. However, the technique of separating the various operators into different productions becomes a little unwieldy if there are a large number of operators in the grammar. For a recursive descent parser, a good compromise would be to include all of the associative operators within a single production, and then perform a 'semantic' check to ensure that each new operator is the same as the first.

8.7 This problem is extremely difficult to solve using the direct approach used in the examples met so far. There are two main difficulties. Firstly, all of the transitions out of any particular state are not all met at once, and thus cannot be directly inserted into a compacted table. Consider an expression with several terms in alternation. There will be several transitions out of the starting state, and yet transitions out of other states will have to be processed first. To solve this problem requires the table to be constructed as an array of lists, with each list holding all the transitions out of a particular state. In that way transitions may be added to the appropriate list, irrespective of the order in which they are actually discovered.

The second, and more serious problem is that when two or more terms are in alternation, the ending state of each chain which recognizes a term must be shared. Since whether or not a particular factor is the last in a term is not known until after the factor procedure has returned, it is sometimes necessary to go back and change a destination state (a so-called backpatching step), or to introduction additional epsilon-transitions.

For an elegant solution to this problem it is best to build a tree data-structure which may then be walked to build the table. Chapter 10 has the details.

8.8   There are essentially two different approaches to this problem, and we sketch both of these.

Approach 1

Suppose a regular expression is formed for the language, expressed in such a form that there is no non-determinism due to different branches of an alternation beginning with the same symbol. (This is always possible, since the language is necessarily LL(1), but perhaps requires some factorization.)

The regular expression may now be directly recognized by a single procedure.

Concatenated subexpressions are recognized by a straight-line code sequence.

A closure on a subexpression is recognized by the construct

while *smbl* **in** *DSet* **do**
    {recognize subexpression}

where, once again, the LL(1) property comes to our rescue.

Finally, an alternation is recognized by a **case** statement, where the branching is based on the current symbol value.

This particular solution is the 'implicit state FSA' referred to in Section 3.3.2. The flow of control in the procedure corresponds to the path through the state diagram.

Approach 2

Form a right-linear LL(1) grammar for the regular language. This is always possible, although sometimes the language must first be extended by the inclusion of an explicit *stopper* symbol.

The productions of this grammar may be directly or indirectly right-recursive, implying the presence of recursive procedure calls in a simple, recursive descent implementation of a recognizer based on this grammar. However, any right-recursion may be converted into an iteration.

The elimination of right-recursion corresponds to a well-known theoretical result on the elimination of 'tail recursion', but a simple demonstration is provided anyway.

Suppose we have a typical set of indirectly right-recursive productions:

$A \rightarrow bB$
$B \rightarrow cC$
. . .
$E \rightarrow aA.$

We may back-substitute these productions in order to arrive at a single right-recursive production,

$A \rightarrow uA$

where u is the string $bc \ldots a$. Since the grammar is clean, and hence necessarily terminating, it is clear that there is at least one other production for A. Let us suppose it is

$A \rightarrow \alpha$.

By assumption, the two productions have distinct director sets, so that we may take the two,

$A \rightarrow uA \mid \alpha$.

and replace them both by the single RRP production which generates precisely the same strings, and is still LL(1).

$A \rightarrow \{u\}\alpha$.

This production may be recognized without the use of any recursion.

8.9   The RRP production was $A \rightarrow \alpha(\beta|\gamma)\delta$. Suppose that we invent the non-terminal symbol B to denote the bracketed factor. The following CFG productions arise

$A \rightarrow \alpha B\delta$.
$B \rightarrow \beta$
$\quad \mid \gamma$.

Provided that neither of the two productions for B have a nullable right-hand side the director sets of the two productions are just $FIRST(\beta)$ and $FIRST(\gamma)$, respectively. If these two sets are disjoint, the original production will be LL(1).

If just one of the terms is nullable, and the director set of the corresponding production for B does not overlap with $FIRST$ for the other production, then the LL(1) property will still be fulfilled. However, if both terms are nullable then the two productions for B will have director sets which have all of the symbols of $FOLLOW(B)$ in common. In this case, the grammar is actually ambiguous, having two different ways to derive the phrase $\alpha\varepsilon\delta$.

The skeleton of the recursive descent procedure to recognize this production would be as follows.

procedure *ARecognize*;
begin
$\quad$ {recognize α};
$\quad$ **if** *symbol* **in** $DSet_1$
$\quad\quad$ **then** {recognize β}
$\quad\quad$ **else** {recognize γ};
$\quad$ {recognize δ}
end;

Chapter 9

9.1 For all of the model solutions for this chapter a slightly different method of forming the characteristic NFSA is employed. This method leads to a slightly easier subset construction procedure, since some states which would have been separate in the method used in the text are merged in the modified method.

Rather than first forming the prefix-recognizing automaton, and then adding the production-recognizing side-chains, the side-chains are formed first. A set of prefix states is formed as for the previous method, and the production-recognizing chains added immediately. The innovation is concurrently to generate the transitions of the underlying prefix-recognizing machine. Whenever a state in the automaton has an out-transition labelled by a non-terminal symbol, that state also has an epsilon-transition added to the corresponding prefix state.

The characteristic NFSA produced by this method for the reverse Polish expression grammar is as shown. In this particular case the NFSA has exactly the same number of states as for the previous method.

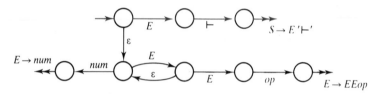

The corresponding DFSA follows, and is seen to have no inconsistent states. Hence the grammar is LR(0).

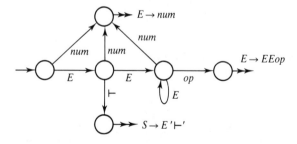

9.2 For the grammar

$S \rightarrow E \vdash.$

$E \rightarrow T \mid T \oplus E .$

$T \rightarrow a \mid T \otimes a.$

it may easily be seen that $FOLLOW(E) = \{\vdash\}$.

The characteristic NFSA and DFSA for this grammar are shown below.

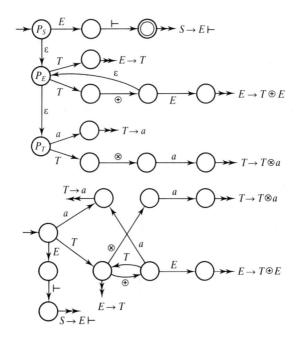

The only inconsistent state has a reduce exit for production $E \to T$, and read transitions on symbols $\oplus$ and $\otimes$. The use of the *FOLLOW* set as reduction lookahead thus resolves the read-reduce conflict, and the grammar is therefore SLR.

9.3 The director sets for the various productions are shown in the following table.

Production	Nullable	FIRST(rhs)	FOLLOW(lhs)	Director set
$G \to S\vdash$	false	$\{a,b\}$	–	$\{a,b\}$
$S \to AaAb$	false	$\{a\}$	–	$\{a\}$
$\to BbBa$	false	$\{b\}$	–	$\{b\}$
$A \to \varepsilon$	true	$\{\}$	$\{a,b\}$	$\{a,b\}$
$B \to \varepsilon$	true	$\{\}$	$\{a,b\}$	$\{a,b\}$

The grammar is seen to be LL(1). The NFSA and DFSA for the characteristic machine are as follows.

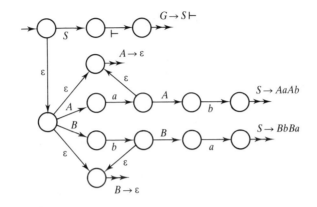

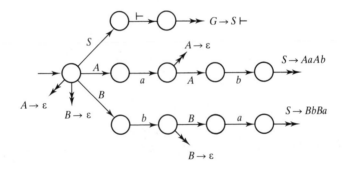

From the *FOLLOW* sets in the preceding table it may be seen that the SLR lookaheads for the two empty reductions in the start state are identical. The grammar is thus not SLR.

However, when the LALR lookaheads are considered it is noted that the reduction $A \rightarrow \varepsilon$ *looks-back-at* (*start,A*), which only reads the terminal symbol a. Correspondingly, the other reduction $B \rightarrow \varepsilon$ *looks-back-at* (*start,B*) which reads b. We conclude, therefore, that the LALR lookaheads resolve the conflict.

9.4 The ambiguous **if-then-else** grammar of Figure 8.23 has the deterministic characteristic machine shown below, where the notation is consistent with that used in Figure 9.11.

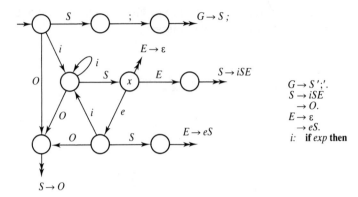

$G \rightarrow S';'.$
$S \rightarrow iSE$
$\quad \rightarrow O.$
$E \rightarrow \varepsilon$
$\quad \rightarrow eS.$
$i:$ if exp then

The state marked 'x' has a read-reduce conflict, since the SLR (and LALR) lookahead of the reduction $E \rightarrow \varepsilon$ is $\{e,;\}$. However, the arbitrary deletion of e from this lookahead set causes the read transition to be taken so long as the next symbol is e (i.e. the symbol is **else** in the full notation). This leads to the usual semantics, as discussed in Section 8.4.

9.5 We reprint the characteristic DFSA for the ambiguous grammar, Figure 9.23.

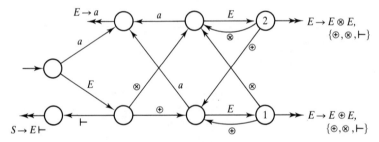

(i) Consider state 1. If the next symbol is $\otimes$, then since this operator is to take precedence, the read transition should be taken rather than the reduction $E \rightarrow E \oplus E$. On the other hand, if the next symbol is $\oplus$, the reduction should be invoked, since we wish '$E \oplus E \oplus E$' to be parsed as $(E \oplus E) \oplus E$.

Similar considerations in state 2 lead to the final disambiguated characteristic automaton shown below.

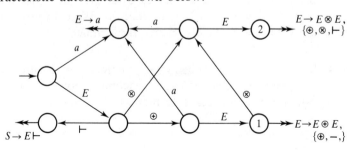

The subtle difference between this diagram and Figure 9.25 should be noted. A suitable string to trace for distinguishing the actions of the two automata is '$a \oplus a \oplus a$'.

(ii) Similar reasoning to the previous case leads to a disambiguated characteristic machine as follows.

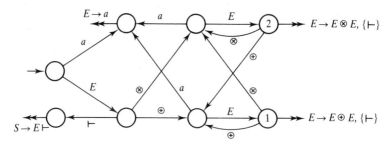

Since each operator asociates so as to cause right-to-left evaluation, no reduction should be performed until the end of the string has been found. In this particular case the operators are not distinguished syntactically, and both could be replaced by a common symbol op leading to the simplified machine shown below.

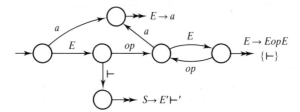

9.6 The diagram of the characteristic machine is shown below. The LALR lookaheads are shown for the reductions in the two inconsistent states. This diagram should be compared to Figure 9.22.

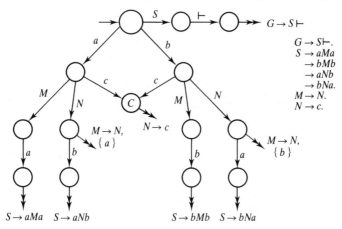

9.7 We deal initially with the case of a right-linear regular grammar. It is also assumed in the statement of the problem that the grammar is LL(1), corresponding to a deterministic FSA. We will assume that, if necessary, the grammar has been augmented by the introduction of an explicit *end* symbol.

We note initially that any conflict in a characteristic machine arises due to the merging of states during the subset construction procedure which converts from the initial NFSA to the characteristic DFSA. It is helpful to concentrate on the kinds of non-determinism which arise in the characteristic NFSA for regular grammars, since it is these features which control the state mergers which will take place.

For a completely general NFSA two kinds of non-deterministic features can occur: there may be more than one transition out of a particular state for any given symbol, or there may be epsilon-transitions.

In the case of the characteristic NFSAs which arise from the very restricted grammars which we are considering here, only one of these kinds of non-determinism can arise. There are certainly epsilon-transitions, but there can be at most a single transition on any given terminal symbol out of any prefix-recognizing state. This is a consequence of the LL(1) property. Each non-terminal symbol may only have a single production starting with a given symbol, and hence the starting symbols of each side-chain out of any particular prefix state are distinct. The diagram illustrates a typical fragment of a characteristic NFSA.

It is important to note also that the epsilon-transitions which do occur in the characteristic NFSA always lead from a state in the middle of a side-chain and a prefix state. The form of the right-linear productions prevents epsilon-transitions from connecting prefix states together.

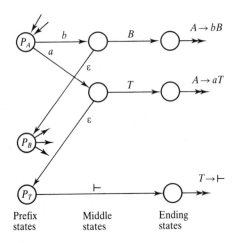

Prefix states   Middle states   Ending states

When the subset construction procedure is applied to such a characteristic NFSA, the only kind of mergers which take place are between prefix states and the middle states of the production side-chains. The state sets which are formed are either singleton sets or pairs consisting of one middle state and one prefix state. In particular, it is never possible to merge a chain-ending state with any other state. We conclude that the states in the DFSA thus have no shift-reduce or reduce-reduce conflicts.

The argument in the case of the left-linear grammars is a little different. Recall that the left-linear grammar arising from an FSA has a syntactic category corresponding to each state except the start state, and the name of the state stands for the syntactic structure already recognized. Unlike the right-linear case, the start state is anonymous and the accept state corresponds to the goal symbol.

The assumption that the FSA to which the grammar corresponds is deterministic prevents any two productions having identical right-hand sides. For example, consider the form of an FSA which possesses two productions with the same right-hand side, $A \rightarrow Cx$ and $B \rightarrow Cx$, say. In this case the state corresponding to category C must have two separate out-transitions labelled x, leading to states A and B, respectively, and thus contradicting the deterministic assumption.

A fragment of the characteristic NFSA corresponding to an LL(1) left-linear grammar is shown in the following figure.

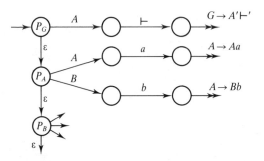

Note that when the subset construction procedure is applied to such an NFSA all of the prefix states will be merged, as will many of the middle states. However, the uniqueness property of the complete right-hand sides prevents the merging of any states with reductions, showing that once again the characteristic machine is LR(0).

In order to illustrate these points we present a complete worked example, an FSA for optionally signed integers. The grammar and characteristic automata are shown first for the right-linear case.

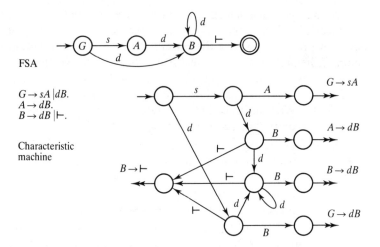

FSA

$G \to sA \,|\, dB.$
$A \to dB.$
$B \to dB \,|\, \vdash.$

Characteristic
machine

The corresponding diagrams for the left-linear case are as follows.

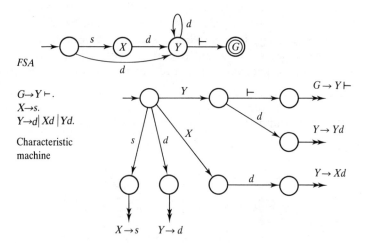

FSA

$G \to Y \vdash.$
$X \to s.$
$Y \to d \,|\, Xd \,|\, Yd.$

Characteristic
machine

Chapter 10

10.2 The IDL description of the tree type is repeated here.

structure *Index*
root *ILIST* **is**
   ILIST ::= *list*;
   list => *asItems* : **seqOf** *ITEM*;
   ITEM ::= *item*;
   item => *lxItemName* : *string*,
          asOccurList : **seqOf** *INTEGER*,
          asSubItems : **seqOf** *SUBITEM*;

SUBITEM ::= *subItem*;
subItem => *lxItemName* : *string*,
             asOccurList : **seqOf** *INTEGER*;
end.

It will be noted that only one level of *subitem* is possible in the structure. A possible tree walker is as follows.

```
procedure WalkSubItem(node : SubItemType);
begin
  WriteName(node.itemName);
  WriteList(node.occurList);
  NewLine;
end;

procedure WalkItem(node : ItemType);
begin
  WriteName(node);
  WriteList(node.occurList);
  NewLine;
  for {every subItem of node} do begin
    indent;
    WalkSubItem(subItem)
    end;
end;

begin (* mainline *)
  for {every item node} do
    WalkItem(item)
end.
```

The code assumes the existence of various procedures which implement the actions described by their names. The details of these various procedures are not shown. They will depend on the way in which the actual tree data-structure is implemented. However, the structure of the tree-walking algorithm itself does not depend on the implementation, but only on the attributes of the abstract tree as described by the IDL.

10.3 The model solution has a single node-class *EXPR*, which has a subclass *BINARY* with one class-member corresponding to each binary operator.

Structure *Polish exp* **root** *EXPR* **is**

EXPR ::= *number* | *ident* | *negate* | *BINARY*;

BINARY ::= *add* | *sub* | *mult* | *divd*;

cont. overleaf

cont.

> *number* => *sm_value* : *Real*; — or whatever.
>
> *ident* => *lx_name* : *String*,
>   . . . ;   — other attributes probably.
>
> *negate* => *as_operand* : *EXPR*;
>
> *add* => *as_left_op* : *EXPR*,
>   *as_right_op* : *EXPR*;
>
> *sub* => *as_left_op* : *EXPR*,
>   *as_right_op* : *EXPR*;
>
> *mult* => *as_left_op* : *EXPR*,
>   *as_right_op* : *EXPR*;
>
> *divd* => *as_left_op* : *EXPR*,
>   *as_right_op* : *EXPR*;
> **end**.

10.4 Suitable type declarations might be as follows.

> **type** *TokenType* = (*num, ident, neg, add, sub,*
>   *mult, divd, eql, endmark*);
>
>   *TagType* = *num..divd*;
>
>   *NodePtr* = ^*Node*;
>
>   *Node* = **record**
>   **case** *tag* : *TagType* **of**
>   *num* : (*value* : *Real*);
>   *ident* : (*rep* : *String*;
>   . . .   );
>   *neg* : (*opr* : *NodePtr*);
>   *add, sub, mult, divd* :
>   : (*opLeft, opRight* : *NodePtr*);
>   **end**;

There must be global declarations of a root-pointer, a global symbol variable, and various procedures associated with the lexical scanner.

The main parsing procedure will be similar to the following.

procedure *Parse*(**var** *root* : *NodePtr*);

   procedure *ExprRecognize*(**var** *subRoot* : *NodePtr*);
    var *ptr* : *NodePtr*;
       oldSymbol : *TokenType*;

```
begin
   oldSymbol := symbol;
   if symbol in [num..divd] then begin
       NEW(ptr); (* allocate maximum size node *)
       ptr^.tag := symbol
       GetSymbol;
   end;
   case oldSymbol of
       num  : {whatever};
       ident : {whatever};
       neg  : ExprRecognize(ptr^.opr);
       add, sub. mult, divd : begin
                   ExprRecognize(ptr^.opLeft);
                   ExprRecognize(ptr^.opRight);
               end;
       eql, endmark : Error; (* not specified here *)
   end;
end;

begin (* parse *)
   {initialize scanner};
   ExprRecognize(root);
   Accept(eql);
end;
```

As usual, we have adopted the convention that the symbol variable already contains the first symbol of the phrase to be recognized prior to the call of the nested procedure. This condition must be established during scanner initialization.

10.5 One of the many sets of possible IDL class and node declarations for this grammar fragment might be as follows.

```
STATEMENT ::= increment | assignment;
EXPRESSION ::= VARNODE | constant | negTerm | sum;
   VARNODE ::= variable;

increment => as_var    : VARIABLE,
             as_step   : EXPRESSION;

assignment => as_lhs   : VARIABLE,
              as_rhs   : EXPRESSION;

       sum => as_terms : seqOf EXPRESSION;
   variable => sm_desc  : Descriptor;        — an external type.
   constant => sm_value : Real;              — an external type.
   negTerm  => as_term  : EXPRESSION;
```

Note that there is no attempt to enforce all of the grammatical rules by means of the tree structure. For example, the grammar requires that only the first child of a sum node may be a *negTerm* node, but the IDL permits any member of the expression class to appear in any position. It is the responsibility of the parser to ensure that only trees corresponding to valid strings get constructed.

10.6 Below we show a typical pair of trees corresponding to the situation in which the transformation may be performed. It will be seen that the key requirement is that the left-hand-side *variable* of the assignment appears within the right-hand-side expression.

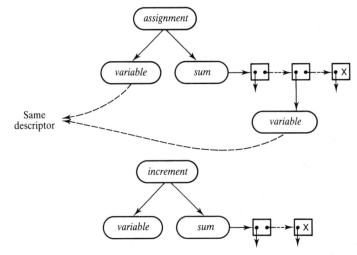

The transformation procedure must see if any right-hand-side *variable* terms have a descriptor field which is the same as the left-hand-side *variable*.

```
procedure TransformToIncrement(root : StmtPtr);
    var found : BOOLEAN;
begin (* assert: root^.tag = assignment *)
    if root^.rhs^.tag = sum then begin (* check *)
        found := FALSE;
        {initialize listGet};
        while{rhs not ended} and not found do begin
            {get next term};
            if (term^.tag = variable) and
               (term^.descriptor = root^.lhs^.descriptor) then
            begin
                found := TRUE;
                root^.tag := increment;
                {delete term from list}
            end; (* inner if *)
        end; (* while *)
    end; (* outer if *)
end;
```

Chapter 11

11.1 For the original grammar fragment, the relevant part of the characteristic machine is

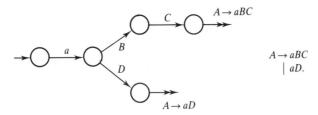

$A \rightarrow aBC$
$\quad | \ aD.$

With the modified grammar, the same fragment is

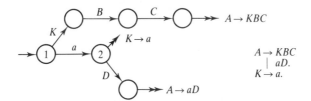

$A \rightarrow KBC$
$\quad | \ aD.$
$K \rightarrow a.$

Assuming for simplicity that neither of the symbols B or D is nullable, then the lookahead for the reduction in state 2 will be $FIRST(B)$. Conversely, the paths which result in recognition of a D symbol will start with $FIRST(D)$. State 2 will, therefore, have no shift-reduce conflict provided $FIRST(B)$ and $FIRST(D)$ are disjoint. This is exactly the condition that the two original productions can be successfully factorized, and a recursive descent translator used.

11.2 If a nullable non-terminal J is introduced, as an alternative to the grammar transformation in the previous exercise, then the characteristic machine fragment is

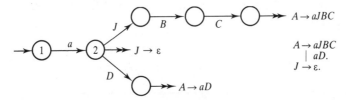

$A \rightarrow aJBC$
$\quad | \ aD.$
$J \rightarrow \varepsilon.$

In this case also, the lookahead of the reduction in state 2 is $FIRST(B)$, so that the condition for the state to be consistent is the same as for Exercise 11.1.

The two previous examples, therefore, illustrate a special case of the general result of Brosgol linking the possibility of introducing marker productions and the LL(1) property.

11.3 In order to simplify the reasoning, we distinguish between the

various roles in which a node may appear as an operand. The left and right operands of an *add* node will be called *augend* and *addend*, respectively, while the left and right operators of a *mult* node will be called the *multiplicand* and *multiplier*, respectively. In effect, we define a type

type *OperandRole* = (*augend*,*addend*,*multiplicand*,*multiplier*).

Tree fragments which include every possible combination of node type and role are shown below, together with the required output string.

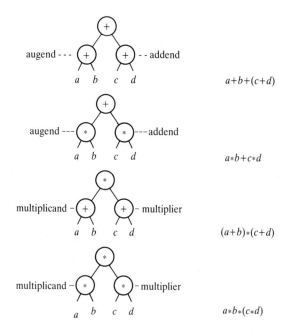

$$a+b+(c+d)$$

$$a*b+c*d$$

$$(a+b)*(c+d)$$

$$a*b*(c*d)$$

In terms of these roles, the need for parentheses is summarized in the table

Role of node	Type of node	
	mult	*add*
augend	*false*	*false*
addend	*false*	*true*
multiplicand	*false*	*true*
multiplier	*true*	*true*

The expression translation procedure in Figure 11.8 must now be modified to pass role information to any recursive calls of itself.

```
procedure ExprTranslate(role : OperandRole);
begin
    case smbl of
        atomsmbl: . . .
        starsmbl  : begin (* parentheses only if multiplier *)
                        GetSymbol;
                        if role = multiplier then Emit(open);
                        ExprTranslate(multiplicand);
                        Emit(multiply);
                        ExprTranslate(multiplier)
                        if role = multiplier then Emit(Close);
                    end;
        plussmbl : begin (* parentheses unless augend *)
                        GetSymbol;
                        if role <> augend then Emit(open);
                        ExprTranslate(augend);
                        Emit(add);
                        ExprTranslate(addend);
                        if role <> augend then Emit(close)
                    end
    end (* case *)
end;
```

11.4 Following on from Exercise 11.3, we assume that the order of precedence is the same for all the 'mulops', and lower but equal for all the 'addops'. We will further assume that parentheses are only required for a negation operand if it is an *addop* node as shown.

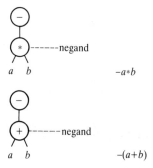

After inventing one further constant of the *OperandRole* type, the table in Exercise 11.3 is modified to read as follows.

Role of node	Type of node	
	mult	add
augend	false	false
addend	false	true
multiplicand	false	true
multiplier	true	true
negand	false	true

The procedure is similar to that in the answer to Exercise 11.3.

11.5 One possible solution is to copy a single line of comment into the usual *buffer* variable and to set the *SymLen* attribute in the usual way. The parser is then able to determine whether or not the comment fragment can fit onto the current line, and the buffer need be no longer than the maximum input line. A suitable set of additional values for the *SymbolType* variable are

```
. . .
newlineComment,    (* start of comment on a new line      *)
embeddedComment,  (* comment not following a line-break *)
commentContinue,  (* continuation of multiline comment   *)
. . .
```

After each call of *WriteGetSymbol*, the next *symbol* value is checked. If it is a *newlineComment*, the comment is immediately written to the output, preceded by a *NewLine* and followed by any comment continuations. On the other hand, if an embedded comment is detected then it may immediately be output, using the code within *WriteGetSymbol* to detect whether a *NewLine* and indent are necessary.

It is possible to do all of this by modifying the code of *WriteGetSymbol* so that it calls itself recursively.

```
. . .
GetSymbol;
if SpaceRequired then
    . . .
if symbol = newlineComment
    then begin
        NewLine;
        WriteGetSymbol(mar + Step);
        while symbol = commentContinue do
            WriteGetSymbol(mar + Step);
        end
```

```
  else if symbol = embeddedComment
    then begin
      WriteGetSymbol(mar + Step);
      while symbol = commentContinue do
        WriteGetSymbol(mar + Step);
    end;
end; (* WriteGetSymbol *)
```

Note carefully that the detection of continuation lines in multi-line comments implies that the scanner must maintain state information *between* calls to *GetSymbol*. Clearly the procedure must know, when it is called, that it is not in the usual start state, but is already inside a comment. The scanner state variable, therefore, cannot be a local variable of the procedure but (in Pascal) becomes yet another global variable which must not be tampered with by any other part of the code. Readers familiar with the history of programming languages will recognize an application for Algol 60's seldom used facility for declaring **own** variables. These were inaccessible except within the procedure in which they were declared, but maintained their value between procedure calls.

Bibliography

Aho, A. V. and Johnson, S. C. (1974). 'LR Parsing' *Computing Surveys*, **6**, 99–124

Aho, A. V. and Ullman, J. D. (1972). *The theory of parsing, translation and compiling*. Vol. 1. Englewood Cliffs, NJ: Prentice-Hall

Aho, A. V. and Ullman, J. D. (1973). *The theory of parsing, translation and compiling*. Vol. 2. Englewood Cliffs, NJ: Prentice-Hall

Aho, A. V. and Ullman, J. D. (1978). *Principles of compiler design*. Reading, Mass.: Addison-Wesley

Aho, A. V., Hopcroft, J. E. and Ullman, J. D. (1983). *Data structures and algorithms*. Reading, Mass.: Addison-Wesley

Aho, A. V., Sethi, R. and Ullman, J. D. (1986). *Compilers: principles, techniques, and tools*. Reading, Mass.: Addison-Wesley

Anderson, T., Eve, J. and Horning, J. J. (1973). 'Efficient LR(1) parsers' *Acta Informatica* **2**, 12–39

Backhouse, R. C. (1979). *The syntax of programming languages*. London: Prentice-Hall

Barrett, W. A. and Couch, J. D. (1979). *Compiler construction, theory and practice*. Science Research Associates

Bentley, J. (1985). *Programming pearls*, see 'column 13'. Reading, Mass.: Addison-Wesley

Brosgol, B. M. (1974). 'Deterministic translation grammars' *PhD Thesis*, Harvard University, Cambridge, Mass.

Brzozski, J. A., (1962). 'A survey of regular expressions and their applications' *IEEE Transactions on Electronic Computers*, **11**, 324–335

Brzozski, J. A. (1964). 'Derivatives of regular expressions' *Journal of ACM*, **11**, 491–494

Chomsky, N. (1959). 'Three models for the description of language' *IRE Transactions on Information Theory*, **2**, 113–124

Ciesinger, J. (1979). 'A bibliography of error handling' *SIGPLAN Notices*, **14**, 16–26

453

Conway, M. E. (1963). 'Design of a separable transition diagram compiler' *Communications of ACM*, **6**, 396–408

DeRemer, F. (1971). 'Simple LR(k) grammars' *Communications of ACM*, **14**, 453–460

DeRemer, F. and Pennello, T. (1982). 'Efficient computation of LALR(1) lookahead sets' *Transactions on Programming Languages and Systems*, **4**, 615–644

Dwyer, B. (1985). 'Improving Gough's LL(1) lookahead generator' *SIGPLAN Notices*, **20**, 16–19

Earley, J. (1983). 'An efficient context-free parsing algorithm' *Communications of ACM*, **26**, 57–61

Evans, A., Jr and Butler, K. J. Eds (1983). *DIANA reference manual*, revision 3. Tartan Laboratories, Pittsburg, PA.

Finn, G. D. (1985). 'Extended use of null productions in LR(1) parser applications' *Communications of ACM*, **28**, 961–972

Gough, K. J. (1981). 'Little language processing, an alternative to courses in compiler construction' *SIGCSE Bulletin*, September

Gough, K. J. (1985). 'A new method of generating LL(1) lookaheads' *SIGPLAN Notices*, **20**, 16–19

Gries, D. (1973). 'Describing an algorithm by Hopcroft' *Acta Informatica*, **2**, 97–109

Hopcroft, J. E. (1971). *An n log n algorithm for minimizing states in a finite state automaton*. In *Theory of machines and computation*. New York, NY: Academic Press

Hopcroft, J. E. and Ullman, J. D. (1979). *Introduction to automata theory, languages, and computation*. Reading, Mass.: Addison-Wesley

Irons, E. T. (1963). 'An error-correcting parse algorithm' *Communications of ACM*, **6**, 669–673

Jensen, K. and Wirth, N. (1974). *Pascal user manual and report*, 2nd edition. New York, NY: Springer Verlag

Johnson, S. C. (1975). '*Yacc*, yet another compiler compiler' *Computing Science Technical Report 32*, AT&T Bell Laboratory, Murray Hill, NJ.

Kastens, U., Hutt, B. and Zimmerman, E. (1982). 'GAG: A practical compiler generator' *Lecture Notes in Computer Science*, New York: Springer Verlag, Vol. 141

Knuth, D. E. (1965). 'On the translation of languages from left to right' *Information and Control*, **8**, 607–639

Knuth, D. E., Morris, J. H. and Pratt, V. R. (1977). 'Fast pattern matching in strings' *SIAM Journal of Computing*, **6**, 323–350

Kohavi, Z. (1978). *Switching and finite automata theory*, 2nd edition, New York, NY: McGraw-Hill

Lalonde, W. R. (1971). 'An efficient LALR parser-generator' *Technical Report Number 2*, Computer Systems Research Group, University of Toronto

Lewis, P. M. and Stearns, R. E. (1968). 'Syntax directed transduction', *Journal of ACM*, **15**, 465–488

McLuskey, E. J. (1965). *Introduction to the theory of switching circuits*. New York, NY: McGraw-Hill

McNaughton, R. and Yamada, H. (1960). 'Regular expressions and state graphs for automata' *IEEE Transactions on Electronic Computers*, **9**, 39–47

Mealy, G. H. (1955). 'A method of synthesizing sequential circuits' *Bell System Technical Journal*, **34**, 1045–1079

Moore, E. F. (1956). 'Gedanken experiments on sequential machines', in *Automata Studies*. Princeton, NJ: Princeton University Press

Naur, P. (ed.) (1960). 'Report on the algorithmic language ALGOL-60' *Communications of ACM*, **3**, 299–314

Naur, P. (ed.) (1963). 'Revised report on the algorithmic language ALGOL-60' *Communications of ACM*, **6**, 1–20

Nestor, J. R., Wulf, W. A. and Lamb, D. A. (1981). 'IDL – Interface description language' *Technical Report CMU-CS-81-139*, Carnegie-Mellon University

Pager, D. (1979). 'Eliminating unit productions from LR(k) parsers' *Acta Informatica*, **9**, 31–59

Reps, T. W. (1982). 'Generating language-based environments' *PhD thesis*, Cornell University. (Also published by MIT Press, 1984.)

Rosenkratz, D. J. and Stearns, R. E. (1970). 'Properties of deterministic top-down grammars' *Information and Control*, **17**, 226–256

Sagar, T. J. (1985). 'A polynomial-time generator for minimal perfect hash functions' *Communications of ACM*, **28**, 523–532

Teitelbaum, T. and Reps, T. W. (1981). 'The Cornell program synthesizer: a syntax-directed programming environment' *Communications of ACM*, **24**, 9

Thompson, K. (1968). 'Regular expression search algorithm' *Communications of ACM*, **11**, 419–422

Unger, S. H. (1969). *Asynchronous sequential switching circuits*. New York, NY: Wiley

Waite, W. M. and Goos, G. (1984). *Compiler construction*. New York, NY: Springer Verlag

Warshall, S. (1962). 'A theorem on Boolean matrices' *Journal of ACM*, **9**, 11–12

Wirth, N. (1968). 'PL-360 – a programming language for the 360 computers' *Journal of ACM*, **15**, 37–74

Wirth, N. (1971). 'The design of a Pascal compiler' *Software Practice and Experience*, **1**, 309–333

Wirth, N. (1977). 'What can we do about the unnecessary diversity of notation for syntactic definitions?' *Communications of ACM*, **20**, 822–823

Index